FOREIGN POLICY AT THE PERIPHERY

FOREIGN POLICY AT THE PERIPHERY

The Shifting Margins of US International Relations since World War II

Edited by Bevan Sewell and Maria Ryan

K UNIVERSITY PRESS OF KENTUCKY

Copyright © 2017 by The University Press of Kentucky

Scholarly publisher for the Commonwealth,
serving Bellarmine University, Berea College, Centre
College of Kentucky, Eastern Kentucky University,
The Filson Historical Society, Georgetown College,
Kentucky Historical Society, Kentucky State University,
Morehead State University, Murray State University,
Northern Kentucky University, Transylvania University,
University of Kentucky, University of Louisville,
and Western Kentucky University.
All rights reserved.

Editorial and Sales Offices: The University Press of Kentucky
663 South Limestone Street, Lexington, Kentucky 40508-4008
www.kentuckypress.com

Cataloging-in-Publication data is available from the Library of Congress.

ISBN 978-0-8131-6847-0 (hardcover : alk. paper)
ISBN 978-0-8131-6849-4 (epub)
ISBN 978-0-8131-6848-7 (pdf)

This book is printed on acid-free paper meeting
the requirements of the American National Standard
for Permanence in Paper for Printed Library Materials.

∞

Manufactured in the United States of America.

Member of the Association of
American University Presses

Contents

Introduction

Bevan Sewell and Maria Ryan

In January 2012, the Obama administration released a new report on defense in an era of austerity. Titled *Sustaining U.S. Global Leadership,* the report stressed "the national security imperative of deficit reduction." In essence, the administration wanted to cut the defense budget—and by extension the national deficit—without seriously imperiling US global leadership. The new era of austerity, catalyzed by congressional concerns about the national debt, forced the Obama administration to outline a vision of US leadership that was more cognizant of limits; one that identified "core" areas of interest in the twenty-first century and core tasks as well as secondary or "peripheral" regions and missions. For the Obama administration, the core regions were the Asian Pacific and the Middle East. The so-called pivot to Asia—the most noted aspect of the new strategy—was premised on "China's emergence as a regional power [that] will have the potential to affect the U.S. economy and our security in a variety of ways." Less noteworthy, and more predictable, was the strategy's emphasis on the Middle East as another core region: the administration would "*continue to place a premium on U.S. and allied military presence in—and support of—partner nations in and around this region.*" However, in more peripheral areas, such as Africa and Latin America, "*we will develop innovative, low-cost, and small footprint approaches to achieve our security objectives.*"[1]

The perceived differences between the importance of certain areas was reflected in Obama's elevation of Pentagon train-and-equip programs in Presidential Decision Directive 23. Assisting indigenous security forces was a more cost-effective way to "disrupt and defeat transnational threats; sustain legitimate and effective public safety, security, and justice sector institution; [and] . . . maintain control of . . . territory and jurisdiction waters, including air, land, and sea borders" in countries where the United States could not or would not put its own boots on the ground.[2] The pinch on resources and American capabilities thus required a more prudent approach to national security—one that paid heed to the fact that, in those areas deemed peripheral, the attainment of US goals would necessitate the utilization of alternative approaches.

Ultimately, however, this most recent approach to core and peripheral regions came undone with the rise of the Islamic State—a virulently anti-American coalition of extremist Sunni insurgents that took control of parts of Iraq and Syria in 2014. Obama was faced with the dilemma of how to preserve vital US interests in a core region of concern when there was little public appetite for further intervention there. The unsatisfactory solution was to send US military advisers to conduct the kind of train-and-equip programs that had really been envisaged for use in more peripheral theaters.

Obama, of course, is hardly the first president to struggle to determine the extent of US interests abroad or establish how they should be secured. When the United States emerged as an economic and military superpower at the end of World War II, its leaders made every effort to actively preserve this preponderance of power. With Washington's interests now defined as truly global in scope, US officials faced the challenge of prioritizing competing interests in different regions of the world, determining the means necessary to defend them, and reconciling this with what was politically and financially possible. But this task was complicated by the emergence of the Soviet Union—a competing superpower promoting an antithetical economic and social system. For the next fifty years, US policymakers attempted to define the core economic, military, and political interests essential to the maintenance of US dominance of the Western world and, if possible, the extension of American influence into newly independent and nonaligned countries.

While the announcement of the Truman Doctrine in March 1947 had potentially committed the United States to an open-ended commitment to "help free peoples to maintain their free institutions and their national integrity against aggressive movements that seek to impose upon them totalitarian regimes," the policy discussions that subsequently took place attempted to define which areas the United States considered to be of core importance and which were more peripheral.[3] George Kennan, who served as head of the Policy Planning Staff under President Harry Truman, sought to tackle this issue by defining a strategy that would allow the United States to identify certain core areas that had to be protected. In doing so, as John Gaddis notes, he outlined the importance of "'strongpoint defense'—concentration on the defense of particular regions and means of access to them, rather than on the defense of fixed lines." Identifying the key areas as being the United States, the Soviet Union, Britain, Germany and Central Europe, and Japan, Kennan argued that, with the Soviet Union out of reach, it was crucial that the United States strive to ensure that the other four areas remained free of Soviet control. With the Truman administration generally agreed that the United States had only limited resources to support its foreign policy ambitions, Kennan's strategy allowed it to pursue a policy that was cognizant of the limited resources available and also to be selective about where else it might oppose Communist threats. The loss of a nation in South Asia to communism was hardly to be welcomed, but nor should it be seen as being more of a threat than it actually was.[4] The focus of this strategy was, primarily, on Europe—an area that, as Anders Stephanson has explained, was driven by a "pronounced concern with European and Western Civilization, the survival of which Kennan considered vital for the United States itself."[5]

In Kennan's formulation, then, the United States could focus primarily on these core areas and adopt a more cautious approach elsewhere. In an inversion of the problem that would later confront Obama, however, major challenges to this approach would soon emerge when communism appeared to be making rapid progress in areas that the United States had previously deemed peripheral. With the American people being informed that communism was a monolithic entity controlled by Moscow and eager to destroy Western civilization, it became hugely difficult for the Truman administration not to respond to Communist advances in places outside Kennan's five vital centers.[6] This was especially true in Korea, where, in June 1950, the Communist North's attack on the South fatally undermined Kennan's strategy.

Previously, in adhering to Kennan's notion that US capabilities were not limitless, Secretary of State Dean Acheson had publicly stated that, in Asia, America's defense perimeter "runs along the Aleutians to Japan and then goes to the Ryukus . . . [and then] from the Ryukus to the Philippine Islands." As for other areas in the Pacific, he went on: "It must be clear that no one person can guarantee these areas against military attack."[7] It was a speech, as Acheson later noted in his memoirs, inspired as much by the innate limits on US power as by any desire to set out America's stall in Asia. "Our defense stations beyond the western hemisphere and our island possessions," he explained, "were the Philippines and defeated, disarmed, and occupied Japan. These were our inescapable responsibilities. We had moved our line of defense, a line fortified and manned by our own ground, sea, and air forces, to the very edge of the western Pacific."[8] Beyond the line thus sketched out, US interests would have to be pursued in other ways that did not involve the use of American forces. The point, as Melvyn Leffler has argued, "was to emphasize that it was a mistake 'to become obsessed with military considerations'": "[Acheson's] concern was with winning the cold war, not waging a hot war."[9]

Following a period in which China had gone Communist following the success of Mao Zedong's forces in the Chinese Civil War and the Soviets had successfully exploded a nuclear device, however, the perception that international communism was on the march prompted an alarmist response to the outbreak of war in Korea. Suddenly, Kennan's more prudent model looked dangerously narrow: if the United States did not oppose Communist expansion in Korea, then, potentially, it would be seen as abandoning the entire region. Communist militarism would have to be met in kind. Distinctions between core and periphery in Cold War strategy thus began to look premature. NSC 68, the revised national security strategy agreed on in the wake of the Korean War, offered a potential solution to this by essentially globalizing America's definition of what could be referred to as a *core area*. Rejecting Kennan's strategy, the new document set out a more expansive vision. "The assault on free institutions is world-wide now," it explained, "and in the context of the present polarization of power a defeat of free institutions anywhere is a defeat everywhere."[10]

But, in spite of this, the maturation of the Cold War into a global struggle between East and West over which model of progress would come to define the future was not as straightforward as that. To be sure, the relationship between the Cold War and the emergence of the so-called Third World soon became inextricably linked. As Robert McMahon has noted, officials in Moscow and Washington "came to see in the dominant trends throughout the developing regions a litmus test of their core ideas about the nature and direction of historical change."[11] Yet, if the Cold War could consequently come to provide the overarching context within which US officials perceived the wider world, this did not mean that the same methods would be used everywhere or that certain areas would not be considered to be of secondary or even tertiary concern to the United States. Though the descent into war in Vietnam could demonstrate the impact of following "the doctrine of national security to its logical conclusion," the pursuit of other tactics and strategies elsewhere in the Global South illustrated that this was not the only way in which US influence would manifest itself.[12] There would, in other words, continue to be areas of the world that were deemed to be peripheral for those determining the course of US policy. And, while *peripheral* is undoubtedly a problematic term, it is useful here in seeking to define why it was that a succession of US administrations intervened militarily in some areas and only indirectly, through nonmilitary means, or not at all in other regions.

Military force would be used to achieve US goals in some areas (most infamously Vietnam). In a host of other situations, however, a range of different factors—from basic security considerations, to economic and development matters, to the role played by transnational organizations and local actors—would all affect the way in which decisions were taken and the methods that were utilized to meet a particular goal. US policy might have had global connotations, then, but this in no way meant that similar approaches would be pursued in all areas of the world. What the Cold War did do, however, was to provide US officials with a reliable framework with which to evaluate its policies. When this started to fracture in the 1970s—as systemic shifts in the global economy, mounting problems in terms of the West's supply of oil from the Middle East, and the rise of transnational humanitarian movements demanded solutions that were not determined by Cold War concerns—a difficult period for US officials was prompted, one that was only partially alleviated by the emergence of human rights as a prominent issue in American policy, which led, in Daniel Sargent's analysis, to "the resurgence of a crusading style in U.S. foreign policy."[13]

Since the protection and promotion of US preponderance was a project that transcended the Cold War, it was also one that outlasted the East-West confrontation. When Soviet communism collapsed, the United States became the world's sole superpower for the first time in its history. Though the removal of the Cold War framework led, to some extent, to greater flexibility in US policy, it also raised new questions: In the absence of an obvious adversary, what was the rationale for global power projection? What issues now defined US foreign relations? National security, economics, humanitarianism, the desire to combat rogue states, democratic enlargement, or some difficult-to-define amalgamation of all these?[14] If this was difficult to define, meanwhile, under what circumstances could post–Cold War US presidents set out in precise terms the areas that they believed to be vital for maintaining the newfound US primacy and the areas (if any) that were peripheral? In the absence of a competing superpower, the administrations of George H. W. Bush and Bill Clinton reflexively sought to protect America's access to the Persian Gulf and its position of influence in that region as well as to prolong its newfound position as the world's sole superpower. But how this latter objective would be achieved in practice was contested by policymakers and intellectuals trying to make sense of a world in which there was no longer an obvious geopolitical adversary against which both to react and to go on the offensive. In some quarters, there was even a degree of nostalgia for the East-West conflict, which was viewed wistfully as an era when decision-making had been simple. Grappling with how to respond to the Bosnian civil war in 1994, Bill Clinton's national security adviser, Anthony Lake, admitted: "Sometimes I really miss the Cold War."[15]

The dilemmas now faced by the United States were both substantial and diverse. If Washington was to perpetuate what one commentator (with a touch of exaggeration) called its "unipolar moment," it needed to define what this meant in practice in every region of the world, including in former Communist and nonaligned states.[16] Under what circumstances would the United States now intervene in these regions, and how? What kinds of political, economic, and military crises constituted challenges to the new order? Which regions were core and which, if any, were peripheral? Indeed, in an era characterized by an aggressive and all-encompassing globalization (of finance, politics, culture, and violence), was there any region that was merely peripheral to US interests? If America was—as both critics and supporters claimed—an empire, then theoretically, at least, its interests could have no geographic limits.

Equally significant in this context is the fact that the areas conjured up by the very term *periphery* have shifted considerably since 2001 and the onset of the War on Terror. From the beginning, the War on Terror was conceived of as a conflict that was potentially global in scope.[17] While Afghanistan and Iraq were the main theaters of action, secondary fronts would quickly open up in the Philippines, across Africa, and, to a lesser extent, in the Caspian Sea region. Thus, whereas in its Cold War context *the periphery* was typically viewed as referring to areas such as South Asia, Latin America, and Africa, the post-9/11 age and the transformations wrought by globalization have seen the emergence of a new conception of what parts of the world are outside Washington's core interests. Indeed, in a world of globalized supply and production lines, some areas of the United States itself, such as Detroit, as well as declining areas of Europe, such as Greece, can now be seen as more peripheral to US interests than once-marginalized areas like the Middle East and Africa.[18]

As Obama's difficulties in 2014 attest, therefore, the problems of determining how the United States should respond to areas of the world outside its core interests—as well as prescribing which areas this applies to—remain as thorny as ever. In order to understand the way in which this problem has evolved, the chapters in this collection wrestle with two key questions related to this broader issue. First, what interests and goals drove US actions toward noncore areas in the years after 1945? Second, how have these changed over time, and how does this alter our perception of US foreign policy across a broader sweep of time?

No single study, of course, can provide a comprehensive answer to these questions.[19] But, whereas previous studies have focused solely on either particular geographic areas or specific periods of time, the chapters contained herein adopt a different tack. Rather than reanalyzing those well-covered flashpoints of US foreign policy in the Global South after 1945—Vietnam, Cuba, Guatemala, Iran, Iraq, and the wider Middle East—they consider the ways in which US policy evolved in areas that were deemed to be beyond Washington's core interests. In this sense, then, the term *periphery* does not refer to the so-called Third World in its entirety but relates instead to those parts of the world considered to be at the margins of US interests and considers the way in which perceptions of and engagement with these regions evolved in the Cold War and beyond. The consequence of this is an account of US policy that is more fractured than many accounts have typically suggested. For, while the policies pursued toward the developing world were often informed by similar principles and ideologies, they were also subject to large variations.

In adopting this approach, the chapters focus on four key themes—strategic concerns, economics, cultural factors, and the role of nongovernment and international actors—all of which had a profound effect on the evolution of the American view of so-called peripheral areas. Furthermore, each of these themes exerted a different influence at different times and in different places. None of them can be traced through the entire period under investigation here and portrayed as recurrent and singular themes in US policy; rather, they have evolved and changed in concert with the changing nature of the broader international context and influenced American perceptions of the wider world in numerous ways.

Geostrategic interests have, of course, exerted a significant influence on how American strategists perceived their foreign policy interests since World War II. Put simply, which areas were necessary to secure—and in what fashion—in order to protect the United States? The same model could, moreover, be applied to the post-1989 era as American policymakers grappled with similar debates. But, even when it comes to such an ostensibly clear-cut set of interests, defining what is a core interest and what is not is far from easy. An area that is believed to be of inordinate importance at one moment may well become less so in later years. Is it then still a core interest? Or are strategic interests more malleable than that? Can an area be considered core at one point but then, later, fade into the periphery? Is the reverse true? Can an area be considered peripheral at one point and become core later on? Western Europe, for one, is an area that, in the early Cold War years, was of extraordinary importance to the United States. Once it had been stabilized and helped toward economic recovery, however, and once the division of Europe became more or less permanent for the foreseeable future, one could argue that Europe's importance to US officials began to decrease. The Cold War still dominated US perceptions of Europe, to be sure, but its importance had undoubtedly altered. It would likely be going too far to suggest that Europe ever truly became peripheral in American eyes; even so, its fluctuating importance highlights the way in which such constructs can be transitory across a broad sweep of time.

At various points since 1989, the same oscillation has been evident. Post–Cold War Europe—in the wake of the collapse of the Soviet Union and its empire and the reunification of Germany—was of the utmost concern to the George H. W. Bush administration. Fast-forward ten years, however, and Europe's importance to the United States—particularly the importance of what Donald Rumsfeld would later chastise as "old Europe"—was evidently in decline. And, if such fluctuations can happen in Europe, what of areas like the Middle East or Africa? In their contributions to this volume, Robert J. McMahon, Tanya Harmer, David Ryan, Hal Brands, Simon Dalby, and Maria Ryan interrogate these evolving notions of a strategic core and periphery and consider the ways in which they evolved throughout the period under examination.

The role of development economics, to take another example, has had a wide-ranging and diverse influence on the way in which US policymakers have viewed the world. As underdevelopment came to replace race as an indicator of backwardness in the early Cold War world, officials in Washington focused their attention on methods by which to solve this endemic problem in order to eradicate the natural breeding ground for international communism. Yet this built on preexisting intellectual threads in American thinking that had been evolving since the United States began to emerge as a genuine world power in the late nineteenth century. The international fallout that followed the collapse in Vietnam seemed, for a time, to have brought about development's fall from grace in American policies toward the developing world. It reemerged with renewed force in the years after 1989, however, as Americans' perceptions about their capacity to shape global development were reinvigorated—first, by the notion of US victory over Soviet communism and, second, by the altered context and new world order imposed by aftermath of the 9/11 attacks and the onset of the global War on Terrorism.[20] Nation building in Iraq and Afghanistan saw a return to the broad-based theories that had underpinned earlier American efforts to foster modernity overseas. Continuities such as these, cannot, however, mask substantial differences. Development and modernization during the Cold War were, after all, built on the foundations of America's innate belief in the superiority of its own economy (despite some evidence by the early 1960s suggesting that this was a distinctly one-dimensional view). Post–Cold War development, on the other hand, came into vogue as certain areas within what had previously been thought of as the core—mainland Western Europe and the United States—fell into the abyss of poverty. Globalization and its attendant constructs have, therefore, altered the context for international development; they have done so, moreover, in a manner that explains away financial collapse in, say, Detroit or Greece as being merely an evolution of the global financial system. As the chapters by David Ekbladh, Christopher R. W. Dietrich, and Dustin Walcher argue, the fluctuation within and the evolution of US economic perceptions of the periphery since 1945 have exerted a substantial influence over American policy.

US relations with the periphery shaped by cultural factors or influenced by international or supranational actors, to take our third theme, complicate our understanding of these issues in a number of important ways. For, if the issues of strategic understanding and economics can be clearly seen to be driven by tangible interests, the roles of cultural factors and non-US actors are much less straightforward. At times, the influence exerted by the way in which US officials perceived other areas of the world—whether that be due to issues relating to race, religion, gender, or even the influence of emotions and the five senses—could alter Washington's approach even if, on the surface, this did not have any clear benefit to the United States. Equally, the role of supranational organizations like the United Nations or the perennial ability that nations across the globe had to pursue their own interests and affect American policy could take the United States in a direction it might not otherwise have followed. Any attempt to understand US conceptions of and policy toward a so-called periphery must, therefore, take into account these much less tangible influences. By doing so, we get a far greater sense of the enormous fluidity that has characterized perceptions of the periphery. In their contributions, Andrew J. Rotter, Alan McPherson, Mary Ann Heiss, Ryan Irwin, and Philip Dow examine the effect that cultural and international actors—and American perceptions of both—have had on US views of the so-called periphery.

In order to achieve this goal, the collection is divided into two sections. The first, featuring chapters by Robert J. McMahon, David Ekbladh, Andrew J. Rotter, Alan McPherson, and Simon Dalby, offers a series of thematic interpretations of evolving US interests as they pertain to peripheral areas. As these contributions note, US perceptions of these issues were subject to considerable change over time. This is vital in seeking to further understand the factors that drove US actions. As these chapters show, issues such as national security, economics and development, culture, anti-Americanism, and intellectual trajectories of imperialism were all, despite clear evidence of continuity, liable to fluctuate as international and domestic circumstances altered. Alan McPherson's assessment of instances of anti-American sentiments, for example, demonstrates that, though US officials' responses to this during the Cold War and after typically remained "defensive and unimaginative," there were also signs that their conception of these issues was becoming far more "comprehensive and accurate." The way in which US officials responded to anti-Americanism, McPherson notes, tells us much about the way in which appraisals of the so-called periphery were changing and the impact that different international and domestic contexts could have on this process. Similarly, as Robert J. McMahon's chapter makes clear, appraising perceptions of the periphery from different standpoints—geostrategic, economic, and cultural—can help explain why it was that in the Cold War all areas of the Global South were lumped together, resulting to some extent in "a false comparability" in historical works dealing with areas such as Asia, Africa, the Middle East, and Latin America. Yet, as McMahon goes on to note, understanding the way this took place in the years after 1945 is far from easy. "To understand the evolution of US strategic thinking in the early postwar era," he explains, "it is essential to recognize that different parts of the Third World became important to US strategists at different times and for quite different reasons." Responses to the periphery in the years after 1945, then, were often different—and we can get varying assessments of these differing responses by focusing on a range of thematic approaches.

The second section, building on these broader thematic assessments, provides a series of case studies that demonstrate the fluctuating nature of US policies in these areas. The chapters by Mary Ann Heiss, Ryan Irwin, Philip Dow, Dustin Walcher, Tanya Harmer, Christopher R. W. Dietrich, David Ryan, Hal Brands, and Maria Ryan engage with the ways in which policies toward peripheral areas emerged out of a range of different factors and were subject to change as the Cold War evolved and then, later, gave way to a new era in international relations. Ryan Irwin demonstrates the ways in which shifting intellectual trends in the United States during and after World War II—as exemplified by the positions taken by Wendell Wilkie and Nicholas Spykman—brought about profound changes in the global geography of American foreign interests. If Irwin's contribution highlights the way in which singular conceptions could emerge out of positions that varied considerably, however, the other chapters in this section demonstrate how, in spite of this, different policies and interests would come to govern US actions in peripheral areas. At times, geostrategic matters related to the Cold War would predominate; at other times, longer-standing economic and commercial interests, fused with newer ideologies of Modernization, would be to the fore; and, at still other times, transnational organizations and local actors would also exert a significant influence over US policymaking. In areas such as Latin America and the Middle East, which ebbed and flowed between being highly important and peripheral, this range of objectives would serve to influence US actions. Once the Cold War was over, meanwhile, officials in Washington would again confront the question of where their interests lay and how they should seek to extend them. The post–Cold War era undoubtedly offered new opportunities in the so-called periphery, as Hal Brands details, but it also continued to pose profound problems when it came to pursuing US objectives.

Ultimately, by adopting this way of considering US policy in areas that American officials considered to be peripheral—that is, of secondary importance when compared to areas believed to be of crucial importance—we can identify new ways of tracing the evolution of Washington's influence in areas once considered underdeveloped or peripheral. Moreover, and despite the contested nature of those terms, it can help to identify how a particular mind-set that grew out of the Cold War—the dated notion that some areas were more worthwhile than others—changed and assumed a new form as one global context was replaced by another. Shifts in US policy after 1945 might have forged the notion of some areas being peripheral, but, as this collection shows, this was not a phenomenon that was bound by the Cold War.[21] Goals and objectives in areas considered to be at the margins of Washington's core areas of concern were pursued by a variety of different means for a variety of different reasons. Finally, such an approach helps us situate US actions in areas such as these within a longer chronological framework, one in which the location of peripheral areas might have changed but one that still helps explain why the United States has continued to find ways of using its power to "influence the world."[22]

Notes

1. *Sustaining U.S. Global Leadership: Priorities for 21st Century Defense* (Washington, DC: US Department of Defense, January 2012), 1–3, http://www.defense. gov/news/defense_strategic_guidance.pdf

2. "Fact Sheet: U.S. Security Sector Assistance Policy" (Washington, DC: White House, Office of the Press Secretary, April 5, 2013), https://www.fas.org/irp/offdocs/ppd/ssa.pdf.

3. "Special Message to the Congress on Greece and Turkey: The Truman Doctrine," March 12, 1947, Gerhard Peters and John T. Woolley, eds., The American Presidency Project, http://www.presidency.ucsb.edu/ws/?pid=12846.

4. John Lewis Gaddis, *Strategies of Containment: A Critical Appraisal of American National Security Policy during the Cold War,* rev. ed. (New York: Oxford University Press, 2005), 54–64, 57. See also Walter Hixson, *George F. Kennan: Cold War Iconoclast* (New York: Columbia University Press, 1989), 49–50.

5. Anders Stephanson, *Kennan and the Art of Foreign Policy* (Cambridge, MA: Harvard University Press, 1989), 136.

6. See Marc Selverstone, *Constructing the Monolith: The United States, Great Britain, and International Communism, 1945–1950* (Cambridge, MA: Harvard University Press, 2009).

7. "Crisis in Asia—an Examination of US Policy: Remarks by Secretary of State Dean Acheson, January 12, 1950," *Department of State Bulletin* 22, no. 551 (January 23, 1950): 111–19.

8. Dean Acheson, *Present at the Creation: My Years in the State Department* (New York: Norton, 1969), 354–58, 357. See also Matthew Jones, *After Hiroshima: The United States, Race and Nuclear Weapons in Asia, 1945–1965* (Cambridge: Cambridge University Press, 2010), 53–56.

9. Melvyn Leffler, *A Preponderance of Power: National Security, the Truman Administration, and the Cold War* (Stanford, CA: Stanford University Press, 1992), 338. See also Bruce Cumings, *The Korean War: A History* (New York: Modern Library Chronicles, 2010).

10. "NSC 68: United States Objectives and Programs for National Security," April 14, 1950, *Foreign Relations of the United States, 1950,* vol. 1, *National Security Affairs; Foreign Economic Policy* (Washington, DC: US Government Printing Office, 1977), 240; Stephanson, *Kennan and the Art of Foreign Policy,* 157–75.

11. Robert McMahon, introduction to *The Cold War in the Third World,* ed. Robert McMahon (New York: Oxford University Press, 2013), 1–10, 3. See also

Odd Arne Westad, *The Global Cold War: Third World Interventions and the Making of Our Times* (Cambridge: Cambridge University Press, 2005).

12. Andrew Preston, "Monsters Everywhere: A Genealogy of National Security," *Diplomatic History* 38, no. 3 (June 2014): 477–500, 479.

13. Daniel Sargent, *A Superpower Transformed: The Remaking of American Foreign Relations in the 1970s* (New York: Oxford University Press, 2015), 4. See also Barbara Keyes, *Reclaiming American Virtue: The Human Rights Revolution of the 1970s* (Cambridge, MA: Harvard University Press, 2014).

14. John Dumbrell, "Was There a Clinton Doctrine? President Clinton's Foreign Policy Reconsidered," *Diplomacy and Statecraft* 13, no. 2 (Spring 2002): 43–56; Hal Brands, *From Berlin to Baghdad: America's Search for Purpose in the Post–Cold War World* (Lexington: University Press of Kentucky, 2008); Douglas Brinkley, "Democratic Enlargement: The Clinton Doctrine," *Foreign Policy*, no. 106 (Spring 1997): 110–27, 114–16.

15. Lake cited in Brands, *From Berlin to Baghdad*, 335. See also Derek Chollet and James Goldgeier, *America between the Wars: From 11/9 to 9/11—the Misunderstood Years between the Fall of the Berlin Wall and the Start of the War on Terror* (New York: Public Affairs, 2008).

16. Charles Krauthammer, "The Unipolar Moment," *Foreign Affairs*, 70, no. 1 (Winter 1990/1991): 22–33.

17. See, e.g., the Authorization for Use of Military Force, September 18, 2001, Public Law 107-40, https://www.911memorial.org/sites/all/files/Authorization%20 for%20use%20of%20military%20force.pdf. This granted the president authorization to use "all necessary and appropriate force" against unspecified "nations, organizations, or persons he determines planned, authorized, committed, or aided the terrorist attacks that occurred on September 11, 2001, or harboured such organizations or persons, in order to prevent any future acts of terrorism against the United States."

18. Robert Ross and Kent Trachte, *Global Capitalism: The New Leviathan* (Albany, NY: State University of New York Press, 1990). On Greece and the notion of a "Eurozone periphery," see Kash Mansori, "Why Greece, Spain, and Ireland Aren't to Blame for Europe's Woes," *New Republic*, October 10, 2011, http://www. tnr.com/article/economy/95989/eurozone-crisis-debt-dont-blame-greece#; Michael Moran, "Peripheral Damage Goes Global, Part II," *Slate*, June 14, 2012, http:// www.slate.com/blogs/the_reckoning/2012/06/14/euro_crisis_with_the_greeks_ voting_peripheral_damage_goes_global_.html; and Mark Mazower, *Governing the World: The History of an Idea* (London: Allen Lane, 2012), 406–29

19. See, e.g., McMahon, ed., *The Cold War in the Third World;* and Mary Ann Heiss and Peter Hahn, eds., *Empire and Revolution: The United States and the Third World since 1945* (Columbus: Ohio State University Press, 2001). One way round this has been for collections to emerge that deal with particular areas or time periods. See, e.g., Gilbert Joseph and Daniella Spenser, eds., *In from the Cold* (Durham, NC: Duke University Press, 2007); Sue Onslow, ed., *Cold War in Southern Africa:*

White Power, Black Liberation (London: Routledge, 2009); Nigel Ashton, ed., *The Cold War in the Middle East: Regional Conflict and the Superpowers, 1967–73* (London: Routledge, 2007); Andrew Johns and Kathryn Statler, eds., *The Eisenhower Administration, the Third World, and the Globalization of the Cold War* (Lanham, MD: Rowman & Littlefield, 2006); Francis Gavin and Mark Atwood Lawrence, eds., *Beyond the Cold War: Lyndon Johnson and the New Global Challenges of the 1960s* (New York: Oxford University Press, 2014); and Andrew Preston and Fredrik Logevall, eds., *Nixon in the World: American Foreign Relations, 1969–1977* (New York: Oxford University Press, 2008).

20. David Ekbladh, *The Great American Mission: Modernization and the Construction of an American World Order* (Princeton, NJ: Princeton University Press, 2010); Michael Latham, *The Right Kind of Revolution: Modernization, Development, and US Foreign Policy from the Cold War to the Present* (Ithaca, NY: Cornell University Press, 2010); Daniel Immerwahr, *Thinking Small: The United States and the Lure of Community Development* (Cambridge, MA: Harvard University Press, 2015).

21. On the temporal nature of the Cold War and the fact that US interests and objectives existed outside the conflict with the Soviets, see Anders Stephanson, "Cold War Degree Zero," in *Uncertain Empire: American History and the Idea of the Cold War,* ed. Joel Isaac and Duncan Bell (New York: Oxford University Press, 2012), 19–51.

22. Westad, *The Global Cold War,* 404.

1

THEMES

How the Periphery Became the Center

The Cold War, the Third World, and the Transformation in US Strategic Thinking

Robert J. McMahon

This chapter presents a critical examination of the relationship between the center and the periphery in US strategic thinking during the Cold War era. It argues that sharp and meaningful distinctions between the periphery and the center largely collapsed during the early Cold War years, leading US policymakers to conflate, and confuse, peripheral with vital interests. The impact of this pronounced shift in American strategic thinking was profound; it permitted countries such as Vietnam, Laos, Angola, Guatemala, Nicaragua, and Afghanistan, among others, to assume outsized significance in American foreign policy while drawing disproportionate US attention and resources.

After acknowledging the ambiguity and elasticity of the term *periphery* and exploring critically the different ways in which that term has been utilized in Cold War historiography, I examine the multiple ways in which the periphery came to be equated with the Third World in US strategic thinking and the process by which the Third World, in turn, came to be seen by American elites as a vast, undifferentiated space—a space populated by racially and civilizationally inferior peoples, wracked by political and social instability, yet possessing a treasure trove of crucial natural resources. Significantly, different parts of the Third World became important to US planners at different times and for quite different reasons.

Since virtually every corner of the Third World came to be viewed by American strategists as vital, or potentially vital, to the overall national security interests of the United States—by no later than the mid- and late 1950s—it is crucial to understand how this blurring of distinctions occurred. American policymakers maintained a clear hierarchy of importance among different Third World areas during the earliest years of the Cold War. The Middle East and Southeast Asia stood at the top of that hierarchy for a confluence of economic and geopolitical reasons; other regions ranked much lower. The present chapter seeks to explicate how that changed: how and why a globalist vision emerged in US policy circles that resulted in the gradual disappearance of distinctions between core and periphery along with the erasure of distinctions *among* peripheral regions and countries. Strategic, economic, ideological, political, and psychological factors seamlessly merged in US strategic thinking, I stress, making *every* corner of the world critical, or potentially critical, to the nation's expansive global interests. That development carried far-reaching ramifications for the Cold War and for America's international role.

Scholars of modern international history have increasingly utilized the term *periphery* in their work. I have bowed to that fashion myself, titling my book on US relations with India and Pakistan between 1947 and 1966 *The Cold War on the Periphery*.[1] In it, I deployed *periphery* both as a description of the region I was examining and as a construct and framework for my analysis.

Yet it bears emphasizing that *periphery* remains an elastic and ambiguous term. It is often used without a clear definition, and it sometimes means strikingly different things to different authors. The formal dictionary definition of the word—"the external boundary or surface of a body; the outward bounds of something as distinguished from its regions or center; [or] an area lying beyond the strict limits of a thing"—hardly hints at the wider meanings *periphery* has assumed among scholars of international history.[2]

For world-systems theorists, *periphery* (along with *core* and *semiperiphery*) constitutes one of the three interconnected spatial and functional constants in a world capitalist system that has existed from the sixteenth century to the present. In his adaptation of this theory to fit the history of US foreign policy since 1945, the historian Thomas J. McCormick describes the peripheral zone of the world system as one that specializes in the production of agricultural commodities and raw materials for the benefit of core countries. He sees *periphery* and *Third World* as synonymous during the Cold War era. Essentially, the periphery/Third World served as the "hewers of wood and carriers of water" for the system's hegemonic power, the United States, as well as for its industrialized, high-technology fellow core states of Western Europe, Canada, and Japan. Throughout the Cold War era, McCormick contends, the Third World's value to the United States derived from the high priority Americans assigned to "the economic integration of the periphery into core market economies—as investment opportunities, as sources of cost-cutting raw materials, as consumer goods markets." During that period, a time in which the United States maintained its position as the world's chief capital exporter, "the Third World absorbed one-third of [US] overseas investments[,] and that one-third generated more aggregate profit than the two-thirds invested in Europe, Japan, and Canada."[3]

For scholars whose work emphasizes the strategic more than the material wellsprings of American foreign policy, *periphery* typically alludes to areas of the world considered to be of secondary or tertiary interest to US policymakers. Thus, foreign relations historians and international relations specialists alike routinely divide US interests in different parts of the world into those that are vital, meaning crucial, or essential, or fundamental (in other words, those that must be preserved in order to sustain the national security), and those that are peripheral, meaning decidedly nonvital, if not marginal, to the national security. The diplomat-scholar George F. Kennan captured this key distinction as well as anyone in several memoranda that he penned and speeches that he delivered in the early post–World War II years. That not all parts of the world were equally vital to American security formed his guiding premise. Rather, he wrote in August 1948: "We should select first those areas of the world which . . . we cannot permit . . . to fall into hands hostile to us, and . . . we [should] put forward, as the first specific objective of our policy and as an irreducible minimum of national security, the maintenance of political regimes in those areas at least favorable to the continued power and independence of our nation."[4]

In a subsequent address at the National War College, the originator of the containment doctrine lent unusual specificity to this concept by identifying what he characterized as the world's five vital power centers: the United States, the Soviet Union, Great Britain, continental Western

Europe (including West Germany), and Japan. Those, Kennan stressed, constituted the only "centers of industrial and military power in the world which are important to us from the standpoint of national security." His reasoning flowed from his calculation that only in those five areas "would [you] get the requisite conditions of climate, of industrial strength, of population and of tradition which would enable people there to develop and launch the type of amphibious power which would have to be launched if our national security were [to be] seriously affected."[5]

John Lewis Gaddis, Kennan's prizewinning biographer and a leading scholar of the Cold War, has peppered his own prodigious scholarship with similar core/periphery, vital/peripheral distinctions. For Gaddis, those US Cold War diplomats who helped conceive and bring to fruition the soundest—and hence most realistic—grand strategies, such as Henry A. Kissinger and Kennan himself, followed this thinking closely. Their success derived in large measure from their recognition of the crucial distinction between the core and the periphery and from their concomitant unwillingness to permit a preoccupation with presumed threats to determine Washington's fundamental interests and priorities. Such statesmen recognized that the ends and means of policy needed to be in balance; resources, since they were always finite, needed to be utilized for the achievement of the most essential policy goals. A multitude of scholars of US foreign relations, many proceeding implicitly from the theoretical assumptions associated with realism, similarly gauge the relative strengths and weaknesses of different American statesmen and presidential administrations in terms of their grasp of the essential distinctions between core and periphery—and especially their ability to differentiate vital from peripheral interests.[6]

In his sweeping account of the national security strategy of the Harry S. Truman administration, Melvyn P. Leffler appropriates such a framework to appraise the combination of wisdom and shortsightedness that he attributes to America's actions in the early Cold War years. While he heaps praise on Truman administration planners for conceiving and implementing policies that strengthened core industrial states while orienting them toward the United States, he faults them for exaggerating and distorting the importance of the Third World periphery. Washington policymakers "attributed excessive value to the Third World," he charges, becoming "ever more determined to preserve stability and thwart the rise of revolutionary nationalism on the periphery." He decries the fact that senior diplomatic and defense officials in the Truman administration became so "obsessed" with the presumed Communist threat to peripheral areas that they even displayed "a willingness to risk atomic war over the periphery." They grievously "misconstrued the intrinsic value of even the most important of these countries," Leffler contends, concluding: "For prudent men to have attributed so much importance to the periphery, for them to have possessed such exaggerated notions of Soviet capabilities in the Third World, and for them to have invested so heavily in strategic overkill was foolish indeed."[7]

Periphery has thus become a veritable synonym for *Third World* among scholars of the Cold War. The initial prospectus for the conference that inspired the present volume well captures that common understanding. "By the early 1950s," the conference organizers noted, "it was becoming clear to officials in both Washington and Moscow that the location for much of the Cold War was going to be the developing world—or, as political scientists would subsequently label it, the *periphery*." Hence, in this standard formulation, the terms *developing world, Third World,* and *periphery* are interchangeable.

Yet the assumptions undergirding this common conceptual usage also suggest a problematic notion of the Third World as *undifferentiated space.* This reductionist usage implies a false comparability between places as diverse as Southeast Asia, Korea, the Middle East, South America, Central America, the Caribbean, and Sub-Saharan Africa.

A partial explanation for the inclination to lump together all Third World territories can be found in the upsurge of recent scholarship in international history that highlights themes of race, development, and culture. In racial terms, the Third World/periphery was of course overwhelmingly nonwhite. US officials, especially during the early phase of the Cold War, frequently thought in terms of racial hierarchies and regularly disparaged nonwhites. Dean Rusk, who worked closely with Secretary of State Dean Acheson and later ascended himself to the top position at the State Department, once observed that Acheson "did not give a damn about the brown, yellow, black, and red people in various parts of the world."[8] And that perception, however harsh, captures the combination of disdain, condescension, and racial stereotyping with which Acheson and an entire generation of US policymakers approached the non-Western world.⁹ For his part, George Kennan regarded "states with colored populations" as "the neurotic products of exotic backgrounds and tentative Western educational experiences." As vice president, Richard M. Nixon once remarked that the people of Africa could hardly be taken seriously since they had only recently come out of the trees, and an Africa specialist in the State Department dismissed African freedom fighters as "black baboons." Those examples can easily be multiplied many times over and just from a modest examination of now-declassified US diplomatic records. More than one scholar, accordingly, borrowing from the cultural theorist Edward Said, has suggested that Americans internalized an Orientalist view of Third World peoples.¹⁰

In developmental terms, US elites inside and outside the government reflexively equated the non-Western world with the planet's poorest and least-developed parts—whether those areas had been independent for generations, as had most of the Latin American republics, or were just emerging from decades of colonial subjugation. Hunger and poverty plagued the diverse peoples who inhabited the peripheral areas of the Global South, according to most Western observers. The non-Western portions of the globe thus appeared conceptually unified, not just by their subordinate economic status relative to the advanced, industrialized West, but by their desperate need for modernization and development. The very existence of those near-uniform conditions of underdevelopment, accordingly, lent additional support to the image of the periphery as an essentially homogeneous space.¹¹

Culturalist work in international history points us toward a set of even broader prejudices feeding US perceptions of the Third World as a locale whose common attributes far outweighed any local or regional distinctions. "To the United States, the Soviet Union, and their respective allies and subordinates, the Third World was by definition an undifferentiated space," emphasizes Andrew Rotter. "It was filled with vital natural resources but inconveniently wracked by instability, presided over by leaders whom First and Second World officials generally considered to be racially or civilizationally inferior to themselves."¹² The culturalist wave in international history points to a wide range of analytic constructs—from gender, race, and religion to language, emotion, and identity—that serve to underscore the subordinate position that the entirety of the periphery held for most US policymakers throughout the Cold War decades.

Yet, if we focus on US perceptions and plans regarding the value of peripheral territories to the overall global interests and strategy of the United States, the picture looks very different. Doing so makes it imperative for us to move away from the notion of undifferentiated non-Western space and instead highlight distinctions and differences. To understand the evolution of US strategic thinking in the early postwar era, it is essential to recognize that different parts of the Third World became important to US strategists at different times and for quite different reasons.

During the Truman administration, certain parts of the Third World—most especially the Middle East and Southeast Asia—assumed great importance in US grand strategy, for an interrelated set of economic and geopolitical reasons, while other parts remained quite marginal. Middle Eastern oil ranked as a crucial resource for the Western powers. It had to be denied to the Soviets and at the same time made available to the energy-starved nations of Western Europe in order to facilitate their economic recoveries. The availability of cheap oil from the Middle East was critical to the success of the Marshall Plan. Indeed, by the early 1950s, Middle Eastern oil supplied fully 70 percent of Europe's total energy needs. World War II had taught that access to and control over petroleum constituted a fundamental component of a nation's military-economic power, a lesson that underlined the strategic import of the Middle East— in wartime and peacetime. That region also contained military base sites that defense officials in the United States considered essential in any hot war with the Soviet Union, further magnifying its criticality.[13]

In similar fashion, US planners valued Southeast Asia for the resources it provided to and the commercial links it maintained with core states, inputs that they judged essential to the economic revival of both Western Europe and Japan. The prewar years had driven home the importance of the rubber, tin, and oil of Southeast Asia. Tellingly, hundreds of millions of dollars in Marshall Plan aid were transferred directly or indirectly to the colonial territories of the Western European powers in an effort to reinforce traditional economic ties. For those broader strategic and economic reasons, Truman-era officials sought to spur closer integration between the developing nations of the Middle East and Southeast Asia and the industrial core states of Western Europe and Japan.[14]

Reflecting those priorities, Secretary of State Dean Acheson devoted far more attention to the Middle East and Southeast Asia during his tenure in office (1949–1953) than he did to any other parts of the Third World. His keen interest in strengthening the fledgling NATO led him to press both the Dutch and the French to pursue more liberal and accommodating approaches to the aspirations for self-rule of Indonesian and Vietnamese nationalists. US policies diverged in the two cases, to be sure, with Acheson pressuring the Dutch to grant independence to moderate nationalists in Indonesia while approving the provision of military assistance to the French in their struggle against the Communist-led Vietminh insurgents. Still, a determination to stabilize the Southeast Asian periphery in order to bolster the military and economic strength of key NATO allies shaped US actions in both instances. Acheson also accorded a high priority to safeguarding access to base sites in North Africa and ensuring access to inexpensive oil in Iran, Saudi Arabia, and elsewhere in the Middle East. For the strategically minded diplomat, the Southeast Asia and Middle East regions constituted essential elements in a grand strategy aimed at guaranteeing a preponderance of power for the West in the Cold War. The interdependence that obtained between those areas and the industrial core states transformed them from peripheral to critical US interests.[15]

The same preoccupation with correlations of power that elevated the Middle East and Southeast Asia to major national security concerns for Acheson and other Truman administration principals, on the other hand, rendered much of the rest of the Third World marginal to US grand strategy. Vast tracts of territory ranging from South Asia to Sub-Saharan Africa to much of Latin America appeared as little more than blips on the radar screens of senior policymakers. The relative neglect of those areas should not be surprising since they possessed few of the attributes most prized by US officials: they offered neither significant military strength nor even fledgling industrial power; they contained neither essential base sites nor indispensable resources. The Soviet Union, moreover, posed no demonstrable threat to any of those regions. Truman administration officials, consequently, were not particularly concerned about developments in the peripheral parts of the Third World. Their plates were already quite full, and there were already too many demands on available American resources.

The South Asia region offers an instructive case in point. At the time of Prime Minister Jawaharlal Nehru's first state visit to the United States in October 1949, some US officials recommended that the administration bolster India as a non-Communist Asian alternative to the new Communist regime of Mao Zedong in China. Nehru's refusal to join a US-dominated alliance system, his insistence on pursuing instead a strategy of nonalignment in the Cold War, and the doubts harbored by Truman, Acheson, and other top officials about India's strategic and economic value combined to render such ideas stillborn. Chester Bowles, Truman's energetic ambassador in New Delhi, sought to gain administration support for a major aid program aimed at fostering Indian economic growth only to be thwarted at every turn. Perceptions of the South Asia region as a strategic backwater persisted into the Dwight D. Eisenhower administration, even after the new president approved a mutual security pact with Pakistan, India's chief regional rival, in 1954. It is telling that the US-Pakistani arms agreement sprang from US conceptions of Pakistan as a useful adjunct to its efforts to defend the Middle East and not from its status as a South Asian nation.[16]

In the mid-1950s, a set of bold diplomatic and economic initiatives undertaken by the Soviet Union and targeting the non-Western world triggered a fundamental shift in prevailing US attitudes and policies toward the periphery. Indeed, Moscow's Third World "economic offensive," as US observers tagged it, deserves recognition as one of the Cold War's key turning points. More than any other event, it was the Soviet campaign to extend its influence throughout the periphery that led to the collapse of previously held distinctions between vital and marginal areas.

The death of the long-serving dictator Joseph Stalin in March 1953 brought to the Kremlin a more flexible and diplomatically adroit Soviet leadership cadre. Communist Party chairman Nikita S. Khrushchev and his colleagues pushed a number of international initiatives aimed alternately at winning the public relations dimension of the Cold War, weakening the cohesiveness of the Western alliance, and putting the United States on the defensive. By the fall of 1955, concerned US analysts began focusing particular attention on a new and apparently ominous aspect of this wider campaign: namely, the friendly Soviet overtures that were being made to various uncommitted Third World nations. The generous aid and trade offers that Moscow was beginning to offer to a number of nonaligned countries in Asia and Africa formed the centerpiece of its economic offensive. By encouraging the neutralist tendencies already evident in those countries, the Soviets could advance their broader goal of diluting Western strength while simultaneously enhancing Moscow's own global power and prestige—or so US observers feared.[17]

On November 1, 1955, the CIA emphasized the gravity of this new development for US security interests in a report presented on behalf of the American intelligence community. It noted that the most "salient feature of the present global situation is a change in the character of the East-West conflict." By demonstrating a break with Stalinist orthodoxy with its aid and trade offers to selected nonaligned states, the Kremlin was seeking to exploit Western vulnerability in the Third World. That vulnerability was exacerbated by Washington's close identification with the now discredited, and frequently despised, colonial powers. America's recently negotiated bilateral and multilateral alliances with certain pro-Western states along the periphery had compounded the problem by alienating many of the nonaligned nations. In addition, the rapid industrialization of the Soviet Union over the past generation offered an appealing model to many aspirant Third World leaders who desired similarly dramatic transformation in their own homelands. A "grave danger" existed, the report concluded, that the new policy being pursued by Moscow "will create an even more serious threat to the Free World than did Stalin's aggressive postwar policies."[18] The April 1955 convocation of the Afro-Asian nations at Bandung, the high-profile trip of Khrushchev and Premier Nikolai Bulganin to India, Afghanistan, and Burma later that year, and the Eastern Bloc arms deal with Egypt's Gamal Abdel Nasser joined with the Kremlin's generous aid and trade offers to highlight what seemed to be an emerging contest for the loyalty of Third World states and peoples.

The alarm that these moves sparked at the highest levels of the Eisenhower administration constitutes a break from previous attitudes toward the periphery in at least two respects. The conviction that the United States and its allies had important strategic and material interests in certain portions of the Third World was certainly not new. Neither was the concern that developments along the periphery might enhance the power of the Soviet Union while correspondingly weakening the power of the West. Indeed, by the late 1940s, those convictions had been commonly accepted by nearly all senior planners in the Truman administration. But US officials now calculated that the *nature* of the Soviet threat in the Third World had changed. They were dismayed by Moscow's newfound tactical flexibility since it appeared to pose a different kind of challenge. They had not in the past needed to contend with an adversary more interested in extending ties to nonaligned states than it was in furthering Communist revolutions in the non-Western areas.

Second, they were concerned that the *direction* of the Soviet threat in the Third World had now changed as well. Throughout the Truman administration, as noted above, senior officials had identified Southeast Asia and the Middle East as the only truly critical parts of the Third World from the standpoint of US security. The absence of critical resources, base sites, and commercial/strategic links with core states, coupled with the absence of a palpable Soviet interest or threat there during the late 1940s and early 1950s, made South Asia, Sub-Saharan Africa, and Latin America seem far removed from the front lines of the Cold War. Officials judged those regions, consequently, to be relatively unimportant to US security. During the Truman years, even modest aid recommendations for those regions never gained traction with high-level policymakers. One administration official who opposed Ambassador Bowles's efforts to garner substantial economic aid for India complained: "We cannot afford an economic development program unrelated to the communist threat."[19] That revealing admission helps explain the relative inattention paid by the United States to much of South Asia, Latin America, and Sub-Saharan Africa throughout the Truman and early Eisenhower years.

By late 1955, however, that complacency was jarred by evidence of a concerted Soviet campaign to win friends and gain allies and trading partners across the vast reaches of the Third World periphery. On November 15, CIA director Allen W. Dulles shared his concern with the National Security Council (NSC), expressing deep apprehension about the Soviet campaign. The Kremlin's varied actions, he emphasized, suggested "a pattern of coordinated long-term and high-level operations designed to advance Communist influence in all of these [peripheral] areas." Taken together, he warned, those actions might ultimately undermine US interests throughout the developing world.[20] A subsequent study commissioned by the White House called the Soviet economic offensive "well-planned and integrated . . . vigorous, selective, and opportunistic"— one that was "global in scope." The offensive's goal, in targeting countries such as India, Burma, and Afghanistan, was "to neutralize U.S. influence and undermine the Western politico-military position in areas adjacent to the [Communist] Bloc." The report concluded with the by-then familiar warning that the United States now faced a grave political and strategic challenge; it stressed that the Soviets aimed not only to undercut US leadership and influence in the underdeveloped areas but in the process also to undermine the Western alliance as well.[21]

Soviet diplomatic and economic opportunism in the developing world had plainly forced US policymakers to reexamine long-held assumptions about the character and gravity of the threat posed by the Soviet Union. The wide-ranging intra-administration debates that surrounded the issuance in February 1956 of a new statement of "basic national security policy" demonstrate the extent to which a significant conceptual shift was taking place at the upper levels of the Eisenhower administration. The NSC Planning Board noted that the principal rationale for proposing significant revisions in a policy paper (NSC 5501) that was only a year old stemmed from the "new methods and more flexible tactics" that the Soviets had unveiled, especially in their bold diplomatic venture into the Third World. In its pursuit of closer ties with certain developing nations, the Kremlin was effectively exploiting the failure of the United States to develop an affirmative "community of interests" with those states. The new policy paper (NSC 5602) laid out the core problem with refreshing directness. "The dangers to free world stability are particularly acute in the less developed areas," it declared, "and are enhanced by recent Soviet initiatives."[22]

A different appreciation of the Soviet threat and of core US national security interests was clearly taking hold in policy circles. In the past, strategists in the United States had viewed the Soviet challenge to US security as primarily geostrategic in character. The principal fear driving US policy in the early postwar period stemmed from the worry that a combination of political instability and economic distress might enable the Soviet Union to gain direct or indirect control over parts of the invaluable Eurasian heartland. That fear had a politico-psychological dimension as well. US analysts worried that Communist successes might encourage neutralist tendencies among free world nations. Even worse, they might spark a bandwagon effect that would enable the Soviets to expand their dominion without firing a shot. Either outcome would erode Western strength, solidarity, and morale. In April 1950, NSC 68 had declared that one of the most essential objectives of US policy was, consequently, to ensure that "our allies and potential allies do not as a result of a sense of frustration or of Soviet intimidation drift into a course of neutrality eventually leading to Soviet domination."[23] In addition to the core areas of Western Europe and Japan, certain regions of the Third World, principally the Middle East and Southeast Asia, were important factors in the containment strategy designed by the Truman administration to counter both the military and the nonmilitary dimensions of the Soviet threat. Vast parts of the Third World, however, remained consigned to the margins—or periphery, if you will—by planners in the Truman and Eisenhower administrations, including such prominent targets of recent Soviet diplomatic activity as India, Burma, and Afghanistan.

In the wake of the Soviet Union's Third World offensive, those countries had for the first time suddenly been transformed into major Cold War prizes. That transformation occurred, not because US officials had revised earlier estimates about the intrinsic strategic and economic value of those lands, but because they had extended earlier calculations about the politico-psychological interconnectedness between core and periphery. The Joint Chiefs of Staff alluded to this shifting assessment in a memorandum of March 12, 1956. Noting with alarm that "the free world situation is gradually deteriorating," they stated their conviction that the threats confronting the United States were now "primarily in the political, social, and psychological, fields."[24]

The revised statement of overall national security policy, which was formally approved by Eisenhower three days later as NSC 5602/1, warned explicitly that the movement of *any* additional state into the Communist camp could harm US security. In a particularly revealing passage, it forecast that the resultant damage "might be out of all proportion to the strategic or economic significance of the territory involved."[25] Given the lessons likely to be drawn by friends and foes alike about the power, resolution, and prestige of the two superpowers from developments taking place even in peripheral parts of the Third World, any areas in which the Soviets had chosen to invest substantial attention or resources thus by definition *became* vital to the security of the United States. Efforts to differentiate between vital and peripheral areas of interest, already partially blurred in such earlier policy statements as NSC 68, were rendered by this logic totally meaningless. Even developments in the far periphery of the Third World could, according to this logic, have a potentially decisive impact on overall correlations of global power.

US leaders reached that conclusion by conflating and exaggerating two distinct types of fears. On the one hand, they feared Moscow's unsheathing of a new economic weapon in its Third World campaign. On the other, they feared that Soviet gains anywhere in the Third World would shape the future loyalties both of other Third World states and of US allies in Europe and Japan. This strategic appraisal, however muddled, exercised a powerful hold on planners in the Eisenhower administration. In their eyes, the Soviet threat encompassed significant new elements that rendered it dangerous in the extreme. It was not only global in character but also so diffuse as to be almost impossible to check. To make matters even worse, this Soviet threat was "less likely to manifest itself through readily identifiable crises," according to NSC 5602/1, "but more likely to lead to gradual erosion of free world position." And the Soviets, of course, as Eisenhower worriedly confided to Secretary of State John Foster Dulles, "had the advantage of the initiative."[26]

Obviously, a different kind of threat demanded a different kind of response. But, just as the debate over the new NSC policy paper revealed a developing consensus within the Eisenhower administration about the changed nature of the Soviet threat and the growing importance of the periphery, so too did those deliberations reveal sharp differences within the administration regarding the specific steps needed to counter that threat. At an NSC meeting of December 8, 1955, Eisenhower had posited that a more aggressive and imaginative use of foreign aid could provide a useful diplomatic counterweapon. It would be advantageous to US security interests, he argued, "to have certain important countries like India strong enough to remain neutral or at least 'neutral on our side.'" Other senior officials, including Secretary of Defense Charles Wilson and Secretary of the Treasury George Humphrey, questioned the propriety of increased aid dollars for any of the nonaligned states; their deeply held convictions ensured that any such initiative would first have to overcome entrenched bureaucratic opposition.[27]

Congress posed an even more serious impediment to an expanded foreign aid effort aimed at the nonaligned nations. The powerful Senate majority leader, William Knowland, a conservative California Republican, doubtless spoke for many of his colleagues when he confided to Eisenhower and Dulles during a private meeting: "It would be bad if the impression got around the world that we reward neutralism."[28] Such sentiments ran deep, leading Congress to slash Eisenhower's proposed foreign aid budgets for the fiscal years 1956, 1957, and 1958.

The president ultimately overcame much of that opposition. By the end of his second term in office, economic assistance to India and other Third World states stood as a centerpiece of the administration's foreign aid program. The US commitment to the developing nations deepened further during the presidency of John F. Kennedy. In 1961, Kennedy's secretary of state, Dean Rusk, proclaimed to the Senate Foreign Relations Committee that the "much enlarged" Soviet effort in the Third World demonstrated that the Soviet-American struggle had shifted "from the military problem in Western Europe to a genuine contest for the underdeveloped countries." He warned: "The battles for Africa, Latin, America, the Middle East, and Asia are now joined, not on a military plain in the first instance, but for influence, prestige, loyalty, and so forth, and the stakes there are very high."[29]

The far-reaching changes in US diplomatic priorities suggested by Rusk's assessment can be traced directly to the Soviet economic offensive of the mid-1950s. US analysts—however illogically—saw that campaign as an insidious threat to US security. Nothing less than a full-scale commitment by the United States to the economic development of the Third World periphery would, they became convinced, be sufficient to counter Moscow's frightening new challenge. Such ideas continued to animate US actions along the Third World periphery right up to the end of the Cold War, as the Ronald Reagan administration's near obsession with the presumed threats to US national security emanating from Central America so plainly demonstrates. The conflation of vital and secondary interests and the concomitant blurring of distinctions between core and peripheral corners of the globe have left a powerful and problematic legacy for the post–Cold War statesmen of our own time.

Notes

1. Robert J. McMahon, *The Cold War on the Periphery: The United States, India, and Pakistan* (New York: Columbia University Press, 1994).

2. *Merriam-Webster's Collegiate Dictionary,* 11th ed. (Springfield, MA: Merriam-Webster, 2003), s.v. *periphery.*

3. Thomas J. McCormick, *America's Half-Century: United States Foreign Policy in the Cold War* (Baltimore: Johns Hopkins University Press, 1989), esp. 3, 135–36 (quote 136).

4. Kennan quoted in John Lewis Gaddis, *Strategies of Containment: A Critical Appraisal of Postwar American National Security Policy* (New York: Oxford University Press, 1982), 30.

5. Ibid., 27–31 (quotes 29).

6. Ibid.

7. Melvyn P. Leffler, *A Preponderance of Power: National Security, the Truman Administration, and the Cold War* (Stanford, CA: Stanford University Press, 1992), esp. 506–11.

8. Dean Rusk, *As I Saw It* (New York: Norton, 1990), 422.

9. Thomas Borstelmann, *Apartheid's Reluctant Uncle: The United States and Southern Africa in the Early Cold War* (New York: Oxford University Press, 1993), 40, 112; Andrew J. Rotter, *Comrades at Odds: The United States and India, 1947–1964* (Ithaca, NY: Cornell University Press, 2000), 159–60.

10. See, e.g., Douglas Little, *American Orientalism: The United States and the Middle East since 1945* (Chapel Hill: University of North Carolina Press, 2008). See also Borstelmann, *Apartheid's Reluctant Uncle,* 112 (Kennan quote); Roland Burke, *Decolonization and the Evolution of Human Rights* (Philadelphia: University of Pennsylvania Press, 2011), 146 (Nixon quote); and Ryan Irwin, *Gordian Knot: Apartheid and the Unmaking of the Liberal World Order* (New York: Oxford University Press, 2012), 82 ("black baboons").

11. See, e.g., Nick Cullather, *The Hungry World: America's Cold War Battle against Poverty in Asia* (Cambridge, MA: Harvard University Press, 2010); David Ekbladh, *The Great American Mission: Modernization and the Construction of an American World Order* (Princeton, NJ: Princeton University Press, 2010); and Michael E. Latham, *The Right Kind of Revolution: Modernization, Development, and U.S. Foreign Policy from the Cold War to the Present* (Ithaca, NY: Cornell University Press, 2011).

12. Andrew J. Rotter, "Culture, the Cold War, and the Third World," in *The Cold War in the Third World,* ed. Robert J. McMahon (New York: Oxford University Press, 2013), 156–77, 160.

13. Leffler, *A Preponderance of Power.*

14. Ibid.

15. Robert J. McMahon, *Dean Acheson and the Creation of an American World Order* (Washington, DC: Potomac, 2009).

16. McMahon, *Cold War on the Periphery.*

17. The section that follows draws on Robert J. McMahon, "The Illusion of Vulnerability: American Reassessments of the Soviet Threat, 1955–1956," *International History Review* 18 (August 1996): 591–619.

18. "World Situation and Trends," National Intelligence Estimate 100-7-55, November 1, 1955, and State Department Paper, October 3, 1955, *Foreign Relations of the United States, 1955–1957,* vol. 19, *National Security Policy* (Washington, DC: US Government Printing Office, 1990), 131–45 (quotes 133, 141), 123–25 (hereafter, e.g., *FRUS, 1955–1957*).

19. Ohly to Elsey, October 1, 1952, India 1952 folder, box 341, W. Averell Harriman Papers, Library of Congress, Washington, DC.

20. Memorandum of Discussion at NSC Meeting, November 15, 1955, *FRUS, 1955–1957,* vol. 10, *Foreign Aid and Economic Defense Policy* (Washington, DC: US Government Printing Office, 1989), 28–31.

21. "The Nature and Problems of Soviet Economic Penetration in Underdeveloped Areas," February 29, 1956, State Department memorandum, Ann Whitman File, Dulles-Herter Series, Dwight D. Eisenhower Papers, Eisenhower Library, Abilene, KS. See also C. D. Jackson to Nelson A. Rockefeller, November 10, 1955, *FRUS, 1955–1957,* vol. 9, *Foreign Economic Policy; Foreign Economic Program* (Washington, DC: US Government Printing Office, 1987), 8–10.

22. Memorandum by the NSC Planning Board, n.d. (forwarded to the NSC February 13, 1956), *FRUS, 1955–1957,* vol. 19, *National Security Policy,* 193–97. A slightly revised version of the paper, approved as NSC 5602/1 on March 15, 1956, is printed in ibid., 242–68. The quote, which remained unchanged in the two versions of the paper, is on p. 250 of the latter.

23. The complete text of NSC 68 is reprinted in Ernest May, ed., *American Cold War Strategy: Interpreting NSC 68* (New York, 1993).

24. Memorandum from the Joint Chiefs of Staff to Secretary of Defense Wilson, March 12 1957, *FRUS, 1955–1957,* vol. 19, *National Security Policy,* 234–38.

25. NSC 5602/1, March 15 1956, ibid., 215–18.

26. Eisenhower to Dulles, December 5, 1955, *FRUS 1955–1957,* vol. 9, *Foreign Economic Policy; Foreign Information Program,* 11.

27. Memorandum of Discussion at NSC Meeting, December 8, 1955, *FRUS, 1955–1957,* vol. 10, *Foreign Aid and Economic Defense Policy,* 47.

28. Notes of bipartisan legislative meeting, May 3, 1955, Whitman File, Legislative Meeting Series, Eisenhower Papers.

29. Rusk Statement, February 28, 1961, *US Senate Committee on Foreign Relations, Historical Series, Executive Sessions,* vol. 13, pt. 1 (Washington, DC: US Government Printing Office, 1984), 187.

2

Peripheral Vision

US Modernization Efforts and the Periphery

David Ekbladh

The past decade has seen the United States struggle with wars in countries that in another era would have been slapped with the label *periphery*. Deep American commitment in places like Afghanistan and Iraq has come with a recommitment to international development and the nation building that comes with it. It all echoes similar efforts in the twentieth century on the periphery to use modernization to extend and legitimate an American world order. As leading international historians have noted, a central element in the contest between ideological systems that was the Cold War demanded intervention in great swaths of the globe.[1] Here, the periphery was not peripheral to US strategy. But many assumptions that enabled American engagement in what would become known as the Third World actually emerged in the crisis of the 1930s. The Depression taught key figures that a vibrant liberal global economy required that nonindustrialized areas of the world—what many often labeled *the periphery*—remain as integrated cogs. They would supply integral raw materials, markets, and labor. If they followed another path marked by other ideologies, the chance was that an integrated, interdependent, and healthy world economy based on liberal principles would be endangered. However, the view of the role development was to play in the periphery was a shifting one. It was a vision that was altered by changing strategic and historical imperatives, by the conceptions and methods dominating the mainstream approaches to development, and by those on the periphery itself.

In the twentieth century, development was called to the colors of national strategy by the United States. Development, defined very broadly as the urge to guide change, has no single clearly defined starting point. Civilizing missions instrumental to nineteenth-century imperialism had developmental facets. The galaxy of progressive reformers active at the turn of the twentieth century blurred domestic and international boundaries with a spectrum of activities rightly called *developmental*. What changed in the mid-twentieth century was a global crisis that brought ideological challengers with their own versions of development face-to-face with liberalism. It forced the crystallization of a set of new ideas and practices that produced a new and influential set of approaches under the rubric *modernization*.

Many of the ideas operating during the Cold War emerged during the crisis of the 1930s. The Depression abruptly ended a period of liberal ascendance. The speed with which the global capitalist economy unraveled and the inability of liberal governments to contain the aftershocks raised sudden and acute questions. Liberals were thrown onto the defensive internationally, embattled on one side by the failures of capitalism and on the other by ideological challengers with convincing claims to have social, political, and economic systems better attuned to modernity. Fascism and communism had dramatic force in a world seeking answers. Each offered utopian visions of the future and promised results with social and economic regimentation discussed in opposition—and, more ominously, as the successor—to a tired, bankrupt liberalism. They had appeal in a world searching for answers. It was the era of the Autobahn, the Agro Pontino, and the Five-Year Plan—state-sponsored development to implant prosperity. Liberal societies had to contend with a spectrum of active and appealing competitors.[2]

As part of their response to these threats, liberals scrambled to demonstrate that they could be masters of modern development. They were drawn to approaches and technologies that their ideological opponents also found indispensable. Collectivist ideas were embraced. State planning, an amorphous concept regarding who controlled key levers of economic life, was given a central role. This easily segued with views increasingly popular among nongovernment groups that were intensively active internationally. Development should be extensive in its reach, seeking to transform economies and societies with the generous application of technology.

For American liberals and internationalists, these ideas were often best demonstrated by the New Deal. Programs like the Tennessee Valley Authority (TVA) with massive technological elements that covered vast territory and actively promoted social change as part of their mission were ecstatically welcomed by liberals at home and abroad. Part of the TVA's appeal was that in its operation the program exemplified plural aspects of liberal societies. Partnerships with universities, businesses, charities, and other nongovernment groups complemented government activities even as the state remained the prime mover. All contributed to the project, and their work became a template for the wider cooperation that would characterize postwar modernization efforts. With such attributes, programs like the TVA were taken as proof that liberals could turn the juggernaut of modern life to beneficial ends. Indeed, by the end of the decade, many internationalists in the United States and Europe highlighted the project as a demonstration that liberal societies could mate economic and social development with forward-thinking planning.[3]

This was connected to a deep sensitivity about the state of the global economy. Many internationalists embraced the view that a healthy world economy demanded the free flow of raw materials, capital, people, and knowledge. If this became common in international life, the fragmentation already wreaked by the Depression would become permanent.[4] Capital and particularly raw materials were spread unevenly across the globe, and the requirement that they move freely and easily could not be guaranteed in the darkening world of the 1930s. This movement was vital if a peaceful, healthy international economy was to be maintained. Cooperation of this sort had the added benefit of constructing a foundation for collective action against totalitarian aggression.[5]

A voice that articulated mainstream views on the maintenance of a healthy world economy was Eugene Staley, a well-connected Tufts University economist who quickly became a fixture at the Council on Foreign Relations and other leading advocacy bodies. Staley's innovative addition to these discussions was the suggestion of a comprehensive program of liberal international development in a form recognizable today. It presupposed systematic intervention in peripheral areas of the globe to guide economic and social change. Through various means, technical knowledge would be injected into poorer areas of the globe to smooth the way for the freer movement of raw materials and commerce, assuring the stability of an open, liberal world order. Planning, made safe for a free society, would make such expansion possible. Staley believed that any effort demanded cooperation across a set of institutions.[6] Internationally, it was the task of governments as well as voluntary and international groups, including the League of Nations, to increase the capacities of the peoples of poorer, often colonial, nations. When explaining his ideas, Staley chose not to dwell on the contradictions emerging from colonial development. Like many predisposed to development, he found his attention drawn to China. It became his example of how international development might be conducted. It was already being offered technical aid by the League and leading American nongovernment groups such as the Rockefeller Foundation.[7] If it received technical assistance on liberal terms that fit its perceived needs, China could eventually become a productive member of a liberal international economy.[8]

Education in the technical arts would eventually create a rank of modern, technologically minded persons with the capital to foster growth. Staley shared the view, common internationally, that development was an interconnected process, linking the economic and the social. "Bringing roads and schools and technical institutes and machinery to China and India and Borneo" would create a "self-reliant generation . . . equipped with modern tools for meeting their own needs and for exchanging with other peoples." There was a further reason to act. If liberal forces did not lead such development, these areas of the globe would fall under the sway of "nationalistic imperialisms." Following these false prophets to the future would bring revolution and war, not only harming peoples in the underdeveloped nations, but also, and perhaps more importantly, continuing dislocation within the international economy. According to Staley, the United States had to be the engine of history and drive the process. The "economic millennium," he scolded, "will not be brought about by hoping for it." American leadership represented an acknowledgment of its considerable economic and technical resources. It also reflected a bleak understanding that, if the United States did not assume the role, someone else—whose goals were deemed less savory—would. By default, global leadership and specifically command of an approach to world development that put great emphasis on those nations on the periphery of the modern industrial world economy lay in the hands of the United States.[9]

Importantly, these budding international development ideas found a pressing strategic rationale. During the critical years from 1937 to 1940, a new geopolitics designed to secure the pale of liberal life emerged. Increasingly, the United States turned to cultural and economic diplomacy as a way to contain German influence in Latin America. By the end of the decade, American agriculturalists were trying to foster village-level transformation in Mexico. Following this was the Institute of Inter-American Affairs (IIAA), which offered US aid to governments across Latin America. These have rightly been seen as the forebears of Cold War–style technical assistance programs. They also reflected broadly similar rural reconstruction projects elsewhere in the world, particularly those of the Rockefeller Foundation in China, which had the ultimate goal of strengthening the Nationalist government. So, even before the United States entered the conflict, clear lines of how development should operate as part of an ideological confrontation were being drawn, and it was clear that the periphery was where this competition would be most starkly demonstrated.[10]

As the techniques evolved on the ground, so did the grand strategy of development. The sort of global vision of development in which Staley had trafficked became common currency in policy discussion. As Europe consumed itself in war in 1939–1941, the call to modernize the periphery as a means to support a revived world economy built to liberal specifications became a well-worn axiom in liberal discussions of the world to come. Many internationalists, spanning an embattled Atlantic, turned to the TVA as a mechanism to carry forward the development of "backward" areas that was one of the "economic essentials of durable peace." South America, Africa, and Asia were all marked for large-scale development on the TVA model. At one 1940 conference, leading figures in international relations promised war-torn China a "T.V.A. for the Yangtze Valley" as part of a general program to revitalize a postwar liberal order.[11] This thinking went beyond academics. In 1941, Winfield Riefler, a former member of Roosevelt's Brain Trust and a leading international economist, proposed a grand vision of an international development authority that would use surpluses to foster investment with the goal of transforming underdeveloped countries. The proposal circulated among key figures in the administration, including the Treasury secretary Henry Morgenthau and Vice President Henry Wallace.[12] Wallace, who had his own affinities for the means (including the TVA) to promote a better standard of living in what he termed the "century of the common man," was partial to such ideas.[13] Of course, none of these plans were implemented in their proposed forms. Nevertheless, these cases show that issues were widely and regularly discussed at diverse and influential centers of power. They reveal that development had become a staple means to transform the peripheral economies so that they could play their part in a liberal world order and thus prevent a repeat of the harrowing raw materials crisis and the depression that came with it.

Development was insinuated into the rehabilitation activities that were to follow the global struggle. The UN Relief and Rehabilitation Administration—created in 1943 to conduct global postwar reconstruction (and one of its early hires was Eugene Staley)—quickly found itself conducting development programs in many parts of the globe. Indeed, its activities influenced many who undertook modernization activities in the postwar years.[14] Beyond recovery, there was a need to reestablish the legitimacy of a liberalism that had staggered through a decade and half of crisis. The process was increasingly labeled *modernization,* and the term became nearly synonymous with economic and social development.

As the brewing Cold War seeped into the globe, areas emerging from colonial rule took on great importance. Their development was for the United States a means to aid the establishment of a global economy set to American liberal principles. Containing the appeal of the Soviet model of development, with its own promises of social and economic progress, was vital from the earliest stages of the struggle. To do so, the American state evolved its own capacities for the task. Among other initiatives was the Economic Cooperation Administration (ECA), the body initially created to oversee the Marshall Plan in Europe. In 1948, its mandate came to include international development. However, American policymakers differentiated between Marshall Plan and modernization activities. Poorer, underdeveloped countries demanded a thorough transformation to achieve modernity.

A defining difference between the core and the periphery was the great gap seen between what developed and underdeveloped nations required in terms of aid. This gap was apparent as American officials confronted the thicket of global issues surrounding relief, recovery, and development across the globe in the years after World War II. Flush with the success of the New Deal, American planners advocated ideas rooted in what has become known as *productionism* to repair and enhance economies in Europe. Here, collaboration among government, business, and labor leaders would assure that harmful disputes and competition over the fruits of industrial production would be curtailed. Contentious issues were to be solved by supposedly impartial forces of engineering, scientific management, and state and regional planning. What once had been political concerns could now be dealt with as technical problems. The result would be the increased productivity that would provide economic benefits for all, easing social divisions. Such ideas were fundamental to the European Recovery Program (ERP). Their apparent success was supremely gratifying to Americans. But there was an early understanding that the reproduction of the ERP was simply not possible outside industrialized areas. Despite the destruction visited on it, Western Europe retained a deep technological and human infrastructure on which to rebuild. The skeletons of factories, power grids, and transportation networks all remained. Even more importantly, large numbers of well-trained and experienced technicians, engineers, managers, and bureaucrats were available. Psychologically, these individuals already held the outlooks and had crafted the institutions that made their societies modern. What the Europeans needed were the funds and the organization to put them back to work.[15]

A perception reigned that Europe—and Japan for that matter—was already modern. Many nonindustrialized societies simply were not and would require a thoroughgoing transformation. This meant that ideas and policy were very different when conversations turned to strategically vital areas, particularly Asia. Programs that offered massive technological as well as social change, like the TVA, were prescribed, rather than replays of the Marshall Plan or the occupation of Japan. Although Germany and Japan received enormous amounts of American aid, they were not considered to require the same depth of transformation as South Korea, China, Iran, and other nations seen in the peripheral vision of Washington. Such assumptions cut across official and unofficial worlds that were adopting new terms for processes finding an important role in an international environment dominated by the Cold War.[16]

A significant moment was President Harry Truman's 1949 inaugural address where he made the famous "Point Four" declaration, promising US-sponsored development assistance to the globe. Importantly, Truman was placing existing approaches to modernization front and center in a US foreign policy geared to the Cold War. Although a number of scholars have seen his declaration as the inception of the sort of modernization that would reign during much of the postwar period, it is interesting to note that many contemporaries did not regard it as much of a departure. The genealogy of Point Four was widely discussed at the time. Speaking a week after his speech, Truman said that it had been percolating in his mind since the start of the Marshall Plan and aid to Greece and Turkey.[17] Whether the president's claim was entirely true is open to question, but those directly involved in the sponsorship of technical assistance at the time saw its origins. In February 1949, the State Department placed Point Four in context with existing programs such as the IIAA, the ECA, and those of the United Nations. The chief of the ECA, Paul Hoffman, later claimed that his organization initiated discussions for a larger technical assistance program. Spectators at the Council on Foreign Relations saw these diverse and deeper historical links. They discussed the "phenomenon of the year" as just "a catalyst that led to the coalescing of many ideas, projects, and drives," but it was "nothing really new" since many of "our fathers were engaged in private point fours for a long while."[18] The response shows that contemporaries were aware of the longer lineage of the development policies they were watching unfold. Nevertheless, Truman's inaugural and the programs it inspired were important. For the first time, there was within the US government an official and permanent bureaucracy focused entirely on international development—specifically, on promoting in the periphery a brand of modernization that had defined, Cold War goals.

By the early 1950s, foreign aid and the social and economic development it was to synthesize were crucial in containing the Soviet threat in strategic areas of the globe. However, many of the assumptions driving the application of liberal development were formulations arrived at during the 1930s. Proof lay in the voices that continued to resonate. Eugene Staley articulated the place and importance of modernization in securing a liberal order against a totalitarian threat in the new world of the Cold War. He continued to haunt the Council on Foreign Relations as the body discussed a topic increasingly important to its members. Someone who had articulated its importance back in the 1930s modulated these voices on the emerging topic of modernization. In this sense, the rise of modernization theory in the 1950s should be seen less as a new beginning than as an intellectual reflection and extension of ideas already in play in public life and foreign policy.[19]

Precisely how rising states on the periphery might chart their own course to economic development and national power made modernization critical to the outcome of the Cold War. Historians increasingly see that global struggle as one between two competing ideologies. The Soviet Union and the United States had to demonstrate that their respective systems had the potential to produce progress to secure their legitimacy. Modernization in the Third World was one way to do so. It was an instrument for cultivating influence. For the United States, aid was an indispensable way to contain the appeal of communism, which was real. Nationalist leaders in the postwar period looked to the Soviet Union and later the People's Republic of China as states that had rapidly overcome backwardness to industrialize through state-led planning. Americans struggled to assure clients that the same could be done through their liberal programs. But this was, in important respects, a continuation of a view that saw countries at the periphery as integral to the stability of a liberal world order tailored to American preferences.

In fact, Staley's 1954 book *The Future of Underdeveloped Countries,* which framed much early Cold War understanding of the issue, displayed the continuity of ideas born in the crisis of depression and war. Voicing assumptions common among his peers, Staley assumed that mechanical technology and the "social technologies" transferred through development left deep imprints on any society they touched. Therein lay the problem; there was the clear and present danger to the West of the competing and attractive model of Soviet communism. Staley was under no illusion that Communist interest in underdeveloped nations was a cloak to enhance Communist power at the center (i.e., Moscow) as part of a long-term global strategy to undermine the global system of liberal capitalism. He reiterated the belief that totalitarian communism was not revolutionary in and of itself. Those committed to the ideology were attempting to capture an ongoing revolution of rising expectations around the globe and turn it to their own ends. World war had changed international conditions, but the enemy remained the same. Staley did not want his readers to forget that the United States had to take the responsibility to halt any movement that "assumes the proportions of a world menace." Fascism was such a peril, but this "totalitarianism of the right" had been duly crushed. A "totalitarianism of left," which "at this moment in history [is] by far the most powerful and virulent menace to free institutions and the most aggressive threat to . . . free nations," remained. Staley marked the Soviet Union as merely the latest variant of an ongoing totalitarian challenge to liberalism.[20]

In this ongoing ideological combat, the question of whose development model would dominate was not tangential. Staley revealed the very stakes of the Cold War itself: "Under which of the two competing systems of life are the underdeveloped areas to be modernized, that of Communism or that of democracy? The issue is terribly important for the future of mankind. For at some point the areas now underdeveloped are likely to hold the balance of power between the two."[21]

Staley summarized the arguments and motivations of many of those anti-Communist liberals who supported development aid. His book was so successful a summary that it warranted a revised edition carrying its conclusions into the 1960s. But if he understood that the Cold War threat was merely a new version of an old enemy, he also knew that the development methods he was advocating were not entirely new either. Like many others, he was mustering existing concepts and setting them to task in an altered world situation. He understood that the principles and institutions at work in the 1950s were linked to the past. The concepts to which he turned were evolving, but they were based on formulations from the 1930s when liberals turned to development programs to contain totalitarian influence. Staley, in agreement with many contemporaries, saw the TVA as a way to demonstrate liberalism's development heft. He was convinced that it did not need the dark political elements contained in totalitarian systems and was certain that "we can have a T.V.A. . . . without nationalizing all the enterprises along Main Street."[22]

The geopolitics of global commitment and the specter of statism evident in the 1930s remained in Staley's articulation of the means and ends of US Cold War modernization policy. While Staley cannot speak for the entire sprawling development community of the time, his views were mainstream and widely shared. His was a call to take up arms against a dangerous ideology, and the weapon of choice was, again, development. The question of which form of development would prevail internationally would frame basic elements of the Cold War. The need to demonstrate the vitality of liberalism globally in the face of ideological challengers had defused from the 1930s into the Cold War of the 1940s. The demonstration site remained the periphery.

The emerging field of development economics aided in the codification of many principles already guiding action. In the 1950s and 1960s, influential economic thinkers like Gunnar Myrdal, W. Arthur Lewis, and John Kenneth Galbraith assured their wide audiences that the governments of the new nations had to perform certain economic and social tasks. Broadly, the view was that development was best done through state planning as the civil societies of the developing states were too weak to perform such tasks. These views represented a consensus, not unchallenged dogma, but even fierce critics admitted that they were fighting dominant trends in economics and international life.[23]

Using modernization as a Cold War weapon required the US government to mobilize the capacities of nonstate groups. Through the interwar years, such actors had cultivated many influential development ideas. Many groups devoted to relief during the war consciously altered their programs to embrace a long-term development mission. Capacity building for overseas development carried over into the United Nations, which had been given a broad development mandate in its charter. In the later 1940s, the United States urged the creation of a number of bodies and commissions within the United Nations that were to be invested with development missions. Among this constellation was the International Bank for Reconstruction and Development—the World Bank. Although it focused on Europe in its first decade, the World Bank shifted its attention to the developing world in the 1950s. By the end of the 1940s, the United States had helped cultivate a diverse set of state and nonstate institutional resources oriented toward the basic task of building modern nations along the periphery.

At the opening of his administration, John F. Kennedy called on the United Nations to declare the whole of the 1960s the "Decade of Development." By the 1960s, modernization framed policy toward emerging post-colonial states structuring policy and the worldviews of policymakers internationally. In the West, the United States dominated the way modernization was conceptualized and practiced. It was the largest single donor, with its development bureaucracy, the US Agency for International

Development (USAID), doling out $2.9 billion in 1962 alone. Modernization was a focal point of US foreign policy in the Third World during the Cold War. The Peace Corps and the Alliance for Progress were given high profiles in US Cold War strategy.

Such emphasis on modernization was apparent in a major US effort in the Third World, the Vietnam War. The war would pull in all aspects of the diverse and interconnected collection of modernizers. Aid from the Eisenhower administration on emphasized the construction of a viable non-Communist state in South Vietnam. The modernization apparatus also relied on a cross section of nongovernment organizations (NGOs) and businesses to execute everything from village-level development to large-scale infrastructural programs. University resources were marshaled to provide area expertise and technical skills. Scholars also generated a growing body of social scientific modernization theory claiming to explicate and legitimate the larger goals of the process on the ground.

These efforts were all tied to the growing American commitment in Southeast Asia. Counterinsurgency leaned heavily on the promises of modernization to win the hearts and minds of people. As troop strength in the region grew, so did the USAID mission, expanding to over seven thousand personnel (including contractors and local staff) with a budget of nearly $500 million by 1967. Intimately connected to the counterinsurgency, modernization also held an important public and strategic position. In 1965, as American troops were openly committed to a ground war, President Lyndon Johnson announced a major initiative to reconstruct South Vietnam and make it into a modern nation. This massive national modernization plan had as its centerpiece a project Johnson hoped would fulfill a vision, "to turn the Mekong into a Tennessee Valley."[24]

War shattered these ambitions and the relationships necessary to bring them to reality. A veteran of modernization activities in Vietnam lamented that the "best and brightest of [US]AID went to Vietnam," to face there the reality that "there was no way anyone could do development in that war zone." Security was a major problem, but the unclear and controversial cause for which the United States fought was a bigger liability. Nonstate organizations that had aided other important Cold War efforts either never joined the operation in Vietnam or abandoned what members of one prominent NGO working at the village level called an "overwhelming atrocity."[25] University and scholarly collaboration with the war effort was subjected to intense criticism, leading many institutions to abandon close cooperation with government programs. USAID came under sustained criticism as long-standing supporters like Senator J. William Fulbright declared foreign aid policy a "shambles." As the 1970s began, US development policy was radically overhauled by an initiative emphasizing "New Directions." USAID's budget and staff were slashed, and the philosophy guiding official US development policy was fundamentally rethought. As its own capacities deteriorated, USAID turned to private organizations, not as collaborators, as it had during the Cold War, but as executors of large segments of its development programs. This has led critics to deride its efforts and see it as little more than a contracting agency.[26]

However, Vietnam was only the most visible part of rising international donor fatigue. Within the international affairs community, there was an acknowledgment that development ideas faced pervasive disillusionment. These concerns mirrored a wider dissatisfaction with the approaches to modernization and economic growth that had predominated in the postwar world. There were ample reasons, evident both at home and abroad, to question modernization. As early as 1967, leading members of the international development community were lamenting that "at present everything is going wrong" as the "Decade of Development" devolved into frustration and recrimination.[27]

Its plight was the result of larger shifts in global affairs. William Pfaff at the Council on Foreign Relations admitted that "the spell was broken" regarding the Cold War. The credibility of both superpowers and their ideologies was strained by the late 1960s. As the United States sank into the mire of Vietnam, the promises of Communist models were further hollowed by the crackdown on the Prague Spring reform movement and the excesses of the Cultural Revolution. Such events further sapped the ideological intensity that had driven commitments to modernization. That waning urge was part of a general crisis of confidence in modern society. In the West, questions and critiques came from diverse directions, and impacts were felt in a host of areas. War, economic stagnation, the realities of racism, an atomized society, changing views of gender, political crisis, spiritual and religious ferment, and environmental despoliation all challenged the faith in progress in which modernization was rooted. If liberal society was imperfect in the West, the logical question was whether its example should be inflicted on the periphery.[28]

There was a paradox. The very importance of modernization in international politics was one reason its limits rapidly became apparent. Attention focused on the issue in the postwar period by institutions worldwide inspired a spectrum of research on its impacts. The 1960s were dotted by research exposing how benchmarks of modernization, particularly those large technological projects foundational to the modernization so many sought to export, could have wide-ranging adverse effects on the environment and many of the populations supposedly being aided. But the legion of negative effects brought by these efforts could no longer be ignored. Dams, for example, could do profound damage to the ecology of various waterways and the populations surrounding them. Initially hailed as almost a miracle, the impacts of DDT on environmental and human health became inescapable. Added to this was massive industrial and urban growth that strained environmental systems worldwide.

None of these issues could be entirely divorced from the technological, social, cultural, political, and ideological issues posed by big development projects. Many problems came to be seen as intractable barriers, while others struck at basic ideas behind modernization. Environmental issues segued easily into many other concerns raised by modernization, ranging from questions of governance to the growing North-South divide, an increasing call for development to focus on alleviating poverty, and the rise of international institutions to increased importance. In this atmosphere, perpetual questions surrounding modernization found renewed relevance. Concerns about population growth that had long stalked the issue of development burst into prominence as commentators fretted that it might limit or even undo development gains. Criticisms about the efficacy of the state's role in economic life found renewed life on the political Right but increasingly moved supporters on the Left away from long-held positions as disenchantment came to partisans. The school of dependency theory gained acceptance with the thesis that the capitalist global economy actually promoted stagnation and poverty rather than growth and prosperity. A renewed feminist movement faulted modernization thinking for regularly overlooking women as actors. Other frustrations lay in the fact that the objects of the development process, the new nations, had not lived up to their high expectations. By the late 1960s, numerous postcolonial states had taken on the trappings of autocracy, and, perhaps more importantly, state-centered approaches to modernization were not bearing the expected fruit. For some, the statism they had embraced seemed to be part of the problem. For all the excitement and effort of the 1940s, 1950s, and 1960s, the promise of the rapid growth and change to be brought by modernization remained unfulfilled.[29]

Critically, American views of development had to contend with increasingly vocal dissent from the periphery itself. From various quarters in the developing world there came new concepts to challenge conventional American and Western development policies. This chorus of critique was amplified in the chambers of important multilateral and international institutions. The UN system reflected how an increasingly diverse international community helped revise development thinking. The rush of newly independent nations profoundly altered the makeup of the General Assembly and the tone of the institution. A "Group of 77," claiming to speak for the interests of the Global South, pressed into discussion fresh voices that were often at odds with reigning assumptions in the West. The body had become an important site for challenges to conventional wisdom that increasingly came from the developing world. Organs like the UN Council on Trade and Development and the Economic Commission for Latin America (ECLA) became hives of research and opinion that challenged reigning assumptions. The ECLA, in particular, provided a platform for critical thinkers. These included the economist Raul Prebisch, who laid out analyses important to dependency theory and other policies running against consensus thinking. The newly formed UN Development Program (UNDP) provided a rostrum for the increasingly plural viewpoints on the issue. Mahbub ul Haq, a Pakistani economist, found a hearing for his trenchant critiques of the Western development mind-set. His work on poverty would inspire the UNDP's "Human Development Reports," which frame the issue today.[30] In many important ways, those on the periphery changed the perception of what sort of development should happen there and, with it, core concepts of what constituted development.

As views changed, so did the policy and institutional relationships within the aid community. Groaning under global commitments, the United States increasingly funneled aid through multilateral institutions as a way of defusing the financial as well as political burdens of global development. Accommodating to international realities, it surrendered its place as leading donor. Into the gap moved the World Bank. Robert McNamara, a refugee from the Vietnam debacle, took the reins in 1968 and transformed the bank's global role. Although he was steeped in the postwar approach to development, the crisis years would alter his perspective, leading him to install an emphasis on alleviating "absolute poverty" to the rhetoric and programs of the bank. He surrounded himself with advisers like ul Haq who were critics of earlier ideas. When he left in 1981, McNamara had increased the bank's annual lending from $900 million to over $12 billion. He also the converted the bank into a fully fledged development agency (providing analysis and technical assistance as well as capital) and made it the central player in the international development community.[31]

All these institutions accepted the turn in development discourse, at least in theory. Extensive planned development to transform societies and grow national economies shifted to a focus on smaller-scale programs centered on basic needs. Uprooting poverty became the least common denominator—even if how poverty was to be undone was not always clear. Barbara Ward, a prominent commentator on global development, captured how quickly the landscape had been altered. She believed that the modernization ethos of the post–World War II years had been undone by critiques displacing the emphasis on the provision of technology, economic growth, and state authority. In 1974, a reeling Ward commented that these views had "destroyed the old consensus" but warily noted that they had "put nothing in its place."[32]

The Vietnam era was a perfect storm. It was the confluence of a set of transformative events and critiques that rearranged international relationships and US aid policy as well as the basic goals of development itself. The belief in broadly conceived development planning centered on the state broke down under critiques emerging from seemingly every quarter.

Modernization—built on promises of constant growth and dramatic change—smashed into a new formulation that such growth could not be maintained perpetually and, in important respects, could be harmful. No longer could the various impacts of development programs be ignored in the calculus. These new outlooks would transform the way in which development programs would be implemented, not only by national and multinational development organizations, but also by the ever-growing numbers of nongovernment groups committed to development. The views appearing in the hothouse of 1960s were the roots of the concept of sustainable development. Given full form by the Brundtland Commission's 1986 report, *Our Common Future,* the fundamental demand of sustainable development was that development programs be economically and socially maintainable over the long term while achieving environmental equilibrium. *Sustainable* became linked to *development,* and the compound was used to suggest a novel approach. However, the regard for the sustainable development paradigm has had a great deal to do with its vagueness and variability as well as the fact that it could coexist with structures created during the postwar consensus. Rather than offering any concrete guide to action, sustainability often operates as a politically flexible and acceptable lingua franca to unite disparate constituencies.[33]

As these views became entrenched in policy, and as actual practices of development changed, *modernization* fell into disuse. A term suggesting the future was consigned to the past. It was increasingly seen as a label for a chauvinistic approach that was too dependent on large-scale technology, Western examples, and Cold War imperatives. *Development* and *modernization,* used nearly synonymously for so long, were decoupled and used distinctly.

Structural changes in the world economy in the 1970s meant wild swings in commodity prices and aid levels for the developing world. Economic trends in some regions slowed or even reversed. Despite remarkable growth in parts of East Asia, there was stagnation in other parts of the world. The Right was able to accelerate attacks on state authority in economic affairs following the Latin American debt crisis. The 1980s offered little relief and have since been lamented as the "lost decade" of development owing to cutbacks in bilateral aid and the damage done by the financial upheaval of the period. This was typically seen as the failure, not of a particular institution, but of the development system and the world economy generally to generate the certain type of prosperity and progress that many sought. Perhaps most importantly, the abrupt end of the Cold War tensions denied supporters of development assistance the Communist specter as an imperative. Without this, the vision of the periphery changed. There was no longer the nagging strategic need to develop the periphery, and, accordingly, engagement there was no priority.

Development did survive the Cold War but with concepts flowing from the crisis of the 1960s and 1970s holding sway. Through the 1990s, many across the political spectrum held great hopes that NGOs would carry out development and other tasks on the world stage that had once been the province of the state. International interventions in Bosnia, Somalia, East Timor, and Haiti during the decade all had development elements. Many of the institutions involved, ranging from the World Bank to the smallest of NGOs, saw the need for development aid to build state capacities and strengthen civil society (all parts of the modernization process) in troubled areas as a means to prevent conflict and build peace. To unify such efforts, the World Bank proposed in 1999 a "comprehensive development framework" to fuse the work of government, international, and civil society groups in a "holistic long-term strategy" to effectively implement programs. Nevertheless, the bank was careful to declare that it was not advocating a return to large-scale development planning. George W. Bush even squeezed development for a dribble of political gain in the 2000 election with an ostentatious stance against nation building.[34]

The easy return of *development* (and with it much modernization jargon) to the international lexicon following wars in Afghanistan and Iraq is a sign of the concept's endurance. The Bush administration abandoned reservations and pressed development into service as a weapon to contain threats it defined as ideological. Engagement on the periphery had again been given a strong strategic rationale. From his 2002 State of the Union Address on, the president described the opponents being faced as "totalitarian." Various other commentators, including some liberals, embraced a mission to confront a "totalitarian wave" building in critical parts of the globe—particularly the Middle East. Militant Islamism was considered an heir to the totalitarian ideologies of the 1930s, although critics found distinct limits to the comparison.[35]

Mobilizing development, the US government implemented a larger and more aggressive aid agenda. A 2002 conference under UN auspices in Monterrey, Mexico, saw Bush and a collection of world leaders recommit themselves to the recently articulated Millennium Development Goals of the United Nations and promise more money for poorer nations. The Bush administration attempted to reform the maligned government foreign aid apparatus. The Millennium Challenge Corporation was established in 2004, separate from the still denigrated USAID. Despite the fanfare, the overall impact of these and other innovations remained unclear as bureaucracies were created and others were shifted even as responsibilities and activities remained convoluted. Nevertheless, in 2005, Secretary of State Colin Powell made it plain that development was seen as an important strategic weapon to contain extremism and a means to shore up the legitimacy of an American world order.[36]

Even as the United States and the international community rushed back to development, the legacies of modernization's crisis remained. There was no clear international consensus on implementation. Strong differences between donors and recipients over what techniques work best are common. Even economists publically clash about the correct formula. Seeing the muddle in what development "is doing, will do, can do, or should do," William Easterly, a former World Bank economist, calls for a more entrepreneurial approach to development in poorer nations. Wielding *planner* as a damning epithet, he dismisses one of his intellectual adversaries, Jeffery Sachs. With an undoubtedly ambitious vision, Sachs sees the end of global poverty within reach if rich nations muster the right technologies, the funds, and simply the will to solve the problem. Struggling for historical proof, he inadvertently betrayed the persistence of some emblems of the past when he highlighted "successful regional development programs [that] help us understand how international development can succeed"—referencing the TVA.[37]

Muddle there may be in concept and method, but, during the first decade of the twenty-first century, extensive development programs had rediscovered utility in foreign policy. The quick and easy reintegration of development practices into various institutions, particularly the US military, demonstrates its utility and its heritage. Despite its prominent place in the US Army's vaunted (and controversial) counterinsurgency doctrine and sometimes formless process of nation building in Iraq and Afghanistan, the actual accomplishments of these policies remained questionable.[38] The chronic economic crisis that gripped the new century at the end of its first decade has also called into question whether renewed commitments to aid and development could be sustained in the face of shrinking budgets and the chant of austerity. But there was one lesson that could not be missed and that would have been clear to many observers from the Depression era on. When an American world order was challenged and the United States had to shore up its interests on a twenty-first-century periphery, development was again vested with significant tactical and strategic importance.

Notes

1. The leading exponent of this view is Odd Arne Westad. See his *The Global Cold War: Third World Interventions and the Making of Our Times* (Cambridge: Cambridge University Press, 2005).

2. On the variety and similarity of reform ideas in the period, see Wolfgang Schivelbusch, *Three New Deals: Reflections on Roosevelt's America, Mussolini's Italy, and Hitler's Germany, 1933–1939* (New York: Metropolitan, 2006).

3. The best example of this is David E. Lilienthal, *TVA: Democracy on the March* (New York: Harper & Bros., 1944).

4. On the impact of autarchy on world affairs, see James Harvey Rogers, *Capitalism in Crisis* (New Haven, CT: Yale University Press, 1938); and Eugene Staley, "What Price Self Sufficiency?" *Christian Science Monitor,* September 22, 1937, and *World Economy in Transition* (New York: Council on Foreign Relations, 1939), 206–22.

5. Eugene Staley, "Economic Foundations of a Just and Enduring Peace," May 30, 1941, box 3, Staley Papers, Hoover Institution on War, Revolution, and Peace Archives, Stanford University, and *Raw Materials in Peace and War* (New York: Council on Foreign Relations, 1937), 55–69.

6. Eugene Staley, "What Types of Economic Planning Are Compatible with Free Institutions?" *Plan Age,* February 1940, 33–50.

7. Frank Ninkovich, "The Rockefeller Foundation, China, and Cultural Change," *Journal of American History* 70 (March 1984): 799–820.

8. Staley, *World Economy in Transition,* 279–81.

9. Ibid., 68, 269–86, 333.

10. Nick Cullather, *The Hungry World: America's Cold War Battle against Poverty in Asia* (Cambridge, MA: Harvard University Press, 2010), 43–71; Nicole Sackley, "The Village as Cold War Site: Experts, Development, and the History of Rural Reconstruction," *Journal of Global History* 6 (November 2011): 481–504; Claude C. Erb, "Prelude to Point Four: The Institute of Inter-American Affairs," *Diplomatic History* 9 (Fall 1985): 249–69.

11. "The Economic and Political Bases of Durable Peace," April 1940, Conference Proceedings, box 12, World Peace Foundation Papers, Swarthmore College Peace Collection.

12. Winfield Riefler, "A Program to Stimulate International Investment," October 4, 1941, box 2, Winfield Riefler Papers, RG 200, National Archives, College Park, MD; Riefler to Wallace, October 2, 1941, and Wallace to Morgenthau, November 14, 1941, reel 40, Henry A. Wallace Papers, Library of Congress, Washington, DC.

13. Henry A. Wallace, *The Century of the Common Man* (New York: Reynal & Hitchcock, 1943).

14. William Adams Brown Jr. and Redvers Opie, *American Foreign Assistance*

(Washington, DC: Brookings Institution, 1953), 111; George Woodbridge, *The History of the United Nations Relief and Rehabilitation Administration,* 3 vols. (New York: Columbia University Press, 1950), 3:476–80.

15. Michael Hogan, *The Marshall Plan: America, Britain and the Reconstruction of Western Europe, 1947–1952* (New York: Cambridge University Press, 1987), 5–25; Charles Maier, "The Politics of Productivity: Foundations of American International Economic Policy After World War II," *International Organization* 31 (Autumn 1977): 607–33.

16. Emblematic of this assumption was the debate over an Asian recovery program within the US government in 1948. See Nitze to Butterworth, "A Coordinated Economic Policy for the Far East," October 26, 1948, and Butterworth, Satterthwaite, Labouisse, and Nitze, "Coordinated Policy for the Far East," November 22, 1948, reel 151, US Delegation Subject Files, 1945–1952, RG 43, National Archives, College Park.

17. Harry Truman, *Memoirs,* vol. 2, *Years of Trial and Hope, 1946–1952* (New York: Doubleday, 1956), 231.

18. Office of Public Affairs, Department of State, "Point Four," Washington, DC, February 1949, Discussion Meeting Report, June 10, 1949, box 3.7, Isaiah Bowman Papers, Special Collections, Johns Hopkins University; Merle Curti and Kendall Birr, *Prelude to Point Four: American Technical Missions Overseas, 1838–1938* (Madison: University of Wisconsin Press, 1954).

19. Eugene Staley, *The Future of Underdeveloped Countries: Political Implications of Economic Development* (1954; rev. ed., New York: Council on Foreign Relations, 1960).

20. Staley, *The Future of Undeveloped Countries,* 5–6, 40, 119–20. See also "Political Implications of Economic Development," Fourth Meeting, June 5, 1952, and Eugene Staley, Working Paper, Study Group on Political Implications of Economic Development, October 28, 1952, Study Groups, box 46, Council on Foreign Relations Records, Seeley G. Mudd Manuscript Library, Princeton University.

21. Staley, *The Future of Undeveloped Countries,* 195.

22. Ibid., 29–35, 190, 236.

23. Gunnar Myrdal, *Development and Underdevelopment: A Note on the Mechanism of National and International Economic Inequality* (Cairo: National Bank of Egypt, 1956), 62; W. Arthur Lewis, *The Theory of Economic Growth* (Homewood, IL: Richard D. Irwin, 1955); Alexander Gerschenkron, *Economic Backwardness in Historical Perspective* (Cambridge, MA: Harvard University Press, 1962); John K. Galbraith, *Economic Development* (New York: Houghton Mifflin, 1962). For the collected views of one of the leading dissenters, see P. T. Bauer, *Dissent on Development: Studies and Debates in Development Economics (*London: Weidenfeld & Nicolson, 1971).

24. *Agency for International Development: Program Presentation to the Congress, Proposed FY 1969 Program,* H-5 (Washington, DC: USAID Library, 1969); Doris

Kearns Goodwin, *Lyndon Johnson and the American Dream* (New York: St. Martin's, 1976), 267.

25. Abraham M. Hirsch, *The USAID Program and Vietnamese Reality*, Doc. PN-ABS-391 (Washington, DC: USAID Library, June 1968); Reminiscences of John H. Sullivan, October 29, 1996, Foreign Affairs Oral History Project, USAID Library.

26. Felix Belair, "Foreign Aid Setup Called 'Shambles' by Senate Group," *New York Times*, April 26, 1971; Vernon W. Ruttan, *United States Development Assistance Policy: The Domestic Politics of Foreign Economic Aid* (Baltimore: Johns Hopkins University Press, 1996), 102–5; *Introduction to the FY 1973 Development and Humanitarian Assistance Program Presentation to Congress* (Washington, DC: USAID Library, 1973), 1–2.

27. Davidson Summers, "Report on Trip to Europe," June 6, 1967, and Summary of Discussions, Meeting on Aid and Development, April 20, 1967, box 13, David Bell Papers, Ford Foundation Archives, New York City.

28. William Pfaff, "The Scope of Our Discussions," December 11, 1969, Discussion Meeting Report, "New Forces in World Politics," Second Meeting, January 15, 1970, and Discussion Meeting Report, "New Forces in World Politics," Third Meeting, February 12, 1970, box 63, CFR, MLP.

29. For a summary of these frustrations, see Michael Latham, *The Right Kind of Revolution: Modernization, Development, and U.S. Foreign Policy from the Cold War to the Present* (Ithaca, NY: Cornell University Press, 2010), 157–85.

30. For Prebisch's views, see Edgar J. Dosman, *The Life and Times of Raul Prebisch, 1901–1986* (Montreal: McGill-Queen's University Press, 2008); and Paul Kennedy, *The Parliament of Man: The Past, Present and Future of the United Nations* (New York: Random House, 2006), 126–29. See also Mahbub ul Haq, *Reflections on Human Development* (New York: Oxford University Press, 1995), 10.

31. Bruce Rich, "World Bank/IMF: 50 Years Is Enough," in *50 Years Is Enough: The Case against the World Bank and the International Monetary Fund*, ed. Kevin Danaher (Boston: South End, 1994), 6–13, 9.

32. Barbara Ward, "Science and Technology: For What?" box 11, Barbara Ward (Baroness Jackson) Papers, Special Collections, Georgetown University.

33. World Commission on Environment and Development, *Our Common Future* (New York: Oxford University Press, 1987).

34. World Bank, "Overview and Background of the CDF" (Washington, DC: World Bank, 1999); James Wolfensohn, "Discussion Paper on the Comprehensive Development Framework" (Washington, DC: World Bank, 1999) (quotes); "The First Gore-Bush Presidential Debate," October 3, 2000, Commission on Presidential Debates, http://www.debates.org/index.php?page=october-3-2000-transcript.

35. Paul Berman, "Liberal Hawks Reconsider the Iraq War," *Slate*, January 12, 2004, http://www.slate.com/articles/news_and_politics/the_angle/2016/07/the_dnc_hack_hillary_clinton_and_michelle_obama_in_slate_s_daily_newsletter.html; Paul Berman, *Terror and Liberalism* (New York: Norton, 2003). For the com-

parison's limits, see Anson Rabinbach, "Totalitarianism Revisited," *Dissent,* Summer 2006, https://www.dissentmagazine.org/article/totalitarianism-revisited.

36. Colin Powell, "No Country Left Behind," *Foreign Policy,* January–February 2005, 28–35.

37. William Easterly, "Introduction: Can't Take It Anymore?" in *Reinventing Foreign Aid,* ed. William Easterly (Cambridge, MA: MIT Press, 2008), 1–44, 4–5; Jeffery Sachs, *Common Wealth: Economics for a Crowded Planet* (New York: Penguin, 2008), 243.

38. See Nathan Hodge, *Armed Humanitarians: The Rise of the Nation Builders* (New York: Bloomsbury, 2011).

3

Narratives of Core and Periphery

The Cold War and After

Andrew J. Rotter

Many social scientists and historians subscribe to Immanuel Wallerstein's division of the international system into core and peripheral areas, and there is undoubtedly some utility in seeing the Cold War world in this way, with economic influence and political power concentrated in First and Second World cores, radiating outward to nations in the Third World, which for the purposes of this chapter I will equate with the periphery. (In fairness, note that Wallerstein's "world-systems" analysis considers more fully the seventeenth century than the twentieth and that Wallerstein posits the presence of a "semiperiphery," though with waning enthusiasm in his more recent work.) Core power might be received with hostility, perhaps with resignation or resistance—but the image was compelling: during the Cold War peripheral nations were as electrons around a nucleus and thus always subordinate to the whims and fortunes and decisions of the Americans, the West Europeans, and the Soviets. "Every system needs a center sometimes," as Thomas McCormick has put it. And world-systems theory challenged historical interpretation that assumed common patterns of political-economic development based on Western models of modernization. That the image of core and periphery has endured for so long suggests that it retains validity as a way to explain international history from 1945 to 1989 and possibly beyond.[1]

Yet the simplicity and apparent common sense of Wallerstein's largely binary formulation ought not to obscure its interpretive shortcomings. For one thing, we know that during the Cold War the core was never unitary—the First and Second Worlds were their own nuclei, each surrounded by their own electron shells. In the First World itself were cracks and fissures. The West Europeans disagreed among themselves and with the Americans over the inclusion of West Germany in Continental defense, the wisdom of retaining empires, diplomatic posture toward China and the Soviet Union, and the desirability of their own political and economic unity. American power wavered over time with the willingness of presidential administrations and the American people to support its military and economic expression. We know also that it is not so easy to map the world into core and peripheral areas. Nations gain power and move toward the core (China) or find their bonds with more powerful states strengthened (South Korea with the United States) or weakened (semiperipheral Czechoslovakia with the Soviet Union) over time and unpredictably. In US relations with Latin America, Steve Stern has written, there has been "an 'expansionist periphery' and a 'decentered center.'" What is regarded as ancillary to one core nation's security is regarded as vital to another's. As Josef Stalin wrote to Harry Truman in 1945: "Poland borders with the Soviet Union, [which] cannot be said of Great Britain and the United States." Above all, power at the core of things has often been less compelling than it looks. Power fluctuates, depends on the will to use it, moves around, and can be blunted or undercut. World-systems analysis is, notes Paul Kramer, "top-down history, with little room for non-elite actors." If there is one thing we have learned about the Cold War and the period since, it is that small states and even stateless groups can display their own kind of power and by their actions vitiate the power of larger polities. During the Cold War, the French, the Americans, and the Russians learned this lesson in Algeria, Vietnam, and Afghanistan, respectively. Handfuls of terrorists have attacked Spain, Britain, Russia, and the United States since the Cold War ended. "Center and periphery may be shifting terrain," concludes Emily Rosenberg, "and what is periphery in some respects may, in fact, take precedence in other areas."[2]

Let me offer five narratives of the Cold War as it took place in the Third World. A few of these narratives largely accept the core-periphery binary as their premise—that is, they assume power at the nucleus and the dependency of the peripheral electrons. Others are inclined to grant greater agency and purpose to the nations on the periphery and thus tend to erode the distinction implied by Wallerstein's terminology. The last of these narratives, which I will call *cultural* and will define presently, offers, in my view, particular promise of revising the core-periphery dichotomy and complicating the periodization of international history after 1945. Though I am distinguishing these interpretations from each other, I see them operating rather as *Annales* school historians imagine the interplay of historical forces, layered and sliding across each other like tectonic plates and thus by no means altogether distinctive explanations of complex phenomena.

The first narrative, which generally reinforces the core-periphery model, is that of national security. According to this version of the Cold War, the United States and the Soviet Union, along with their allies and subalterns, believed that their adversaries genuinely threatened their safety and conducted themselves accordingly in peripheral theaters. Indeed, some have argued, the colonial, postcolonial, and newly independent states in Asia, Africa, and Latin America were little more than arenas for Cold War contestation. Determined to assure their security by building enormous nuclear arsenals, but fearing the consequences of a nuclear exchange, the powers instead fought by proxy in the Third World. It was cheaper to spend Vietnamese, Angolan, and Cuban lives than to commit American and Soviet forces to combat. It also seemed less dangerous. When great power forces were sent to fight wars abroad, their governments generally took care to limit their missions. In Korea, the Americans managed not to antagonize the Soviets into intervening directly, though they failed to prevent Chinese involvement when they misread Beijing's warnings to stay away from the Yalu River. Nikita Khrushchev backed down in Cuba in 1962 rather than risk a possible nuclear exchange over the placement of Soviet missiles there. These conflicts, and others on the periphery, were fought chiefly because the powers viewed the Cold War as a constant-sum game: thus, the loss of even a remote outpost of core influence might be perceived as a threat to the core state's security. When the core power believed, in addition, that the loss of such an outpost would lead to the collapse, by whatever mechanism, of nearby states as well—

the domino theory, as applied by the Americans to Southeast Asia and the Soviets to Central Asia—its security fears intensified. The sound of dominoes falling on the periphery was audible at the core.[3]

The second Cold War narrative emphasizes the economic roots of the conflict. There is an unsophisticated version of the economic interpretation of the Cold War, largely behind us now, that framed the contest as one between ossified capitalism, engorging itself on the Third World raw materials it craved, and socialism or communism, either equally ossified or regnant in its revolutionary form, a rival vision of anti-imperialism and human equality. A more subtle and persuasive version of the economic narrative placed the Cold War in the context of the Great Depression of the 1930s, which made the United States and Western Europe leery of a world system left atrophied by Soviet-style autarky or political instability. As some historians pointed out, the record is largely innocent of statements by US policymakers that the Soviets represented a security threat, in Europe or elsewhere. But officials were much concerned that, if the United States and the West Europeans lost access to the periphery's raw materials—rubber, tin, copper, uranium, and oil, for example—their economies would collapse to Depression-era levels. The Marshall Plan was, for instance, less about the defense of Western Europe than about the revival of West European industry and especially markets for US exports. Economic aid for the developing world aimed to accommodate Western investment, encourage the growth of extractive industries, and prompt the consumption of finished goods imported from the United States and Europe. To find power, "follow the money," advised Walter LaFeber a few years ago. That remains sound advice.[4]

Elements of both the national security and the economic narratives are captured in a third: ideology. Defined, by Michael Hunt, as "an interrelated set of convictions or assumptions that reduces the complexities of a particular slice of reality to easily comprehensible terms and suggests appropriate ways of dealing with that reality," the concept of ideology is sufficiently grand to encompass a broad range of ideas and practices yet analytically parsimonious enough to get one's head around. William Appleman Williams wrote of an American weltanschauung that featured economic thinking but not only that. Those who apply an ideological interpretation to the Cold War stress expressions, on both sides, of distrust for the values and behaviors of the other. For the Americans, the

Cold War was a battle against communism, which empowered the state at the expense of individual enterprise, destroyed personal freedom, and was by nature militarily aggressive. For the Soviets, the Cold War was a battle to prevent American hegemony, the triumph of the rich few over the impoverished many, and what one commentator later called "the Coca-Colonization of the world." The ideological contest was played out on the periphery; even if the security of core states remained relatively unaffected, their values were at odds in the contest for the hearts and minds of Latin Americans, Africans, and Asians. Lately, historians have located the language of modernization in the realm of ideology. There was widespread expectation in Washington during the 1950s and 1960s especially that developing nations should be induced to grow along liberal-capitalist lines, their economies boosted to take off by free enterprise, their political systems embracing representative government, or its promise, in their rejection of communism. Ideology thus encompasses in some measure the national security narrative (core values are under threat everywhere) and the economic one (free enterprise is the one best system). It is a flexible narrative.[5]

These three narratives are mostly based on the assumption that the core-periphery model effectively and fundamentally explains the workings of the international system during the Cold War years. They tend to treat those outside the so-called West as bit players in the drama, disempowered subjects of those residing in the metropole. Many have argued that this view is simplistic. A fourth narrative of the Cold War shifts the lens to the lands outside the First and Second Worlds and focuses on them, not as spaces that entertained clashes of other nations' armies or values, or as mere containers of raw materials, but as places full of people with agency. The Cold War overhung the world system, yet the most significant force in the lives of millions was the rise of nationalism and the related effort to drive imperialism (or neoimperialism) out of Asia, Africa, and Latin America; decolonization is the fourth narrative. Long before the conflict between the First and the Second Worlds hardened in the late 1940s, people of color across the globe had taken up the struggle against foreign rule. In Indochina, the Dutch East Indies, and India, in Algeria, Ghana, and Kenya, and in Cuba, nationalists demanded liberation from outside domination. Some used the Wilsonian rhetoric of self-determination; others raised the banner of Lenin. The Cold War presented challenges to the forces of nationalism, amplifying local conflicts into international ones. And it provided opportunities to nationalists who were able to play the powers off against each other in their search for assistance. But it was never as powerful as nationalism itself. The most important story of the period 1945–1965 is the movement for independence in what was known as the Third World.[6]

The fifth and final narrative—one that complicates even more fully the core-periphery binary—concerns *culture*. I offer the broadest possible definition of this much-contested term: *culture,* according to the anthropologist Clifford Geertz, constitutes the "webs of significance" spun by human beings. "Cultural signification and interpretation," writes John Tomlinson, explicating Geertz, "constantly orientates people, individually and collectively, towards particular actions." The definition encompasses much that was long left out of analyses of the Cold War and international history generally: language, symbols, gestures, prejudices, and stereotypes or, more concretely, categories of analysis including gender, race, religion, maturity, and identity. These are analyses united by their constructedness and significance, by their basis in contingency, ambiguity, and the multiplicity of historical meanings. The connections between the culturalist narrative and that of decolonization are many. Yet culture is perhaps the more promising approach to the study of the Cold War in its apprehension of the interplay between deep forces lying beneath the surface of events, its disrespect for the artificial boundaries that mapmakers and scholars have imposed between nations, and its sympathy for the psychological processes at work in the minds of men and women who made decisions concerning the international system. The culturalist approach is more sensitive to the agency of those on the so-called periphery and to some extent less beholden to the traditional division of the post-1945 period into the Cold War years and after. It suggests, for example, that cultural productions in the metropole were not merely "imperialist impositions but . . . collaborative processes involving complicated . . . transnational exchanges," as Seth Fein has described the presence of US film propaganda in Cold War Mexico. Let me offer some examples of how culture changes our view of the Cold War period as it constructively subverts the core-periphery binary and demands that we take fully into account the activism of those once designated (by Jawaharlal Nehru, with disdain) "the playthings of others."[7]

Let us first consider race. White racism was an undercurrent of the Cold War, used at first to justify the domination by whites of people of color, then later to explain why white tutelage of darker-skinned people was alleged to be necessary. Statements of outright racism are not hard to find in the diplomatic record of the 1940s. George Kennan attributed the sins of the Soviet Union to its leadership's "Oriental" or "semi-Asiatic" character, while George McGhee, who served in a variety of diplomatic posts in Asia and the Middle East, once told Mahatma Gandhi's son (!) that racial "differences really did exist . . . [as] illustrated by the fact that Africa had always been retarded in its development." Such statements became unfashionable by the 1950s and were less often uttered on the record. To some extent racism moved underground, merging with the rhetoric of modernization to stigmatize nonwhite societies as underdeveloped or (more charitably) developing; inferiority, while still present, was fungible, perhaps no longer inherent in people of color. Along with that, segregationist practices in the United States damaged the nation's standing with people of color abroad and thus became a liability in the contest for standing in the Third World. (The Cold War overhang is prominent here.) Reluctantly or otherwise, US presidents from Truman to Nixon pursued civil rights at home in order to rectify America's image abroad. White policymakers recognized, for example, that African American musicians might, by their performances in African or Asian countries, help persuade people that the United States was just as free as their jazz compositions and surely tolerant of *them*.[8]

Race was an equally complicated affair within the Third World, and it shaped initiatives and responses both within and outside the area. African societies were in general not monolithic racial or ethnic entities, and their experiences with colonialism had left them with different attitudes toward mixed-race citizens or those whose skins were white or brown. Culture is never static; as in the United States, racial attitudes in Africa, for example, changed over time. Ghana's Kwame Nkrumah, who spent ten years in the United States and experienced racism there, nevertheless avoided the subject in his autobiography; his concerns were more about political economy than race. On the other hand, forces fighting for the liberation of Angola from Portugal in the 1970s readily accepted help from Fidel Castro's Cuba in the name of racial solidarity, and blacks in southern Africa celebrated the news that, as one paper put it, "Black troops—Cubans and Angolans—have defeated White troops in military exchanges" there. During the 1950s and 1960s, residents of India, whose skin color ranges from light to very dark, expressed in racial terms their support for black Africans seeking liberation from the white empires. They were chastened by black African charges that Indians in Africa had long collaborated with white ruling elites, exploited black consumers, and quietly sought acceptance from whites while denigrating blacks. Nehru's decision to liberate Goa from the Portuguese in late 1961, seemingly in contradiction of his pleas for nonviolence during the Cold War, came about largely because Africans still under Portugal's control challenged him to act determinedly on behalf of people of color everywhere by doing what they themselves could then only dream of doing: throwing the colonialists out.[9]

Perceptions based on gendered thinking also shaped behavior across boundaries and independently of the Cold War. As Frank Costigliola has demonstrated, the gender-inflected language of American policymakers suggests they hoped that their wartime and Cold War initiatives were forceful and manly and that they feared they might not be. George Kennan (useful for our purposes once more) warned in his famous "Long Telegram" (1946) of the Soviet Union's "unceasing pressure for penetration," and he construed the Russian people as feminine victims of sexual assault by their hypermasculine leaders. The application of counterforce was in part a masculine response to Soviet aggression. The occupation and reconstruction of Germany and Japan were predicated on representing menacingly masculine recent adversaries now as feminine victims in need of guidance and sustenance. Members of the Dwight Eisenhower administration regarded the Iranian leader Mohammed Mossadeq as effeminate—he appeared publicly in his pajamas and wept before cameras, behavior that fed their mistrust of him and helped rationalize his ouster. US officials regarded Arabs as *irresponsible, feckless,* and *overwrought,* emotional descriptors usually assigned to women. Though raised in decidedly different environments, both John F. Kennedy and Lyndon Johnson brought masculine sensibilities to the making of foreign policy. Kennedy's self-proclaimed toughness came of his experience in male-only schools and university secret societies, his own military service, and his fear, during the Red and Lavender Scares of the early 1950s, of being judged soft on communism and a bit too chummy with men to be fully reliable. Johnson's manhood was a product of rural Texas culture, in which men drank and hunted and brawled, scorned the allegedly effeminate among them, and adored women, frequently several at once. Both men thus regarded the Vietnamese rebellion as an affront to their masculinity, a challenge, physical and psychological, to their self-images as men. (Johnson famously boasted that he had "Ho Chi Minh's pecker in [his] pocket" and promised to seduce the Vietnamese leader by "going up Ho's leg one inch at a time.") A gendered, Cold War–era counternarrative was provided by an inclusive, nurturing, maternal discourse, on display, as Christina Klein has shown, in popular Broadway musicals such as *South Pacific* and *The King and I,* both of which urged American audiences to embrace Asians rather than fight them, though not necessarily on equal terms.[10]

Gender often worked differently outside the United States. Latin American and African societies have their own versions of machismo, and, when their nations were in their view abused or made to feel dependent on the United States, the Soviet Union, or Europe, they lashed back. Israelis created and cultivated a self-image as plucky, masculine frontiersmen to win sympathy in Washington and, in part, to insulate themselves against the trauma of the Holocaust. The Palestinians were for decades less successful because they depicted themselves as victims, mainly an effeminate category if unleavened with a vocabulary of heroism. The Hindu majority (and leadership) in India had its own version of masculinity, one based not on sharp opposition to the feminine or effeminate but on the ability to encompass both the masculine and the feminine, to incorporate into India's political culture values of modesty, humility, and diplomacy in its rejection of bellicosity. The Pakistanis, by contrast, fashioned for themselves an identity as tough-talking, hard-drinking, resolute fighters who would not blink in the face of the responsibility to fight Communists—as long as the Americans supplied them with the modern weapons to do so.[11]

It is increasingly common to find scholars writing about the presence of religious thinking in international relations. Religion is, like race and gender, a category of culture, a human construct having to do with beliefs, attitudes, and behaviors in all realms of life. The Cold War was in part a religious contest, or at least the Americans saw it that way. Leading US policymakers were themselves religious men: the secretaries of state Dean Acheson, John Foster Dulles, and Dean Rusk were sons of clergymen and had considered the pulpit themselves. Dulles especially configured the Cold War as a battle between good and evil, with the atheistic Communists in the latter role. After 1945, social distinctions faded between the largest American religions—Protestantism, Catholicism, and Judaism—as commentators such as Will Herberg stressed the participation of all three in the Americanization of immigrants. The periphery offered both threat and opportunity to Christian policymakers. Long a target of Christian missionaries, Asians, Africans, and Latin Americans could, the United States feared, be turned in their ignorance or heathenism to the false religion communism—or might, they hoped, because of their own religiosity of whatever description, find the American appeal to an omnipotent God more compelling than the Communist claim to science.[12]

Such a contest was played out in South Asia. To US officials, India seemed in its foreign relations to reflect the moral uncertainty and spiritual apathy of its dominant Hindu religion. Hindus had many gods, not one, and thus multiple versions of the truth. This, thought the Americans, predicted an inability to be decisive or to choose the right position on straightforward matters of right and wrong. There could be no polytheists in Cold War foxholes. Hindus do, in fact, tend to resist absolutes and have an abhorrence of moral certitude. Nehru objected to the Americans' "narrow religious outlook on politics" and their "desire to force [their] will on the other person or the other nation." The Pakistanis, by contrast, appeared to Americans to manifest the decisiveness of monotheistic Islam. As Muslims, they believed, said Prime Minister Liaquat Ali Khan in 1950, "in the supreme sovereignty of God." They were thus willing to stand with the Americans against atheistic communism, especially if it meant that they would thereby receive some of the latest in military technology—which might be used, in the event, not against the Russians (who were not expected in Karachi anytime soon) but against India. Islam was incompatible with communism, or at least the Pakistanis were willing to insist it was, and the Americans were willing to believe them.[13]

The religious factor was also involved in US policy toward Vietnam during the 1950s. Desperately seeking a leader who could rally at least the southern Vietnamese against the Communist-led Vietminh, the Americans chose Ngo Dinh Diem to create a government in Saigon. Diem was on the whole not well regarded in Vietnam. His nationalist credentials were underdeveloped, as were his political skills, and he had not fought the French, as had his Communist counterpart Ho Chi Minh. Diem's Catholicism was a liability to the Buddhist majority of South Vietnam, who believed, with some justice, that his policies favored his coreligionists. But, as Seth Jacobs has argued, Diem appealed to influential Americans because he was a Catholic, having swept floors in a New Jersey monastery with the novices. He was familiar, someone who worshiped as Americans did, or at least as did fellow Catholics Francis Cardinal Spellman, Mike Mansfield, and John Kennedy. He was, said the publisher Henry Luce in 1955, "a Roman Catholic and a simon-pure Vietnamese nationalist, thus doubly proof against communist force." For this reason and others, the Americans hitched their wagon in Vietnam to Diem's star. By the time they became disillusioned with him and midwives to his assassination in 1963, they had become, through their attachment to him, enmeshed in the Vietnam War.[14]

Before moving on to the post-1989 period and thus to my conclusion, I would like to note explicitly one point of contact between the culturalist narrative and that of national security, in part to show that what we think of as the separate realms of power and culture are not in fact unrelated. How a nation defines its national security needs, and thus how it formulates its strategic thinking, is shaped in part by culture. The term *strategic culture* means "the body of attitudes and beliefs that guides and circumscribes thought on strategic questions, influences the way strategic issues are formulated, and sets the vocabulary and the perceptual parameters of strategic debate," according to Alastair Iain Johnston. Since societies and nations have different "attitudes and beliefs," it follows that their foreign policy strategies proceed from different assumptions. Thus do the Chinese, writes Simei Qing, look at the world political economy believing that their *national* freedom and equality of status are of overwhelming importance, while Americans use their foreign policy to promote *individual* freedom all over, making the world safe for democracy. In the United States and India, strategic culture is predicated on different ideas about space: while Americans view space—the frontier, places across seas, even outer space—as beckoning, an exciting opportunity for expansion, Hindu India long felt threatened by it, the dangerous areas beyond its borders, and thus harbored no expansionist dreams. This perception is part of Hindu cosmology, and it was reinforced by India's susceptibility to invasion by outsiders. During the period of the Cold War, US policy appeared to Indians as aggressive, while India seemed to the Americans passive, its strategic culture wan and without ambition.[15]

How have things changed in the world since 1989? The end of the Cold War has forced the revision of several of its narratives and particularly of the ways in which we understand the core-periphery binary. Let us briefly revisit them.

The quest for national security changed markedly after 1989. US power was no longer threatened by the Soviet Union; as many commentators noted, the world was unipolar. The Americans did not have to go it alone in their military ventures, as the 1991 Gulf War demonstrated, but they could if they wished to, and they all but did so in Iraq in 2003. Yet the apparent decline in the security threat from other core states was offset by new dangers from the periphery. The very singularity of US power after 1989 meant that no nation imagined itself to have more at stake in the world than the United States. Resentment of the extension of power by the United States resulted in what Chalmers Johnson (and the CIA) called *blowback* against perceived American influence and arrogance. The attacks of September 11, 2001, brought home to Americans the staggering reality that the end of the Cold War had not made them safer—indeed, it seemed, quite the opposite. The containment strategy undertaken between 1945 and 1989 was directed by the United States at the Soviet Union— and, ironically, was developed by the Americans *and* the Soviets for use against the residents of their volatile peripheries.[16]

The economic realities of the Cold War were supposed to change once it ended as Americans anticipated a "peace dividend" with a diminution of expensive competition with the Soviets across the globe. The dividend never came. Instead, the contest for resources and export markets has intensified. Economists observing the recent global crisis worry about the long-term prosperity of the United States, which is more than ever tied to international forces, not just domestic ones. Despite recent trends, energy independence seems ultimately an illusion; surrendering dollars, arms, and influence to buy access to oil is more than ever the American way of doing business with the so-called periphery. In economic terms, which Wallerstein emphasized, the core-periphery distinction is less valid than ever. Some of the fastest-growing economies are Asian, residents of the Cold War periphery: China, Mongolia, India, Taiwan, Singapore, and South Korea. Brazil had until recently moved forward. Even some of the nations of Sub-Saharan Africa, long relegated to the status of basket cases, have shown surprising rates of growth. Walk into a train station in a medium-sized American city and one of comparable size in East Asia and try to decide which one is of the core and which of the periphery.

Insofar as the Cold War was an ideological struggle for the hearts and minds of those in the Third World, communism pretty much lost. But one can reasonably ask whether liberal capitalism therefore won. Certainly, the effort to promote American values on the periphery did not end in 1989. One of the most striking features of US foreign policymaking during the period 1990–2010 was what James Mann has termed *the rise of the Vulcans,* a group of Straussian moralists (Dick Cheney, Paul Wolfowitz, Condoleezza Rice) who saw the demise of the Soviet Union as an opportunity for the United States to implant democracy across the globe. Even before the Cold War ended, there were refreshing signals that the United States had begun to distance itself from kleptocrats, like the Philippines's Ferdinand Marcos, who had purchased US support with their devoutly expressed anticommunism. By the beginning of the new century, the Vulcans were in power, and they attempted to fashion a version of American democracy wherever a chance arose. The war with Iraq in 2003 was designed, in part, to create democracy in that nation, with the hope that it would then spread to other nations in the Middle East. (It turns out that democracy tends not to work that way. Neoconservative efforts to link the encouraging Arab Spring of 2011 to US intervention in Iraq have foundered on matters of logic and evidence as few of those involved in the uprisings have had anything good to say about the American military presence nearby and no one wishes to claim custody of the debacle in Syria.) Indeed, the American military in Afghanistan abandoned plans to import into dangerous cities like Marja and Kandahar "government in a box," as if government was a meal ready to eat. It was much easier to fight ideological battles when the adversary was just one place and believed just one repugnant thing.[17]

The narrative of nationalism and decolonization—which grants agency to those outside the core—is by definition dissociated from the Cold War, so 1989 did little to change its trajectory. It could be said that both forces had won out by end of the twentieth century: formal empires were all but nonexistent, nationalism given its due as a force more powerful than any international regime that hoped to control it. Questions remained about the pace and impact of decolonization. Looking back, some South Asians charged that the British quit India too abruptly, leaving Muslims and Hindus to fight a bloody struggle as independence dawned for India and Pakistan. In Africa, the tardiness and bad grace with which the French, British, Belgians, and especially the Portuguese retreated from their colonies left economies in ruins and political culture rudimentary. The legacy of colonialism remains bitter; it is the cause of resentment directed at the United States and Europe and thus another source of blowback from the periphery to the core.

Finally, if the culturalist narrative of the Cold War unsettled the core-periphery binary, its growing acceptance recently would seem to undo it entirely. Tension over religious difference has exacerbated relations between states with large Christian or Jewish populations and those with large Islamic ones. But this is not a reductionist argument, for other cultural constructs have proved as troublesome in their way. While racism or the perception of racism seems to have abated as a factor of consequence in the world system, neither has gone away entirely: witness the anger of many African states over the apparent hypocrisy of NATO intervention against Serbian-led genocide in the former Yugoslavia in the absence of any similar action to prevent genocide in Rwanda at roughly the same time or Sudan or the Congo more recently. Perceptions based on gender have also remained influential in the post–Cold War world. If a single emotion has proved durable in recent years, surely it is the humiliation felt by men who consider themselves to have been emasculated and thus disempowered by others. A variety of causes move al-Qaeda, Hamas, Hezbollah, the Taliban, and the poisonous Islamic State. Prominent in every case is the sense that their people, especially their men, have been shamed and humiliated by Western (including of course Israeli) domination, occupation, or victory in battle. One hears this from unemployed Palestinians in Gaza, prisoners released from Abu Ghraib or Guantanamo, even the late Osama bin Laden, who turned against the Americans when his own country allowed US troops to mass on its soil prior to the liberation of Kuwait—a humiliating admission that Saudi Arabia could not handle Middle Eastern problems itself.

One last point about culture. The dissolution of the core-periphery binary in recent years has to do with the movement of ideas and people and money across national borders, leading some to question the long-term efficacy of borders themselves. This process is called roughly *globalization,* a "fashionable buzzword of contemporary political and academic debate," according to William Scheuerman, but a real presence nonetheless. Globalization has multiple features—the increased speed with which goods and ideas are transmitted, the creation of transnational networks, the transformation of individual and collective identity—all with the result of dissolving boundaries that separate people by nation-state, ethnicity, and of course culture. Especially culture. As John Tomlinson has written: "A world of complex connectivity . . . links the myriad small everyday actions of millions with the fates of distant, unknown others and even with the possible fate of the planet. All these individual actions are undertaken within the culturally meaningful context of local mundane lifeworlds in which dress codes and the subtle differentiations of fashion establish personal and cultural identity." Cultural flows in a globalized world are perhaps heaviest from places of wealth and power, but these currents do not exhaust the flow of influence. More and more, the outcome of globalization is cultural hybridity, whereby contact creates a mélange of substance and style. Chinese teenagers listen to hip-hop, but it may be Japanese hip-hop. McDonald's goes kosher in Israel, sells beer in Germany, and offers teriyaki burgers in East Asia. Curry is Britain's national dish. During the US war in Iraq, thousands of South Asian and Arab workers did manual labor on American military bases, and in the evenings they watched Bollywood movies, sometimes joined by the Americans. The world is not, as Thomas Friedman has put it, flat; mounds of money and the jutting contours of tanks and jets persist in making its landscape uneven. Yet there are few genuinely homogeneous places left on earth. The hierarchical divisions that once seemed immutable have gone—though, as I have argued, one could see this prefigured in the Cold War period. For better or worse, in cultural terms, there is now no core, no periphery.[18]

Notes

1. Immanuel Wallerstein, *The Modern World-System: Capitalist Agriculture and the Origins of the European World-Economy in the Sixteenth Century* (New York: Academic, 1974), *The Modern World-System II: Mercantilism and the Consolidation of the European World-Economy, 1600–1750* (New York: Academic, 1980), and *World-Systems Analysis: An Introduction* (Durham, NC: Duke University Press, 2004); Paul A. Kramer, "Power and Connection: Imperial Histories of the United States in the World," *American Historical Review* 116, no. 5 (December 2011): 1348–91; Thomas

J. McCormick, "'Every System Needs a Center Sometimes': An Essay on Hegemony and Modern American Foreign Policy," in *Redefining the Past: Essays in Diplomatic History in Honor of William Appleman Williams,* ed. Lloyd C. Gardner (Corvallis: Oregon State University Press, 1986), 195–220.

2. Steve J. Stern, "The Decentered Center and the Expansionist Periphery: The Paradoxes of Foreign-Local Encounter," in *Close Encounters of Empire: Writing the Cultural History of U.S.–Latin American Relations,* ed. Gilbert M. Joseph, Catherine C. LeGrand, and Ricardo D. Salvatore (Durham, NC: Duke University Press, 1998), 47–68; Walter F. LaFeber, *America, Russia, and the Cold War, 1945–2000,* 9th ed. (Boston: McGraw-Hill, 2002), 18; Kramer, "Power and Connection," 1386; Emily S. Rosenberg, "Turning to Culture," in Joseph, LeGrand, and Salvatore, eds., *Close Encounters of Empire,* 497–514, 507; Anthony Beevor, *Berlin: The Downfall, 1945* (London: Penguin, 2007), 183 (Stalin quote).

3. See, e.g., John Lewis Gaddis, *Strategies of Containment: A Critical Appraisal of Postwar American National Security Policy* (New York: Oxford University Press, 1982); Melvyn P. Leffler, *A Preponderance of Power: National Security, the Truman Administration, and the Cold War* (Stanford, CA: Stanford University Press, 1992); Robert J. McMahon, *The Cold War on the Periphery: The United States, India, and Pakistan* (New York: Columbia University Press, 1994); and Odd Arne Westad, *The Global Cold War* (New York: Cambridge University Press, 2005).

4. Harry Magdoff, *The Age of Imperialism: The Economics of U.S. Foreign Policy* (New York: Monthly Review Press, 2000); Joyce Kolko and Gabriel Kolko, *The Limits of Power: The World and United States Foreign Policy* (New York: Harper & Row, 1972); Thomas J. McCormick, *America's Half-Century: United States Foreign Policy in the Cold War* (Baltimore: Johns Hopkins University Press, 1989); Michael J. Hogan, *The Marshall Plan: America, Britain, and the Reconstruction of Western Europe, 1947–1952* (New York: Cambridge University Press, 1987); Walter F. LaFeber, "Technology and U.S. Foreign Relations," *Diplomatic History* 24, no. 1 (Winter 2000): 1–19. (This note offers a progressively denatured version of Marxist economic analysis as it moves along.)

5. Michael H. Hunt, *Ideology and U.S. Foreign Policy* (New Haven, CT: Yale University Press, 1987), xi; William Appleman Williams, *The Tragedy of American Diplomacy* (New York: Dell, 1959); Reinhold Wagnleitner, *Coca-Colonization and the Cold War: The Cultural Mission of the United States in Austria after the Second World War* (Chapel Hill: University of North Carolina Press, 1994); Frank Ninkovich, *The Wilsonian Century: U.S. Foreign Policy since 1900* (Chicago: University of Chicago Press, 2001); Michael E. Latham, *Modernization as Ideology: American Social Science and "Nation Building" in the Kennedy Era* (Chapel Hill: University of North Carolina Press, 2000); David C. Engerman, Nils Gilman, Mark H. Haefele, and Michael E. Latham, eds., *Staging Growth: Modernization, Development, and the Global Cold War* (Amherst: University of Massachusetts Press, 2003).

6. On Vietnam, see Mark Philip Bradley, *Imagining Vietnam and America: The Making of Postcolonial Vietnam, 1919–1950* (Chapel Hill: University of North Car-

olina Press, 2000). On Algeria, see Matthew Connelly, *A Diplomatic Revolution: Algeria's Fight for Independence and the Origin of the Post–Cold War Era* (New York: Oxford University Press, 2002).

7. Clifford Geertz, *The Interpretation of Cultures* (New York: Basic, 1973), 5, 14; John Tomlinson, *Globalization and Culture* (Chicago: University of Chicago Press, 1999), 24; Rosenberg, "Turning to Culture"; Edward Said, *Orientalism* (New York: Pantheon, 1978), and *Culture and Imperialism* (New York: Vintage, 1993); Seth Fein, "Everyday Forms of Transnational Collaboration: U.S. Film Propaganda in Cold War Mexico," in Joseph, LeGrand, and Salvatore, eds., *Close Encounters of Empire*, 400–50, 403; Andrew J. Rotter, *Comrades at Odds: The United States and South Asia, 1947–1964* (Ithaca, NY: Cornell University Press, 2000), xiii–xxix, 39 (Nehru quote). Or as the preeminent scholar of world-systems theory has put it: "Our cultures are our lives, our most inner selves but also our most outer selves, our personal and collective individualities." Wallerstein, *The Modern World-System II,* 65.

8. Thomas Borstelmann, *The Cold War and the Color Line: American Race Relations in the Global Arena* (New York: Oxford University Press, 2001), 50; Rotter, *Comrades at Odds,* 159 (McGhee quote); Hunt, *Ideology and U.S. Foreign Policy,* 46–91; Mary L. Dudziak, *Cold War Civil Rights: Race and the Image of American Democracy* (Princeton, NJ: Princeton University Press, 2000); Penny M. Von Eschen, *Satchmo Blows Up the World: Jazz Ambassadors Play the Cold War* (Cambridge, MA: Harvard University Press, 2004); John Lewis Gaddis, *George F. Kennan: An American Life* (New York: Penguin, 2011), 150 (Kennan quote).

9. Kwame Nkrumah, *Ghana: The Autobiography of Kwame Nkrumah* (New York: International, 1957), 42–43, 46; Piero Gleijeses, *Conflicting Missions: Havana, Washington, and Africa, 1959–1976* (Chapel Hill: University of North Carolina Press, 2002), 8 (newspaper quote); Rotter, *Comrades at Odds,* 176–87.

10. Frank Costigliola, "'Unceasing Pressure for Penetration': Gender, Pathology, and Emotion in George Kennan's Formation of the Cold War," *Journal of American History* 83, no. 4 (March 1997): 1309–39; Petra Goedde, *GIs and Germans: Culture, Gender, and Foreign Relations, 1945–1949* (New Haven, CT: Yale University Press, 2003); Naoko Shibusawa, *America's Geisha Ally: Reimagining the Japanese Enemy* (Cambridge, MA: Harvard University Press, 2006); Mary Ann Heiss, *Empire and Nationhood: The United States, Great Britain, and Iranian Oil, 1950–1954* (New York: Columbia University Press, 1997); Douglas Little, *American Orientalism: The United States and the Middle East since 1945* (Chapel Hill: University of North Carolina Press, 2002), 26–27; Robert D. Dean, *Imperial Brotherhood: Gender and the Making of a Cold War Foreign Policy* (Amherst: University of Massachusetts Press, 2001), 240 (LBJ quotes); Christina Klein, *Cold War Orientalism: Asia in the Middlebrow Imagination, 1945–1961* (Berkeley and Los Angeles: University of California Press, 2003).

11. Frederick Cooper, *Africa since 1940: The Past of the Present* (New York: Cambridge University Press, 2002), 126; Michelle Mart, *Eye on Israel: How America*

Came to View the Jewish State as an Ally (Albany: State University of New York Press, 2006); Rotter, *Comrades at Odds,* 188–219.

12. Will Herberg, *Protestant, Catholic, Jew: An Essay in American Religious Sociology* (Chicago: University of Chicago Press, 1955); Martin E. Marty, *Modern American Religion,* vol. 3, *Under God, Indivisible, 1941–1960* (Chicago: University of Chicago Press, 1996); Andrew Preston, "Bridging the Gap between the Sacred and the Secular in the History of American Foreign Relations," *Diplomatic History* 30, no. 5 (November 2006): 783–812; William Inboden, *Religion and American Foreign Policy, 1945–1960: The Soul of Containment* (New York: Cambridge University Press, 2008); Gary Scott Smith, *Faith and the Presidency: From George Washington to George W. Bush* (New York: Oxford University Press, 2009); Andrew Preston, *Sword of the Spirit, Shield of Faith: Religion in American War and Diplomacy* (New York: Knopf, 2012).

13. Andrew J. Rotter, "Christians, Muslims, and Hindus: Religion and U.S.–South Asian Relations, 1947–1954," *Diplomatic History* 24, no. 4 (Fall 2000): 593–613, 607 (Khan quote), and *Comrades at Arms,* 241 (Nehru quotes); Matthew F. Jacobs, "The Perils and Promise of Islam: The United States and the Muslim Middle East in the Early Cold War," *Diplomatic History* 30, no. 4 (September 2006): 705–39.

14. Seth Jacobs, *America's Miracle Man in Vietnam: Ngo Dinh Diem, Religion, Race, and U.S. Intervention in Southeast Asia* (Durham, NC: Duke University Press, 2004), 12, 76, 209.

15. Alastair Iain Johnston, *Cultural Realism: Strategic Culture and Grand Strategy in Chinese History* (Princeton, NJ: Princeton University Press, 1995), 1–6 (quote 5); Simei Qing, *From Allies to Enemies: Visions of Modernity, Identity, and U.S.-China Diplomacy, 1945–1960* (Cambridge, MA: Harvard University Press, 2007), 11–17; John Lewis Gaddis, "New Conceptual Approaches to the Study of American Foreign Relations: Interdisciplinary Perspectives," *Diplomatic History* 14, no. 3 (July 1990): 402–24; Rotter, *Comrades at Odds,* 37–76.

16. Chalmers Johnson, *Blowback: The Costs and Consequences of American Empire* (New York: Metropolitan, 2000).

17. James Mann, *Rise of the Vulcans: The History of Bush's War Cabinet* (New York: Viking, 2004).

18. William Scheuerman, "Globalization," in *Stanford Encyclopedia of Philosophy,* http://plato.stanford.edu/entries/globalization; Tomlinson, *Globalization and Culture,* 25–26; Akria Iriye, "Global History," in *Palgrave Advances in International History,* ed. Patrick Finney (Houndmills: Palgrave Macmillan, 2005), 320–44; Lane Crothers, *Globalization and American Popular Culture,* 2nd ed. (Lanham, MD: Rowman & Littlefield, 2010), 17–18, 29, 133, 196; Thomas Friedman, *The World Is Flat: A Brief History of the Twenty-First Century* (New York: Farrar Straus Giroux, 2005).

4

US Government Responses to Anti-Americanism at the Periphery

Alan McPherson

In the 1963 cinematic version of Eugene Burdick and William J. Lederer's didactic novel *The Ugly American* (1958), the new US ambassador to the fictional Southeast Asian nation of Sarkhan, Harrison Carter MacWhite, arrives at the host airport only to be greeted by a life-threatening anti-US riot. Enraged crowds rock his car and smash and spit on the windows. MacWhite and his entourage barely escape with life and limb. Played with restrained intensity by Marlon Brando, the ambassador remains calm during the riot but later angrily confronts his new staff after summoning them to the embassy on a Sunday. He is furious at them for knowing there was to be a demonstration and not predicting it might escalate into a riot. He exposes their ignorance and their self-imposed isolation from the Sarkhanese.

"The only thing that is clear is that there's no clarity at all," MacWhite tells his staff, adding that he's more scared of their complacence than he is of the rioters. Reflecting the "vital center" liberal optimism of his time, MacWhite offers a solution: better information gathering. "Confusion, ignorance, and indifference will cease as of this moment," he orders. Yet, in that meeting, never does he suggest that the cause of the riot might be US policy, nor does he propose any changes to that policy. Improved two-way communication would have to do.[1]

The scene encapsulates well an abiding pattern in US government responses to anti-Americanism at the periphery: US thinking in the face of evidence of the rejection of US influence remained fundamentally defensive and unimaginative even while Washington's data-collection efforts grew more comprehensive and accurate. This was the case during the Cold War, when concerns over periphery-wide anti-Americanism first emerged. And it has been the case since, culminating in the years following September 11, 2001, and the US invasion of Iraq. Only in recent years has the US government proved more open to acknowledging the demonstrated sources of anti-Americanism.

The pervasiveness and persistence of this willful blindness among US policymakers offers historians an opportunity to shed light on the difficulty of managing effectively the anti-US sentiment that has emerged from most regions of the world. As former deputy director of the CIA Richard Bissell reasoned: "Anti-Americanism is generally perceived as a cultural or sociological phenomenon; at some point during its accumulation, its impact on the conduct of US foreign policy has to be recognized."[2] Historians would do well to conceive of anti-Americanism not simply as a one-way street of criticism of the United States. It is, rather, a back-and-forth interaction in which foreigners express hostility, US officials and the public read that hostility and respond to it, foreigners respond to US responses, and so on. The response of the US government—what we might call *anti-anti-Americanism*—matters.

Bissell's entreaty implies that, just as anti-Americanism opens windows into the identities of those who express it, so too does the US response to anti-Americanism allow us to peer into the depths of US national identity. US government responses to anti-Americanism at the periphery reveal much about the psyche of the United States in the world. Rather than take on the near-impossible task of providing comprehensive evidence for all US responses to anti-US events from the Cold War until today, this chapter will instead offer some anecdotal evidence of this psyche, from the 1950s to the 2010s. It skips over some years and even the entire 1990s, which is not to suggest that anti-Americanism did not exist during these periods but rather to reflect that they seemed to contain no notable shift in US government responses to the phenomenon at the periphery. As a whole, this survey suggests that US policymakers who responded to anti-Americanism harbored an abiding exceptionalism and a disdain for the "decent respect to the opinions of mankind," as Jefferson put it the Declaration of Independence.

A final few words of explanation are in order. *Periphery* is defined here as the areas outside North America, Europe, Australia, Japan, and the Sino-Soviet bloc using a hybrid politicoeconomic framework that emphasizes the consequences of powerlessness. Such a framework is relevant because, first, these areas made up a world whose grievances against the United States stemmed from common frustrations arising from being underdeveloped in the face of a great accumulation of wealth in industrialized nations. Second, these areas also largely suffered from marginal political status in the Cold War, which, as Odd Arne Westad has demonstrated, stood in sharp contrast to their centrality as battlefields of that same East-West struggle. And I still define *anti-Americanism,* as I first did over a decade ago, as "the expression of a disposition against U.S. influence abroad."[3] I hold fast to that definition because of its breadth: *expression* includes verbal, physical, and policy modalities; *disposition* can describe a range of ideological positions from a well-informed opinion to outright bias; and *US influence* can refer to "hard" and "soft" power, including military interventions, political arm-twisting, economic domination, and cultural hegemony.

The 1950s

Washington began paying attention to anti-Americanism all along the periphery—and not merely in one area such as Latin America—following a confluence of events that included the Chinese Revolution of 1949, the successful testing of a Soviet nuclear bomb that same year, the death of Joseph Stalin in 1953, and the growing decolonization struggles in Asia and Africa in the late 1940s and early 1950s. All of a sudden, it seemed that communism was not only spreading in popularity but also possibly overtaking the soon-to-be former colonies of Europe. At first, anti-Americanism appeared to Washington to be a subset of communism, an ideological muddle of images that the Sino-Soviet bloc and its minions around the world used to manipulate a portion of the masses. It seemed to have the particular potential to bridge the sharp ideological precepts of Communist cadres and the vague discontent of peripheral societies and then to direct that discontent against the United States.

Many in Washington thought a response to anti-Americanism imperative. To better measure public sentiment abroad and respond to it, the US government founded the US Information Agency (USIA) in 1953. That same year, the National Security Council (NSC) gave the Psychological Strategy Board (PSB) the task of explaining the declining prestige of the United States, stating that it noted a growing anti-Americanism around the world. C. D. Jackson of the Operations Coordinating Board introduced the report in September, defining *prestige* as "our ability to influence other people because of their attitudes toward us, as distinguished from our ability to exert influence through the use of special incentives." The definition was close to that of what we now call *soft power,* and much of the evidence of this decline was what we now term *anti-Americanism:* public opinion polls that expressed significant negative opinion of the United States as a whole. Reflecting the area studies epistemology of the Cold War, the report analyzed polls by region—Europe, the Far East, South Asia, the Arab World, and Latin America.[4]

Data collection showed promise in the early Cold War years. The USIA, for instance, relied on social scientists such as William Buchanan and Hadley Cantril to understand the nature of stereotypes and on professional pollsters such as Lloyd Free to argue for the importance of negative foreign public opinion. Buchanan and Cantril had developed the image of "maps in our heads," a cognitive concept that, for instance, prevented nations from accurately processing contradictory new information. They also used some of the first world opinion polls, conducted by the United Nations in the late 1940s. In the Dwight Eisenhower administration, these advocates for appreciating "how others see us," in Buchanan's phrase, enjoyed the backing of prominent Republicans such as Nelson Rockefeller.[5]

However, several red flags already indicated some logistic but also some ideological obstacles to collecting and analyzing data about anti-Americanism. First was the East-West framing of the prestige issue: the PSB addressed only the supposed US decline among Cold War allies, who were also supposedly concerned only that Washington had not been decisive enough against Communist bloc advances in Soviet satellites in 1944 and the Korean Peninsula in 1950. Second, budgets for polling were small: in 1958, while the Soviets spent $500–$750 million on "propaganda, student exchange, etc.," according to USIA director George Allen, the USIA in contrast had a budget of only $95 million. Third, even if polls could be funded, collecting a representative sample of foreign populations proved challenging. The report on decline, which summarized reports from US foreign service officers in the field, admitted: "Inevitably, American contacts are disproportionately with educated, articulate sectors of the population, and one must guard against attributing to an entire populace sentiments expressed by this relatively small group." In Latin America, a 1955 USIA report polled a broad cross section of four thousand Mexicans but queried only eight hundred "opinion leaders" in Brazil. In the Arab world and Indonesia in 1957–1958, the USIA took no poll because anti-Americanism was *too* prevalent there.[6]

A few years earlier, the USIA had polled itself, asking 142 of its officials in Washington and abroad to evaluate the agency in a six-volume self-study. As the historian Max Friedman noted: "Their findings were devastating: the Agency did not know whether its news coverage was impartial or biased, whether its anti-Communist messages were subtle or blatant, whether its impact was 'important' or 'infinitesimal.'"[7]

As a result of such incompetence, and despite the nevertheless unprecedented polling ability, US opinions toward negative foreign opinion remained complacent. The 1953 report on prestige stated: "It would be false to draw the conclusion that there is anything durable or fundamentally wrong in the relationships between the United States and other countries." The explanation amounted to psychobabble filtered through the lens of international relations: "A debtor never loves a creditor and those who receive bounty rarely feel lasting gratitude to the giver; states which quickly assume commanding positions in the world are viewed with jealousy and suspicion by those who lately exercised great power and who by force of circumstances have lost it; the devastation and disillusionment of war, bring to victor and vanquished alike, psychopathic conditions, which superimposed on economic and social stress and strain, tend to exaggerate international friction." Nowhere were policy issues discussed. As Friedman has demonstrated in many episodes of the Cold War, others rejected from the start the mission to gather the "opinions of mankind" because they refused to acknowledge the Jeffersonian need to "respect" them. "In many areas of the world it makes little or no difference what overt acts we undertake," wrote a US colonel the year of the USIA's founding. "No matter what we do or what we say in these areas, the peoples of these areas will spare no love for the U.S. We should not be concerned with this but should recognize it as one of the facts of international life."[8] The colonel's remarks were doubly discouraging because he worked for the PSB.

In another telling episode from the 1950s, it became clear that any semblance of a US government employee giving credence to foreign criticism—perhaps even suggesting a change in policy—was likely to meet with hostility from the top. When Jackson presented a survey of foreign attitudes to the NSC, Eisenhower "said that he had almost blown his top when he first read this report." The president blamed negative foreign reporting on New Dealers in overseas posts out to do harm to the Republican Party. He even suggested sending out "observers who were really loyal to the new Administration" to "find out who are the traitors in these various missions." Rather than defend his report, Jackson agreed and blamed "termites" in Washington and "disgruntled eggheads" overseas. Secretary of State John Foster Dulles was more measured, calling the report "a correct reflection" of State Department reporting. But Dulles, a believer in secrecy, also warned of "great damage" were the report released.[9]

As a result, major recommendations of 1950s reports were to change no policies or even attitudes. They instead suggested that the government institute purely public relations changes meant to soften Cold War rhetoric. In one instance, C. D. Jackson counseled that the US government should dissociate itself from McCarthyism and "avoid outright condemnation of 'neutral countries' or rigid insistence that they must be 'for us' or 'against us.'" This resilience in the face of foreign hostility came partly from the assumption—for instance, by Buchanan and Cantril—that "the stereotype can be more flexible than is often assumed." In other words, Washington believed that it could massage the message, so public diplomats embraced a superficial approach to selling the United States to the rest of the world. Correspondingly, the language of movies and public relations pervaded discussions about anti-Americanism. In the 1950s, for instance, the *Saturday Evening Post* characterized "America's reputation abroad" as "our overseas box office."[10]

Secretary of State Dean Acheson also counseled diversionary rhetoric in a 1950 circular to eight Middle East posts. After noting bombings, "vitriolic public statements," "diatribes and fantastic rumors," and other evidence of anti-Americanism in the Arab world, he admitted no fault in US policy, only the possibility of "a sincere objection to America's part in Palestine developments." Otherwise, he blamed anti-American "emotional-ism" on "Communists or Moslem extremists," "irresponsible journalists," and "weak government officials." It was an instance of the often-reiterated idea that anti-Americanism was the province of emotion, extreme ideology, and political opportunism. Acheson suggested countering with "corrective versions," which should aim to "re-direct the attention of Arab peoples to their own internal problems."[11]

In 1957–1958, the USIA's budget shrank by 16 percent, and the agency almost abandoned its only worldwide opinion polls, the Barometer Surveys, when the word came down to cut the Research and Intelligence Division by half. Nelson Rockefeller wrote urgently to Eisenhower and obtained a reduction of only a quarter. Yet what was left indicated a persistent disinterest in foreign opinion: apart from two surveys per year covering four European countries, there was only one covering two Latin American countries and two covering one Far Eastern country. So much for the periphery.[12]

Caracas, 1958

A worldwide *Newsweek* map of anti-US disturbances around the world in 1957 did not even include Latin America. That changed after the May 13, 1958, attack on Vice President Richard Nixon in Caracas, Venezuela. That assault on Nixon's motorcade, a fourteen-minute ordeal more dangerous than the fictional riot in *The Ugly American* was made even more dramatic by the coincidence of other anti-US demonstrations on the same day in Lebanon, Algeria, and Burma.[13]

The mounting evidence of widespread anti-US sentiment on the periphery sparked a set of discussions within the Eisenhower administration. George Allen made several iterations of a presentation called "The Image of America." In them, Allen proved humble, agreeing that US officials boasted too much about their power and civilization. He was also focused, identifying the most important anti-Americanism as what emerged not from the Kremlin but from potential allies with "cleaner hands" such as "Afro-Asians." "The Image of America" was essentially a revision of the prestige report, but this time Eisenhower was less partisan and dismissive. He called the report "interesting" and "valuable."[14]

Discussions notably prompted some reevaluations of data gathering.

The Nixon trip reinvigorated the practice of drawing up lists of Latin American grievances and attitudes toward the United States. Perhaps for the first time, the USIA focused its energy on a social group, in this case "the university students, labor and 'intellectual' groups in Latin America." Spurred again by the fear that the Soviets were winning the information struggle in a peripheral region, an NSC report assessed that "these politically active groups are increasingly numerous and have more leisure as Latin American education and industrial development become more widespread." The USIA planned more exchanges, binational centers, and textbooks and other publications. By 1958, it and other organizations had professional local pollsters who could query hundreds of people in a few days in major Latin American cities, all in Spanish, and supposedly without the appearance of working for the US government.[15]

Some policies changed. In diplomacy, Nixon counseled giving dictators a firm handshake and democrats a warm embrace. He also recommended that educational exchange programs should be "at least doubled." NSC meeting notes suggest that officials planned to "organize" pro-US groups among students and intellectuals, who would then be "bought." Soon, the administration took steps in all these directions. They also suddenly lent an ear to Presidents Juscelino Kubitschek of Brazil and Alberto Lleras Camargo of Colombia, who seized the moment and proposed a program of public investment that later became Operation Pan-America, the genesis of the Alliance for Progress.[16]

Yet, in the end, the post-Caracas moment came and went, with little to no change in policy. US resilience carried the day in the face of foreign criticism. "Our failures are principally psychological," concluded Roy Rubottom of the State Department in August 1958. "We should not, through excessive reluctance to enter into the argument or a feeling of guilt, appear to accept the prevalent Latin American argument that it is entirely *our* fault that *they* have failed to solve *their* problem." Throughout the Nixon trip and the White House debates and policy changes that followed, exceptionalism ruled, and the denial of imperialism persisted. They characterized every government agency, Democrats and Republicans, officials and journalists, public and private comments. Allen himself remarked that accusations of imperialism were "surprising, because no American is conscious of any effort or desire to create an American empire beyond our present boundaries." Eisenhower himself was mostly interested in "correcting misunderstandings of the true American position." And, as in the early 1950s, domestic politics entered the fray. Republicans accused Democrats of exploiting the "Image of America" talk to argue that Eisenhower had presided over the deterioration of that image.[17]

1960s

The 1960s only increased the incidence of anti-Americanism. The spread of the ideology of the Cuban Revolution and the militaristic response of Washington at the Bay of Pigs, the peaking decolonization struggle in Africa and the manipulation of it by the CIA in the Congo, the rise of the neutralist movement, the incipient civil wars in Southeast Asia, and the funding and other encouragement of all these movements by the newly adventurous Soviets expressed themselves partly as anti-Americanism. From 1956 to 1965, one study counted 171 attacks on US facilities or citizens around the world; from 1968 to 1979, the CIA estimated that they had grown to 1,418.[18]

Data collection improved during the 1960s but remained limited. In 1963, the USIA conducted its own worldwide poll, called the World Survey. It included, outside Europe, four countries from Latin America, five from the Far East, and two from the Near East, including the first ever poll of Tehran. Paul Nitze, then assistant secretary of defense, called the poll "useful to us as general background information." The agency—and others in the US government—investigated the impact of specific US institutions or policies—for instance, Hollywood movies abroad or agricultural assistance—on, again, "the American image." US officials also, for perhaps the first time, communicated their findings to the public, or at least the academic world. Yet, as the USIA itself admitted, "existing survey organizations [were] inadequate to provide genuine world-wide evaluations": only cities were counted, and pollsters stayed out of Africa altogether. Conceptual problems equally persisted. The USIA continued to be interested exclusively in the periphery as a constituency in the Cold War and not in North-South issues per se.[19] The area studies approach also reinforced the inability to frame overall issues—of development and democracy, for instance—that might be of interest to the entire developing world.

The Kennedy presidency was especially mired in a tug-of-war

between being proactive against anti-Americanism at the periphery and just throwing up its hands and accepting its inevitability. On one hand, the USIA was optimistic. Its new director, Edward R. Murrow, wrote Kennedy to crow that there was finally a US propaganda program enjoying a preponderance of symbolic power. "The Russians are really squealing about the Peace Corps," he noted. "They can and do compete with us in the field of periodicals, books and broadcasts, but they can not risk sending their youth abroad except under conditions of strict control." On the other hand, Senator George Smathers complained to the president-elect that events in Cuba, the Congo, Iraq, and the United Arab Republic made the USIA look as if it were "apologizing for the United States and giving the benefit of the doubt to America's detractors." Reflecting Eisenhower's rhetoric from the early 1950s, Smathers wanted to ensure the loyalty of US "propagandists," suggesting that they be trained as a "hard core of dedicated pro-Americans." Shopworn ideological failures persisted through the 1960s. Much of the new so-called sensitivity of US policy toward the periphery was rhetorical. Witness a 1961 list of suggested linguistic changes targeted to Americans abroad: "developing" should replace "underdeveloped, backward"; "non-allied" was now better than "neutralist, non-aligned"; and "citizens (preceded by nationality)" was to replace "natives, aborigines, indigenous population." And, again, the politicization of US government responses was always a danger. In 1964, the Republican presidential candidate, Barry Goldwater, attacked Democrats and especially the CIA for saying that US prestige was once again in decline.[20]

Exceptionalism and the US Response

What nerves did anti-Americanism touch in the US body politic? What defense mechanisms did it trigger? How can we best describe how criticisms of the United States in the developing world—or elsewhere in the free world, for that matter—disturbed the US official psyche so deeply as to prevent an open-minded response? Even before the Cold War, the US response to foreign criticism proved resilient against the rise and ebb of foreign hostility. This resilience appeared felicitous and robust to US patriots yet arrogant and provincial to US critics. Such is nevertheless the portrait that emerges from the history of US responses, and such a history seems to evoke a larger debate over US exceptionalism. As the scholar Rob Kroes has asserted, while anti-US criticism is inherently international and averse to looking inward, it "ironically reintroduces an exceptionalist element" because it highlights unique ways in which the United States has projected the notion of America and how the world has received it.[21] A few trends of the US response thus stood out.

The first was the intensity of US emotions stirred by the very existence of criticism abroad, especially among allies. US emotionalism was paradoxical, given the US penchant for dismissing anti-Americanism itself as overly emotive. Yet US policymakers consistently expressed shock at not being liked. "We feel that anyone in his right mind ought to like us, or at least understand us," admitted the editors of *America* in 1953. "After all, aren't we the most 'normal' people in the world?" Partly, hurt feelings resulted from the universalism of US political beliefs. US citizens held that what was good for them was good for the world and that therefore the world looked to them to exemplify moral foreign policy making. Poll analysts in the 1960s found that US citizens were largely ignorant of the world outside their borders yet highly concerned with their image abroad and the respect they garnered there.[22]

Second, the charge of imperialism leveled against the US government throughout the twentieth century particularly sparked pleas of innocence. US officials recoiled at the thought that, as former colonies, the United States would be accused of colonialist aspirations. US textbooks expunged the word *imperialism* when speaking of any period after the 1920s. The historian Samuel Flagg Bemis even said in the 1940s that the US role in the Caribbean prior to the 1920s was to promote "imperialism against imperialism." Debates over whether the United States was at any time imperialistic have continued ever since.[23]

1970s

The ideological and political constraints on US government responses helped paralyze Washington during one of the Cold War's most important peripheral anti-American events: the Iranian Revolution, which expressed much of the periphery's anti-Americanism during the 1970s. The defeat in Vietnam, the relative economic decline of the United States vis-à-vis Western Europe and Japan, the breakdown in domestic political discourse exemplified by Watergate, and the growing assertiveness of decolonized nations taking advantage of the détente between the superpowers all created a context in which the United States appeared to be a weakening yet still aggressive hegemon.

It was no surprise that Iran became the poster child for anti-Americanism at the end of the decade. It was the site of the CIA's first successful coup d'état in 1953, and Washington had taken relatively little notice of the hostility among the Iranian masses that had been slowly building since. Some of the Iranian students who took over the US embassy in Tehran in November 1979 had been fed a steady diet of fierce anti-US propaganda, blaming the United States, which they dubbed the "Great Satan," for every misfortune that had befallen not only Iran but also much of the periphery in the previous generation. They seemed convinced that the CIA, especially, was literally the source of all evil in the modern world and that it controlled far more than it actually did. The hostage takers could not bring themselves to believe that only three embassy employees were spies and that, being new to the posting, they knew yet little about Iran. Iranians particularly saw themselves as spokespersons for all Third World resistance movements against US imperialism, so their struggle helped spread much of the rhetoric about US responsibility for the misery within the periphery. The vehemence of the anti-Americanism emerging from Iran made it nearly impossible for US government officials to be open-minded, especially when colleagues were being held in captivity.[24]

An October 1978 cable by Victor Tomseth, the US consul in Shiraz, revealed some US ideological assumptions at the foreign service officer's level. Tomseth met with US academics visiting a local Iranian university who warned him of "growing anti-American sentiment at the university and throughout much of Iranian society," especially after President Jimmy Carter had once again declared his support for the hated shah. Tomseth, as a State Department employee, clearly found himself bound to note these intellectuals' "naïveté about the realities of inter-governmental relationships." He cautioned against overt statements of support but not against support itself. Months later, the shah fell, and months after that the revolution turned violently anti–United States.[25] Tomseth himself was taken hostage in November 1979.

This hesitancy on the part of US government employees came just as

US data collection on anti-Americanism grew by leaps and bounds. A fascinating report emerged on December 4, 1979, a month after the Iranian taking of the embassy. The USIA's director had asked that the staff put together an analysis of worldwide anti-Americanism to see whether Iran signaled a broader shift. The task fell to Leo Crespi, who had conducted polls since the early 1960s. Crespi looked back at fifteen years of global polls to identify possible trends in anti-Americanism.[26]

As in the past, the exercise denoted an increasing sophistication and comprehensiveness in polling foreign public opinion. The USIA now had twenty-five years of surveys in fifty countries to pull from. Crespi likened world opinion around the Iranian Revolution to that around the Vietnam War a decade earlier: it was important, he said, "to distinguish anti-Americanism from criticism of US foreign policies." Earlier polls showed that most countries opposed the war but still harbored pro-US opinions. "Perhaps we have all become sophisticated enough," he added, "to realize that anti-American demonstrations, such as these in Iran, do not prove the existence of general anti-Americanism in public sentiment." Another USIA employee even admitted the conceptual difficulties: "What is this thing called . . . anti-Americanism?" It was "difficult to find as hard evidence of the ideas in people's minds," he wrote. "It exists, instead, in the form of campaigns and communications, as policy of parties and themes of speeches."[27] In other words, careful USIA employees came to similar conclusions that scholars did a generation later in the face of worldwide condemnation of US actions in the Middle East.

Yet other conclusions from the analysts were strikingly familiar. Their tone was one of innocence abroad, blaming the Iranian Revolution not on US policy but on "the confluence of historical streams which were looking for targets against which to express their frustrations." A broader problem was that, as the CIA's Bissell wrote, "those in the US government who consider the issue of anti-Americanism to be a priority are not in major policymaking positions." For all Washington's increasing knowledge on the matter, concern with anti-Americanism was still largely limited to bureaucrats in the field of public affairs, especially those at the USIA. Bissell's dispirited assessment, written in 1985, was a case in point: it was probably the only published essay on the US government's response to anti-Americanism up to that point in the Cold War.[28]

Early Twenty-First Century

The late 1980s and the 1990s certainly showcased episodes of anti-Americanism, but it was the dramatic worldwide upsurge in anti-Americanism following the 2003 invasion of Iraq that showed perhaps the greatest dissonance between the ability to expertly poll foreign publics and the inability of US government officials to acknowledge their policies' part in angering those publics. Polls unequivocally demonstrated a sharp decline in favorable opinions toward the United States, to the point where several countries now showed, for the first time, an overall negative opinion. From 1999 to spring 2003, when the US government launched its attack on Saddam Hussein's forces, the favorability rating of the United States declined from 56 to 34 percent in Brazil, from 75 to 15 percent in Indonesia, and from 77 to 27 percent in Morocco. Peoples throughout the periphery expressed disdain for the George W. Bush administration's unilateralism and militarism and fear that their country would be its next target.[29] The US response to the developing world's resentment became all the more important because, after the Cold War, the nerve centers of anti-Americanism moved from the Soviet-China-Cuba axis of propaganda and the intelligentsia of Western Europe to nonstate actors in the developing world such as al-Qaeda, media outlets such as Al Jazeera and various Internet sites, and the demagogic leaders of regional powers such as Iran and Venezuela. In other words, in the post–Cold War world, the periphery took over the center of anti-Americanism.

Felicitously, in the first decade of the twenty-first century, world polling came into its own. There remained some information gaps: for instance, sending poll takers into bastions of anti-Americanism such as Cuba and North Korea remained impossible. But, overall, data and analysis about anti-Americanism in the periphery became plentiful and accessible. Major news organizations now conducted deep and accurate polls of foreign publics, such as the Iraqis themselves, and the private Pew Research Center for People and the Press and Gallup organizations did the broadest, most relevant polls of anti-Americanism ever. The US government also increasingly enjoyed sophisticated two-way communication tools. Though the USIA no longer existed after 1999, by 2011 no fewer than sixty-six agencies undertook international exchange and training programs, and dozens of them engaged in public diplomacy. There also now existed an undersecretary for public diplomacy whose budget at middecade was nearly $700 million. The funds paid for new glossy magazines, radio programs, student and scholarly foreign exchanges, and frequent high-level trips to the Middle East.[30]

Still, little of these new resources seemed to translate into changes in US attitudes toward the relationship between their own policies and anti-Americanism. While 81 percent of Middle East respondents believed that US policy had caused the attacks of September 11, 2001, that number in the United States was merely 18 percent, and US responses to anti-Americanism at the periphery mirrored this dissonance. Secretary of State Colin Powell's first appointment as undersecretary for public diplomacy was the Madison Avenue executive Charlotte Beers, whom Powell entrusted with the mission to "rebrand American foreign policy," suggesting that the public relations response to anti-Americanism was alive and well.[31]

Karen Hughes was the most notorious undersecretary because of a "listening tour" she undertook in the Middle East in response to a crescendo of criticism in 2005. The tour was part of her plans for a rapid response to counter false stories in Middle East media and to train diplomats to deliver rebuttals in Arabic. Hughes did do some listening, and the tour included some heartwarming images of her hugging schoolchildren. She also tried to connect to Middle Eastern mothers through her own identity as a working mother. Yet she spent much of her "listening" tour informing Arab women that they led unfulfilled lives. In Jeddah, Saudi Arabia, she told an audience that they should drive and "fully participate in society." A member of the audience responded: "The general image of the Arab woman is that she isn't happy. Well, we're all pretty happy." Hughes was also poorly informed. She told audiences that George W. Bush was the first president to support an independent state for Palestine—that was Bill Clinton. She also falsely claimed: "Our constitution cites 'one nation under God.'" Even State Department employees traveling with Hughes were embarrassed.[32]

2010s

The presidency of Barack Obama made some, though limited, headway toward addressing the US government's role in creating anti-Americanism at the periphery. In the heady days following the 2008 election, after

Obama had promised in his campaign to "restore America's standing in the world," it seemed like anti-Americanism might just vanish into thin air after the departure of the hated Bush regime. Throughout the world, the new president raised US favorability ratings. The Middle East remained skeptical, but other Muslim countries such as Indonesia, where Obama lived as a boy, saw his favorability rise from 15 to 64 percent. In March 2011, a Gallup poll revealed that the United States was the most popular world power, with a rating of 47 percent, 14 points higher than its rating during the Bush administration.[33]

Yet the cloud of anti-Americanism did not completely lift from the periphery. Obama's foreign policies often continued those of his predecessors. There were also ideological remnants of anti-Americanism. Venezuelan president Hugo Chávez declared that Obama still carried the "stench" of Bush, whom Chávez infamously said in 2006 had left the UN speakers' podium smelling of sulfur. After all, Chávez added of Obama, "this is the U.S. Empire we're talking about." During Obama's first years, Chávez continued to speak of building anti-US alliances with countries such as Iran, Russia, China, and Belarus.[34]

The response to anti-Americanism by the Obama administration, however, included a clever rhetorical strategy aimed especially at the sins of the past committed by the US government. While the strategy of the Clinton presidency—and even of Secretary of State Powell—toward US-supported Cold War coups—for instance, in Guatemala and Chile—was to express regret, Obama's response was to refuse to dwell on the past and instead reset relations for the future with an emphasis on bilateral relations of "mutual interest and mutual respect." At the Summit of the Americas in Trinidad and Tobago in April 2009, Obama responded to lectures about the Bay of Pigs with the comment: "I didn't come here to debate the past, I came here to deal with the future." He added: "We must learn from history. But we can't be trapped by it." This rhetorical insistence on acknowledging the tensions—even US responsibilities—of the past half century while simultaneously encouraging the periphery to move past them became a standard in the Obama administration's rhetoric, one that, considering the dismissive nature of past US government strategies, seemed like an improvement. In Ecuador in 2010, Secretary of State Hillary Clinton even turned a common theme of anti-Americanism on its head: "Sometimes, we in America are accused of not paying enough attention to our history. But the obverse can also be true. Sometimes people are captives of their history." Other administration officials reiterated these themes.[35]

The US government arguably perfected this rhetoric at Cairo University in Egypt on June 4, 2009, when Obama delivered perhaps his most effective public relations response to anti-Americanism at the periphery. He first acknowledged the "great tension between the United States and Muslims around the world" rooted partly in historical mistakes by the United States. He also addressed anti-Americanism head-on, saying: "America is not the crude stereotype of a self-interested empire." Yet, unlike previous acknowledgments of anti-Americanism, in his Obama asserted that "we must face these tensions squarely" and explicitly listed their sources: violent extremism, Israel, Iran's nuclear ambitions, democracy, religious freedom, women's rights, and development. He emphasized the historical and cultural ties between the United States and Islam and called for enhanced collaboration based on those ties. Refreshing in the speech was the lack of exceptionalism in Obama's tone.[36]

To be sure, the more subtle, forbearing response to anti-Americanism at the periphery under Obama emerged from US weakness. Fed images of an exhausted military and ballooning deficit, many no longer believed that the United States was the all-powerful hyperpower of the 1990s. Majorities in Pakistan, Mexico, and of course China believed that China would eventually replace, or had already replaced, the United States as "the World's Leading Superpower."[37]

"US prestige abroad . . . is extremely complicated. Based as it must be on a heterogeny [sic] of causes, it eludes simple analysis or generalization. There are serious reasons for concluding that perhaps there are no universal criteria for measurement."[38] So spoke a US Air Force colonel in 1953 in connection with that year's prestige report to the NSC. His statement suggested how challenging it would be for intelligence analysts and public diplomacy officers even to obtain accurate information about anti-Americanism in the world, not to mention to convey that information to leaders who were wary, for political and ideological reasons, of allowing it to modify policy. That dynamic lasted throughout the Cold War, and it has survived it.

Certainly, we cannot assume that anti-US opinions should be the guiding force in US policymaking or that countering false information is not a prerogative of the US government. But there is more than this at work in addressing anti-Americanism through the US government; there is also US foreign policy ideology. There has long existed in Washington an inability to admit that foreign public opinion might be wiser than US public opinion. It is something deep within the exceptionalism of US ideology that prevents US policymakers—and the US public—from taking the leap. Delving into the history of US responses to anti-Americanism might be a step toward that leap.

This chapter is meant to encourage further research into the largely neglected topic of US government responses to anti-Americanism. Up to the turn of the millennium, anti-Americanism as a field of knowledge remained largely the province of academics and journalists, who not only rarely inquired into the response of the US government to the phenomenon but also seldom used the useful research methods of that government. They relied instead on scattered interviews with foreign opinion makers, historical analysis, and their own broad generalizations about developing societies.[39] There have been clear improvements ever since the events of September 11, 2001, spawned a cottage industry of serious research on anti-Americanism. There are more systematic use of polls, historical case studies, and theoretical analysis and a general attempt to divorce scholarship from ideological battles.[40] Yet there is still a dearth of written work on US responses to that phenomenon. Focusing on that response should help bring out its assumptions, processes, and successes and failures.

Notes

1. The expression *vital center* comes from Arthur M. Schlesinger, *The Vital Center: The Politics of Freedom* (Boston: Houghton Mifflin, 1949); the quote comes from *The Ugly American,* dir. George Englund (1963; DVD, Universal City, CA: Universal Studios, 2003).

2. Richard Bissell, "Implications of Anti-Americanism for U.S. Foreign Policy," in *Anti-Americanism in the Third World: Implications for U.S. Foreign Policy,* ed. Alvin Z. Rubinstein and Donald E. Smith (New York: Praeger, 1985), 249–58, 249.

3. Odd Arne Westad, *The Global Cold War: Third World Interventions and the Making of Our Times* (Cambridge: Cambridge University Press, 2005); Alan McPherson, *Yankee No! Anti-Americanism in U.S.–Latin American Relations* (Cambridge, MA: Harvard University Press, 2003), 5.

4. PSB, Memo to Enyart, August 3, 1953, folder PSB 092 (1), box 17, Central Files Series, Psychological Strategy Board, and C. D. Jackson, Memo to NSC, Washington, September 23, 1953, folder PB 381 United States, box 26, Psychological Strategy Board (PSB) Central Files Series, both in National Security Council Staff: Papers, 1953–61, White House Office (hereafter WHO), Dwight D. Eisenhower Library, Abilene, Kansas (hereafter DDEL); Joseph S. Nye Jr., *Soft Power: The Means to Success in World Politics* (New York: Public Affairs, 2004).

5. See William Buchanan and Hadley Cantril, *How Nations See Each Other: A Study in Public Opinion* (Urbana: University of Illinois Press, 1953). Unesco conducted polls in 1948 in Australia, Britain, France, Germany, Italy, the Netherlands, Norway, and the United States. William Buchanan, "How Others See Us," *Annals of the American Academy of Political and Social Science* 295 (September 1954): 1–11; Streibert, Memo to Henry Loomis, January 10, 1956, folder USIA, box 9, Records of the Intelligence Bureau, Office of the Director 1949–1959, Record Group (RG) 59, National Archives, College Park, Maryland (hereafter NARA II).

6. PSB, Memo to Enyart (n. 4 above); George Allen, "The Image of America," September 30, 1958, folder United States Information Agency (1) [1954–60], box 18, NSC Series, Briefing Notes Subseries, NSC 5819, folder NSC 5819 (5), box 8, NSC Series, Status of Projects Subseries, and "Reported Decline in US Prestige Abroad," folder Miscellaneous (3) [September 1953], Subject Subseries, NSC Series, all in Office of the Special Assistant for National Security Affairs: Records, 1952–61, WHO, DDEL; USIA, "Stereotypes—Their Nature, and Function in International Communication with Selected Material on Foreign Images of the U.S.," folder S-9–55, box 10, and S. I. Nadler, "Attitude toward Americans in Recent Surveys," July 18, 1958, folder S-11–58, box 15, both in Office of Research Special Reports, 1953–63, RG 306, NARA II.

7. Max Paul Friedman, *Rethinking Anti-Americanism: The History of an Exceptional Concept in American Foreign Relations* (Cambridge: Cambridge University Press, 2012), 120.

8. "Reported Decline in US Prestige Abroad"; Max Paul Friedman, "Bernath Lecture: Anti-Americanism and U.S. Foreign Relations," *Diplomatic History* 32, no. 4 (September 2008): 497–514; Enyart, Memo to Mr. Reckerd, August 4, 1953, folder PSB 092 (2), Box 17, Central Files Series, Psychological Strategy Board, National Security Council Staff: Papers, 1953–61, WHO, DDEL.

9. Gleason, NSC meeting notes, folder 164th Meeting of NSC October 1, 1953, box 4, NSC Series, Eisenhower Papers as President, 1953–61, DDEL.

10. C. D. Jackson, Memo to NSC (n. 4 above); USIA, "Stereotypes—Their Nature"; "'Liberal' Horror Stories about U.S.A. Aren't Helping Our Reputation Abroad," *Saturday Evening Post*, January 16, 1954, 12.

11. Acheson, Airgram to "certain American diplomatic and consular offices," Washington, May 1, 1950, National Security Archive, http://www.gwu.edu/~nsarchiv/NSAEBB/NSAEBB78/docs.htm.

12. NSC 5819, folder NSC 5819 (5), box 8, NSC Series, Status of Projects Subseries, Office of the Special Assistant for National Security Affairs: Records, 1952–61, WHO, DDEL; [Henry Loomis, Office of Research and Intelligence, USIA?], Memo to Nelson Rockefeller, June 17, 1957, folder Image of America, box 3, OCB Series, Subject Subseries, Office of the Special Assistant for National Security Affairs: Records, 1952–61, WHO, DDEL.

13. "'Anti-Americanism' Abroad," *Newsweek,* June 10, 1957, 51–53; McPherson, *Yankee No!* 26–32; Whitman Diary, May 13, 1958, folder May, 1958—ACW Diary (1), box 10, Ann Whitman Diary Series, Eisenhower Papers as President, 1953–1961, DDEL.

14. George Allen, "The Image of America," folder Image of America, box 3, OCB Series, Subject Subseries, Office of the Special Assistant for National Security Affairs: Records, 1952–61, WHO, and Eisenhower in Gleason, NSC meeting notes, folder 381st Meeting of NSC October 2, 1958, box 10, NSC Series, Eisenhower Papers as President, 1953–61, both in DDEL.

15. See, e.g., USIA, "Prevalent Opinions Held by Latin Americans about the People of the US," April 10, 1962, and USIA, "Some Contemporary Prevalent Attitudes of Latin Americans toward the US," April 16, 1962, both in folder RO/LA 1962 1/38, box 2, Requestor Only Reports, 1956–1962, Office of Research, RG 306, NARA II; USIA, "Latin American Opinion—a Current Assessment," July 1, 1959, folder P-32–59, box 7, Production Division Research Reports, 1956–1959, Office of Research, RG 306, NARA II; NSC 5819, folder NSC 5819 (5), box 8, NSC Series, Status of Projects Subseries, Office of the Special Assistant for National Security Affairs: Records, 1952–61, WHO, DDEL. See also Mark Haefele, "John F. Kennedy, USIA, and World Public Opinion," *Diplomatic History* 25, no. 1 (Winter 2001): 63–84, 67.

16. Cabinet meeting notes by Art Minnich, May 16, 1958, folder C-45 (1) May 16 and 23, 1958, box 5, Cabinet Series, Office of the Staff Secretary: Records 1952–1961, WHO, DDEL; NSC meeting notes, May 23, 1958, folder 366th Meeting of NSC May 22, 1958, box 10, NSC Series, Eisenhower Papers as President, 1953–1961, DDEL. For details on what was done, see Stephen Rabe, *Eisenhower and Latin America: The Foreign Policy of Anti-Communism* (Chapel Hill: University of North Carolina Press, 1988), 111–12; Richard Roy Rubottom Jr., interview by John Luter, December 22, 1969, August 11, 1970, DDEL; Snow to Cushman, September 22, 1958, folder 1958 Nixon Trip to South America, box 7, lot 60D553, Subject Files, Records of Roy Rubottom, RG 59, NARA II; and Joseph S. Tulchin, "The United States and Latin America in the 1960s," *Journal of Interamerican Studies and World Affairs* 30, no. 1 (Spring 1988): 1–36, 10.

17. Rubottom to Smith, August 11, 1958, folder Latin America—General 1958, box 7, Office Files of Henry A. Hoyt, 1956–1958, lot 60D513, RG 59, NARA II; Allen, "The Image of America" (n. 14 above); Gleason, NSC meeting notes, folder 381st Meeting of NSC October 2, 1958 (n. 14 above); Persons, Memo, Washington,

January 18, 1961, folder USIA (1), box 37, Administration Series, Eisenhower Papers as President, 1953–61, DDEL.

18. Tai Chong-Soo, Erick J. Peterson, and Ted Robert Gurr, "Internal versus External Sources of Anti-Americanism: Two Comparative Studies," *Journal of Conflict Resolution* 17, no. 3 (September 1973): 455–88, 463; D. Kumamoto, "International Terrorism and American Foreign Relations, 1945–1976" (Ph.D. diss., University of California, Los Angeles, 1984), 1–2, 336–37.

19. Nitze, letter to Murrow, Washington, September 21, 1963, and Wilson, Memo to Kennedy, July 10, 1963, both in folder ZW6301 9 Multi Area Jan.–Feb. 1963 World Survey I: General Attitudes (xx15), box 8, Multi Area (World) Project Files, 1953–63, Office of Research, RG 306, NARA II; USIA, "The Impact of Hollywood Films Abroad," July 1961, folder PMS-50, and USIA, "Posts' Assessment of the Impact of Hollywood Films Abroad," September 1961, folder PMS-54, both in box 2, Program and Media Studies, 1956–1962, Office of Research, RG 306, NARA II; "The Impact of Achievements in Science and Technology upon the Image Abroad of the United States," folder PCIAA study No. 23, and "Agricultural Technical Assistance and the American Image," 8 August 1960, folder PCIAA Study no. 39, both in box 13, NSC Registry Series, 1947–62, Office of the Special Assistant for National Security Affairs: Records, 1952–61, WHO, DDEL; George V. Allen, "The Overseas Image of American Democracy," *Annals of the American Academy of Political and Social Sciences* 366 (July 1966): 60–67; USIA, "Free World Opinion on Selected International Issues," June 14, 1960, folder RN-25–60, box 3, Office of Research, Research Notes, 1958–62, RG 306, NARA II.

20. Murrow, Memo to Kennedy, Washington, March 21, 1961, and Smathers, Memo to Kennedy, n.d. [November 1960–March 1961], both in folder USIA 1960 and 1/61–6/61, box 91, President's Official Files, Departments & Agencies, Papers of President Kennedy, John F. Kennedy Library, Boston; Tubby, Memo to Murrow, August 21, 1961, folder USIA, box 355, lot 62D187, Public Affairs Subject Files, 1957 to 1961, Executive Office, Office of the Assistant Secretary for Public Affairs, RG 59, NARA II; Chase, Memo to Redmon, October 5, 1964, folder Central Intelligence Agency Vol. 1, box 8, Agency File, National Security Files, Lyndon B. Johnson Library, Austin, TX.

21. Rob Kroes, "American Empire and Cultural Imperialism: A View from the Receiving End," in *Rethinking American History in a Global Age,* ed. Thomas Bender (Berkeley and Los Angeles: University of California Press, 2002), 295–314, 296. For scholarly debates, see Michael Kammen, "The Problem of American Exceptionalism: A Reconsideration," *American Quarterly* 45 (March 1993): 1–43; Michael Denning, "'The Special American Conditions': Marxism and American Studies," *American Quarterly* 38 (1986): 356–80; and Joseph Lepgold and Timothy McKeown, "Is American Foreign Policy Exceptional? An Empirical Analysis," *Political Science Quarterly* 110 (Autumn 1995): 369–84.

22. Editorial, "Learning about 'Anti-Americanism,'" *America,* December 26,

1953, 330; Lloyd A. Free and Hadley Cantril, *The Political Beliefs of Americans: A Study of Public Opinion* (New York: Simon & Schuster, 1968), 77–78.

23. Bemis cited in Mark Gilderhus, "Presidential Address: Founding Father: Samuel Flagg Bemis and the Study of U.S.–Latin American Relations," *Diplomatic History* 21 (December 1997): 7. See also Robin Winks, "The American Struggle with 'Imperialism': How Words Frighten," in *The American Identity: Fusion and Fragmentation,* ed. Rob Kroes (Amsterdam: Amerika Instituut, Universiteit van Amsterdam, 1980), 143–77, 146; and Amy Kaplan, "'Left Alone with America': The Absence of Empire in the Study of American Culture," in *Cultures of United States Imperialism,* ed. Amy Kaplan and Donald E. Pease (Durham, NC: Duke University Press, 1993), 3–21.

24. For more details, see Mark Bowden, *Guests of the Ayatollah: The Iran Hostage Crisis, the First Battle in America's War with Militant Islam* (New York: Grove, 2006).

25. Tomseth, Airgram to Department of State, Shiraz, October 30, 1978, http://www.gwu.edu/~nsarchiv/NSAEBB/NSAEBB78/propaganda%20137.pdf.

26. Burnett, Memo to Director of USIA, December 5, 1979, folder S-19–79, box 20, Office of Research, Special Reports, 1964–82, RG 306, NARA II.

27. Crespi, "The Extent of Anti-Americanism Abroad in the Wake of Iranian Developments," December 4, 1979, folder S-11–79, box 19, Office of Research, Research Reports, 1964–82, RG 306, NARA II; Burnett, Memo to Director of USIA (n. 26 above).

28. Burnett, Memo to Director of USIA (n. 26 above); Bissell, "Implications of Anti-Americanism," 249.

29. "Global Opinion: The Spread of Anti-Americanism," January 24, 2005, http://www.people-press.org/files/2011/02/104.pdf.

30. For examples of media polls, see "Most Iraqis Favor Immediate U.S. Pullout, Polls Show," *Washington Post,* September 27, 2006 http://www.washington-post.com/wp-dyn/content/article/2006/09/26/AR2006092601721.html; and "Poll Shows Dramatic Decline in How Iraqis View Lives, Future," *Washington Post,* March 20, 2007, http://www.washingtonpost.com/wp-dyn/content/article/2007/03/19/AR2007031900421.html. For polls by the Pew Research Center, see http://people-press.org. For Gallup, see "Global Views of U.S. Leadership," http://www.gallup.com/poll/142631/Worldwide-Leadership-Approval.aspx. Thanks to Professor Bruce Gregory of Georgetown University for the number of agencies. See also Lucy Jones, "Karen Hughes' 'Listening Tour' and Its Aftermath: Selling America to the Muslim World," *Washington Report on Middle East Affairs,* December 2005, 24–26, http://wrmea.com/archives/December_2005/0512024.html.

31. "Global Opinion"; Clay Risen, "Re-Branding America," March 13, 2005, http://www.boston.com/news/globe/ideas/articles/2005/03/13/re_branding_america.

32. Steven R. Weisman, "Diplomatic Memo; On Mideast 'Listening Tour,' the

Question Is Who's Hearing," *New York Times,* 30 September 2005, www.nytimes.com/2005/09/30/international/middleeast/30hughes.html; Jones, "Karen Hughes' 'Listening Tour.'"

33. "China Seen Overtaking U.S. as Global Superpower," July 13, 2011, Pew Research Center, http://www.pewglobal.org/2011/07/13/china-seen-overtaking-us-as-global-superpower; Jon Clifton, "Worldwide Approval of U.S. Leadership Tops Major Powers," March 24, 2011, Gallup, http://www.gallup.com/poll/146771/Worldwide-Approval-Leadership-Tops-Major-Powers.aspx?utm_source=tagrss&utm_medium=rss&utm_campaign=syndication&utm_term=All%20Gallup%20Headlines.

34. Cited in Frida Ghitis, "World Citizen: Latin America's Tempered Obama-Mania," *World Politics Review,* January 22, 2009, http://www.worldpoliticsreview.com/articles/3193/world-citizen-latin-americas-tempered-obama-mania; Jon Lee Anderson, "Fidel's Heir," *New Yorker,* June 23, 2008, 46–57.

35. "Remarks by President Obama on Latin America in Santiago, Chile," March 21, 2011, White House, Office of the Press Secretary, http://www.whitehouse.gov/the-press-office/2011/03/21/remarks-president-obama-latin-america-santiago-chile; "Clinton Apologizes to Guatemala," *Democracy Now,* March 11, 1999, http://www.democracynow.org/1999/3/11/clinton_apologizes_to_guatemala; "Secretary of State Colin L. Powell Interview on Black Entertainment Television's Youth Town Hall," February 20, 2003, Federation of American Scientists, http://www.fas.org/irp/news/2003/02/dos022003.html; Mark S. Smith, "At Summit, Obama Gets Friendly with Chávez," *Miami Herald,* April 18, 2009; "[Secretary Clinton's] Policy Address on Opportunity in the Americas," June 8, 2010, US Department of State, http://www.state.gov/secretary/20092013clinton/rm/2010/06/142848.htm. See also, e.g., "Does the U.S. Have a Policy toward Latin America? Assessing the Impact to U.S. Interests and Allies," Testimony of Arturo A. Valenzuela, Assistant Secretary, Bureau of Western Hemisphere Affairs, US Department of State, February 15, 2011, http://www.state.gov/p/wha/rls/rm/2011/156598.htm; Mark Feierstein, Assistant Administrator, Latin America and the Caribbean, USAID, Congressional Testimony, *Congressional Record,* 112th Cong., 1st sess., February 17, 2011; and Joe Biden, "A New Day for Partnership in the Americas," op-ed, March 27, 2009, UN Dispatch, http://www.undispatch.com/joe-bidens-latin-america-op-ed.

36. "Remarks by the President at Cairo University, 6-04-09," White House, Briefing Room, June 4, 2009, https://www.whitehouse.gov/the-press-office/remarks-president-cairo-university-6-04-09.

37. "China Seen Overtaking U.S. as Global Superpower."

38. Enyart, Memo to Reckerd (n. 8 above).

39. Examples from journalists include James Saxon Childers, *The Nation on the Flying Trapeze: The United States as the People of the East See Us* (New York: David McKay, 1960); John C. Merrill, *Gringo: The Americans as Seen by Mexican Journalists* (Gainesville: University of Florida Press, 1963); Thomas Morgan, *Among the*

Anti-Americans (New York: Holt, Rinehart & Winston, 1967); Carlos Rangel, *The Latin Americans: Their Love-Hate Relationship with the United States,* trans. Ivan Kats (New York: Harcourt Brace Jovanovich, 1977); Stephen Haseler, *The Varieties of Anti-Americanism, Reflex and Response* (Washington, DC: Ethics and Public Policy Center, 1985), and *Anti-Americanism: Steps on a Dangerous Path* (London: Institute for European Defence and Strategic Studies, 1986); and Peter Rodman, "The World's Resentment: Anti-Americanism as a Global Phenomenon," *National Interest* 60 (Summer 2000): 33–41. A small sampling of works by scholars includes William M. Baker, "The Anti-American Ingredient in Canadian History," *Dalhousie Review* 53 (1973): 57–77; G. T. Hollyday, *Anti-Americanism in the German Novel, 1841–1862* (Berne: Peter Lang, 1977); David Strauss, *Menace in the West: The Rise of French Anti-Americanism in Modern Times* (Westport, CT: Greenwood, 1978); Alvin Z. Rubinstein and Donald E. Smith, eds., *Anti-Americanism in the Third World: Implications for U.S. Foreign Policy* (New York: Praeger, 1985); Denis Lacorne, Jacques Rupnik, and Marie-France Toinet, eds., *The Rise and Fall of Anti-Americanism: A Century of French Perception* (New York: St. Martin's, 1990); Paul Hollander, *Anti-Americanism: Critiques at Home and Abroad, 1965–1990* (New York: Oxford University Press, 1992), and *Anti-Americanism: Irrational and Rational* (New Brunswick, NJ: Transaction, 1995); and Dan Diner, *America in the Eyes of the Germans: An Essay on Anti-Americanism,* trans. Allison Brown (Princeton, NJ: Marcus Wiener, 1996).

40. See e.g., Jean-François Revel, *Anti-Americanism,* trans. Diarmid Cammell (San Francisco: Encounter, 2003); McPherson, *Yankee No!* Russell A. Berman, *Anti-Americanism in Europe: A Cultural Problem* (Stanford, CA: Stanford University Press, 2004); Paul Hollander, ed., *Understanding Anti-Americanism: Its Origins and Impact at Home and Abroad* (Chicago: Ivan R. Dee, 2004); Barry Rubin and Judith Colp Rubin, *Hating America: A History* (New York: Oxford University Press, 2004); Andrew Ross and Kristin Ross, eds., *Anti-Americanism* (New York: New York University Press, 2004); Alan McPherson, ed., *Anti-Americanism in Latin America and the Caribbean* (New York: Berghahn, 2006); Brendon O'Connor and Martin Griffiths, eds., *The Rise of Anti-Americanism* (New York: Routledge, 2006); Philippe Roger, *The American Enemy: The History of French Anti-Americanism* (Chicago: University of Chicago Press, 2006); Glenn E. Schweitzer with Carole D. Schweitzer, *America on Notice: Stemming the Tide of Anti-Americanism* (Amherst, NY: Prometheus, 2006); Peter J. Katzenstein and Robert O. Keohane, eds., *Anti-Americanisms in World Politics* (Ithaca, NY: Cornell University Press, 2007); Andrew Kohut and Bruce Stokes, *America against the World: How We Are Different and Why We Are Disliked* (New York: Macmillan, 2007); Ivan Krastev and Alan McPherson, eds., *The Anti-American Century* (Budapest: Central European Press, 2007); Denis Lacorne and Tony Judt, eds., *With Us or Against Us: Studies in Global Anti-Americanism* (New York: Palgrave Macmillan, 2007); Andrei Markovits, *Uncouth Nation: Why Europe Dislikes America* (Princeton, NJ: Princeton University Press,

2007); Brendon O'Connor, ed., *Anti-Americanism: History, Causes, Themes,* 4 vols. (Oxford: Greenwood, 2007); Giacomo Chiozza, *Anti-Americanism and the American World Order* (Baltimore: Johns Hopkins University Press, 2009); Friedman, *Rethinking Anti-Americanism;* and Monti Narayan Datta, *Anti-Americanism and the Rise of World Opinion* (Cambridge: Cambridge University Press, 2014).

5

Peripheral Places/Global War

Simon Dalby

Thus has it ever been since the days of Thucydides the Athenian, that democracies at home consorted with dictators and became tyrannies abroad, though still cloaking their interests in the rhetoric of "spreading democracy."
—Christopher Bayly and Tim Harper, *Forgotten Wars*

Contemporary Geopolitics

In the aftermath of September 11, 2001, numerous claims to novelty were made concerning wars of various sorts, ones that were apparently global in some important senses. With the benefit of hindsight and the application of critical analysis to the War on Terror, claims to both novelty and globality now look increasingly suspect. In the initial rhetorical efforts to frame the War on Terror as a new form of war, many lessons of past wars were lost, only to be subsequently rediscovered when the terrain of conflict turned out to be very different from the initial global geopolitical projections. Once the initial enthusiasm for the apparent success of the high-technology weapons of the Revolution in Military Affairs (RMA) with its apparently quick and easy victories faded, the miseries of military occupation in distant lands became apparent. War on the frontier was, as ever, a murky and messy business. A decade after the removal of the Taliban from Kabul, Western soldiers and journalists in Afghanistan were apparently once again reading Winston Churchill's *The Story of the Malakand Field Force* in search of insight into conducting irregular warfare on the North-West frontier.[1]

Thus, what initially was portrayed as a new and global war turned out to have many historical parallels with earlier small imperial wars conducted in peripheral places on the frontier of civilized settlement.[2] The US military has a long history of these imperial wars, from the wars of conquest in the nineteenth century, to the wars mostly of regime change and pacification in the twentieth, and now the wars in Asia in the twenty-first. One key geographic factor was apparently clear, and it shaped much of the American strategy after 9/11. Threats from peripheral "ungoverned areas" may, the new doctrines of the War on Terror asserted, be more serious than the interstate threats for which conventional military thinking in metropolitan states had previously planned and built forces to fight. Nonetheless, those forces were the military machine that was turned loose on Afghanistan, then Iraq, and to a lesser extent Yemen, Somalia, and Libya as the "long war" unfolded. Much of the justification for these interventions goes back to the logic of regime change in Afghanistan because it harbored al-Qaeda. But, ironically, these interventions in peripheral places may yet lead back to a situation of military confrontation between metropolitan great powers as wars in the Middle East once again polarize international politics. While Afghanistan might be peripheral in many ways, the Middle East region is much less peripheral owing to the presence of both Israel and petroleum in key parts of it.

Democratic polities at the center of global affairs are frequently related to the violent politics and wars of plunder on the periphery even if the argument that they rarely fight each other remains mostly correct.[3] In the War on Terror, peripheral places quickly got mapped in the traditional ways as wild zones in need of taming, reprising a long-standing pattern in American strategic thinking of distant places being understood as zones of danger and turmoil that either directly or indirectly threaten metropolitan order.[4] The September 11, 2001, attacks very powerfully reinforced this theme. But the intervention in Iraq and revived support for Israel's policies in the region quickly extended the violence of the War on Terror into a region that has strategic significance precisely because of its oil wealth. Subsequently, the airstrikes against the Islamic State of Iraq and Syria (ISIS) in 2014 and 2015 extended this pattern of high-technology warfare against local militias.

Now, however, peripheries are frequently referred to simply as *ungoverned spaces* or *ungoverned areas*.[5] In them, the rules of state sovereignty apparently only sporadically apply, and force is thus appropriate as a mode of dealing with the turmoil understood as having its source in these wild zones. As the War on Terror unfolded, states that were seen as unfriendly, or at least not willing to accede to American and in a few cases French and British policies, were targeted too, as the case of Libya in 2011 made clear. Ungoverned areas thence became linked to the supposed failure of governments to live up to the terms specified in the doctrine of the responsibility to protect and hence to situations where intervention could be justified.[6]

These geographic contextualizations matter because how the arena of conflict is specified is related to the modes of conduct deemed appropriate *there*. Geographic analogies are frequently invoked in political discussion; analyzing how these contextualize political conduct provides a useful mode of doing geopolitical critique.[7] Mappings and tactics are also related to the historical narratives as to how the arenas so mapped are created in the first place. Likewise, a crucial matter of the strategy in the War on Terror is how these arenas are supposedly to be reshaped by the practices of violence in various interventions to produce places that are no longer threatening. This is all necessary as part of the discussion of peripheral wars because the question of empire is back in focus in contemporary discussions of geopolitics.[8] This has reaffirmed the importance of understanding geopolitics in terms of metropolitan attempts to assert control over an unruly world.[9]

This chapter focuses on the geopolitical framings of the discussion of the War on Terror. It starts with the discussion of "new wars," the complicated violence mostly in peripheral places in the global political economy since the end of the Cold War. It extends Derek Gregory's threefold categorization of war into spaces of targets, alien places, and spaces of exception to the largest-scale geopolitical framing in terms of empire. It also considers the links between imperial framing and development discourse and specifically the logic of remaking peripheral societies as liberal polities.[10] In the process, contemporary violence is understood in terms of the problem of applying a war machine designed for major wars to the very different situations of limited war and to the circumstances in spaces of occupation. How all this is contextualized is crucial to understanding both the arguments in play and the contemporary violence in peripheral places.

New Wars

Mary Kaldor notes the classic Clausewitz formulation of warfare as "an act of violence designed to compel our opponent to fulfil our will." She suggests that this assumption of a contest of wills may not be enough; another definition of war may be necessary to encompass contemporary violence. War is "an act of violence involving at least two organised groups framed in political terms." Looking at so-called ethnic conflicts, Kaldor suggests that war may actually be a mutual enterprise, a violent collusion to manipulate grievance and rule violently not least by perpetuating the fear of dangerous others. This is political violence in which victory may not be the goal but rather something closer to Clausewitz's notions of limited warfare, of politics by other means. Indeed, in some ways, victory might actually be counterproductive: "Defeating the enemy is the justification not the goal of war. Indeed the warring parties share a mutual need for justification and consequently, they may actually reinforce each other. Through war and violence, the armed actors transform themselves from marginal extremists into mainstream power brokers. By producing fear and hatred, they construct exclusive ethnic or religious ideologies that underpin their power. Understood in this way, war is not about genuine grievances or 'root causes'—it is about manipulating and instrumentalising grievance."[11]

The crucial point here is that the assumption of violence as the key to victory actually misconstrues the purposes to which violence is put in using it as a method of terror and in assuming that it is the most important thing to focus on in terms of peacemaking. Enemies are frequently more useful as objects of enmity and targets for military action than they are as entities that must be defeated; in David Keen's terms, such enemies are useful.[12]

This is related to the colonial optic through which so much of the contemporary thinking about war is viewed. James Renton has been back to look again at the assumptions in the discussions of the British Palestine mandate that led to the pattern of violence there and the subsequent tragedy for the Palestinian people.[13] Focusing on the elites and the leaders and assuming that peace or control is possible only through elite compliance and, if necessary, defeat and replacement in the face of noncompliance are old imperial tactics. But they presume that political rule is about compulsion and, insofar as they focus on only this theme, miss the larger dynamics of societal forces and frequently perpetuate violence. Israeli prime minister Netanyahu's assumption that force is key to imposing peace is, Renton argues, the imperial view inherited from Mandate times. As Kaldor points out, this use of violence against Hamas in particular and the complete failure to consider a serious negotiation in the region because victory is assumed to be necessary prior to negotiation and only the terms of surrender will be up for discussion perpetuate the state of the new war.

The issue is complicated by the overlay of UN and international security arrangements in the region.[14] The assumption on the part of many of the parties has long been that periodic bouts of violence will last long enough to change some matters on the ground but be neither severe enough nor protracted enough to drastically alter the political map. At least some strategic thinkers have long wished to change the political leaderships in the region without fundamentally redrawing most boundaries.[15] The assumptions in the territorial covenant of the United Nations is that, while violence may happen, the shape of the political map is permanent and that the status quo ante is more or less the shape of any final settlement.[16] Thus, limited wars are allowed, but major fights to the finish, in which the victor imposes a solution and the map is drastically redrawn, are apparently not. The boundaries in Palestine are thus especially contentious given the larger norm of boundaries' supposed fixity.

Such standoff situations have obvious economic payoffs for some of the participants, albeit at the cost of economic dislocation for many of those caught in these situations. Focusing on extremists because of the assumption that they are the power brokers simply reinforces the pattern of war rather than looking at the social processes that perpetuate the recruitment opportunities for the extremists. Oliver Richmond suggests that the process of liberal institution building that has been tried in many postconflict conditions is not working for anyone except the elites and that in many places the population that was the key reason legitimizing the intervention has little to show for the interventions: "The shock of conflict has been used to liberalise, modernise, marketise, develop, democratise, and to remove any older political agencies and resiliencies that appeared to be an obstacle to this process. What began as a humanitarian project has turned into an insidious form of conversion and riot control which has had many casualties. It has been profoundly anti-democratic in many cases, including in Bosnia, Afghanistan, and Iraq. From the ground, for many of its recipients, the various iterations of this liberal peace project have taken on a colonial appearance."[17]

None of this would come as a surprise to Michael McKinley, who understands contemporary liberal globalization as war and war in the classic Clausewitzian sense of compelling an opponent to fulfill your will. But in his case the will that is to be fulfilled is that the other become part of the globalized economy, and, if that requires structurally adjusting a population and removing social safety nets, changing social relations to make the poor even more vulnerable, then that is the price of victory. In this logic, peripheral places must be forcefully incorporated into metropolitan economic arrangements to ensure their successful pacification.[18]

What is not so clear in much of this material is the clear congruity between these formulations of liberal economies, elite rule and the integration into the global economy, and the explicit articulation of precisely such a desideratum as the necessary requirement for winning the American long war, the struggle to end tyranny on earth, as the official policy documents from the latter years of the Bush administration articulated matters. This point can be extended without difficulty to argue that the Bush doctrine was indeed a form of economic warfare by other means, one that sees nothing less than the transformation of the global economy into one led by the United States as final victory, the triumph of the liberal peace, and the end of the scourge of warfare.[19]

Her analysis of the post–Cold War conflicts Kaldor termed *new wars* suggested that war no longer has the neat geographies of state territories or the simple modern aim of winning battles and controlling places.[20] Instead, she suggests that commodity chains, violence to control populations, and struggles over resources and diaspora-led funding arrangements to support identity struggles "back home" have made for a much more complicated geography of conflict. Nonetheless the violent spaces of these new wars are mostly a matter of peripheral locations in the global political economy even if the support and financing come through global economic connections. The geography of all this matters greatly and is part of the reason why the many conventional accounts of the War on Terror that gloss over the contexts of violence in favor of simplistic moralistic formulations lacked the analytic rigor needed to understand how war on the periphery works either in the early years of the twenty-first century or more generally in imperial history.

War and Peace

Derek Gregory's conceptualization of contemporary war and peace juxtaposes the RMA, with its high-technology killing machines and satellite surveillance of much of the world, with Mary Kaldor and other new wars thinkers interested in looking at the contemporary nature of violence and the geographies of death and destruction that happen when the two modes of warfare bleed into one another.[21] The distinction between periphery and metropolitan spaces became much more difficult following Osama Bin Laden's attack on New York and Washington in September 2001 and the specification of the response as a *global* war.[22] Gregory suggests that this complexity can be analyzed by looking at a threefold typology of the resultant spaces: target spaces, alien places of the enemy, and the space of the exception, a space where law is suspended and lethality happens. Then, he argues, a series of countergeographies can be brought to bear on these spaces to challenge the legitimacy claims that structure their construction. Gregory's title, "War and Peace," is, he tells us, drawn from Picasso rather than Tolstoy, but the imbrication of the two is key to the analysis; Orwell's formulation in *Nineteen Eighty-Four*, "War is Peace," is more telling in that the supposed antonyms are understood as suffused within each other rather than separate categories.

Given the widespread coding of war as a problem and peace as a virtue in modern states, the necessity to legitimize warfare in terms of either its necessity or its promise of producing peace, this entanglement is now not at all surprising. Gregory goes back to the Kellogg-Briand Pact of 1928—when states explicitly condemned the recourse to war—to situate the moral arguments against war and to ruefully note that the sentiments of peace and the profound declarations of the rejection of war as a mode of policy did not last long in the 1930s. The adoption of peace as a desideratum and the use of Picasso's dove as a symbol became macabre in the Cold War, although Gregory does not note that a reproduction of Picasso's *Guernica* hangs to this day in the lobby of the UN building in

New York to remind all who enter of the horrors that the institution was established to prevent.

Neither does the crucial point about the UN charter precluding war as policy and allowing only self-defense get much comment. The *nuclear age* is a term that has long since been rendered unfashionable, but in the 1940s war departments got turned into defense departments and formal declarations of war became a thing of the past. Security trumped notions of war and likewise linked numerous matters of economics, politics, and crucially technology explicitly to the calculus of geopolitics. Such is the language of the United Nations; international and global security is the primary motivating logic of diplomatic activity now tied into the powerful norms of stable international boundaries. There is a more complicated history to the terms *war* and *peace* than this brief synopsis can elucidate, but the key point is that war and peace are not so simple, and the meshing of these in terms of security has set in motion a complicated series of discursive innovations that neither adequately encompass the violence of the present nor provide any obvious geographic specification of the terrain of that violence.

Target Spaces

Perhaps the most obvious interpretation of novelty in discussions of strategy and the violence of the so-called War on Terror is to note that this violence is new insofar as it is different from the wars that the American military planned to fight in the last decade of the Cold War. In that crucial sense, the wars of the present are new in that all sorts of high-technology weapons are involved, and that alone suggests a novel state of affairs. Drones, cell-phone intercepts, geocoded target data sets, online recruitments, and real-time aerial surveillance fed directly into targeting systems shortens the decision loops and the kill chains in a way that at least appears novel to the proponents of high-technology weapons systems. Indeed, it is precisely these weapons systems that make possible the construction of particular targets; the contemporary technology of destruction is a legacy of innovations stretching back many years.

Gregory bypasses the Cold War confrontation to concentrate on more recent wars and the ongoing political violence, both in the Kiplingesque "Savage Wars of Peace"—the interventions and conquests of modern forces in less powerful places—and the legacies of violence that these leave in their wake. He also notes that the contemporary violence might be traced to the dramatic innovations of the Napoleonic wars and their inclusion of many distant places in the logic of European confrontations. While these transformations were important, the subsequent industrialization of slaughter and the innovations of science in propulsion, munitions, and communications transformed the capabilities for violence beyond all recognition, reaching their apotheosis in 1945 with the use of nuclear bombs to destroy Hiroshima and Nagasaki.

Technologies make certain forms of violence possible, and it is noteworthy that the War on Terror has led to the acceleration of war robots in particular in response to the difficulties of dealing with ungoverned areas. But this is not a new fact of war. Weapons systems are designed and built for particular purposes. Eliot Cohen's important point is that militaries are built to fight certain kinds of wars in particular circumstances and hence that it is necessary to put the RMA in geopolitical context.[23] His example of the 1930s, when Germans assembled panzer divisions but the Japanese built aircraft carriers, is simple but apposite. Technologies for fighting wars are in part determined by the assumptions concerning the context within which struggles will be played out. War in Europe in the 1940s was likely to be substantially different from war in the Pacific, and these contextual assumptions were key to the procurement decisions of the respective militaries. This is of course especially important in the case of the discussions of the RMA because which weapons are needed relates to where the hostilities are likely to be, who the likely opponents are, and how they are equipped.

The legacy of the Cold War left not only an American military shaped to fight a major conventional war against a similarly equipped foe but also a military with a global reach and communications, logistics, and surveillance capability that can go anywhere and fight anytime, more or less.[24] During the latter stages of the Cold War, a smaller professional force faced a numerically superior Red Army in Europe, and clearly in the event of hostilities the US forces needed superior technological capabilities to defeat more numerous Red Army forces in Germany. The air-land battle doctrine and the use of high-tech sensors and communications systems to see the battlefield and direct munitions accurately were key to all this. Nuclear weapons that could be used precisely in counterforce roles rather than countervalue city busters were also part of these innovations, and cruise missiles added a new dimension to precision warhead delivery.

Once the Cold War was over, these innovations provided technical capabilities for warfare that then shaped the American way of war and facilitated not only the destruction of Iraqi forces in 1991 but also the subsequent application of dial-a-bomb techniques with the special forces targeting Taliban forces on behalf of the Northern Alliance in Afghanistan in 2001 and subsequently in Iraq and elsewhere. The weapons were much more accurate and could hence be used for precise targeting and at least supposedly minimize collateral damage and the costs to civilians of interventions to depose regimes or kill terrorist operators. However, by targeting the electrical and communications infrastructure that supports regimes under attack, a strategy "to switch societies off," as Stephen Graham puts it, then suffering and a civilian population death toll are inevitable when sewage systems and hospitals are nonfunctional, despite the implicit counterclaims about the limited casualties that directly result from surgical strikes, precision operations, and supposedly prompt lethality.[25]

Alien Places

The global panopticon of the US military implies hierarchical arrangements of opponents, ones that have an address and a headquarters and can be compelled to surrender after their forces have been defeated in combat. In short, the utility of these high-technology weapons is Clausewitzian. This is a clean war, violence to a clear end, a virtuous use of force. It depends on the distinction between civilian and combatant and the powerful reinforcement of such things by media-generated images of virtuous Westerners and evil others who neither play fair, fight by those rules, nor abide by the supposed clear distinctions that Western legal categories drawn from the Geneva Conventions apply universally. These themes are complicated further by the political insistence in much of the rhetoric of Western interventions that the population is not the target, that these interventions are in one way or another about protecting the population from tyrants or human rights disasters; targeting the military forces that perpetuate tyranny or abuse is done in the name of liberating or protecting the people who are in need of either or both from afar. Add to this the military codes of the Western forces—the insistence that casualties be minimized, that no Western soldier be left behind in a distant battlefield, and that tactics, sometimes using overwhelming firepower to control dangerous spaces, be designed with this force protection priority clearly in mind—and the moral landscapes of interventionary violence become even more complicated.[26]

Despite the technical capabilities of the surveillance systems, the irony is that so many peripheral parts of the world are effectively unknown to the panoptically viewing experts mapping the global War on Terror. Unknown spaces have to be fitted into the scheme. Wolfram Lacher's analysis of the securitization of the Sahara, which preceded the war on Libya, and the rearticulation of insecurities of various sorts, not least the Malthusian fears of populations in Niger, Mali, and Algeria, suggested an even more interesting twist on the global discourse.[27] Precisely their lack of legibility in recent years, the anxiety because they were not known, regulated, and administered in various practices of security caused the construction of these spaces as such. They became the breeding grounds for terrorists, and the new AFRICOM command area for the US military is tasked with security management.

Lacher noted that the universal specification of the region as dangerous runs counter to the diverse heterogeneous interests at play there and warned against the conflation of too many things into the language of security, where development has morphed into security discourse: "Securitization, then, denotes the process by which, in the quest for security, a governable entity is constituted. Security and its corresponding development, that is, are not merely conservative forces. By deploying their apparatuses of knowledge and government, they transform their field of intervention—with uncertain outcome."[28] The process here is about making things and peoples legible and hence facilitating their conduct being conducted, as it were. In the terms of contemporary politics, this is in part a matter of immigration and the unknown, of governing unease, that apparently has to be tackled by rendering the other known within the legibility of security and hence that which can be governable because known.[29]

The multiplicity of development programs, the diversity of interests and contestations of these projects, suggests that the implicit assumption that they work in some way that coheres is not a sensible conclusion, although one that discourse analysis is always in danger of perpetuating. In some cases, the lack of clear authority in ungoverned areas and the confused violence of many spaces where interventions are called for and sometimes happen suggest a medieval arrangement, one where there is no monopoly of violence over a defined territory, the quintessential definition of the modern state derived from Max Weber. Multiple armed forces and competing loyalties to various authorities, combined with the intermittent presence of professional armies, marked the period prior to the Treaty of Westphalia of 1648, at least in some loose approximation. The parallels with the new wars suggest similar patterns in contemporary peripheral places.

Now, the presence of international professional troops is also part of contemporary violence, even if the authority they at least supposedly support is the United Nations or NATO, not the Holy Roman emperor, but the term *neomedieval* has crept into the literature. Ostensibly, the polity in existence prior to Westphalia was an imperial form, albeit one that frequently had very considerable difficulty asserting any effective control over fractious Christian princes. This Eurocentric formulation leaves out of the picture numerous other polities whose imperial powers might have many other models of authority, but it does clearly suggest the inadequacy of the Westphalian model. Interventions and the suspensions of territorial sovereignty, only to have it reasserted immediately after a regime change, suggest just how contested contemporary global governance mechanisms actually are.[30]

Exceptional Spaces

The discussion of new wars suggests that the violence in many places is not the kind of war that these high-technology forces are designed to fight. David Chandler suggests that in fact the global war discussions are in part confused because the opponents are not those that are can be tackled in conventional modes of strategic encounter.[31] The discourse of global security, the struggles to control and regulate at the global level, is analogous in some ways to war as a struggle for geopolitical control, but a simple scaling up from the nation-state to the globe is not helpful, especially when supposedly critical theorists take these claims at face value.

To put his point bluntly, Chandler notes that exceptional spaces require a notable lack of reflection on their contextualizations. He invokes Hardt and Negri's discussion of global war as an attempt to constantly shape the social by military and police actions.[32] This is a process that Hardt and Negri see as never ending. Specifically, Chandler cites Vivien Jabri's argument:

> The discourse from Bosnia to Kosovo to Iraq is one that aims to reconstruct societies and their government in accordance with a distinctly Western liberal model the formative elements of which centre on open markets, human rights and the rule of law, and democratic elections as the basis of legitimacy. The aim is no less than to reconstitute polities through the transformation of political cultures into modern, self-disciplining, and ultimately self-governing entities that, through such transformation, could transcend ethnic or religious fragmentation and violence. The trajectory is punishment, pacification, discipline, and ultimately "liberal democratic self-mastery." Each step in turn services wider, global remits so that the pacified, the disciplined, the self-governing of the liberal order can no longer pose a threat either to their own or to others.[33]

Chandler's argument suggests that interventionary acts are based on values rather than a clear strategic conflict over interests. The lack of planning for postconflict situations in Afghanistan, Kosovo, Iraq, and elsewhere is, he argues, a consequence of this situation.

But in Jabri's terms there is a clear aim to reconstitute the other as the image of the liberal self. Danger lies in the illiberality of others, security in their incorporation into our political order. The fact that this was grossly mishandled in both Afghanistan and most notably in Iraq is beside the point.[34] Chandler is much less sure, suggesting that the new wars of the post–Cold War period are not about strategic competition or the dangers of defeat in a major war:

> In this sense, global wars reflect the fact that the international sphere has been reduced to little more than a vanity mirror for globalized actors who are freed from strategic necessities and whose

concerns are no longer structured in the form of political struggles against "real enemies." The mainstream critical approaches
to global wars, with their heavy reliance on recycling the work
of Foucault, Schmitt and Agamben, appear to invert this reality, portraying the use of military firepower and the implosion
of international law as a product of the high stakes involved in
global struggle, rather than the lack of clear contestation involving the strategic accommodation of diverse powers and interests.[35]

What Chandler's analysis does not go on to say is that, at least in terms of
the Bush administration's large picture of the global War on Terror, the
critics are quite correct; eliminating opposition to liberal rule is seen as
essential to the long-term success of American-led modernity; pacification
of the periphery is essential to the peaceful existence of those behind the
frontier.[36] In the terms of the Bush administration's formulation, this is
all necessary to eliminate tyranny on earth, the task that was the ultimate
goal of American foreign policy, at least as codified in the 2006 Quadrennial Defense Review.[37] International relations theory conveniently
supports the logic of this with discussions of the liberal peace, noting
that democracies mostly do not go to war with each other. Therefore, the
enlargement of democracy, the foreign policy priority of the 1990s Clinton administrations, must be continued but with the use of force where
necessary to produce compliant regimes abroad that will happily facilitate
the expansion of the liberal prosperity that supposedly follows from the
removal of dictators and nationalist tyrants.

Exceptional spaces are therefore those where liberal rule has not been
established, territories where state integrity can be suspended while being
reasserted simultaneously, in the service of the larger liberal project apparently.[38] All this suggests something more reminiscent of Carl Schmitt's
infamous Nomos and his concern at the lack of a world order in the aftermath of the demise of the European order of the nineteenth century, or
a situation where all non-Western democratic spaces can potentially be
exceptions should circumstances require.[39] But this is little more than
a return of imperial rule to a disorganized periphery. Chandler's point
about this not being a strategic contest in the classic Clausewitzian sense
of major war is accurate, but the point that the means of warfare let loose
by the American forces are those designed to prosecute that war has got

lost in his analysis, and this point matters greatly, as the debate about counterinsurgency, rather than counterterror strategies, makes clear.[40] The American military has the technical ability to kill terrorists, whether using special forces, drone weapons, or now the armory of global strike. But occupying territory and changing political arrangements to undercut support for an insurgency are very different matters.[41]

Empire Redux

On the fringes of empire, peripheral peoples resist the impositions of imperial rule and in some cases fight back, provoking violence from the center in the struggle to rid their lands of foreign troops and comprador elites. Palestinians most notably have been struggling against the appropriation of their lands and towns, which, when viewed in imperial terms, looks very like many other colonizations of the last few centuries.[42] Viewed in terms of imperial power, the presence of American troops in the Middle East can also be seen as part of an old pattern. But, precisely because of the repeated assertion that the United States is not an empire, and, as George W. Bush put it in the 2003 State of the Union address, not so precisely because the United States does not conquer territory, it was difficult to interpret opposition from al-Qaeda in these terms.

The explicitly geopolitical strategy of the original al-Qaeda declaration of war on America in 1996 is easy to read as anticolonial.[43] Whatever it may have morphed into subsequently—and over the years Bin Laden's statements covered many themes—back then his logic was simple. The task was to remove the infidels from the land of the two holy places. This is a simple geography of removing foreign presence and the hopelessly corrupt comprador elite of the House of Saud. If that required attacking the distant enemy (America) in such a way as to bring the full force of its might to bear on the region and indirectly on the near enemy (corrupt apostate local rulers in the Middle East) and trigger enough destabilization so that the near enemy would lose control, then that is what needed to be done. The upshot of the American wars in the region might yet yield that result if political regimes, shaken by the war in Iraq in particular, unsettled by the global financial chaos of 2008, and in disarray as a result of the rise of ISIS and the consequences of the Syrian civil war, crumble under further assaults.

Subsequently, this key geographic point got lost in the discussion of the War on Terror. In his historical perspective on terrorism, Christopher Fettweis suggests that Robert Pape's much-cited analysis of suicide bombings and the suggestion that the tactic is nearly always used in opposition to what is understood as an external presence of occupation force are wrong. Instead, he suggests that al-Qaeda is in fact a religious terrorist organization and not one that might plausibly be about nationalist opposition to foreign occupation.[44] On the other hand, if the geographic lenses are focused on the War on Terror as all about what Robert Fisk calls, in the subtitle of his book, "the conquest of the Middle East," then the geography of Bin Laden's strategy seems a very old-fashioned anticolonial struggle.[45] The unholy alliance of the House of Saud with the American oil corporations and the famous deal between Roosevelt and Ibn Saud in 1945 can then be seen in terms of one more proxy colonization whereby the American forces gradually superseded the British in the Middle East and brought colonizing corporate practices to the kingdom.[46] Viewed this way, they are consistent with Pape's analysis of the implicit geography of suicide terror. The only thing that was different in September 2001 was that the suicide bombers used hijacked aircraft and operated at a greater distance from their home base than is usually the case.

Given the nearly unquestionable support of America for Israel, the whole Middle East looks like a colonization project; after all, it is not difficult to read the construction of Israel as the establishment of the last of the white settler colonies. This is especially irritating to Arab nationalists who were being colonized just as their nationalist peers were extracting themselves from European domination farther East in the late 1940s. No wonder Palestinian language uses apocalyptic tropes to discuss the events of this period. While the Israelis technically declared independence from the British, they took over their imperial mode of administration as soon as they established an effective occupation of the territory and have ever since used such colonial modes of asserting power in the region.

Geopolitical Spaces

This chapter has suggested that, in the discussion of war, the implicit geographies matter and that the appropriate geographic contextualizations are frequently given much less attention in the discussion than seems to be necessary to piece together a clear understanding of either novelty or the specificity of what counts as warfare in peripheral places in the twenty-first century. Clearly, organized political violence is part of current global politics, and the use of the War on Terror as a pretext for geopolitical intervention lasted for well over a decade. The nightmare scenario is that this militarization of many things and the insistence on the part of American policymakers that the Iranian regime be either tightly constrained or preferably changed altogether will lead to a more explicitly geopolitical realignment in the coming years. One of the problems with contemporary militarization is, to borrow once again Derek Gregory's formulation, that, if you look at alien spaces through a gun sight long enough, the whole world starts to look like a target where exceptional action is apparently needed in perpetuity.

American attempts to remake the Middle East have been justified repeatedly by the argument that threatening weapons from there will ultimately endanger the rest of the world. Hence the necessity to suspend the normal function of state sovereignty and invoke the higher priority of exceptional circumstances requiring punitive actions. Rivalries in peripheral places causing states to consider core interests in ways that lead to arms races and related social pathologies are alas not new either. In the case of the Middle East, however, given the importance of the petroleum supplies that come from there to fuel the global economy, the stakes are now huge. While the chances of a major conflict with Iran lessened in early 2015, the presupposition that the American navy can keep the Straits of Hormuz open, as it did in the 1980s, intercept Iranian missiles targeting the oil infrastructure on the south coast of the Gulf, and keep local elites in power in the face of popular unrest caused by further military action in the region may underpin strategic calculations in Washington but, in a crisis, is likely to be greeted with much skepticism elsewhere.[47]

The danger of this actually spilling over into hostilities is very considerable, albeit reduced by extended negotiations between Iran and Western powers in early 2015. Should hostilities with Iran happen, other states may finally decide that the Americans' insistence on suspending international law when it suits them—of claiming the sovereign right to act on behalf of the system of states and launching one more assault on a peripheral place in the name of civilization, the international order, or even the United Nations itself—requires some form of response. Then, should other major states decide that the possibilities of constraining the United States by diplomatic means are exhausted and that Americans understand only force, the potential for a realignment in global geopolitics and a new cold war between Asian states and much of the rest of the world looms.

None of this has to happen, but a more complicated geopolitics and the recognition that imperial optics from metropolitan centers frequently obscure the practicalities of politics in particular peripheral places are needed if the simple verities of wars for civilization and assumptions of the rivalries of elites as the only political game that matters are to be transcended. The politics of this also suggests that the simple triumph of neoliberalism cannot be a strategically rational mode of thinking if the long-term security of most of the world's peoples is taken seriously.[48] Rendering peripheral spaces as targets requiring exceptional action is not a mode of intellectual or practical activity that can provide security for peoples anywhere in the long run, however efficacious it may be in the short term for political elites anxious to hang on to the perquisites of power in the face of a rapidly changing world.

Notes

The epigraph for this chapter is from Christopher Bayly and Tim Harper, *Forgotten Wars: The End of Britain's Asian Empire* (London: Penguin, 2008), 549.

1. Robert Kaplan, "Man against Afghanistan," *Atlantic Monthly,* April 2010, 60–71.
2. Max Boot, *The Savage Wars of Peace: Small Wars and the Rise of American Power* (New York: Basic, 2002).
3. Philippe Le Billon, *Wars of Plunder* (London: Hurst, 2012).
4. Max Singer and Aaron Wildavsky, *The Real World Order: Zones of Peace, Zones of Turmoil* (Chatham, NJ: Chatham House, 1996).
5. Anne L. Clunan and Harold A. Trinkunas, eds., *Ungoverned Spaces: Alternatives to State Authority in an Era of Softened Sovereignty* (Stanford, CA: Stanford University Press, 2010).
6. Paul D. Williams and Alex J. Bellamy, "Principles, Politics and Prudence: Libya, the Responsibility to Protect, and the Use of Military Force," *Global Governance* 18 (2012): 273–97.
7. John Agnew, "Making the Strange Familiar: Geographical Analogy in Global Geopolitics," *Geographical Review* 99 (2009): 426–43.
8. Simon Dalby, "Political Space: Autonomy, Liberalism and Empire," *Alternatives: Global, Local, Political* 30 (2005): 415–41.

9. Ronnie Lipschutz, *The Constitution of Imperium* (New York: Paradigm, 2009).

10. Derek Gregory, "War and Peace," *Transactions of the Institute of British Geographers* 35 (2010): 154–86. On empire as geopolitics, see Noel Parker, "Empire as a Geopolitical Figure," *Geopolitics* 15 (2010): 109–32.

11. Mary Kaldor, "Reconceptualising War," February 24, 2010, Open Democracy, http://www.opendemocracy.net/5050/mary-kaldor/reconceptualising-war.

12. David Keen, *Useful Enemies: When Waging Wars Is More Important Than Winning Them* (New Haven, CT: Yale University Press, 2012).

13. James Renton, "Forgotten Lessons: Palestine and the British Empire," March 19, 2010, Open Democracy, http://www.opendemocracy.net/opensecurity/james-renton/forgotten-lessons-palestine-and-british-empire.

14. Barry Buzan and Ole Waever, *Regions and Powers: The Structure of International Security* (Cambridge: Cambridge University Press, 2003).

15. The classic document cited in this regard is Richard Perle, Douglas Feith, and David Wurmser, *A Clean Break: A New Strategy for Securing the Realm* (Washington, DC, and Tel Aviv: Institute for Advanced Strategic and Political Studies, 1996), which advocates a balance-of-power approach in contrast to policies of peacemaking.

16. Mark Zacher, "The International Territorial Order: Boundaries, the Use of Force, and Normative Change," *International Organization* 55 (2001): 215–50.

17. Oliver P. Richmond, "Liberal Peace Transitions: A Rethink Is Urgent," November 19, 2009, Open Democracy, http://www.opendemocracy.net/oliver-p-richmond/liberal-peace-transitions-rethink-is-urgent. See more generally Oliver P. Richmond, *Failed Statebuilding: Intervention, the State, and the Dynamics of Peace Formation* (New Haven, CT: Yale University Press, 2014).

18. Michael McKinley, *Economic Globalisation as Religious War* (London: Routledge, 2007).

19. Simon Dalby, "Regions, Strategies, and Empire in the Global War on Terror," *Geopolitics* 12, no. 4 (2007): 586–606.

20. Mary Kaldor, *New and Old Wars: Organized Violence in a Global Era* (Stanford, CA: Stanford University Press, 2007).

21. Gregory, "War and Peace."

22. Simon Dalby, "Calling 911: Geopolitics, Security and America's New War," *Geopolitics* 8, no. 3 (2003): 61–86.

23. Eliot Cohen, "Change and Transformation in Military Affairs," *Journal of Strategic Studies* 27 (2004): 395–407.

24. Simon Dalby, "Geopolitics, the Revolution in Military Affairs and the Bush Doctrine," *International Politics* 46 (2009): 234–52.

25. Stephen Graham, *Cities under Siege: The New Military Urbanism* (London: Verso, 2010).

26. Simon Dalby, "Warrior Geopolitics: *Gladiator, Black Hawk Down* and *The Kingdom of Heaven*," *Political Geography* 27 (2008): 439–55.

27. Wolfram Lacher, "Actually Existing Security: The Political Economy of the Saharan Threat," *Security Dialogue* 39 (2008): 383–405.

28. Lacher "Actually Existing Security," 386.

29. Didier Bigo, "Security and Immigration: Toward a Critique of the Governmentality of Unease," *Alternatives: Global, Local, Political* 27 (2002): 63–92.

30. Stuart Elden, *Terror and Territory: The Spatial Extent of Sovereignty* (Minneapolis: University of Minnesota Press, 2009).

31. David Chandler, "War without End(s): Grounding the Discourse of 'Global War,'" *Security Dialogue* 40 (2009): 243–62.

32. Michael Hardt and Antonio Negri, *Multitude: War and Democracy in the Age of Empire* (New York: Penguin, 2004).

33. Vivienne Jabri, *War and the Transformation of Global Politics* (Basingstoke: Palgrave, 2007), 124–25, quoted in Chandler, "War without End(s)," 248–49.

34. Rajiv Chandrasekeran, *Imperial Life in the Emerald City* (New York: Knopf, 2006).

35. Chandler, "War without End(s)," 259.

36. Thomas Barnett, *The Pentagon's New Map* (New York: Putnam's, 2004).

37. Dalby, "Geopolitics."

38. Elden, *Terror and Territory*.

39. Carl Schmitt, *The Nomos of the Earth in the International Law of the Jus Publicum Europaeum* (New York: Telos, 2003).

40. David Kilcullen, *The Accidental Guerilla: Fighting Small Wars in the Midst of a Big One* (New York: Oxford University Press, 2009).

41. Jenna Jordan, "Attacking the Leader, Missing the Mark: Why Terrorist Groups Survive Decapitation Strikes," *International Security* 38, no. 4 (2014): 7–38.

42. Derek Gregory, *The Colonial Present: Afghanistan, Palestine, Iraq* (Oxford: Blackwell, 2004).

43. Dalby, "Calling 911."

44. Christopher Fettweis, "Freedom Fighters and Zealots: Al Qaeda in Historical Perspective," *Political Science Quarterly* 124 (2009): 269–96; Robert A. Pape, *Dying to Win: The Strategic Logic of Suicide Terrorism* (New York: Random House, 2005).

45. Robert Fisk, *The Great War for Civilization: The Conquest of the Middle East* (London: Harper Collins, 2006).

46. Robert Vitalis, *America's Kingdom: Mythmaking on the Saudi Oil Frontier* (Stanford, CA: Stanford University Press, 2007).

47. Caitlin Talmadge, "Closing Time: Assessing the Iranian Threat to the Straits of Hormuz," *International Security* 33, no. 1 (2008): 82–117.

48. Paul Rogers, *Global Security and the War on Terror* (London: Pluto, 2008).

2

CASE STUDIES

6

Whistling in the Dark

US Efforts to Navigate UN Policy toward Decolonization, 1945–1963

Mary Ann Heiss

Among the many issues that received concerted attention from the UN General Assembly during its early decades was the broad issue of decolonization. Indeed, the spectacular increase in UN membership from 51 original members in 1945 to 113 in 1963 occurred in large part as a result of the first great wave of colonial independence movements.[1] Decolonization progressed as Cold War tensions were solidifying, and at times the two developments became linked. The superpower competition for the allegiance of the world's newest nations has been reasonably well covered in the literature.[2] Less well studied is the intersection of decolonization and the Cold War at the United Nations during the years when the organization's mechanisms for dealing with non-self-governing territories were evolving. In seeking to address that historiographic gap, this chapter illuminates US efforts to manage UN interest in decolonization in ways that suited—or at least did not harm—US Cold War interests. In the end, US policymakers could not break free of the East-West conflict as they navigated the UN role in decolonization despite the hopes of both nonaligned nations on the periphery and those states that were gaining independent nationhood as a result of decolonization. In putting traditional great power–based Cold War interests first, Washington ultimately lost credibility with the very states that it sought so fervently to court and suffered a loss of standing with non-European nations that was not easily regained.

Given their role in drafting the UN Charter, the great powers (including the United States) shaped its provisions for dealing with non-self-governing territories in ways that protected their positions as colonial administrators.[3] Consequently, the Charter limited international trusteeship to only the remaining League of Nations mandates and the territories seized from Italy and Japan (Germany had lost its colonies after the First World War). Chapters XII and XIII, which set forth the framework for the international trusteeship system, therefore conspicuously excluded the colonies of the victorious Allies. Although all the Western colonial powers were invited to place their territories under trusteeship, predictably, not one did. UN involvement in the trust territories, which was managed by the relatively powerful Trusteeship Council, included the hearing of local petitioners, the sending of UN missions to individual trust territories, and the monitoring of progress toward self-government.[4]

Dependent territories not covered under the new trusteeship system—essentially the colonies of the victorious Allies and a few other areas—fell under the purview of Chapter XI of the Charter. Formally titled "Declaration Regarding Non-Self-Governing Territories," Chapter XI spelled out the responsibilities of administering states and set forth the hope of eventual self-government—albeit not necessarily independence—for territories that did not yet possess it. Article 73 of Chapter XI affirmed that the interests of the non-self-governing territories were "paramount" and instructed the administering powers to foster "political, economic, social, and educational development" in their colonies. To ensure that the administering states were meeting their responsibilities, section (e) of Article 73 put forth the only obligation to be imposed on the administering powers by requiring them to "transmit regularly to the Secretary-General . . . statistical and other information of a technical nature relating to economic, social, and educational conditions in the territories for which they are responsible." Significantly, no provision was made for the transmission of information on political conditions or progress toward self-government, even though Article 73 had earlier made reference to "political" development alongside development in "economic, social, and educational" areas.[5]

Guided by an activist interpretation of how to implement the Charter's provision for UN interest in the non-self-governing territories, in 1946 the General Assembly voted to establish a committee to examine the information that the administering states were to transmit under Article 73(e). What ultimately came to be called the Committee on Information from Non-Self-Governing Territories was to be composed of one representative from each of the eight administering nations and an equal number of representatives from nonadministering states. As a condition for their participation in the committee's work, the administering states won General Assembly agreement that it would not consider political or constitutional information or approve resolutions dealing with specific territories.[6]

The work of the Committee on Information between 1946 and 1963 demonstrates the evolution of the UN role in the nontrust non-self-governing territories. Initially, while the Western states maintained a majority in the General Assembly, the committee's work was procedural and relatively circumscribed. Beyond studying the information transmitted in conformity with Article 73(e), it early on enumerated what factors made a territory non-self-governing, established standards for declaring when a territory had ceased to be non-self-governing, and drew up a procedure for determining when a member state administered territories that fell under the auspices of Chapter XI, activities that were all related in some way to the Charter's expression of UN interest in the non-self-governing territories. None of these undertakings threatened the administering states' positions or sought to interject the United Nations into the colonial relationship. As the anticolonial element in the General Assembly grew, however, so did calls to minimize—or even to erase entirely—the distinction between Chapter XI, dealing with the non-self-governing territories, and Chapters XII and XIII, pertaining to the trust territories to allow for the hearing of petitioners from the non-self-governing territories, the sending of UN missions to them, the setting of timetables for the granting of independence to nontrust non-self-governing territories, and other measures.[7] Despite the lack of success of these endeavors, they painted in bold relief the growing popularity at the United Nations of an expansive conception of the proper international role in the non-self-governing territories that sought to move from interest to actual involvement.

The strength of the anticolonial faction within the General Assembly from 1960 on ensured that UN involvement in the non-self-governing territories would become manifest. Resolution 1514 (XV) in December of that year, titled "Declaration on the Granting of Independence to Colonial Countries and Peoples," asserted that "all peoples have an inalienable right to complete freedom," "self-determination," and "the exercise of their sovereignty." It amounted to a declaration of war on colonialism as well as a de facto promise of UN support for indigenous independence drives and revealed how far the United Nations had come since its Charter merely posited the organization's interest in the non-self-governing territories.[8] Resolutions 1654 (XVI) in November 1961 and 1810 (XVII) in December 1962 worked to put Resolution 1514 (XV) into practice by creating and then expanding what became known as the Decolonization Committee (first the Committee of 17 and then the Committee of 24), which was empowered to hold meetings outside UN headquarters (even in individual territories themselves) and to make recommendations directly to individual administering states.[9] Finally, in 1963, General Assembly Resolution 1970 (XVIII) dissolved the balanced Committee on Information from Non-Self-Governing Territories and transferred its functions to the more broadly conceived Decolonization Committee.[10] This final step marked the culmination of an evolving UN policy vis-à-vis the non-self-governing territories that witnessed the steady shift from simple international interest in moving territories along toward self-government and even independence to actual involvement in that process.[11]

UN concern with the plight of the world's non-self-governing territories presented the Truman, Eisenhower, and Kennedy administrations with serious challenges.[12] As an administering power itself, the United States had to formulate concrete policies for meeting the UN Charter's expectations when it came to colonial administration.[13] At the same time, the larger implications of a UN role in the non-self-governing territories created for policymakers in all three administrations a dilemma of the highest order. On the one hand, they sought to minimize the consequences of such interest for the nation's Western European NATO allies, whose global positions and contributions to free world defense were largely dependent on their overseas colonies and the products they produced. On the other hand, US officials sought to placate the peripheral states that formed the backbone of the anticolonial movement at the United Nations—and later the states that gained independence as a result of decolonization—so as not to lose them to communism or push them toward extreme anticolonial nationalism or neutralism. In practice, however, the US approach to colonial questions at the United Nations bowed to Cold War considerations and leaned more toward the position of the administering states than toward the idea of greater international action on behalf of colonial peoples.

The Truman administration's stance on colonialism in general as well as on the specific matter of a UN role in the non-self-governing territories was guided in large part by the geostrategic realities of the developing Cold War. In April 1945, just ten days before Roosevelt's death, the Office of Strategic Services had argued that US interests lay in "the maintenance of the British, French and Dutch colonial empires," not in their liquidation.[14] Many of the nation's most important European allies depended on their colonies for raw materials and military bases and could find their own security compromised if those colonies were lost. Such developments could have an attendant deleterious effect for the United States, which would then be forced to take on a greater share of defending its allies. But the end of the European empires could be doubly disastrous for the United States if resource-rich former colonies became associated with the Soviet bloc and thereby weakened the West's defensive—and potentially offensive—capabilities while augmenting those of the East. When forced therefore to choose "between a . . . desire to help the colonial peoples toward independence," which comported with US traditions, and "strategic inter-dependence with the colonial powers which derived their strength from their colonies," owing to security concerns Washington leaned in the latter direction.[15] Its efforts to avoid weakening the Western European colonial powers while at least paying lip service to independence movements around the world led the administration to plow a careful middle ground at the United Nations between its colonial allies and the developing anticolonial bloc designed to balance the legitimate interests of both sides while alienating neither.[16]

The fact that the nonadministering majority at the United Nations had not yet developed a strongly anticolonial stance made the Truman administration's efforts to sell its middle course to the Western European allies easier than would be the case for its successors. There were, to be sure, efforts to expand the powers of the Committee on Information to make it more like the Trusteeship Council, but they were fairly handily defeated during the period when Western states dominated the organization. And, to head off radical proposals, US officials worked for an "improvement in [the] attitude" of the nation's allies when it came to colonial matters at the United Nations by encouraging them to accept UN interest in the non-self-governing territories, cooperate in efforts to bring those territories along toward self-government and, where appropriate, independence, and thereby demonstrate the sort of enlightened and positive attitude that would foster the goodwill of the nonadministering majority at the United Nations.[17]

In an indication of the role that East-West considerations played in shaping their thinking regarding colonial questions at the United Nations, US policymakers developed a multipronged propaganda campaign for countering Soviet efforts to capitalize on the issue of the non-self-governing territories for Cold War purposes. One element would "focus attention . . . on Soviet actions which frequently violate human rights," or what US officials were increasingly dubbing the "conspiracy of Soviet imperialism." This strand of US policy, which highlighted the "number of independent countries [that] had recently become dependent, thus reversing [the] world trend," would become increasingly important as time went on. A second element of US policy at the United Nations would play up "the constructive efforts of the free world . . . to promote the welfare of non-self-governing peoples" as a way of debunking Soviet claims to the contrary. And a third would seek to "keep discussion . . . on substantive questions" in order to prevent political discussions that could open the door to Soviet propagandizing in the first place.[18]

Agreeing on the need to combat Soviet efforts to hijack colonial matters at the United Nations was ultimately easier for administration officials than hewing to the middle course, which occasioned a vigorous debate among the State Department's various geographic and functional elements. Ridgway Knight of the Office of European Regional Affairs, for example, bowed to the Cold War concerns that shaped US policy toward Western Europe in arguing for "full cooperation" and "the friendliest possible relations with [the nation's] European allies." Although he acknowledged that "the sympathy of the American people for dependent peoples [was] a fact of life," he believed that that sympathy had to be subordinated in the short term to the nation's larger security needs. Officials from other areas of the State Department disagreed. Ruth Bacon of the Office of Far Eastern Affairs considered Knight's views "short-sighted and dangerous" and believed that his call for "subservience to the policies of the other NATO powers" would be "repugnant to the American people." Ambassador at Large Philip C. Jessup emphasized the importance of placating not only the "dependent peoples" but also their periphery-based "champions" at the United Nations; he therefore called for more robust US efforts to convince the Western European allies that the development of the non-self-governing territories constituted an international responsibility "which we all must meet together." Similar sentiments were expressed by analysts with responsibility for dependent areas or UN affairs who by nature of their positions took a wider view of US interests than did Knight. In a prescient prediction of things to come, they warned that the "policy of unqualified support of the colonial powers" that Knight advocated "would alienate hundreds of millions of newly independent peoples who are fundamentally opposed to colonialism." It also ran the risk of alienating large segments of the American and Western European populations by portraying NATO as "an old-fashioned alliance designed to maintain the *status quo* at any cost" and creating a situation where "liberal opinion in the world will no longer be influenced by [American] leadership."[19]

The concerns of non-European-oriented officials notwithstanding, a State Department working group concluded that the nation's best strategy remained "a middle of the road position with respect to colonial problems." This meant continuing to serve as an "'honest broker' between what sometimes appear[ed] to be extreme positions taken by both the colonial and the anti-colonial groups" and was more or less the approach the United States had employed since the first UN session in 1946. Advocates of the balanced approach well recognized that this middle course was "difficult" and "uncomfortable" and "may in particular cases make [the United States] unpopular with both extremes." It might also fail miserably at "moderating [either] the conservative approach of some of the administering countries" or "the extremism of the anti-colonial majority." Nevertheless, it remained the preferred course of US policy for the whole of the Truman administration, whose officials always hoped that its "wisdom" would be "apparent to moderate opinion" and ultimately appreciated "in wider circles."[20]

Although when it came to colonial matters the Eisenhower administration eschewed its predecessor's middle-of-the-road efforts at the United Nations—efforts that Secretary of State John Foster Dulles called "unnecessarily ambiguous"—for all practical purposes it adopted the same strategy.[21] To be sure, US rhetoric on colonialism stiffened after 1953—and especially after 1956, when the Suez crisis laid bare the folly of staking the free world's defenses on Western European ties to the colonial or developing states.[22] Yet there was never any thought within the administration of wholesale US endorsement of anticolonialism for fear that such a step could encourage what US leaders believed would be reckless or precipitate independence movements that might lead to Communist gains. The Soviet-American tensions that began during the Truman years emerged full-blown during the Eisenhower era, and, as the Cold War's battleground began shifting to the developing world, the Western European empires became hotly contested real estate for both sides. Accordingly, it became all the more important to control the pace and direction of independence movements so that only those likely to result in non-Communist governments achieved success. It was also important to counter Soviet claims of championing independence and self-government.[23]

One of the first strategies toward the United Nations that the new administration implemented was more active use of the organization as a propaganda forum. Influenced by his own journalistic background, US ambassador to the United Nations Henry Cabot Lodge saw the organization as a bully pulpit from which to strike at the Soviet bloc whenever possible, scoring points not only with other members of the General Assembly but also with peoples around the world who would be exposed to his remarks in their local newspapers.[24] What was ultimately dubbed the Lodge Project constituted an all-out offensive effort to embarrass the Soviet Union on the world stage of the United Nations. "Specifically 'anti-communist' rather than 'pro-US,'" the campaign focused on several areas where Soviet policy was considered vulnerable, including Moscow's "absorption of [the] Baltic States and other territorial accessions in Europe" and its "domination of European satellites," actions US policymakers came to describe as *imperialist*. "While the Soviet Union preaches its concern for the liberation of dependent peoples," propaganda staff working with Ambassador Lodge asserted in an early articulation of what would become a major element of the US propaganda effort both within and outside the United Nations, "it has ruthlessly converted every territory over which it has acquired domination into a vassal of the Soviet state." "It might be desirable for us to highlight this practice," US officials asserted, "and to contrast it with the steady evolutionary progress toward self-determination which has been made under western auspices since World War II."[25]

Yet there were those in the administration, particularly within the Psychological Strategy Board, who considered Lodge's Cold War–oriented publicity campaign ill conceived, if not totally misguided. Edward P. Lilly, for example, lamented Lodge's apparent intention to focus on a negative anti-Communist campaign and advised instead an effort to highlight American accomplishments in the field of human rights, which would in practice also shed light on Soviet failings in that area. Arthur M. Cox went even further, questioning the efficacy of any Soviet-focused propaganda campaign. In a prescient identification of the ultimate reception of the administration's propaganda efforts at the United Nations, he proclaimed: "I think we have made a great mistake as a nation of assuming that because Soviet power and subversion is the greatest problem facing us today, it is therefore the greatest problem facing everybody else." "No amount of horror stories demonstrating the crimes of the Kremlin will convince millions of people in the free world that Soviet-inspired Communism is their main problem," he warned, "because they know that it is not."[26] Such warnings fell on deaf ears, however, as the administration went on to make the Cold War a centerpiece of its UN propaganda.

Cold War considerations also motivated the administration's decision to maintain its predecessor's middle-of-the-road approach to colonial questions at the United Nations. In arguing for this course, Mason Sears, the face of US policy on colonial questions at the United Nations, painted it as "the only position that is always damaging to Soviet operations," thus indicating the Cold War considerations that shaped US thinking. But, in an implicit nod to Arthur Cox's assertion that communism was not the bogey man for the rest of the world that it was to the United States, Sears also suggested that more needed to be done to educate the rest of the world about "why communism is so repugnant to national freedoms everywhere." "The continuing efforts of the Soviets to take over one small nation after another," he purported, "represent[ed] . . . the greatest and only important road block to the ultimate achievement of a secure independence by any dependent or newly-liberated people." While conceding that more rapid progress was required in the drive toward independent nationhood for the non-self-governing territories, he cautioned against "disorderly progress" in that direction, which merely played into the Soviets' hands, a stance that would become increasingly anathema to the growing anticolonial majority in the United Nations.[27]

The nation's traditional ideological affinity for peoples seeking independence and self-government notwithstanding, the Eisenhower administration deemed adoption of "a doctrinaire anti-colonial position across the board" unwise. Although such a course could likely lead to wider support for the United States at the United Nations—"and ease its troubled national conscience in the bargain"—it would also mean "abdicating the bulk of [the nation's] other responsibilities and commitments, not to mention [its] judgment." Most State Department policymakers doubted that more vigorous American anticolonialism would do much to push the Western European colonial administrators toward greater liberality or more rapid independence for their territories, fearing that it might, in fact, have just the opposite effect. Nor was it likely to do much to win the United States immediate support among what the State Department referred to as "the Afro-Asian bloc." "Even if all colonial issues could be settled suddenly to [the] satisfaction [of] that bloc, [it was] still doubtful [that the United States] would have much greater influence because of [its] association with [the] 'hated' West and because of other differences in [its] approach to international problems." And as an administering state itself the United States was bound to be associated with the Western European colonial powers regardless of any rhetorical efforts it might make to distance itself from them. Consequently, the "precarious" and "thankless" middle course on colonial questions that the United States had steered at the United Nations since its founding was seen as the nation's only option.[28]

Consideration by the Fifteenth General Assembly, the last to be held during the Eisenhower presidency, of what became Resolution 1514 (XV) demonstrated clearly the fiction of the middle course. On October 23, Soviet premier Nikita Khrushchev personally introduced a declaration on the granting of independence to colonial peoples to the General Assembly. In a long speech laced with harsh denunciations of Western colonialism, he called on the United Nations to urge the administering states to undertake negotiations with local governments in the non-self-governing territories to effect independence and self-government at the earliest possible moment and suggested UN "assistance, moral and material," if the administering powers dragged their feet. The Soviets deliberately sought consideration of the proposal in plenary session of the General Assembly rather than by one of its functional committees in order to highlight the measure's importance as well as their role in bringing it to the fore. In this way, they hoped to maximize their propaganda gain, both within the assembly and in the wider world.[29]

US officials developed two strategies for neutralizing Khrushchev's initiative. One was portraying the Soviet Union itself as a colonial power and thereby taking the wind out of the declaration's sails. "We should not neglect [any] opportunity," Secretary of State Christian Herter advised the US mission to the United Nations, "[to] condemn Communist colonialism to [the] fullest, pointing out [that the] Soviet Union is not only [the] largest existing colonial power, but [the] only colonial regime that is still expanding and [that] has never granted independence or self-government to any subject people."[30] The second line of attack focused on countering the Soviet declaration on colonialism with an alternative proposal, preferably drafted by the Asian and African states (though possibly with US assistance or input), that condemned both the sort of colonialism the Soviet Union had practiced in the Baltic states and Central Asia and "the more commonly experienced mercantile colonialism which has been primarily of European origin." A balanced declaration against all forms of colonialism, argued John M. Steeves of the State Department's Division of Far Eastern Affairs, was the only chance of securing broad support within the General Assembly. It was also Washington's best hope of currying favor with the assembly's anticolonial majority, which would surely look askance at any US efforts to dilute international efforts to bring the colonial system to an end.[31]

Subsequent debate manifested both US efforts. Numerous delegations criticized Soviet colonialism, both implicitly and explicitly. The Colombian representative Antonio Alvarez Restrepo, for example, noted the gradual elimination of "political colonialism" but lamented the simultaneous advance of what he termed "the colonialism of souls" that "keeps watch over man's conscience, suppresses his freedom, and utterly destroys the life of the spirit." Other states were more direct in condemning the Soviets, as Honduras's Francisco Milla Bermudez did in declaring that "the nation least morally qualified to propose [a declaration on the ending of colonialism was] the Union of Soviet Socialist Republics."[32] US efforts to defuse the Soviet effort were also advanced by the Afro-Asian draft resolution, ultimately cosponsored by forty-three states, which presented a balanced call for an end to all forms of colonialism. Borrowing heavily from the Bandung declaration signed by twenty-nine nonaligned nations in 1955,[33] the draft resolution spoke broadly of self-government and independence as "fundamental human rights," affirmed the right of all people to "freely determine their political status and freely pursue their economic, social and cultural development," declared that "inadequacy of political, economic, social or educational preparedness should never serve as a pretext for delaying independence," and directed that "all armed action or repressive measures of all kinds directed against dependent peoples shall cease." Tunisia's Mongi Slim, whose delegation was among the more than two dozen original sponsors of the draft resolution, summed up the sentiments of the resolution's supporters when it came to efforts to turn the drive to end colonialism into an explicit Cold War question, as Khrushchev's proposal had done. "We do not want to give this debate," he cautioned, or by extension "this whole process of decolonization, an ideological character, which would link it to the struggle at present going on between East and West" and "make [it] a propaganda issue."[34]

The submission of two different proposals to end colonialism created a minor fracas within the assembly. Despite the hopes of the Afro-Asian bloc, the Soviets would neither withdraw their measure nor agree that it could be voted on second. After receiving significant criticism for its contentious tone and clear Cold War inspiration during General Assembly debate, the Soviet declaration failed to win even simple majority support. Reaction to the forty-three-power draft resolution was much more positive, and, as its sponsors had hoped, it won General Assembly approval without a dissenting vote. That is not to say that all delegations voted to approve it, however, as nine, including Great Britain and the United States, chose to abstain.[35]

The US decision to abstain on what became Resolution 1514 (XV) made clear the difficulty of squaring the US relationship with Western Europe with the growing importance of the developing world. It was not easy for the administration to settle on an abstention. Indeed, the initial inclination was to vote in the affirmative while also qualifying US support for each paragraph of the draft resolution. Although no US policymaker believed that the draft resolution was ideal—Secretary of State Christian Herter described it as "exceedingly badly worded"—all agreed that it was preferable to the Soviet declaration. It was also a product of US lobbying with the Afro-Asian bloc, the members of which would likely resent a lack of US support when it came time to vote. Finally, the measure was certain to win approval by a huge margin, and Washington's failure to join with the majority could redound negatively and effect its overall world position. Nevertheless, in the end, President Eisenhower succumbed to Prime Minister Harold Macmillan's plaintive plea that Britain and the United States "stand together" and instructed the US mission to abstain. It was difficult to go against the nation's "strongest ally," the president concluded, particularly when US officials had themselves noted shortcomings in the draft resolution.[36]

In choosing to abstain rather than vote yes, the administration, and particularly Eisenhower himself, made clear that maintaining harmonious relations with key allies, and particularly Great Britain, was more important than the symbolic step of supporting an end to colonialism at the United Nations. Given the fact that the draft resolution was bound to pass handily even without US backing, the practical effect of the US vote was nil. As the "audible gasp of surprise followed by [a] diminishing murmur of whispered comments" that erupted after the US representative cast the abstention made clear, however, it was nevertheless important. US representative to the United Nations James Wadsworth had been "shocked and disheartened" by the decision to shift from support for the draft resolution to abstention and warned of the likely repercussions of siding with the "colonial powers which even we recognize as such" over the "Asians and Africans." The "immediate, strong, sometimes emotional, and invariably negative" reaction to the abstention seemed to justify Wadsworth's fears. "'How could you vote this way?'" asked Ghana's Alex Quaison-Sackey. "'Are you trying to commit political suicide?'" wondered Nigeria's C. O. Ifeagwu. Turgut Menemencioglu of Turkey called the vote simply "'unbelievable and incomprehensible.'" Added to the general disbelief was a clear appreciation for the way in which the vote played into Soviet hands in the General Assembly. Liberia's T. O. Dosumu-Johnson lamented that the United States had "'handed [a] propaganda victory to [the] USSR without reason,'" while Tunisia's Zouhir Chelli predicted that the vote would give "'ammunition to [the] USSR across the board.'" Regardless of its reasons, the administration's decision to abstain on Resolution 1514 (XV) belied its long-standing commitment to steering a middle course when it came to colonial questions at the United Nations and placed it squarely in the colonialist camp. Just as Ambassador Wadsworth had warned, it also weakened the US position with the anticolonial UN majority.[37]

By the time the Kennedy administration assumed office, debate over the UN stance on colonial questions was reaching a head. The lopsided vote on Resolution 1514 (XV) had starkly revealed the growing General Assembly support for UN involvement in the non-self-governing territories. And the Eisenhower administration's last-minute abstention on that resolution had "severely damaged" US "prestige and influence among [the] Afro-Asian group."[38] Yet wholesale support for the anticolonial majority in the General Assembly to redress the balance was out of the question, as was unqualified support for the Western European administering states. As the Bureau of European Affairs within the State Department noted in March 1961: "The best long-range approach [was] to endeavor to work out adjustments between European countries and the Afro-Asian states rather than to side decidedly with one or the other party."[39] In other words, the new administration would continue the middle ground pursued by its predecessors, making clear the need for "both the colonial and [the] emergent nations" to accept certain "restraints and responsibilities."[40]

In fleshing out what they described as a more "forward-looking policy on colonial questions," Kennedy administration officials emphasized the need to seek concessions from the administering and nonadministering states alike.[41] As Richard F. Pedersen of the US mission to the United Nations noted in June 1962, the United States had to "stand for early progress [in the non-self-governing territories] and take risks with [its] European allies." "There will be some scars," he admitted, "but in the long-run the sooner this era [of colonialism] is ended the sooner Western-Afro-Asian Relations can be put on a sound basis."[42] Yet, at the same time, administration policymakers appreciated the need for moderation by those on the anticolonial side of the aisle. "Irresponsible Afro-Asian actions," warned a strategy paper for the Seventeenth General Assembly, "can lead to noncooperation by the administering powers," "the disregard[ing] and downgrading of Assembly recommendations," and ultimately "the weakening of the Assembly" itself.[43] As its continuance of the middle-ground position on UN interest in the non-self-governing territories makes clear, for all its talk about a new vision for US foreign policy, the administration was guided by the same sorts of Cold War considerations as its predecessors and ultimately refused to come down squarely on the side of the non-self-governing territories.

Rather than emphasizing the idea that the Soviets were colonialist or imperialist, as their predecessors had done, officials in the Kennedy administration repurposed the free world/slave world dichotomy articulated in the 1947 Truman Doctrine and set out to paint the West as a land of freedom, opportunity, and choice, in contrast to the East, where oppression, despair, and lack of choice were the norm. As the State Department's Policy Planning Council explained in November 1961: "To emergent leaders, colonialism is one thing and communist expansionist policies are another. . . . The key factor is that colonialism has been experienced whereas Soviet imperialism has not. We must accept this hard fact and act accordingly." Secretary of State Dean Rusk had foreshadowed this new approach in May 31 testimony before the Senate Foreign Relations Committee. He declared: "[The United States] seek[s], above all, a world of free choice in which a great diversity of nations, each faithful to its own traditions and its own genius, will learn to respect the ground rules of human survival. . . . Against the world of coercion, we affirm the world of choice." It was no accident, US officials noted, that people were fleeing Communist-controlled areas in droves, some twelve million since World War II. The August 1961 construction of the Berlin Wall merely confirmed their claims regarding Soviet repression and gave credence to the new US propaganda effort to deflate Soviet claims of supporting self-government and independence for colonial peoples by pointing directly to the oppression inherent in Communist societies.[44] And, when, during the Seventeenth General Assembly, which concluded in late 1962, "some ten delegations made a point of referring to the dependent status of Soviet satellites, and to the subject people inside the Soviet Union itself," US officials were gratified.[45]

The work of the Committees of 17 and 24 over the years, however, proved problematic for the United States. First off, both committees allowed for Soviet and Soviet bloc participation in a way that the Committee on Information had not for a number of years. Unlike the latter, whose nonadministering members were popularly elected, all the members of the Committees of 17 and then 24 were appointed by the president of the General Assembly with an eye toward geographic balance reflective of the many constituencies of the United Nations. Consequently, those entities were dominated from the start by anticolonial states, including the Soviet Union and Poland on the Committee of 17 and those two states plus Bulgaria when the committee was expanded to twenty-four members in 1963. US officials bemoaned that, much as it had done in outlining its declaration on ending colonialism in 1960, the Soviet Union used the Committees of 17 and 24 for Cold War purposes, engineering the introduction of stridently anticolonial—and anti-Western—resolutions that the African, Asian, and Latin American members of the committee were reluctant to oppose lest they be branded "'soft on colonialism.'"[46] A second problem for the United States was the fact that, in keeping with its charge, the Decolonization Committee conducted in-depth investigations into individual territories, visited various territories in Africa, and issued recommendations on specific territories directly to the administering states, things that the Committee on Information had never had the authority to do and that the United States considered a violation of the UN Charter. Moreover, many of the resolutions endorsed by the committee called for "immediate independence" in various individual territories, regardless of conditions on the ground, which the United States found unrealistic and irresponsible.[47] Finally, in another move the United States deemed unacceptable, for the first time in its history the General Assembly, on the recommendation of the Committees of 17 and 24, began passing resolutions that included recommendations for sanctions against member states. Problematic under any circumstances, resolutions recommending sanctions were particularly unseemly when they involved condemnations of South Africa's apartheid policy, which US officials considered a matter of domestic jurisdiction and not something that fell within the purview of the United Nations. US officials were also no doubt concerned that, if the United Nations could recommend sanctions against South Africa for its domestic racial policies, it might move at some point against Jim Crow segregation in the South, a portentous prospect that had to be resisted at all costs, even if it meant forcing Washington to join Pretoria in opposing the overwhelming majority support for action against apartheid.[48]

In large part, the General Assembly's interest in apartheid was fueled by the overall success of the decolonization movement. As the number of territories gaining self-government and independence increased, UN efforts shifted from effecting decolonization to racial issues, particularly the suppression of black majorities by white-minority populations.[49] Mounting African opposition to "the hard-core racial issues in the southern third of [the continent]," the State Department's Harlan M. Cleveland noted in November 1963, replaced calls for self-government and independence, forcing US officials to consider the wider ramification of their reluctance to apply sanctions to racist regimes like South Africa and Portuguese Angola. Holding firm in this regard might cost the United States African backing on other questions, such as the still-vital question of the admission of Communist China to the United Nations.[50] It would also shine a spotlight on racial discrimination in the United States itself, an unpleasant reality that numerous African diplomats had experienced firsthand and one that the administration feared could harm the nation's overall international position.[51] In 1963, apartheid became "the real gut issue" of the Eighteenth General Assembly for what US representative to the United Nations William Attwood described as "the dark-skinned delegations," exposing Washington's previous reluctance to speak out against South Africa, and convincing Attwood of the need to alter course, just as the nation had recently done when it came to domestic civil rights. "We have tended to treat the apartheid issue in the U.N. as an exercise in parliamentary tactics," he averred. "But it is more than ever an emotional issue that can no longer be side-tracked or dispelled by maneuvers, no matter how skillful."[52] To put it another way, the administration needed to adopt a more progressive and forthcoming stance on racial questions at the United Nations if it was to maintain any modicum of credibility with the anticolonial majority—and with the nonwhite world writ large.

Growing support within the General Assembly for universal human rights—and, indeed, for a UN convention on racial discrimination—was another potential problem for US officials by 1963. Human rights had been a UN concern from the start, and US officials had always offered consistent, but not enthusiastic, support for human rights measures. They remained moderately supportive of such initiatives in the early 1960s but feared, probably with more than a little justification, that any UN-sponsored campaign against racial discrimination would complicate "the domestic debate on civil rights legislation." In the end, the US delegation did support the Universal Declaration against All Forms of Racial Discrimination but made clear in the process that the United States intended "to carry out its terms in accordance with [US] constitutional processes."[53] In other words, support for the general principle of racial equality would not mean the wholesale implementation of that principle at home. Shielded behind the domestic-jurisdiction clause of the UN Charter, the United States would continue to insist that what happened within its own borders was not a legitimate concern of the United Nations.

For US officials, the growing UN concern with issues such as racial discrimination and human rights signaled an important and not entirely welcome shift in the organization's orientation and makeup. Reflecting by 1963 the concerns of the "underdeveloped 'south,'" debate in the General Assembly came increasingly to revolve around the differences between the haves and the have-nots and to present new challenges for the United States when it came to protecting its core interests. US officials often found it difficult to break out of the East-West mind-set that had dominated foreign policy thinking in Washington since the conclusion of World War II. And, even when they did appreciate how disinterested much of the rest of the world was in the Cold War, their own policy choices remained shaped by the superpower struggle.[54]

As we have seen, officials in the Truman, Eisenhower, and Kennedy administrations pursued a middle ground on colonial questions at the United Nations that abjured outright endorsement of anticolonialism but also sought to avoid too close an identification with the administering states. Guided largely by Cold War considerations, all three administrations counseled moderation on the part of both factions in order to prevent the Soviet Union from capitalizing on anticolonial sentiment in ways that would improve its strategic position vis-à-vis the West. But, because their primary concern was protecting the Western security position, US officials perforce viewed everything, including the drive for decolonization, through Cold War glasses. As a result, at the United Nations, they were unwavering in defending responsible colonial administration, warning against the dangers of premature independence drives, and, beginning in 1953, mounting a propaganda campaign designed to expose the evils of communism and highlight the virtues of Western liberal capitalism. The general lack of success of these US initiatives demonstrated the strength of anticolonialism, laid bare the growing isolation of the colonial powers on the world stage, and served as a harbinger for a widening global divide between the developed North and the developing South as well as US

Whistling in the Dark   143

alienation from much of the developing world. The Cold War consider-ations that drove the US approach to UN handling of questions related to non-self-governing territories mattered little to the anticolonial majority, particularly to leading states on the periphery, such as India, that sought to avoid allegiance to either superpower and pursued neutralism instead. Despite the growing popularity of anticolonialism in the General Assem-bly, US officials through three presidential administrations effectively supported great power autonomy when it came to the non-self-governing territories at the expense of world opinion. As the diminishing success of this strategy from 1946 to 1963 makes plain, however, it amounted to little more than whistling in the dark.

Notes

I thank the Harry S. Truman Library Institute, the Kent State University Research Council, and the Kent State University Department of History for travel support.

1. The growth of the United Nations can be followed at http://www.un.org/en /sections/member-states/growth-united-nations-membership-1945-present/index .html.

2. See, e.g., Scott Bills, *Empire and Cold War: The Roots of US–Third World Antagonism, 1945–47* (New York: St. Martin's, 1990); Geir Lundestad, *East, West, North, South: Major Developments in International Politics since 1945,* trans. Gail Adams Kvam, 4th ed. (New York: Oxford University Press, 1999); and Odd Arne Westad, *The Global Cold War: Third World Interventions and the Making of Our Times* (Cambridge: Cambridge University Press, 2005).

3. For a recent rendering of this argument, see Mark Mazower, *No Enchanted Palace: The End of Empire and the Ideological Origins of the United Nations* (Prince-ton, NJ: Princeton University Press, 2010).

4. Chapter XIII of the UN Charter, "International Trusteeship System," http:// www.un.org/en/sections/un-charter/chapter-xii/index.html; Chapter XII of the UN Charter, "The Trusteeship Council," http://www.un.org/en/sections/un-charter/ chapter-xiii/index.html. Early US trusteeship plans to place all colonial territories under international supervision can be followed in Ruth B. Russell, *A History of the United Nations Charter: The Role of the United States, 1940–1945* (Washington, DC: Brookings Institution, 1958), 75–77, 84–86, 88–91. See also Victor Pungong, "The United States and the International Trusteeship System," in *The United States and Decolonization: Power and Freedom,* ed. David Ryan and Victor Pungong (New York: St. Martin's, 2000), 85–101.

5. "Declaration Regarding Non-Self-Governing Peoples, Article 73, UN Char-

ter," in *Charter of the United Nations: Commentary and Documents,* 3rd., rev. ed., ed. Leland M. Goodrich, Edvard Hambro, and Anne Patricia Simons (New York: Columbia University Press, 1969), 448–49.

6. Discussion of establishment of the Committee on Information can be followed in the record of the Fourth Committee of the General Assembly, A/C.4/Sub.2. See also UN General Assembly Resolution 66(I), "Transmission of Information under Article 73(e) of the Charter," December 14, 1946, http://www.un.org/en/ga/search/view_doc.asp?symbol=A/RES/66(I); and UN Charter, in *The Charter of the United Nations: A Commentary,* ed. Bruno Simma (New York: Oxford University Press, 1995), xxxii. The eight administering powers were Australia, Belgium, Denmark, France, the Netherlands, New Zealand, the United Kingdom, and the United States. The eight nonadministering powers elected to the committee were Brazil, China, Cuba, Egypt, India, the Philippines, the Soviet Union, and Uruguay. After its establishment in 1946, the committee was renewed annually until 1949 and then given three-year terms in 1949, 1952, 1955, and 1958. The renewal in 1961 contained no terminal date and stated instead that the committee would continue "until such time as the General Assembly has decided that the principles embodied in Chapter XI of the Charter of the United Nations . . . have been fully implemented." UN General Assembly Resolution 1700 (XVI), "Question of the Renewal of the Committee on Information from Non-Self-Governing Territories," December 19, 1961, http://www.un.org/en/ga/search/view_doc.asp?symbol=A/RES/1700(XVI).

7. For one accounting of the committee's work, see Emil J. Sady, *The United Nations and Dependent Peoples* (Washington, DC: Brookings Institution, 1956).

8. UN General Assembly Resolution 1514 (XV), "Declaration on Granting of Independence to Colonial Countries and Peoples," December 20, 1960, http://www.un.org/en/ga/search/view_doc.asp?symbol=A/RES/1514(XV).

9. See UN General Assembly Resolution 1654 (XVI), "The Situation with Regard to the Implementation of the Declaration on the Granting of Independence to Colonial Countries and Peoples," November 27, 1961, http://www.un.org/en/ga/search/view_doc.asp?symbol=A/RES/1664(XVI); and UN General Assembly Resolution 1810 (XVII), "The Situation with Regard to the Implementation of the Declaration on the Granting of Independence to Colonial Countries and Peoples," December 17, 1962, http://www.un.org/en/ga/search/view_doc.asp?symbol=A/RES/1810(XVII).

10. See UN General Assembly Resolution 1970 (XVIII), "Question of the Continuation of the Committee on Information from Non-Self-Governing Territories," December 16, 1963, http://www.un.org/en/ga/search/view_doc.asp?symbol=A/RES/1970(XVIII).

11. For various aspects of the UN role in decolonization, see Roland Burke, *Decolonization and the Evolution of International Human Rights* (Philadelphia: University of Pennsylvania Press, 2010); and Vrushali Patil, *Negotiating Decolonization*

in the United Nations: Politics of Space, Identity, and International Community (New York: Routledge, 2008).

12. For the three administrations' general approaches to the United Nations, see John Allphin Moore Jr. and Jerry Pubantz, *To Create a New World? American Presidents and the United Nations* (New York: Peter Lang, 1999), 1–170.

13. The United States administered the following non-self-governing territories in 1945: Alaska, American Samoa, Guam, Hawaii, the Panama Canal Zone, Puerto Rico, and the Virgin Islands. See UN General Assembly Resolution 66 (I) (n. 6 above).

14. OSS Memorandum, April 2, 1945, cited in Christopher Thorne, "Indochina and Anglo-American Relations, 1942–1945," *Pacific Historical Review* 45 (February 1976): 73–96, 96. See also Tony Smith, *The Pattern of Imperialism: The United States, Great Britain, and the Late-Industrializing World since 1815* (New York: Cambridge University Press, 1981), 172.

15. "Minutes of the Twenty-Fifth Meeting of the United States Delegation to the Third Regular Session of the General Assembly, Paris, Hotel d'Iéna, November 3, 1948, 9:15 A.M.," November 3, 1948, US Department of State, *Foreign Relations of the United States, 1948,* vol. 1, *General: The United Nations* (Washington, DC: US Government Printing Office, 1975), 284 (hereafter, e.g., *FRUS, 1948*).

16. These issues are dealt with in Dean Rusk Memorandum, "Long-Range Policy with Respect to Emergent Nations," July 27, 1948, with attachment, Philip C. Jessup (Acting US Representative to the United Nations) to Rusk, July 20, 1948, International Organization: Bureau of UN Affairs, Henry L. Abbott Files, box 15, Record Group (RG) 59, lot 55 D 323, National Archives, College Park (all subsequent references to RG 59 relate to this archive); and Central Intelligence Agency, "The Break-Up of the Colonial Empires and Its Implications for US Security," ORE 25-48, September 3, 1948, Papers of Harry S. Truman, President's Secretary's File: Intell, box 214, O.R.E.: 1948: 21–29, Harry S. Truman Library, Independence, MO.

17. R. R. Robbins (UNA) Memorandum, "UNA Meeting, Mr. Hickerson's Office, 3 P.M. Monday, January 23, 1950—Subject: Colonial Policy," January 19, 1950, RG 59, Sandifer Files, box 7, folder: Colonial Policy, Misc. Memos, 1949–1952. See also Margaret Joy Tibbetts Memorandum, "Colonial Questions and the United Nations," Enclosure to US Embassy, London, Dispatch 2535 to State Department, May 24, 1950, RG 59, 741.022/5-2450.

18. Unsigned Discussion Brief for Colonial Talks, "Item IV (b) 8—More Effective Measures to Counter Soviet-Inspired Propaganda Activities in Colonial Areas and Soviet Exploitation of the Theme of 'Western Imperialism' in Their Propaganda," September 4, 1951, US Department of State, *FRUS, 1951,* vol. 2, *The United Nations: The Western Hemisphere* (Washington, DC: US Government Printing Office, 1979), 643. See also Harold Karan Jacobson, "Decolonization," in *Soviet and American Policies in the United Nations: A Twenty-Five Year Perspective,* ed.

Alvin Z. Rubinstein and George Ginsburgs (New York: New York University Press, 1971), 73–93.

19. Knight (Acting Deputy Director of the Office of Western European Affairs) Memorandum, "Preliminary Thoughts on the Subject of a US Policy towards Colonial Areas and Colonial Powers," April 21, 1952, US Department of State, *FRUS, 1952–1954,* vol. 3, *United Nations Affairs* (Washington, DC: US Government Printing Office, 1979), 1104, 1105, 1103–4; Ruth E. Bacon (FE) Memorandum for Allison (FE), "UNA and EUR Memoranda on Colonial Policy," May 20, 1952, RG 59, 700.022/5-2052; Jessup (Ambassador at Large) Memorandum, "United States Policy towards Colonial Areas and Colonial Powers," April 30, 1952, and Draft Memorandum Prepared in the Office of Dependent Area Affairs and in the Office of United Nations Political and Security Affairs, "EUR Memorandum on 'US Policy towards Colonial Areas and Colonial Powers,'" May 8, 1952, *FRUS, 1952–1954,* vol. 3, *United Nations Affairs,* 1108–9, 1112–14.

20. "Minutes of Meeting of the Working Group on Colonial Problems, Department of State, August 19, 1952, 10:30 A.M. to 12:15 P.M.," September 24, 1952, *FRUS, 1952–1954,* vol. 3, *United Nations Affairs,* 1140; Memorandum of Conversation, "Belgian Attitude toward Certain Assembly Resolutions Relating to Non-Self-Governing Territories," February 20, 1952, RG 59, 700.022/2-2052; "EUR Memorandum" (n. 19 above); Perkins (Assistant Secretary of State for European Affairs) Memorandum to Matthews (Deputy Undersecretary of State), "US Colonial Policy,'" June 4, 1952, and "Memorandum Prepared in the Office of Dependent Area Affairs: Fourth Committee," n.d. [summer of 1952], *FRUS, 1952–1954,* vol. 3, *United Nations Affairs,* 1118, 1172.

21. Dulles in "Report on the Near East," *US Department of State Bulletin* 28 (June 15, 1953): 833–34.

22. Eisenhower's sentiments can be followed in Eisenhower to Winston S. Churchill, July 22, 1954, Ann Whitman File, International Series, box 19, folder: Churchill, July-December 1954 (1), Dwight D. Eisenhower Library, Abilene, Kansas (hereafter DDEL); and Eisenhower to General Alfred M. Gruenther (Supreme Commander, SHAPE), November 30, 1954, Whitman File, DDE Diary, box 8, folder: DDE Diary—November 1954 (1), DDEL.

23. For the competing pressures on the Eisenhower administration in the area of colonial policy, see Caroline Pruden, *Conditional Partners: Eisenhower, the United Nations, and the Search for a Permanent Peace* (Baton Rouge: Louisiana State University Press, 1998), 178; and Lawrence D. Weiler and Anne Patricia Simons, *The United States and the United Nations: The Search for International Peace and Security* (New York: Manhattan, 1967), 388–95.

24. See Charles R. Norberg (Acting Deputy Assistant Director, Office of Coordination) Memorandum, "Program for Psychological Support for Ambassador Lodge during the 8th Session of the UN General Assembly," January 10, 1953, Records of the Psychological Strategy Board, box 23, folder PSB 334 UN (1), DDEL; Charles R. Norberg (Acting Deputy Assistant Director, Office of Coordination) Memoran-

dum for Mr. McNair, "Intelligence Support for Working Group for 8th Session of the UN General Assembly (WGUN)," April 8, 1953, PSB, box 23, folder PSB 334 UN (1), DDEL; and A. P. Toner, "Notes on Ambassador Lodge's Meeting with Contributors to GA Project," August 4, 1953, PSB, box 23, folder PSB 334 UN (6), DDEL.

25. Memorandum of May 15, 1953, Conversation, "Valley Forge Problem: 'Human Rights' Project," May 18, 1953, Jackson Records, box 4, folder: Lodge; Unsigned Memorandum, "List of Soviet Vulnerabilities for Possible Exploitation at the UN," April 30, 1953, Jackson Records, box 4, folder: Lodge, and Unsigned Memorandum, "COSMOS," July 13, 1953, Enclosure to Richard Hirsch Memorandum to Byron K. Enyart, "COSMOS," August 27, 1953, PSB, box 23, folder PSB 334 UN (9), DDEL. For propaganda policy generally during the Eisenhower administration, including Lodge's efforts at the United Nations, see Kenneth Osgood, *Total Cold War: Eisenhower's Secret Propaganda Battle at Home and Abroad* (Lawrence: University Press of Kansas, 2006).

26. Arthur M. Cox Memorandum to Mr. Browne, "Mr. Irwin's Attached Draft Paper on the Lodge Project," June 3, 1953, PSB, box 23, folder PSB 334 UN (2), DDEL. See also Edward P. Lilly (PSB) Memorandum to H. S. Craig and W. Irwin Jr., "Lodge's Human Rights Project," May 21, 1953, PSB, box 23, folder PSB 334 UN (1), DDEL; Edward P. Lilly Memorandum, "Lodge Project within the United Nations," Enclosure to Lilly Memorandum to Wallace Irwin, "The Lodge Program in the U.N.," July 14, 1953, PSB, box 23, folder PSB 334 UN (5), DDEL; and Edward P. Lilly Memorandum to Byron K. Enyart (Acting Assistant Director for Plans, PSB), "Mr. Irwin's Memoranda on the Lodge Project," September 3, 1953, White House Office Files, National Security Council, OCB Sec, box 4, folder: Lodge's Human Rights Project (2), DDEL.

27. Mason Sears (US Representative on the UN Trusteeship Council) Memorandum, "United States Policy on Colonial Issues," August 18, 1953, and Mason Sears Memorandum, "Notes on United States Approach to Colonial Issues," September 22, 1953, *FRUS, 1952–1954,* vol. 3, *United Nations Affairs,* 1162–63, 1165–66.

28. State Department Memorandum, "Evaluation of Role of US in 10th General Assembly," February 9, 1956, Enclosure to Bloomfield Memorandum, February 15, 1956, RG 59, Office Files of Francis O. Wilcox, 1954–1957, lot 60 D 113, box 44, folder: Studies; State Department Memorandum, "Outline for Report on Colonialism," Enclosure to E. G. Mathews Memorandum to Nunley, "Proposed NAC Statement on Colonialism," May 15, 1956, RG 59, 700.022/5–1556.

29. "Soviet Declaration on the Granting of Independence to Colonial Countries and Peoples, Submitted by the Chairman of the Council of Ministers of the Union of Soviet Socialist Republics at the 869th Plenary Meeting of the General Assembly," September 23, 1960, in "Agenda Item 87: Declaration on the Granting of Independence to Colonial Countries and Peoples," UN Doc. Annexes (XV) 87, 6. See also Nikita S. Khrushchev, *Khrushchev in New York: A Documentary Record of Nikita S. Khrushchev's Trip to New York, September 15th to October 13th, 1960,*

Including All His Speeches and Proposals to the United Nations and Major Addresses and News Conferences (New York: Crosscurrents, 1960), and *Freedom and Independence for All Colonial Peoples: Solve the Problem of General Disarmament* (Moscow: Foreign Languages, 1962).

30. US Embassy, Moscow Tel. 617 to US Del. to UN, October 6, 1960, RG 59, 321.4/10-660; State Department Tel. 804 to US del to UN, November 1, 1960, RG 59, 321.4/10-2560. See also State Department Policy Information Statement IO-78, "The Colonial Issue in the United Nations General Assembly," November 28, 1960, Enclosure to Acting Secretary of State C. Douglas Dillon Circular Instruction CA-4808, November 29, 1960, RG 59, 511.00/11-2960.

31. John M. Steeves (FE) Memorandum to Wallner (IO), "Soviet Draft Declaration on the Granting of Independence to Colonial Countries and Peoples," October 10, 1960, RG 59, 321.4/10-1060.

32. Antonio Alvarez Restrepo (Colombia) Remarks to 929th Plenary Meeting of the General Assembly, November 30, 1960, UN Doc. A/PV.929, par. 81, 83; Francisco Milla Bermudez (Honduras) Remarks to 930th Plenary Meeting of the General Assembly, December 1, 1960, UN Doc. A/PV.930, par. 17. The Turkish, Japanese, Guatemalan, Filipino, and Irish delegations also spoke out against Soviet colonialism. See Verbatim Record of the 932nd, 933rd, and 935th Meetings of the General Assembly, December 2, 5, 1960, UN Docs. A/PV.932, 933, 935.

33. See Richard Wright, *The Color Curtain: A Report on the Bandung Conference* (New York: World, 1956).

34. "Declaration on the Granting of Independence to Colonial Countries and Peoples: Draft Resolution," November 29, 1960, UN Doc. A/L.323; Mongi Slim (Tunisia) Remarks to 929th Plenary Meeting of the General Assembly, November 30, 1960, UN Doc. A/PV.929, par. 28. See also Christopher J. Lee, *Making a World after Empire: The Bandung Moment and Its Political Afterlives* (Athens: Ohio University Press, 2010); and Burke, *Decolonization and the Evolution of International Human Rights,* esp. 35–58.

35. Roll-call voting records on the anticolonialism measures can be followed in Verbatim Record 947th Plenary Meeting of the General Assembly, December 14, 1960, UN Doc. A/PV.947, par. 1-163. The other states abstaining were Australia, Belgium, the Dominican Republic, France, Portugal, Spain, and South Africa.

36. Record of Telephone Calls, Thursday, December 8, 1960, Christian Herter Papers, Misc Memos, box 10, folder: Pres Tel Calls, 7/1959–1/20/1961, DDEL; Prime Minister Harold Macmillan to President Dwight Eisenhower, December 9, 1960, US Department of State, *FRUS, 1958–1960,* vol. 7, pt. 2, *Western Europe* (Washington, DC: US Government Printing Office, 1993), 876; Record of Telephone Calls, Friday, December 9, 1960, Herter Papers, Misc Memos, box 10, folder: Pres Tel Calls, 7/1959–1/20/1961, DDEL.

37. Wadsworth (US Mission to UN) Tel. 1775 to State Department, December 15, 1960, RG 59, 321.4/12-1560; William T. Nunley (EUR) Memorandum to Mr. Kohler (EUR), "UN Events during Your Absence," January 5, 1961, RG 59, 310/1-

561; Wadsworth (US Mission to UN) Tel. 1744 to State Department, December 14, 1960, RG 59, 321.4/12-1460.

38. Adlai Stevenson (US Representative, UN) Tel. 2182 to Secretary of State Dean Rusk, February 11, 1961, RG 59, 321.4/1–2261.

39. Foy D. Kohler (EUR) Memorandum to Mr. Cleveland (IO), "US Position at Resumed Session of the UN General Assembly on Establishment of Target Dates for Self-Determination by Dependent Territories," March 1, 1961, RG 59, Office of UN Political Affairs, Country Files, 1946–1968, box 1, folder: Resolution 1514.

40. State Department Policy Planning Council Draft Paper, "US Policy toward Anti-Colonialism," November 3, 1961, RG 59, Bureau of European Affairs—Subject File of the UN Advisor, 1955–1965, lot 69 D 486, box 1; Benjamin Gerig Memorandum for the Secretary of State, "New United States Approach on the Colonial Question in the United Nations," April 28, 1961, RG 59, Office of UN Political Affairs, Country Files, 1946–1968, box 1, folder: Colonial Issue.

41. Adlai Stevenson (US Representative, UN) Airgram A-273 to Department of State, April 19, 1962, US Department of State, *FRUS, 1961–1963*, vol. 25, *Organization of Foreign Policy; Information Policy; United Nations; Scientific Matters* (Washington, DC: US Government Printing Office, 2001), doc. 201, https://history.state.gov/historicaldocuments/frus1961-63v25/d201.

42. Pedersen Memorandum, "United States Policy as Seen from New York," June 15, 1962, NSF Series 5, box 311, folder: Subjects UN (United Nations) General 6/62, John F. Kennedy Library, Boston (hereafter JFKL).

43. State Department Paper, "United States Strategy at the 17th General Assembly," August 16, 1962, Enclosure to George W. Ball (Acting SecState) Memorandum for the President, "The Seventeenth General Assembly," August 16, 1962, RG 59, 320/8-1662.

44. "US Policy toward Anti-Colonialism" (n. 40 above); Rusk Statement to Senate Foreign Relations Committee, "Building the Frontiers of Freedom," *Department of State Bulletin* 44 (June 19, 1961): 948. See also Arthur M. Schlesinger Jr., Memorandum to the President's Special Assistant for National Security Affairs McGeorge Bundy, "The Rusk-Morrow Memorandum on 'An Effective Counter-theme to Peaceful Coexistence,'" June 19, 1961, National Security Council Action Memorandum no. 61, "An Effective Countertheme to 'Peaceful Coexistence,'" July 14, 1961, and Bureau of International Organization Affairs Memorandum for President Kennedy, "United States Strategy at the Sixteenth General Assembly," n.d. [fall 1961], *FRUS, 1961–1963*, vol. 25, *Organization of Foreign Policy; Information Policy; United Nations; Scientific Matters*, docs. 124, 126, 174, http://history.state.gov/historicaldocuments/frus1961-63v25/d124, http://history.state.gov/historical-documents/frus1961-63v25/d126, and http://history.state.gov/historicaldocuments/frus1961–63v25/d174.

45. Secretary of State Dean Rusk Memorandum for the President, "The 17th General Assembly: A Summary Round-Up," n.d. [late 1962], *FRUS, 1961–1963*, vol. 25, *Organization of Foreign Policy; Information Policy; United Nations; Scientific*

Matters, doc. 232, http://history.state.gov/historicaldocuments/frus1961-63v25/d232. For the importance of enlisting other states in the campaign to "plac[e] [the] Soviets on [the] defensive," see Department of State Tel. 769 to US Mission, UN, October 2, 1961, RG 59, 320/10-261.

46. Department of State Circular Airgram CA-2368, "Committee of 17 in the Seventeenth United Nations General Assembly," August 30, 1962, RG 59, 320/8-3062. See also Bureau of Intelligence and Research Memorandum RSB-148, "Soviet Tactics on Some Major Issues at the 17th UN General Assembly," August 27, 1962, *FRUS, 1961–1963,* vol. 25, *Organization of Foreign Policy; Information Policy; United Nations; Scientific Matters,* doc. 219, http://history.state.gov/historicaldocuments/frus1961-63v25/d219.

47. See Department of State Tel. 422 to US Mission at UN, August 13, 1962, *FRUS, 1961–1963,* vol. 25, *Organization of Foreign Policy; Information Policy; United Nations; Scientific Matters,* doc. 261, http://history.state.gov/historicaldocuments/frus1961-63v25/d261; Airgram CA-2368, "Committee of 17" (n. 46 above); and Department of State Paper, "First Session of the Committee of 24 (February 20–May 10, 1963)," [May 1963], *FRUS, 1961–1963,* vol. 25, *Organization of Foreign Policy; Information Policy; United Nations; Scientific Matters,* doc. 255.

48. See State Department Talking Paper, "US-UK Talks on Africa (December 4 & 5, 1962): Afro-Asian Voting Patterns in the UNGA," December 1, 1962, RG 59, Office of UN Political Affairs, Country Files, 1946–1968, box 4, folder: US-UK Talks; Evan Luard, *A History of the United Nations,* vol. 2, *The Age of Decolonization, 1955–1965* (New York: St. Martin's, 1989), 187–95; and James H. Mittelman, "Collective Decolonization and the U.N. Committee of 24," *Journal of Modern African Studies* 14 (March 1976): 41–64.

49. Harlan M. Cleveland (Assistant Secretary of State for International Organization Affairs) Memorandum to Secretary of State Dean Rusk, "Current Issues before the United Nations," November 27, 1963, *FRUS, 1961–1963,* vol. 25, *Organization of Foreign Policy; Information Policy; United Nations; Scientific Matters,* doc. 282, http://history.state.gov/historicaldocuments/frus1961-63v25/d282. See also David A. Kay, "The Politics of Decolonization: The New Nations and the United Nations Political Process," *International Organization* 21 (Autumn 1967): 786–811.

50. Cleveland Memorandum (n. 49 above).

51. For some of the literature linking racial concerns to foreign policy, see Mary L. Dudziak, *Cold War Civil Rights: Race and the Image of American Democracy* (Princeton, NJ: Princeton University Press, 2002); Carol Anderson, *Eyes Off the Prize: The United Nations and the African American Struggle for Human Rights, 1944–1955* (New York: Cambridge University Press, 2003); and Thomas Borstelmann, *The Cold War and the Color Line: American Race Relations in the Global Arena* (Cambridge, MA: Harvard University Press, 2003).

52. William Attwood (US Representative, UN), "Memorandum on Apartheid," November 7, 1963, Enclosure to Attwood Memorandum to McGeorge Bundy,

"Memorandum on Apartheid," November 8, 1963, NSF Series 5, box 311a, folder: UN (United Nations) General 10/63–11/63, JFKL.

53. Cleveland Memorandum (n. 49 above); George Ball (Acting Secretary of State) Memorandum to the President, "The Current Session of the United Nations General Assembly," December 13, 1963, *FRUS, 1961–1963,* vol. 25, *Organization of Foreign Policy; Information Policy; United Nations; Scientific Matters,* doc. 289, http://history.state.gov/historicaldocuments/frus1961–63v25/d289.

54. Cleveland Memorandum (n. 49 above). See also Department of State Paper, "United States Strategy at the 19th General Assembly," Enclosure to Dean Rusk Memorandum for the President, "Strategy for the Eighteenth General Assembly," August 30, 1963, NSF Series 5, box 311a, folder: Subjects UN (United Nations) General 9/1/63–9/8/63, JFKL.

7

One World?

Rethinking America's Margins, 1935–1945

Ryan Irwin

> Do you realize that we have now made the circuit of the world, and that every system is now a closed system, and that you can now alter nothing without altering the balance of everything, and that there are no more desert shores on which the jetsam of incomplete thought can rest undisturbed?
> —Halford Mackinder (1919)

On a cold afternoon in early autumn 1942, Wendell Willkie strolled quietly along the western side of the Volga River in Kuybyshev, Russia. Located eight hundred kilometers north of Stalingrad, where Nazi soldiers had commenced the siege that would change the course of World War II, the city served as an informal marker between the Soviet state and its eastern hinterland. Behind Willkie stretched the Zhiguli Mountains and the wheat fields of Eastern Europe; before him lay the steppe of Central Asia, extending across Russia's southern rim toward Mongolia. As Willkie walked among dockworkers, soldiers, and shepherds, his mind began to wander: "I could see, it seemed to me, [an] entire generation of men and women who had been destroyed, families that had been scattered, loyalties that had been broken, [and] the thousands who had died . . . in the name of revolution." The region, visibly remade by a confluence of urbanization and ideology that was just twenty-five years old, was now "composed almost entirely of people whose parents had no property, no education, and only a folk heritage." Surveying these surroundings, a conclusion slowly dawned on the young American: these people—without history, desperate for the trappings of a better, more modern life—would shape the fate of the postwar world.[1]

Willkie was in the midst of a forty-nine-day trip across Eurasia that took him from the Mediterranean through Russia and into China's interior. Although he had lost the US presidential election to Franklin Roosevelt in 1940, he now served his commander in chief as a roaming diplomat, meeting with world leaders, and promoting America's wartime interests. *One World,* the subsequent book about his travels, was part travelogue and part treatise, and it helped pioneer a new vocabulary about the world beyond US borders. "England and America are parts," Willkie announced on his return to the United States. "Russia and China, Egypt, Syria, and Turkey, Iraq, and Iran are also parts." "It is inescapable," therefore, "that there can be no peace for any part of the world unless the foundations of peace are made secure throughout all parts of the world." Washington, in his mind, needed to adopt a mind-set that matched the newly interdependent nature of global affairs. The outcome at Stalingrad mattered, but the stakes of this larger drama could be seen on the streets of Kuybyshev: "A great process has started which no man—certainly not Hitler—can stop. After centuries of ignorant and dull compliance, hundreds of millions of people in eastern Europe and Asia have opened the books. . . . They are no longer willing to be Eastern slaves for Western profits. They are beginning to know that men's welfare throughout the world is interdependent. They are resolved, as we must be, that there is no more place for imperialism within their own society than in the society of nations."[2]

At nearly the same moment in New Haven, Connecticut, a young professor at Yale University, Nicholas Spykman, worked fervently on his own vision of the "one world" idea. Spykman was dying of cancer, and his manuscript, which he must have known would be his last, had been presented in draft form to his peers a few months earlier, just as Willkie strolled along the Volga. His words echoed the rhetoric of his better-known contemporary. "The total of the earth's surface has, today, become a single field for the play of political forces," he wrote. Consequently: "The conditions of power on one continent are inevitably reflected in the distribution of power on another and the foreign policy of any state may be affected by events taking place throughout the world." In Spykman's formulation, however, US leaders needed to focus not on the people of Eurasia but on the possibility that a single state might emerge from this region to project power into both Europe and East Asia. Connecting his thoughts directly to those of the famed British geographer Halford Mackinder, Spykman concluded that the "rimlands"—the territory stretching from the Mediterranean through Asia, which Willkie had traversed in late 1942—would be the focal point of global affairs after the Second World War: "If there is to be a slogan for the power politics of [this] Old World, it must be 'Who controls the rimland rules Eurasia; who rules Eurasia controls the destinies of the world.' . . . [I]t is the co-operation of British, Russian, and United States land and sea power that will control the European littoral."[3]

Spykman and Willkie were born months apart in the early 1890s, and they died in 1943 and 1944, respectively, one of cancer, the other of an unexpected heart attack. Their views dramatized the contested possibilities of American internationalism at the twentieth century's midpoint. Willkie spoke in the language of populist anti-imperialism and viewed the war as a chance to replace European imperialism with cosmopolitan Wilsonianism; Spykman saw events through the prism of geopolitics. Yet the two shared a vocabulary of the world as a single unit of analysis—to be studied holistically—and agreed that the United States needed to lead global affairs in the postwar era. In both their accounts, new communication technologies had eliminated the logic of US isolationism, and, while they calibrated the balance between territory and people differently, they shared the conclusion that Southern and Central Eurasia would be the central battlefield of American globalism after World War II. Washington's actions in this critical region would anchor its policies in the so-called Old World.

This chapter explores the intellectual scaffolding that supported these conclusions. My analysis is not comprehensive; it is designed merely as a partial exploration of some Americans who wrestled with the boundaries of American power at a time of rapid change. Using the community that surrounded Spykman as a microcosm—particularly the well-connected scholars who worked under the auspices of the Yale Institute of International Studies (YIIS) from the late 1930s through the mid-1940s—the chapter explores the mental maps deployed in the debate over US world power. It unfolds in three sections, explicating some of the baseline assumptions at YIIS before turning attention to themes of geography, institutions, and power. In later years, Cold War social scientists framed this conversation as a fight between idealism and realism, emphasizing the gap between Willkie's high-minded rhetoric and Spykman's unsentimental realpolitik, but such distinctions became potent only in the second half of the twentieth century. Reading the YIIS conversation forward—placing it within a milieu of midcentury policy thinkers—hints at the elastic nature of liberal internationalism at the century's midpoint. Willkie and Spykman were participants in a wide-ranging conversation about Washington's influence along its margins, and their differences, while important, do not erase a fundamental point of agreement: the geographic horizon line of American foreign relations.

Common Assumptions

Could man control the social forces of modern life? The question captured the imagination of many scholars in the early twentieth century, especially Nicholas Spykman. Born in the Netherlands at the highpoint of European imperialism, Spykman developed a worldview that flowed from a dramatic sense of the present. "Western civilization has reached a crisis," he wrote in the mid-1920s. "Society, the great superindividual structure of man's own making, has become so large, so intricate, so complex, so independent of its maker that it threatens to overwhelm him and to make him the victim of his own creation." Although Spykman had avoided the horrors of World War I, spending his twenties instead in what was then the Dutch East Indies, his words captured the anxieties of his generation. Events moved quickly in the early twentieth century, perhaps too quickly, and while interconnection had bolstered the West's power—through new communication and military technologies and cross-border migration and trade—it had done so at the expense of individual autonomy and social stability. Everything seemed to be bound up in everything else, making contemporary leaders "slaves of [a] great leviathan" that they could not comprehend, let alone control.[4]

In the face of this world, Spykman drifted toward the field of sociology. Settling at the University of California after World War I to pursue a doctorate in political science, his research interests moved between non-Western nationalism and sociological methodology. The connection, in his mind, was self-evident. With proper effort, scholars could understand and control the social structures of modern life. All that was needed was "an earnest desire" for comprehension "on the part of the individuals composing society, a consensus of opinion among the majority with regard to the ends to be obtained, and an adequate knowledge with regard to the means to these ends." Spykman tackled the obvious question— what defined "adequate knowledge"—in his first book, *The Social Theory of George Simmel,* which interpreted the work of a prominent yet rarely translated German sociologist who had spent his career wrestling with the methodological intricacies of studying society and culture. Simmel's scholarship, for Spykman, not only equaled the pathbreaking work of Émile Durkheim and Max Weber but also exemplified the rigor necessary to create usable knowledge. By rejecting the notion of a societal zeitgeist— a shared "social mind" with tangible ontological existence—Simmel illuminated society as a set of interlocking parts in motion. "Group unity is . . . a functional unity, not a substantial unity," Spykman explained in 1925. If conceptualized as "a process [rather than] a thing," modern life—the condition we have come to associate with globalization—could be broken into component parts and then diagnosed, understood, and controlled by experts.[5] For Spykman, this project was the raison d'être of modern sociology.

Spykman's move from the University of California to Yale gave him a larger canvas to work with. He arrived in New Haven in 1925 and successfully lobbied the university to hire several like-minded peers, first Arnold Wolfers and Frederick Dunn, and later Samuel Flagg Bemis, Percy Corbett, and A. Whitney Griswold. Having emerged from a common generational milieu, most of these men agreed that "the pursuit of panaceas" through natural law "had to give way before the hard labor of rigorous political analysis" and saw Spykman's brand of sociological analysis— in contrast to "the traditional concentration on a legal or institutional approach"—as the key to making sense of the world they had inherited together. A full analysis of this dichotomy is outside my parameters here, but this attack on natural law was critically important.[6] It oriented Spykman's efforts and guided the group's early agenda. Their argument to the university was straightforward. If Yale collected "a group of scholars with complementary skills" to work "together in the same place" toward the common goal of explaining society's different moving parts, it would be possible to develop a vocabulary to explain the global condition of the early twentieth century.[7] Dubbed the "State Department" by colleagues and students, Spykman's cohort quickly came to dominate the university's intellectual life. The historian Robin Winks later reflected:

> A self-styled "Tory-Liberal" with two doctorates, Wolfers was [the] natural mediator. Tall, aristocratic, well-dressed, he glittered when he walked, and his crisp, light voice turned quickly from person to person, rather like a searchlight. . . . A bit deaf, Dunn, [in comparison,] mastered the art of agreeing with one before a sentence was finished, replying with a touch of Celtic crispness, by which those who didn't know him thought him always on the verge of taking offense. . . . [They were a sharp contrast to] the very Dutch Spykman, who sought to forestall arguments by beginning his sentences with the declaration, "Of course this is so." Here was a group with a capacity for controlled tension, hard work (and grace) under pressure, and a worldly knowledge of languages.[8]

For Spykman, systemizing this group's insights was the key to widening sociology's influence among elite Americans. In 1935, he received a $100,000 grant from the Rockefeller Foundation to create the YIIS. The institute would not only build consensus about Washington's national imperatives, he explained, but also "search for means toward [these] specific ends," utilizing a methodology akin "to engineering or medicine" to illuminate the "behavior of man manifest in [the] behavior of states." Again, this "sociological approach" was "distinguished from the legal approach to international relations," and it promised to yield "generalized knowledge rather than particular information about passing situations." With the West at a historic watershed, "officials beyond the clerical level" now faced "invariably novel" questions that could no longer "be disposed of simply by reference to past events." Moreover, the "unsettled state of Europe and Asia" ensured that "creative work based on impartial research" had to come from the United States and that any "future peace policy" would be "very largely determined by the attitude" of America's intelligentsia. All this presented Yale with an opportunity. By teaching future leaders *how* to think, the university—with Rockefeller Foundation support—might cultivate leaders with the power to shape social forces at home and predict human behavior abroad. "Upon the completion of their training," Spykman wrote, "[Yale students would be] not merely social philosophers who agree with Mr. Stalin or Mr. Hoover, but experts who have learned a technique that can be used by either."[9]

This premise—that rigorous thinking would uncover usable truths about modern life—was not unique to Yale in the middle decades of the twentieth century. In part, it elaborated an older European discourse about expertise's relationship to political power. In the North Atlantic world, for instance, the rise of the progressive movement had promulgated the view that reform-minded experts could temper the excesses of industrial capitalism, specifically urban blight, class conflict, and immigrant strife. In the colonized world, too, planners were attempting to ameliorate regional unrest—compensating for the violence of European conquest—through education programs, infrastructure projects, and land reforms. Although this project differed across regions, it was connected by a common view that elites with specialized knowledge could identify, understand, and resolve the problems stemming from modern industrial capitalism.[10] Like the Council on Foreign Relations and the Institute for Government Research (later renamed the Brookings Institution), Spykman's YIIS reflected this mind-set and expanded its ambitions, promising to deliver nonpartisan insights to government planners so that America's elites might better calibrate means with ends and control the underlying social processes that characterized modern life.[11] More than any specific argument or policy proposal, this way of thinking—sitting at the heart of the New Deal and other state-led experiments throughout the 1930s—animated the YIIS intellectual agenda and formed the motif of the group's engagement with American internationalism.

Common Geographies

Under Spykman's directorship between 1935 and 1940, the institute built bridges in several directions. As master of Yale's Pierson College, Wolfers turned his home into "a center for campus entertainment second only to the president's residence" and hosted a cross section of statesmen, policymakers, and opinion leaders, including Dean Acheson, George Kennan, Hanson Baldwin, and Grayson Kirk, among others.[12] YIIS members, in turn, lectured regularly at the State and War Departments in Washington, DC, and participated in discussions at the Council on Foreign Relations in New York City. On campus, the group's workshops featured a combination of professors and practitioners and covered topics ranging from nationalism in the Western Hemisphere to geopolitics in Central Eurasia. In the public sphere, YIIS pioneered a collaborative research model, spearheaded by Yale faculty, and backed by a team of student researchers.[13] Some international relations insiders later attached the label *power school* to YIIS's efforts, but Spykman and his colleagues explicitly saw themselves engaged in the "study of the strategy of peace." They hoped to move beyond the simplistic framework that pitted isolationists against internationalists or lauded the merits of idealism versus those of realism.[14] The institute posed large questions: What determined state behavior? What constituted good foreign policy? What were Washington's core interests? And developed answers that eschewed neither international organizations nor military coercion. Groping toward objective rationalism, it saw as its end goal a durable consensus about America's "proper" role in the world.[15]

Two organizing debates framed YIIS's investigation of the strategy of peace. The first was geographic: Where were the margins of American power? In one of the first books sponsored by the YIIS, *A Navy Second to None,* George T. Davis tackled this question by providing a comprehensive overview of recent US naval policy, explicating both the intellectual impact of Alfred Thayer Mahan on US policy and the economic imperatives underlying Washington's military-industrial complex. Davis did not like what he saw. "The American people live in the safest country on the face of the earth," he announced in 1940. "It is important that Americans realize this situation and free themselves from the hobgoblin fantasies which have so often figured in our debates on naval policy." For him, everything turned on the "Asia question." Davis argued that American military entanglements in China sapped resources from the theater that truly mattered: Latin America. Already within Washington's historic and geographic sphere of influence, the Western Hemisphere was the ballast of US foreign policy, an arena that reflected American legal and political norms in a way that contrasted with the naked imperialism of Germany and Japan. With "sea power adequate to guard [this] New World," it seemed unlikely that any great power would "make any threat to our island empire," Davis contended. "Let us not squander the wealth of our people upon needless armament which may jeopardize the stability of our institutions or tempt us to pursue the will-o'-the-wisp of economic ambitions or power politics in distant parts of the world."[16]

Pan-Americanism also seeped into the writings of Samuel Flagg Bemis and A. Whitney Griswold. Bemis's YIIS-sponsored *The Latin American Policy of the United States,* for instance, reified Davis's depiction of the "American hemisphere," coupling a lengthy explanation of North America's social advancements with a sanguine assessment of Washington's record in Central and South America. Bemis celebrated the emergence of the "absolute nonintervention" doctrine and chided the "myth" of economic imperialism.[17] Retracing Davis's steps, Griswold similarly argued that Mahan's recommendations had proved "correct upon the defensive and incorrect upon the offensive," meaning that American leaders were wise to build up a hemispheric network but foolish to follow Mahan's teachings "to their imperialist periphery" in Asia.[18] Griswold's *Far Eastern Policy of the United States,* in turn, explored the factors that led American missionaries and policymakers into East Asia in the first place, lingering on the development, contradictions, and evolution of the so-called Open Door policy. The contrast with Washington's Latin America policy was stark:

> From 1900 to 1932 American efforts . . . had passed through a number of cycles, all ending in failure. With what consequences?—jeopardizing the security of America's own territorial integrity . . . encouraging Chinese patriots to hope for, if not count on, a type of American support that never materialized; obstructing the most profitable trend of American commerce and investment in the Far East which since 1900 had been toward Japan, not China; rendering the exclusion of Japanese immigrants, in Japan's eyes, the addition of insult to injury, and the whole having a baleful effect on every phase of Japanese-American relations; stimulating naval rivalry between the two nations; involving the United States in European politics via the backdoor in Eastern Asia.[19]

The takeaway seemed obvious. The geography of peace was hemispheric, and, while prudence demanded that American leaders stay wary of events in Eurasia, wisdom pointed toward a New World order—a community of independent states, interconnected under Washington's leadership—that would serve as a beacon for the so-called Old World.[20] The events of 1941 did not end this mind-set. Spykman's widely read (YIIS-funded) *America's Strategy in World Politics,* published in 1942, was first and foremost a celebration of Pan-Americanism, with nearly four hundred pages devoted to the economic, cultural, and political nature of US relations in Latin America. The book's novelty stemmed from its support of an offensive war against Germany and Japan. "Hemisphere defense is no defense at all," Spykman wrote. Although the central priority of the United States remained "hold[ing] South America," the Axis entente—a step toward a new Eurasian power structure—meant that the American hemisphere was now threatened on its Atlantic and Pacific flanks. In a world where everything was connected, the smartest response was, according to Spykman, to defeat Germany and Japan in Europe and Asia, respectively, and use America's military power to create a political system that halted the rise of a single Eurasian hegemon and legitimized Washington's sole authority over the Western Hemisphere.[21]

For Spykman, Mackinder's ideas were a means toward this end. Although Mahan had developed a language of naval globalism in the 1890s, Mackinder was the first scholar to "detail the relations between land and sea power on a truly global scale," as Spykman put it. By illuminating the tensions between politics and geography, he had shown modern statecraft to be a competition for the Old World's heartland: the region stretching from the Black Sea across Siberia into East Asia. Spykman expanded this insight in a series of articles and lectures during the late 1930s and early 1940s that delineated the world's major climate and rainfall zones, wheat and rice production sites, and coal and iron deposits. Viewed through an environmental prism, the world's natural power centers came into relief as "the Atlantic coastal region of North America, the European littoral and the Far Eastern coastland of Eurasia, together with a fourth and minor sector, India, which may increase in power in the future." Like Mackinder, Spykman saw Central and Southern Eurasia as the main battleground between these power centers. Whether Washington liked it or not, the Old World was two and a half times larger than the New World with ten times the population and almost equal potential for energy output. The US hold over the Americas was contingent on "prevent[ing] the unification of the Old World centers of power in a coalition hostile to her own interests."[22]

Common Tools

All this points toward the second axis of debate within the institute: the tools of peace. For Spykman, the central failure of the Versailles order was that it "reverse[d] the historical trend toward larger political units" that reflected these natural power centers. Article X of the League of Nations covenant, which promised that every state within the international community would unite against any form of aggressive behavior anywhere, was a "pious fraud" that ignored the "discrepancy between the legal fiction of universality and the political fact of regionalism." Most governments, Spykman argued, had "little interest in the territorial security of states on far-away continents, and distance restricted the possibility of exerting effective restraints on aggressors."[23] Airpower was not the panacea of this problem. "The silver birds soaring against a blue sky may be a symbol of freedom, of the conquest of space," but planes were "bound by invisible strings to their base of operations and beyond that the wooden derricks in the Texas oil fields, the concrete mountains of the power dams, and the bauxite deposits along the muddy rivers of the Guianas." The United States needed to pursue "the same formula by which her power [had] been extended to the Bahamas and South America, that is, by means of the leasing of land for the establishment of [military] bases without the transfer of sovereignty over the territory."[24] This approach—cast as distinct from European-style imperialism—would be legitimized through regional institutions, following the model of the Pan American Union, and would then lead to a more workable style of collective security. Spykman's proposals did not "preclude the eventual development of [wider] federal patterns of political organization"; they merely recommended checks and balances in the short term that accurately reflected (and balanced) the world's true power centers.[25]

These arguments hinted at a wider conversation about international law at Yale. Before arriving in New Haven in the mid-1930s, Dunn, Wolfers, and Corbett had spent their formative years not only teaching at John Hopkins University, the Hochschule für Politik, and McGill University, respectively, but also practicing law at the League of Nations and

the US State Department. Like Spykman, they embraced sociology—
"sociological jurisprudence," specifically—and traded the theoretical for-
malism of natural law for an approach that revealed the political and
social context around legal decisions. Viewed in sociological terms, international law was recast as a reflection of Spykman's geopolitical realism.
"Does this mean there can be nothing but anarchy in a world still organized on national lines?" Wolfers asked in the mid-1930s. "Does it mean
that all efforts to promote peace [through law] . . . are doomed from
the outset and unworthy of serious attention?" The emphatic answer was
no. Conflict's form mattered as much as its location, and, while international law would never abolish war, it provided an irreplaceable lever to
influence how states engaged one another in a global arena. Law's utility,
in other words, stemmed from its ability to suggest norms of acceptable
behavior. Rejecting Spykman's proposal that regional unions alone would
accomplish this end, Wolfers, Dunn, and Corbett attempted to rehabili-
tate the League of Nations as an invaluable "meeting-place and forum for
regular consultation." Its "universality" remained a "hindrance to common action," but dialogue, as a functional end in itself, was essential.
Without the backing of a robust and legitimate international institution,
legal structure—a touchstone of political exchange—would be an empty
vessel.[26]

For its advocates, this approach built logically on Spykman's analysis
while charting a middle way between fascism and communism. Dunn's
Peaceful Change and Wolfers's *Britain and France between Two Wars,* published just before and after the outbreak of World War II, examined the
problems facing the League at its twenty-year anniversary. The authors
articulated comparable conclusions. Focusing on raw materials, population density, and industrial production, Dunn cast the German-Japanese
entente as an inevitable response to geopolitical reality and argued that
League diplomacy alone could alter the existing order in a peaceful manner. At the global level, the organization could replace imperial war with
legal procedure, "harmoniz[ing] the interests in trade and investment of
the nationals of the great states . . . with the interests of nationals of
the lesser and non-European states" in a way that balanced local sovereignty with the demographic needs of powerful states.[27] At the regional
level, the League gave diplomats a way to consider "possible solutions in a
calmer atmosphere," one in which they could "point out the general inter-

est before individual national interests [became] too firmly set."[28] Wolfers agreed and claimed that it had been British and French incompetence—specifically, their unwillingness to make Weimar Germany a legitimate member of the international community—that facilitated Hitler's rise to power. The problem, in Wolfers's mind, was not the League but the contradictory policies of its two most vocal members, specifically, France's commitment to creating an alliance that undermined Germany's support for the status quo and Britain's unwillingness make this alliance a genuine deterrent against German belligerence.[29] With Washington, Moscow, Berlin, and Tokyo on the sidelines, the shortsightedness of these policies went unchecked through the 1930s, leading Wolfers to an obvious conclusion: international institutions were only as good as the governments that controlled their agendas.

Dunn extended these arguments into the public arena during the early 1940s. As YIIS's second director, he shifted resources from book-length projects to confidential memoranda that summarized the group's monthly seminar, "Where Is the World Going?" Usually running between ten and fifteen pages, these papers advanced theses about current events in a format that was easily accessible to scholars, policymakers, journalists, industrialists, and financiers. The topics ranged from Britain's future as the junior partner in the Atlantic alliance to China's potential as a first-ranking power, but they echoed familiar themes about the form and focus of America's world role. In discussing the future of international order, for instance, William Fox charted a middle path between Spykman, Dunn, and Wolfers: "Ten years of the Good Neighbor policy [had] shown how an organization pattern—the much ballyhooed inter-American conferences—[could] tacitly permit great power preponderance while [preserving] publicly the amenities of ceremonial equality." Adopting this approach at the international level would enable the "super-powers"—a term coined by Fox to describe the United States, the British Empire, and the Soviet Union—to take ownership of regional security problems without jettisoning an institutional architecture that fostered "habits of collaboration" with small nations.[30] As the war turned in America's favor in 1943, a conceptual synthesis emerged at Yale. "The sensitivity of the weaker powers to anything that suggests disregard of their equal rights or their dignity may seem at times to be excessive and is often extremely annoying," Wolfers wrote that year. But "privileges accorded the super-powers in one particular direction"—in the form of postwar military bases and security pacts—had to be matched with an institution that allowed "lesser powers" to "find real satisfaction" and "ceremonial equality" in "such matters as public health, relief or communications."[31]

By the end of the war, two conclusions reigned in New Haven. First, the United States had to become a transhemispheric power. The competing internationalisms that marked early disagreements within Yale—with Davis's fortress America pitted against Spykman's Eurasian rimland—gave way under Dunn's stewardship to a new sense that Spykman was correct. To prevent America's geographic encirclement, Washington had to embrace a more expansive understanding of its spatial boundaries and work with London and Moscow to shape events in the world's great borderland: Southern and Central Eurasia. Second, Washington needed to reform the League of Nations fundamentally. For YIIS members, American planners had to construct a responsive institution that reflected geographic reality, acknowledged the difference between large and small states, and replaced universal collective security with a workable police system. If these three goals were met through a legal system that limited the functional autonomy of the great powers, the result would be an institution that worked. The United States, the British Empire, and the Soviet Union could collaborate to curtail another cataclysmic war yet bind themselves to a superstructure that reflected the norms of the countries at their margins. It was a system that both Willkie and Spykman could support.

Common Legacy

But was anyone listening? In Dunn's words, his tenure, specifically his memoranda policy, was a "striking success." Requests for the essays grew exponentially after December 1941, "purely on the basis of unsolicited demand," and the papers were "carefully read not only by scholars, but also by policy-makers and their advisers."[32] Sumner Wells, Alger Hiss, George Kennan, Viscount Halifax, and John Foster Dulles asked regularly for YIIS memoranda, and Walter Lippmann told the Rockefeller Foundation that the series was "a most compelling presentation" of conclusions he was toying with himself that would eventually culminate in his landmark *U.S. Foreign Policy*.[33] (Subtitled *Shield of the Republic,* the book popularized ideas that had become commonplace at Yale by 1944.)

Several American officials celebrated the memoranda as "the best being produced anywhere in the world," and British diplomats praised the YIIS's "realistic approach," similarly concluding that the documents were "the very best productions . . . [coming] out of America."[34] YIIS's David Rowe and Grayson Kirk served as US representatives at Dumbarton Oaks and San Francisco, and nearly half of YIIS's members attended the UN Conference on International Order in San Francisco in 1945. By the end of the war, Yale president Charles Seymour was bold enough to announce that the institute's ability to stay in "constant conference with government officials" had given it unparalleled influence over the "currents of active diplomacy." Yale's complete "independen[ce] [from] government" provided YIIS faculty with the freedom "to attack delicate issues which the diplomats themselves would fear to raise."[35] For Seymour, the institute had become the quintessential think tank.

Yet things unraveled quickly. The group's zenith came immediately after World War II as it deepened its connections with the US State Department and launched *World Politics,* which quickly became one of the most widely circulated international relations journals in the United States. YIIS's conclusions took on new urgency as US-Soviet relations soured in the late 1940s. However, Griswold's 1951 appointment as Yale's sixteenth president sparked an internal feud over the inherent merits of group-led, policy-oriented research. Having worked alongside institute members since the mid-1930s, Yale's new president turned against the YIIS's founding premise during the war—bristling perhaps at the growing star power of its more famous faculty—and worked quickly to push Dunn and his colleagues out of New Haven under the pretense that Yale had to focus resources on undergraduate education.[36] Princeton absorbed most YIIS members in the early 1950s, creating the Center of International Studies within the Woodrow Wilson School, and members of the group moved on to different pursuits at the Institute for War and Peace Studies at Columbia and the Center for International Studies at the Massachusetts Institute of Technology.[37] Dunn, Wolfers, Fox, Corbett, and YIIS's other faculty continued to enjoy prolific careers, but the cohesion of their time at Yale was not repeated. For a brief and critical moment—as the world itself seemed to remake itself in the face of current events—they groped together for insights about political power and articulated common conclusions about the geography and tools of American world power.

The YIIS was not a lone voice in the late 1930s and the early 1940s. With Rockefeller backing, Edward Mead Earle bolstered the field of security studies at MIT and Princeton—countering YIIS's State Department connections with even deeper relations at the War Department—and the University of Chicago became a nexus of social science research in these years, anchored by such luminaries as Harold Lasswell, Hans Morgenthau, Frederick Schuman, and Quincy Wright, among others.[38] Nor did the institute determine America's subsequent grand strategy in the Cold War. Several institutions and ideas competed to shape and legitimize the scope and content of US foreign relations during the late 1940s. The YIIS's importance stemmed from its place as a microcosm that reflected on the contours of midcentury liberal internationalism. In context, the group's writings revealed the middle space between Wendell Willkie and Nicholas Spykman, a space replete with gray hues and complex arguments about Pan America's past and Eurasia's future. Self-determination and ceremonial equality blended as constitutive concepts within this space, creating shared assumptions about the institutions that established (and policed) habits of exchange at the international level. The YIIS's conclusions anticipated many of the ideas in Hans Morgenthau's landmark 1948 *Politics among Nations*[39]—a canonical text among Cold War realists—and exposed the clumsiness of later binaries that cast the United Nations as an idealist project and dramatized the space between isolationists and interventionists. None of the scholars at YIIS questioned the innate importance of international institutions; they debated the best way to calibrate international law with the lessons of modern sociology. Similarly, none of the scholars advanced an isolationist policy in the years before World War II; they merely disagreed over Washington's interests outside the Western Hemisphere.

This look at the YIIS provides a mere glimpse of US policy thinking between 1935 and 1945. But it highlights the scholarly vocabulary that accompanied a wider debate about America's role in the postwar world. Often placed on different ends of the intellectual spectrum, Wendell Willkie and Nicholas Spykman—like so many others—shared complementary, reinforcing views about the spatial scope and political instruments of US power. Born at the end of the nineteenth century into a world dominated by industrial imperialism, they had together inherited a flawed political order based on universal natural law.[40] While the two men used different words, their ideas pointed toward a sociological alternative where America's political and intellectual authority would be extended through regional security pacts and collaborative institutions—where America would adapt itself to the world that was. This mind-set, reflected and formalized at YIIS, formed the central pillar of the emerging UN system. America's full-throated commitment to this new, pragmatic organization—and its willingness to see Eurasia as a vital battlefield of American globalism—was neither preordained nor uncontested. It was the product of a layered conversation that evolved among US elites in the late 1930s and early 1940s. Understanding this conversation provides contemporary scholars with a way in which to better appreciate the changing nature of America's margins in the Cold War and beyond.

Notes

1. *Prefaces to Peace: A Symposium Consisting of the Following: One World by Wendell L. Willkie, The Problems of a Lasting Peace by Herbert Hoover and Hugh Gibson, The Price of Free World Victory by Henry A. Wallace, and Blue-Print for Peace by Sumner Welles* (New York: Simon & Schuster/Doubleday, Doran/Keynal & Hitchcock/Columbia University Press, 1943), 44–46.

2. Ibid., 146–47.

3. Nicholas John Spykman, *The Geography of Peace* (New York: Harcourt, 1944), 35, 43.

4. Nicholas J. Spykman, *The Social Theory of Georg Simmel* (Chicago: University of Chicago Press, 1925), v. For some interesting context, see Martti Koskenniemi, *The Gentle Civilizer of Nations: The Rise and Fall of International Law* (Cambridge: Cambridge University Press, 2001); and Martin Geyer and Johannes Paulmann, eds., *The Mechanics of Internationalism: Culture, Society, and Politics from the 1840s to the First World War* (Oxford: Oxford University Press, 2001).

5. Spykman, *The Social Theory of Georg Simmel*, xxxviii, 264.

6. Frederick Sherwood Dunn, "The Growth of the Yale Institute of International Studies," November 7, 1950, folder 4949, box 417, Yale Institute of International Studies Records, Yale University Manuscripts and Archives (hereafter YUMA). There is some excellent new scholarship on this topic, including Koskenniemi, *The Gentle Civilizer of Nations;* Antony Anghie, *Imperialism, Sovereignty and the Making of International Law* (Cambridge: Cambridge University Press, 2007); and R. B. J. Walker, *After the World, Before the Globe* (London: Routledge, 2009).

7. Dunn, "The Growth of the Yale Institute of International Studies."

8. Robin W. Winks, *Cloak and Gown: Scholars in the Secret War, 1939–1961* (New Haven, CT: Yale University Press, 1987), 41–42.

9. Memorandum from Nicholas Spykman to the Rockefeller Foundation, n.d., folder 47, box 7, Yale Institute of International Studies Records, YUMA. See also Program for the Period of July 1, 1941–June 30, 1944, folder 47, box 7, Yale Institute of International Studies Records.

10. For introduction of themes, see Frederick Cooper and Randall Packard, eds., *International Development and the Social Sciences: Essays on the History and Politics of Knowledge* (Berkeley and Los Angeles: University of California Press, 1997); David Ekbladh, *The Great American Mission: Modernization and the Construction of an American World Order* (Princeton, NJ: Princeton University Press, 2010); Fred Kaplan, *Wizards of Armageddon* (Stanford, CA: Stanford University Press, 1991); Thomas McCraw, *Prophets of Regulation: Charles Francis Adams, Louis D. Brandeis, James M. Landis, Alfred E. Kahn* (Cambridge, MA: Harvard University Press, 1984); and Daniel Rodgers, *Atlantic Crossings: Social Politics in a Progressive Age* (Cambridge, MA: Harvard University Press, 1998).

11. For introduction of themes, see, among others, Donald Abelson, *American Think-Tanks and Their Role in U.S. Foreign Policy* (London: Macmillan, 1996); Edward Berman, *The Influence of the Carnegie, Ford, and Rockefeller Foundations on American Foreign Policy: The Ideology of Philanthropy* (Albany: State University of New York Press, 1983); Donald Critchlow, *Brookings Institution, 1916–1952: Expertise and the Public Interest in a Democratic Society* (DeKalb: Northern Illinois University Press, 1985); Inderjeet Parmar, *Foundations of the American Century: The Ford, Carnegie, and Rockefeller Foundations in the Rise of American Power* (New York: Columbia University Press, 2012); and Michael Wala, *The Council on Foreign Relations and American Foreign Policy in the Early Cold War* (Providence, RI: Berghahn, 1994).

12. Winks, *Cloak and Gown*, 42–43; Parmar, *Foundations of the American Century,* 72–73.

13. The Influence of the Yale Institute of International Studies, 1948, folder 38, box 7, Report for the Year, 1943–44, and Report for the Year, 1944–45, folder 28, box 5, Yale Institute of International Studies Records.

14. William Olson and A. J. R. Groom, *International Relations Then and Now: Origins and Trends in Interpretation* (New York: Taylor & Francis, 1991), 99; Memorandum from Nicholas Spykman to the Rockefeller Foundation (n. 12 above).

15. For general histories of YIIS, see Paulo J. B. Ramos, "The Role of the Yale Institute of International Studies in the Construction of United States National Security Ideology, 1935–1951" (Ph.D. diss., University of Manchester, 2003); and Emily Bowersock Hill, "American Intellectuals and International Politics in the Interwar Years" (Ph.D. diss., Yale University, 1998), esp. chap. 5.

16. George T. Davis, *A Navy Second to None: The Development of Modern American Naval Policy* (New York: Harcourt, 1940), 430, 432.

17. Samuel Flagg Bemis, *The Latin American Policy of the United States: An Historical Interpretation* (New York: Harcourt, 1943).

18. A. Whitney Griswold, "The Influence of History upon Sea Power: A Com-

ment on American Naval Policy," *Journal of the American Military Institute* 4, no. 1 (Spring 1940): 1–7, 6.

19. Alfred Whitney Griswold, *Far Eastern Policy of the United States* (New York: Harcourt, 1938), 467.

20. For interesting context, see Mark Gilderhus, *Pan American Visions: Woodrow Wilson in the Western Hemisphere, 1913–1921* (Tucson: University of Arizona Press, 1986).

21. Nicholas J. Spykman, *America's Strategy in World Politics: The United States and the Balance of Power* (New York: Harcourt, 1942), 446–48.

22. Spykman, *The Geography of Peace*, 35, 45, 33, 45.

23. Nicholas John Spykman, "Frontiers, Security, and International Organization," *Geographical Review* 32, no. 3 (July 1942): 436–47, 442–43.

24. Spykman, *The Geography of Peace*, 47, 58.

25. Spykman, *America's Strategy in World Politics*, 471–72.

26. Arnold Wolfers, "National Foreign Policies and the Strategy of Peace," *Pacific Affairs* 7, no. 2 (June 1934): 139–52, 141, 150.

27. This point is made most forcefully in Frederick Sherwood Dunn, *Protection of Nationals: A Study in the Application of International Law* (Baltimore: John Hopkins University Press, 1932), 355–58.

28. Frederick Sherwood Dunn, *Peaceful Change: A Study of International Procedure* (New York: Council on Foreign Relations, 1937), 151.

29. Arnold Wolfers, *Britain and France between Two Wars: Conflicting Strategies of Peace from Versailles to World War II* (New York: Harcourt, 1940).

30. William T. R. Fox, "Anglo-American Relations in the Post-War World," May 1, 1943, Yale Institute of International Studies Confidential Memoranda 1–10, YUMA. Fox was not alone in articulating this argument, of course. By the mid-1940s, George Kennan had adopted the "spheres of influence" prescript, and Maksim Litvinov, who served as the Soviet foreign commissar until Vyacheslav Molotov took his place in spring 1939, advocated a sphere-of-influence-style postwar allotment of geographic authority.

31. Arnold Wolfers, "The Small Powers and the Enforcement of Peace," August 1, 1943, Yale Institute of International Studies Confidential Memoranda 1–10.

32. The Influence of the Yale Institute of International Studies (n. 3 above), 3.

33. Report for the Year, 1944–45 (n. 18 above); Lippmann quoted in Hill, "American Intellectuals and International Politics," 289. See also Walter Lippmann, *U.S. Foreign Policy: Shield of the Republic* (Boston: Little, Brown, 1943).

34. Untitled and undated document, folder 65, box 8, Yale Institute of International Studies Records; Playfair to Coulson, August 19, 1943, FO 371/35397, British National Archives.

35. "Seymour Sees Youth Training as Vital Need," *New Haven Journal Courier*, December 8, 1944, folder 7, box 1, Yale Institute of International Studies Records.

36. Clippings, *Yale Herald*, April 23, 1951, folder 90, box 6, Arnold Wolfers Papers, YUMA. For further explanation, see Hill, "American Intellectuals and

International Politics," 287, speculating that Griswold felt spurned by some members of YIIS after the publication of *Far Eastern Policy of the United States*.

37. Ramos, "The Role of the Yale Institute," 132.

38. David Ekbladh, "Present at the Creation: Edward Mead Earle and the Depression-Era Origins of Security Studies," *International Security* 36, no. 3 (Winter 2011/2012): 107–41; Parmar, *Foundations of the American Century*, chaps. 2–3; Hill, "American Intellectuals and International Politics," chaps. 4–5.

39. Hans Morgenthau, *Politics among Nations: The Struggle for Power and Peace* (New York: Knopf, 1948).

40. Mark Mazower, *Governing the World: The History of an Idea* (New York: Penguin, 2012), esp. chaps. 3–6.

8

Accidental Diplomats

The Influence of American Evangelical Missionaries on US Relations with the Congo during the Early Cold War Period, 1959–1963

Philip Dow

In August 1959, the newly appointed CIA chief of station was talking with a colleague in Washington about his upcoming tour in the Belgian Congo. While aware that all was not well, the unmistakable impression Larry Devlin was given of the Congo was one of a generally placid "diplomatic backwater." "There are a lot of black-tie dinners," warned his colleague. "Take two tropical dinner jackets so you can have one at the cleaners at all times. And, by the way, you'll be on the golf course by two o'clock every afternoon."[1] As things turned out, Devlin would not have much time for golf. By the time he arrived in July 1960, the once sleepy colony had already begun a startling descent into anarchy that would catapult the new nation to the forefront of the world's attention and make it the African focal point in the global Cold War.

Although he did not recognize it then, it was entirely appropriate that the first Americans Devlin would meet on entering the Congo were evangelical missionaries.[2] For, although they had starkly contrasting goals and methods and rarely, if ever, intentionally acted in concert, the CIA and American missionaries proved to be equally critical to their nation's ultimate Cold War triumph in the Congo. For good reason, a considerable body of literature has been produced by scholars and journalists anxious to assess the CIA's role in the Congo crisis.[3] The same cannot be said concerning the influence of evangelical missionaries, about whom not a single scholarly article, let alone monograph, has been produced. As has previously been noted, this omission in the literature of American foreign relations is particularly glaring in view of the fact that the Cold War witnessed the greatest outpouring of Christian missionary zeal in the history of the modern world, that this explosion of missionary activity was dominated by zealously anti-Communist American evangelicals, and that these patriotic missionaries were often particularly involved in significant Cold War hot spots such as the Congo.[4] This chapter will argue that, during the turbulent independence period, from 1959 to the end of the Katangan secession in January 1963, American evangelical missionaries played a major role in US-Congolese relations and that they did so in three important ways: by helping influence Congolese public opinion in a generally pro-American direction, by informing and influencing American public opinion on the Congo, and, finally, by acting as an important diplomatic bridge between Congolese and American policymakers.

Why Africa Suddenly Mattered

Prior to the mid-1950s, neither superpower had shown much interest in Sub-Saharan Africa; the late 1950s saw them frantically making up for lost time.[5] The Soviet Union first signaled a serious interest in Africa on February 26, 1957, with the convening of the Soviet Africanist Co-Ordinating Conference.[6] This groundbreaking event was followed by the creation of the African Department within the Soviet Ministry of Foreign Affairs (1958), the formation of the influential African Research Institute (1959), and Ivan Potekhin's *Africa Looks to the Future*—a monograph that acted as the blueprint for Soviet strategy in Africa during the 1960s.[7]

For their part, the Americans could at least boast of significant and long-term unofficial ties to the continent. Thanks to the repatriation of former slaves in Liberia and a century's worth of substantial American missionary activity, portions of the American public could claim at least an anecdotal understanding of the region.[8] Nevertheless, it was not until 1957 that the State Department created its Bureau of African Affairs, and it was not until 1959 that the CIA launched its Africa Section.[9] Indeed, in 1957, when the Bureau of African Affairs was initiated, the State Department had more Foreign Service officers assigned to West Germany than it had in the entire African continent.[10] Consequently, as the Cold War spilled over into the periphery, the ignorance of both superpowers, combined with the continent's fragile political institutions, created a climate of acute uncertainty, exacerbating Cold War anxieties, and fueling a new scramble for Africa.

Why the Congo Mattered

There are a number of reasons why the Belgian Congo quickly became the focal point of the Cold War in Africa. Near the top of the list was its violent history of racially based oppression, which made it especially susceptible to anti-Western sentiment and, therefore, particularly appealing to Soviet policymakers.[11] Political naïveté and a lack of vested interests by the Congolese elite also made the Congo particularly vulnerable to Cold War intrigues. Unlike many British and French colonies, where limited elections and the development of democratic institutions were well under way by the late 1940s, the first experience that some Congolese had of democratic participation was in May 1960, scarcely a month prior to independence.[12] Regarding leadership development and intellectual capital, the story was largely the same. Until the 1950s, almost no effort was made by the Belgian administration to encourage the training of students beyond the level of basic literacy required to serve as clerks or minor functionaries within the colonial system.[13] The result was the infamous distinction of having produced at the time of independence approximately one university graduate for every million Congolese and a Congolese elite with virtually no vested interest in the socioeconomic status quo—a circumstance that, as President Eisenhower later remarked, made "political stability almost impossible."[14]

The nation's mineral wealth also acted to solidify the Congo's Cold War pedigree. Relative to the rest of Central Africa, the Congo's economic promise was legendary. In addition to its potential as a world leader in the production of industrial diamonds, by the 1950s the Congo was producing 10 percent of the planet's copper, the majority of Belgium's zinc, and approximately two-thirds of the world's cobalt.[15] Complementing the Congo's remarkable mineral resources were its size, strategic location, and potential for hydroelectric power, which, according to a CIA report produced in 1959, equaled 20 percent of the world's hydroelectric potential, or just under half the potential of the entire African continent.[16]

Further, because it was the second-largest nation in Africa, located at the heart of the continent and surrounded by nine economically subservient nations, it was assumed that whoever controlled the Congo would control the economic and political pulse of Central Africa.[17] Yet these ingredients alone did not guarantee the central place the nation was to take in the Cold War. In the end, it was the startling chain of events that transpired between 1959 and 1963 that turned this potentially combustible diplomatic backwater into the most important theater of the early Cold War period in Africa.

Arguably the pivotal moment in modern Congolese history, and the spark that touched off the wildfire that was independence-era Congo, was the speech delivered by the newly elected Congolese prime minister at the nation's independence ceremony on June 30, 1960. In front of the media, the Belgian king, and a host of international diplomats, the mercurial Patrice Lumumba rejected reconciliation with his former colonial rulers and angrily denounced the "ironies, insults, and blows which we had to undergo morning, noon and night because we were Negroes."[18] Igniting both latent anger and extravagant hopes for independence, Lumumba's speech was greeted enthusiastically by many Congolese listening to it on the radio.[19] Within a week, their expectations for immediate promotion and privilege having gone unheeded, a section of the Congolese army in Thysville mutinied. On July 6, the mutiny spread to the capital city of Leopoldville and then on to other areas of the country, where often-intoxicated and leaderless soldiers perpetuated a series of violent attacks on European residents that induced widespread lawlessness and an economically destabilizing mass exodus of the expatriate community from the country.[20] Less than a week later, the country's wealthiest province (Katanga) seceded, devastating whatever hopes remained for a stable and self-reliant nation.[21] Between the Katangan secession and the withdrawal of UN forces on January 24, 1963, the Congo saw almost half its provinces temporarily secede, the assassination of its prime minister, multiple tribal conflicts, and almost uninterrupted lawlessness.[22] It was this domestic political chaos, within the larger context of the Congo's economic and symbolic significance, that attracted superpower attention and secured the nation's prominent place in the Cold War.

Nevertheless, even before the Congo had begun to unravel, the Soviets and their allies had been preparing the ground for significant influence in the new nation. As early as the Brussels conference on Congolese independence in January and February 1960, the Soviets were actively recruiting Congolese leaders of whom over a hundred appear to have been sent to Czechoslovakia and East Germany for political and military training in the months preceding independence.[23] By the time independence arrived on July 1, 1960, the perceived radical makeup of Lumumba's inner circle was also proving to be a source of profound unease in the West.[24] In addition to a host of radical Ghanaian and Guinean advisers, Lumumba confidants included Serge Michel, an anti-West French leftist, Antoine Gizenga, Lumumba's radical deputy premier, and Madame Andrée Blouin, his bitterly antiwhite and anti-Western chief of protocol.[25] The presence of Soviet advisers in the Sûreté Nationale, Congo's internal security service, only added to the distinct suspicions at the CIA that the Soviets had much more than a passing interest in the Congo.[26] These suspicions seemed to be confirmed in mid-July 1960 when, within the space of three days and after a considerable increase in contact with high-level Communist bloc diplomats, Lumumba broke off diplomatic relations with Belgium and called for Soviet intervention.[27] Over the course of the next two months, these rhetorical moves were complemented by the arrival of up to one thousand Soviet bloc technical advisers and a stockpile of weapons and military supplies.[28] By mid-August, the CIA station chief was panicking. "Congo experiencing classic communist effort takeover government," Devlin cabled. "Anti-West forces rapidly increasing power Congo and there may be little time left in which take action avoid another Cuba."[29]

Over the next three years, the Congo was almost constantly in the news. *Time,* for instance, averaged a substantial article on it at least once every other issue during 1960 and 1961, including two cover articles.[30] Policymakers in Washington and Moscow were no less attentive. As the US assistant secretary of state for African affairs, G. Mennen Williams, summed up in his memoirs, during the early 1960s "Congo, along with Cuba and Vietnam, [was] a top foreign policy problem for the United States."[31] Playing a surprisingly significant role in the midst of this high-stakes Cold War contest were a group of generally unassuming American evangelical missionaries. Just how significant a part they played becomes clear only when we consider the multitude of factors working against pro-Western sentiment within the Congo.

The Context of Anti-Americanism in Independence-Era Congo

As we have seen, a tradition of explicit and racially based political oppression had made the Congo a tinderbox of anticolonial and anti-Western sentiment. Ironically, this latent antagonism toward the West was often bolstered by the divided religious loyalties of the Congolese population.

As early as the 1890s, American Protestant and Belgian Catholic missionaries were in conflict, with the Belgian Catholics zealously supporting King Leopold's administration and the American Protestants acting as the colonial government's most outspoken critics.[32] American anticolonial rhetoric and the revolutionary activities of several caustically anticolonial religious movements with ties to American missions further exacerbated Belgian Catholic mistrust of the American missionary enterprise in the Congo during the three decades immediately preceding the Cold War.[33] Throughout the Second World War, this long-standing religious antagonism increasingly found an outlet in Belgian Catholic accusations that American missionaries were, among other things, avoiding wartime mail censorship, undermining the colony's de facto color line, encouraging Congolese opposition to the Belgian war effort, supporting an important Congolese soldier mutiny, and organizing prayers for an American invasion of the Congo.[34] By 1944, the rumors and formal accusations had progressed to the extent that the American consul was forced to intervene on behalf of the embattled American missionaries and their Congolese converts.[35]

The most explosive ingredient in the cocktail that was independence-era anti-American sentiment, however, may have been the mixture of syncretistic religious movements with the population's extravagant expectations for independence. Ironically, as early as the 1920s, the tendency toward critical thinking and egalitarianism in American Protestantism had combined with colonial oppression and indigenous religions to produce in the Congo religiopolitical movements with a markedly anti-Western flavor. The largest and most significant of these was the Kimbanguist movement, which was started in the early twentieth century by a Congolese converted by American Baptist missionaries. By the 1920s, Kimbanguism had become a mass protest movement against Belgian, and by extension white, power in the Congo.[36]

As Congolese independence grew closer, the potency of this religiopolitical mix began to be taken seriously by American diplomats.[37] In one of many other similar independence-era examples, the Foreign Service officer Richard Sanger expressed at length his alarm at the success of operatives led by the Lumumba confidant Antoine Gizenga in utilizing radical religious sentiment in support of the strongly anti-Western Parti Solidaire Africain (PSA). Sanger noted that, in early 1960, the PSA was consciously and successfully building political support on the Kimbanguist spiritual narrative of a black redeemer who would drive the whites from the land.[38]

Ethnic loyalties were another unexpected source of anti-American feeling in many parts of the Congo. From the beginning, American policymakers had largely agreed that only a Congo united under a strong central government would be able to produce the stability the United States believed was in its interests.[39] Thus, when within six months of independence the Congo had disintegrated into four tribally based rival governments, American support for the central government had, by default, pitted several powerful tribes against the United States—including, ironically, the otherwise pro-West leadership of the powerful breakaway provinces of Katanga and South Kasai.[40] By early in 1961, America's perceived complicity in the murder of Patrice Lumumba and its unwavering support for the moderate Kasavubu/Adoula government had also unleashed rabid anti-American anger in several additional Congolese provinces.[41] As one American missionary administrator confirmed in a confidential letter shortly after Lumumba's death: "Even though our missionaries have avoided political issues, the very fact that they are Americans has labeled them with the United States Government policy of favoring the Kasavubu regime, which, of course, is violently opposed both in the Kivu and Orientale Provinces."[42]

In this religiously and ethnically anti-American context, it is not surprising that the increasing Communist propaganda in the Congo during the late 1950s and early 1960s found an enthusiastic audience. While attempts by the Soviets and the Chinese at using printed propaganda were often amateurish, their use of the radio was highly effective.[43] In a still largely localized and oral society where the spoken word had retained its aura of authenticity, the radio held enormous power to influence Congolese public opinion.

Whether the source was external Communist propaganda or the

voices of Lumumba's radical supporters speaking on local stations, the anti-West message was often the same. Shortly after independence, Lumumba's chief of protocol, Andrée Blouin, for instance, was regularly on the radio lambasting the Western imperialists and ordering the population to "set up roadblocks to intercept whites fleeing with the country's gold."[44] As one missionary described Congolese radio in the early days of independence: "All day long the local radio is broadcasting violent hatred against all whites . . . and telling the most stupid stories and flagrant lies, in order to excite the mass[es] against all whites."[45] After visiting a rural church that had been started by his organization, one American missionary reported: "Upon our arrival [the entire town] met us with shouts and curses. Africa Inland Mission [AIM] was but an instrument of the imperialists. . . . 'Take your Bible, and your lying missionaries, and your Jesus Christ, and get out of our village right now. If you don't, we will kill you!'"[46]

Colonial brutality, institutionalized racial prejudice, historical antagonism between Catholics and Protestants in the Congo, a potent cocktail of religiously infused political radicalism, early postindependence US policy, and radical propaganda, thus, combined to create a context in which anti-Americanism was the default mind-set for many Congolese. Nevertheless, thanks to the long-standing and intimate relationship between significant portions of the Congolese population and American missionaries, a considerable residue of pro-US sentiment remained—and this would prove to be a critical component in the Cold War battle for Congolese hearts and minds.

The Missionary Factor in the Battle for Congolese Hearts and Minds

The story of American missionary influence in the Congo can be traced back to the beginning of the Congo's modern history—that is, the inception of King Leopold's Congo Free State in 1884. Because the United States was the first nation to officially recognize Leopold's claim to the Congo, the staunchly Catholic monarch reluctantly opened the colony's doors to American Protestant missionary activity.[47] The American missionaries did not tarry. In just over a decade, there were at least eight different American missionary organizations active in the Congo, including the American Baptists (1886), the American Methodists (1886), the Christian and Missionary Alliance (1889), the Southern Presbyterian Church of the United States (1891), and the Disciples of Christ (1895).[48]

Significantly, American missionary activity in the Congo continued to grow over the next several decades. As the records of the US Consulate in Leopoldville indicate, as of the 1940s almost all significant American activity within the Congo included Protestant missionaries, of whom virtually all would have been theologically conservative evangelicals.[49] By 1949, the Presbyterians alone could boast of 124 full-time missionaries, and, by 1960, the total number of American missionaries active in the Congo was approaching 2,000, giving that country one of the largest concentrations of American missionaries in Sub-Saharan Africa.[50] Just as important as the large number of American missionaries in the Congo was their longevity. It was not uncommon, for instance, for a missionary couple to spend their entire adult lives there.[51]

If the large number of American missionaries in the Congo and the longevity of their stay there made it likely that their influence on the Congolese people would be significant, the nature of their work made it virtually inevitable. The very foundations on which the evangelical missionary enterprise rested assumed a remarkable degree of intimacy with the people. Whatever their personal prejudices, these missionaries believed in a fundamental spiritual equality of humanity under a creator God for whom there was, according to the Apostle Paul, "neither Jew nor Greek, slave nor free, male nor female . . . you are all one in Christ."[52] As one missionary writing to his colleagues in the midst of the Congo crisis put it: "Regardless of any other factors which might tend to separate us from our Congolese brethren, may we be truly 'TSHINTU TSIMUE,' one in Christ, made one in redemption by His blood to newness of life, brought together into one by the fellowship of His service for His Church in the Congo."[53]

That is not to say that American missionaries were devoid of a sense of cultural superiority or racial prejudice.[54] Nevertheless, American missionaries generally speaking stood out as racial progressives in a colony dominated by the color line. Indeed, the willingness of American missionaries to challenge the Belgian racial hierarchy seems to have been a primary cause of much of the mistrust that had existed between the missionaries and their Belgian neighbors well into the Cold War. In one of several similar episodes, the American missionary H. E. Griggs was refused reentry into the Belgian Congo by colonial officials precisely because he was undermining the colony's racial hierarchy. As the US consul general informed Griggs, according to the colonial administration: "Your manner of life [i.e., 'living on the native level economically'] casts discredit on persons of the white race and threatens to compromise public order and security."[55]

The relatively egalitarian perspective of the American missionaries was, perhaps, most explicit in the area of church governance. Well before the Belgians were seriously contemplating Congolese independence, American missionaries were consciously applying the democratic structures and practices they had grown up with to the Congolese church. Soon after World War II, most American missionary groups were holding elections in order to choose African leaders for church leadership. By the mid-1950s, even the politically conservative AIM could, with obvious pride, claim: "The Church is emerging as a separate entity [from the mission] but the Government will not recognize it as such." The document continued: "On all the Councils of the Church, the mission is represented by a minority in an advisory capacity [including the power of the purse]. The Church has for long been responsible for its own financial matters."[56] The personal practice of democracy that hundreds of thousands of Congolese experienced within American-influenced Protestant congregations across the Congo not only created a close association between the United States and political independence; it also provided virtually the only training in Western-style democratic institutions available in preindependence Congo.[57] In short, within the context of the pre-1959 Belgian Congo, in which the Congolese were entirely excluded from positions of leadership and, by design, virtually no political education was taking place, the Africanization and democratization of the Congolese Protestant church initiated by American Protestant missionaries was paradigm altering.[58]

It was, however, the consistent tradition of humanitarianism and the personal relationships that developed over the years between the American missionaries and the Congolese that gave the egalitarianism and the democratization of the Protestant church their potency.[59] In the Congo, this tradition of American missionary humanitarianism was principally seen in the medical and educational fields. In almost every case, when a new American missionary group arrived in the Congo, its explicitly religious activities were complemented by the building of hospitals and schools. This pattern applied to even the most theologically conservative missions, such as the AIM, whose first hospital, built in 1922, preceded its first explicitly religious school.[60]

Thanks to their desire to give the Congolese the ability to read the Bible for themselves, American missionaries also poured considerable energy and resources into education.[61] For instance, by 1941, in an official report to the American consul, the Presbyterians could claim to have trained 1,535 Congolese teachers who were annually educating over 35,000 students.[62] Just five years later, the American-dominated Council of Protestant Missions of Congo released a report that documented a total of 11,455 Protestant missionary-run schools that were educating almost 350,000 Congolese.[63] Thus, by the time of independence, it can be conservatively estimated that American Protestant missions were responsible for having provided at least a primary-level education to approximately one million Congolese.[64]

The case of missionary efforts in the area of medicine was equally transformative. One particularly telling example is that of the work of Dr. Carl Becker. First arriving in the Congo in 1929, Becker was immediately confronted with a host of staggering health-care challenges. Malaria and blackwater fever were rampant, child mortality was nearly 50 percent, and in some areas it was estimated that nearly 40 percent of the population was afflicted with leprosy.[65] While Becker acted to address each of these crises, his work in the field of leprosy treatment is noteworthy. By the onset of World War II, the young American physician had established three leprosy colonies in northeast Congo that not only treated the afflicted but also acted as research centers where he and his team of Congolese and American assistants pioneered the cultivation of leprosy bacillus—a process that helped transform the way leprosy was understood and treated around the world.[66]

Becker's accomplishments were unusual both in scale and in quality. That said, virtually every American mission in the Congo had a substantial medical program. At the time of independence, for instance, the Presbyterians had eight hospitals and ten dispensaries placed throughout southern Congo, treating over fifty thousand patients a year. Significantly, five of these hospitals were also teaching hospitals responsible for producing over 150 new nurses each year.[67] Owing to their extensive networks of outpatient clinics, other American missions served considerably larger numbers.[68]

Considering the longevity, scale, and quality of the American missionary humanitarian effort in the Congo, it is not surprising that the American diplomatic establishment saw in the actions of these accidental diplomats the foundation for a close relationship between the United States and the newly independent nation. In the official American statement congratulating the Congo on its upcoming independence, the president's representative, the Honorable Robert D. Murphy, went out of his way to draw special attention to the American missionary tradition in the country. Murphy remarked: "Hundreds of American missionaries . . . have [since 1885] come to this country to open schools and hospitals and to contribute to the welfare of the people. Through the years they have grown to love the Congo and its people and have created the basis of a lasting friendship between our two countries."[69]

Of course, the American missionaries who worked in the Congo were not there to promote American interests or to create pro-American sentiment. Nevertheless, it is not surprising that their religious and humanitarian efforts had produced a significant reservoir of promissionary and therefore often pro-American feeling among the wider population. The evidence of promissionary sentiment, in particular, during the immediate aftermath of independence is abundant.

In mission stations across the Congo, it was often Congolese Christians, afraid for the safety of their American friends, who first warned the missionaries of impending threats and pleaded with them to flee. Significantly, it was these reports coming in from across rural Congo that gave the State Department a sense of the breadth and scale of the developing crisis.[70] Also confirming the depth of mutual loyalty that existed between the two groups were the multiple reports coming out of the Congo following the first major missionary evacuation in late July 1960 describing around-the-clock security patrols being set up by local Congolese to protect the homes and property of the missionaries. As one missionary organization could report: "Pastors and Christians on each of these stations have set up a 24 hour watch to prevent looting of the station and the missionaries homes."[71] And, again, after Lumumba's murder had forced a second evacuation in February 1961, a reconnaissance trip by a second missionary organization found: "In all the places we visited there are guards in all the missionary residences [and an] . . . earnest group of men there who are conscientiously trying to guard all mission property."[72] In the context of widespread looting of European businesses and homes during this period, the contrasting treatment of the property of American Protestant missionaries is significant.

In addition, the larger local communities, who saw the missionary departure as a loss of medical care and education, were often equally vocal in their calls for the missionaries to stay. In several instances, local officials ordered missionaries to stay or pleaded with missionary administrators for their return.[73] The president of the Congo, Joseph Kasavubu, was only the most prominent official to do so when, in July 1960, he visited the American Baptist Mission to plead with the missionaries to stay despite a recent violent attack on their colleagues in the area.[74] Significantly, even when balanced against the rising threat of violence against American citizens, the State Department, as late as July 22, 1960, saw the benefits of a continuing American missionary presence and counseled against a hasty withdrawal stating that, "where possible," the missionaries "should continue occupying mission properties."[75] Finally, despite examples of antimissionary rhetoric and violence in some areas, the sense of mutual affection and loyalty between the US missionaries and the Congolese people was confirmed as missionaries across the Congo returned—often within several weeks of their initial departure—to a generally warm welcome.[76]

The special consideration given by the Congolese to American missionaries was not lost on the US State Department, which noted the largely positive reception received by missionaries returning to otherwise hostile areas and the mysterious resilience of "goodwill and respect" for the United States in the now predominantly anti-Western Congo. As one US embassy report concerning the tense atmosphere in the Congo after Lumumba's death observed: "While Americans head the propaganda list . . . a considerable reservoir of goodwill does exist for Americans. Provincial President Manzikula, who last time was less than friendly, greeted the reporting officer on this trip like a long lost brother and praised the work of American missionaries. Louis Lumumba, brother of Patrice and influential Provincial Minister of Interior, also praised American missionaries."[77] In a letter the following month to Congressman Arends, Assistant Secretary of State Brooks Hays noted in specifically Cold War terms: "American (and European) missionaries have been doing a most effective job for many years in combating communism in the Congo. It is significant in this connection that a great majority of the Congo's present leaders are markedly anti-communist. This can certainly be ascribed, at least in part, to the fact that many of them were educated by missionaries."[78] Again, a year later, the American consul working in the breakaway province of Katanga reiterated what by then seems to have been the widespread conclusion: "There still remains . . . a reservoir of goodwill which will serve us in the future when the current nastiness of UN/GOK conflict passes. The missionaries must be given credit for this basically charitable attitude among the Katangans."[79]

In sum, as the Congo moved toward independence, a host of toxic forces were acting against the development of a pro-Western and pro-American sentiment within the Congolese population, including a colonial past filled with racially based violence and prejudice, a host of ethnic and religious tensions, Congolese political naïveté, and an effective program of radical and Communist propaganda. Thanks to this volatile cocktail, for many independence-era Congolese, anti-American feeling was virtually a birthright. Yet, in the midst of this hostile context, US diplomats consistently noted the persistence of pro-American sentiment, even in the most otherwise hostile regions of the country. As American diplomats themselves concluded, this resilient sympathy for the United States among both the grassroots and the elite of Congolese society was largely the result of several generations of American missionary work in the country.

The Influence of American Missionaries on US Public Opinion on the Congo

Through regular communication with their broad network of supporters in the United States, American missionaries also played an important role in shaping US public opinion on the Congo. Generally speaking, while missionary news that reached the American public during this time included information related to the political upheaval, it reflected the essentially religious perspective of the missionaries.[80] The important exception to this rule was the very public and surprisingly effective campaign waged by American missionaries on behalf of the critical breakaway province of Katanga.

The two principal causes for missionaries' activism in Katanga were their close identification with the Katangan people and the outspoken anticommunism of the American missionary–educated Katangan leaders.[81] For several generations, American missionaries had lived among the Katangans, educating their children, caring for their sick, and preaching Christianity. Like the Methodist Howard Brinton, whose childhood playmates included several of the province's key leaders, for many American missionaries the Katangans had become like family.[82] Therefore, when US-supported UN forces took action on behalf of the ideologically ambiguous central government and against the explicitly anti-Communist Katangan secession, American missionaries, to the considerable displeasure of the US government and even their own mission boards back home, aggressively lobbied both the American public and the political elite for a change in US policy.

Missionary activism took a variety of forms. Missionaries at home on furlough often used speaking engagements to argue on behalf of a pro-Katangan change in US policy.[83] In addition, letters to churches and supporters sent by the numerous American missionaries still in Katanga informed their readers, in often heart-wrenching detail, of American-backed UN violence against both the missionary community and the Katangan people.[84] Other letters detailed the bombings of a Katangan hospital by the United Nations, the mounting death toll, and indigenous outrage that the United States would return Katangan affection with violence.

Significantly, the missionary letters coming out of Katanga often made reference to the American Christian education of the province's leaders and the Christian faith of President Moise Tshombe in particular. For instance, in a letter describing the visit of the Katangan president and three of his cabinet to a Methodist conference in 1961, Everett and Vera Woodcock noted sympathetically: "[Tshombe] paid high respect to the church, and mentioned how his experience as a lay leader in the annual conference helped prepare him for the problems in his present position. After telling how much his Bible and faith in prayer meant to him and foreign minister Kimba during their arrest by the central government, he appealed to the whole church to work harder than ever and pray fervently for the advancement of God's kingdom."[85]

Missionaries and an increasing number of engaged supporters in America were also an important component of the powerful Katanga lobby led by Michel Struelens in Washington.[86] This composite of generally conservative opposition to American policy in the Congo drew heavily on the missionary testimonials of pro-American sentiment in Katanga, the anti-Communist credentials of the province's American missionary-educated leaders, and the highly critical missionary accounts of the UN action in the region. Together with a successful letter-writing campaign to influential US politicians such as Vice President Nixon, Senator Dodd of Connecticut, and Senator Russell of Georgia, as well as to policymakers such as US ambassador to the UN Adlai Stevenson, the missionary lobby had become a real threat to US policy in the Congo.[87]

The reaction of US diplomats and policymakers to the unusual activism of the missionaries in the region speaks volumes about the perceived political threat the missionaries posed to US policy. One particularly telling example of the tension that had built up between American policymakers and missionaries in Katanga is a confidential letter from the US consul in the province's capitol, Elizabethville, to the Congo desk officer, Sheldon Vance. In it, the consul, Lewis Hoffacker, bitterly accused the missionaries of being virtually treasonous and the worst enemies of US policy in the region. "Cowardice and disloyalty to their country," wrote Hoffacker, "are obviously qualities with which they can sanctimoniously live. One hears them speak of 'our country,' which usually means Katanga, not the U.S." Giving "the devil his due," Hoffacker did reluctantly concede that "the American missionaries' work in the educational field has apparently been good (they have educated not only Tshombe but also Sendwe and other leaders of the province)." Nevertheless, he concluded, something had to be done, and "conceivably only mission headquarters at home are in a position to do anything constructive in this respect."[88]

The bitter sarcasm of Hoffacker's letter was not the only indication that the missionary lobby was frustrating US policymakers. By 1961, Undersecretary of State George McGhee and Assistant Secretary of State G. Mennen Williams were aggressively courting American mission boards in the United States as a means of neutralizing the political threat posed by the missionaries in Katanga.[89] By early 1962, Williams had met personally with every denomination "with any sizable missionary representation in Katanga."[90] In addition, Sheldon Vance, Frank Carlucci, and Williams had begun to use division within the missionary community to their advantage, stressing in public comments that, in general, only the Katanga missionaries were staunchly pro-Tshombe while American missionaries in other regions of the Congo were sympathetic to US policy.[91]

The potential influence of American missionaries on public opinion was also a matter of serious concern as Williams and his colleagues at the State Department began preparations for congressional hearings on US Congo policy—hearings that, it should be added, were initiated largely by missionary appeals to Senator Dodd.[92] Concerning Williams's testimony, Frederick Dutton suggested that he stress the missionary divisions in the Congo, which, Dutton argued, "in a public sense . . . could be the most critical point in the latter stages of the Congo hearings."[93] Complementing State's strategy of aggressively countering US missionary influence was its effort to secure the testimony of the respected Methodist missionary Howard Brinton. A close childhood friend and confidant of the Katangan president, Brinton nevertheless remained cautiously sympathetic to US policy in the Congo and was, thus, seen as a critical player in the push for congressional support.[94]

In the main, the influence of American missionaries on US public opinion concerning independence-era Congo was benign and apolitical. Outside religiously inspired concerns about the increasing instances of Communist propaganda and descriptions of their evacuations, in their letters and publications, the missionaries continued to focus on spiritual and humanitarian concerns. Significantly, the positive stories about the Congolese Protestant church that came from missionary sources helped balance the image of chaos and barbarism that was the staple of the international media and implicitly encouraged a continued US presence in the new nation. The case of Katanga was, of course, the important exception. And, here, the missionary influence was explicitly political, outspokenly critical, and surprisingly potent. The fact that the breakaway province was able to withstand intense American and UN pressure for more than two years was due at least in part to the activism of a small group of American missionaries and their evangelical supporters at home in the United States.

The Influence of American Missionaries on the Perceptions of US Policymakers

Long before the Congo became a focal point of the global Cold War, American missionaries and diplomats had enjoyed a close and mutually beneficial relationship.[95] For instance, in the capital of Leopoldville prior to independence, it was not unheard of for missionary friends to act as stand-ins for American diplomats at official functions.[96] Visits by the American consul to American missionary stations in "the bush" were also not uncommon and provided an excellent opportunity for American diplomats to both monitor missionary humanitarian efforts and make an appraisal of the sociopolitical realities of rural Congo.[97] In this social context, it was almost inevitable that a significant exchange of information would take place between the American diplomatic and missionary communities.

With the advent of the Cold War in the Congo in 1960, this history of close missionary-diplomat interaction would significantly aid the American effort to make sense of the Congolese chaos. It was, for instance, American missionaries working in southern Congo who first alerted US diplomats to the scale and national significance of the intertribal violence taking place in that region. Calling the Lulua-Baluba conflict "virtually insoluble" in a report to the US consulate in Leopoldville, one American missionary described what would now be referred to as *ethnic cleansing,* including the widespread burning of Lulua homes by the Baluba, multiple murders, and the mass exodus of the Lulua from Baluba-majority areas.[98] Two months later, in August 1960, after the mass evacuation of most Europeans from the region, it was again missionaries remaining behind who reported to the consul general that large numbers of the Baluba were moving toward areas bordering Katanga and that this movement was a possible precursor to a politically potent merger between the Lunda (Tshombe's indigenous majority tribe in Katanga) and the Baluba (the politically influential tribe with minorities in Katanga and a majority in Kasai Province) in reaction to the US-backed central government.[99] In September, it was yet another American missionary who reported that troops loyal to Lumumba were engaging in massive retaliatory executions of Baluba tribespeople.[100] Close communication between American missionaries and the US embassy in Leopoldville concerning these events in Kasai and others across the Congo continued throughout the period with the US ambassador and other American diplomats sitting in on mission meetings and occasionally being shuttled around various Congolese hot spots in missionary planes.[101]

Just prior to independence, American missionaries were also the key sources for intelligence that drew US attention to the proliferation of anti-Western and antiwhite religious movements across the Congo. Unlike their secular compatriots in the State Department, not only did the missionaries take the spiritualist movements seriously in their own right, but they also understood the significant power of those movements to shape politics within the Congolese context. Thus, in June 1960, Mennonite Brethren missionaries in the Kikwit area were the first to report the potential political consequences of the close relationship between the leftist PSA and a local spiritualist movement.[102] It was likely this intelligence that led to the "Secret" report by Richard Sanger in August confirming in great detail the political threat that the movement and others like it posed to US aims in the Congo. It is noteworthy that, like other American government analysts trying to make sense of the Congolese chaos, Sanger was led by his investigation to conclude that, if the United States hoped to make sense of the Congo, missionary knowledge and expertise would continue to be indispensable.[103]

As it became increasingly clear throughout the summer of 1960 that the lives of American missionaries were in real danger, the already significant volume of information exchanged between the two communities grew exponentially. The principle reason for this increase was, of course, the protection of American lives, and in this regard the information flow was largely initiated by the American embassy. For instance, at 1:30 A.M. on the night of July 7–8, as soon as the embassy had confirmed reports of the spread of the soldier mutiny toward Leopoldville, the ambassador called the missionary head of the Council of Protestants in Congo to his residence in order to develop contingency plans for a mass evacuation of American missionaries in the country.[104]

However, the increased contact with American missionaries also served the additional function of keeping the State Department informed on the movement of various political and tribal factions as well as the ebb and flow of political sentiment in a number of Congolese regions where the US government had almost no reliable sources of information. In the particularly volatile Lumumba strongholds of Orientale and Kivu Provinces, for instance, the US embassy in neighboring Kampala remained "in constant contact" with American missionaries, which, by December 1960, meant that the missionaries were in direct contact with the US ambassador twice a day.[105] The same level of diplomatic communication was characteristic of American missionaries on the Congo-Sudan border the following year; they could also report that they were in "constant touch" with the American ambassador.[106]

Facilitating this important exchange of information was a highly effective radio network that connected American mission stations across the Congo. Over the years, a variety of American missionary groups had come together to develop a system of radio communication that had allowed them to organize national meetings of the Protestant church, cooperate in handling medical and humanitarian crises, and help each other keep abreast of significant events in the colony. During the independence-era crisis, this missionary radio network also became an indispensable source of information for American policymakers, who regularly eavesdropped in order to monitor the fluid political situation in rural Congo.[107] Whether the result of long-standing personal relationships and historical ties between the two American communities or the unique demands for immediate information brought on by the independence-era crisis, there was during this period an important and extensive exchange of information between US diplomats and missionaries, and this exchange appears to have significantly influenced official American perceptions of events in the Congo.

Missionaries and Formal Diplomacy

As has been noted, thanks to their long and intimate history with the Congo, American missionaries played a critical role in promoting pro-US sentiment at the grassroots level. Perhaps even more significant, however, was the influence that they had on some members of the Congolese political elite. Whether the result of religious, medical, or educational ties, it was not uncommon for these missionaries to be on first-name terms with the nation's new African leaders. As a result, in a manner and to a degree that most official diplomats could not match, a number of American missionaries wielded a considerable amount of political influence. As early as the Brussels Roundtable leading up to Congolese independence, American diplomats were taking note of the diplomatic potential of the missionary community. In a cable written to Washington on March 23, 1960, American ambassador to Belgium William Burden was emphatic: "I am impressed by [the] surprising effectiveness, importance, and influence of US Protestant missionaries in Congo. . . . Believe appropriate use should be made in the future of their knowledge and contacts."[108] Nevertheless, perhaps because of their generally apolitical perspective or the rigid separation of church and state to which many of the more conservative among them fiercely held, American missionaries rarely sought or accepted prominent roles in formal US diplomacy. There were, however, exceptions. The most important of these was the role played by the Methodist missionary Howard Brinton in US attempts to resolve the Katangan secession. In January 1962, Brinton surfaced as a major player in the high-stakes standoff between the US-backed Congolese government and the UN forces supporting it and Tshombe's breakaway province of Katanga.

A number of factors combined to make the Katangan secession the centerpiece in the Congolese independence-era crisis. Early in the Congo crisis, both pro-Western Congolese leaders and American policymakers had concluded that a successful Katangan separation would be devastating for Congolese economic stability and dramatically increase the new nation's vulnerability to external Communist influence.[109] The Katangan secession also represented a major threat to national, regional, and continental political stability.[110] For American policymakers concerned that a descent into anarchy would create an opening for significant Communist intervention in Africa, the potential Balkanization of the continent was a serious threat to their Cold War objectives.

Finally, the Katangan secession was further complicated by the question of race. Therefore, when the Katangan president, Tshombe, recognizing the paucity of qualified African civil servants, elected to retain a considerable number of European functionaries and advisers, he became a potent symbol of neocolonialism and was easily characterized by domestic political enemies and the Communist bloc as a traitor to the cause of African nationalism.[111] In short, the Katangan secession sat at the economic, political, and symbolic heart of the larger Cold War drama that was independence-era Congo, and at the very center of that crisis stood an otherwise unassuming Methodist missionary.

A number of factors made Reverend Brinton an ideal candidate for the backchannel diplomacy that took place between the United States and Tshombe. Having grown up in Katanga as the child of Methodist missionaries and then returning as a Methodist missionary himself, Brinton had an understanding of the language and culture of the province unmatched by any US diplomat either on the field or in Washington.[112] Significantly, Brinton could also claim lifelong friendships with many of Katanga's most prominent leaders, including President Tshombe and the Congolese vice premier, Jason Sendwe—friendships that were very much alive as the Katanga crisis unfolded.[113] Finally, and perhaps most importantly from the perspective of Washington, unlike the majority of American missionaries in the province, because of his close relationship to the Katangan people and its leaders, Brinton was not antagonistic toward America's larger policy aims in the Congo.[114] In short, in Brinton, both parties had a trusted ally and someone personally invested in seeing a mutually beneficial solution to the crisis.

A trail of government documents stretching throughout 1962 depicts Brinton as a disinterested peacemaker earnestly trying to create a legitimate foundation of trust between the two parties. To American policymakers, he consistently portrayed Tshombe as a reasonable and pragmatic pro-Western leader, willing to compromise for the good of the Congo— provided that structures were put in place to ensure that a fair portion of political autonomy and Katangan wealth remained within the province.[115] Stressing the Katangan leader's knowledge of the American system, he also regularly voiced Tshombe's claim that he sought for Katanga only what the federal system in the Constitution had provided for Americans.[116] In a similarly sympathetic manner, Brinton appears to have been a powerful advocate of America's good intentions and its willingness to support the legitimate interests of the Katangans within a unified and centralized Congo.[117]

The fact that both sides placed a great deal of trust in Brinton is evident from the virtually unlimited access he had to Tshombe and the host of American diplomats whom he briefed or who sought out his advice during the prolonged negotiations.[118] Between January and September

1962, Brinton met personally with a veritable who's who of the US policy-making establishment, including, among others, the American consul in Katanga, Lewis Hoffacker, US ambassador Gullion, Assistant Secretary of State for African Affairs Williams, the Congo desk officer and future ambassador to the nation Sheldon Vance, Senator Thomas Dodd, and US secretary of state Dean Rusk.[119]

In the end, Brinton's significant efforts to bring a peaceful and mutually beneficial solution to the Katangan secession met with failure. American impatience with the pace of African-style diplomacy and fears of being painted with the brush of neocolonialism, combined with the withdrawal of Belgian support for Tshombe's government, led to a conclusive US-supported UN military effort in January 1963 that forcibly reunited the province with the rest of Congo and sent Tshombe temporarily into exile. Nevertheless, the ultimate failure to find a peaceful solution to the crisis should not obscure an important historical reality. For almost a year, American and Katangan policymakers at the highest level had placed much of their hope for a peaceful resolution to the Congo crisis on an unassuming Methodist missionary who, at key moments in that process, came surprisingly close to achieving that unlikely goal.

Between the beginning of 1960 and the end of the Katangan secession in January 1963, twenty-three African nations became independent. In taking almost everyone by surprise, the rapid decolonization of the continent stoked the flames of the Cold War and created a heightened sense of anxiety within the policymaking establishment of both superpowers—an anxiety reflected by President Eisenhower, who in his memoirs described African nationalism as a "flood force" and "a torrent overrunning everything in its path."[120] Within this geopolitically turbulent atmosphere, Congo, Africa's symbolic heart and economic treasure, began to unravel. Whereas it was viewed as a quiet diplomatic backwater only months before, its descent into anarchy seemed to compel superpower intervention and pushed the young nation into the spotlight of the global conflict.[121] In the high-stakes conflict-by-proxy that erupted between the two superpowers in the Congo, the usual suspects were joined by an unlikely and often reluctant group of accomplices.

American evangelical missionaries played a central role in the unfolding drama that was the Congolese independence-era crisis. First, as a result of their consistently intimate and humanitarian involvement with the people of the Congo over the course of several generations, American missionaries played a critical, if unintentional, role in promoting among many Congolese pro-American sympathies and political sensibilities that proved decisive in the otherwise anti-Western environment of independence-era Congo. Second, acting out of character but in line with the deep bonds they had developed with portions of the Congolese people, missionaries in Katanga also aggressively lobbied US politicians and public opinion for a change in America's Congo policy and, in doing so, became a major threat to US policy objectives in the region. Finally, and conversely, thanks to their unparalleled understanding of the Congo and a simultaneous loyalty to both the United States and the Congo, some American missionaries, such as Howard Brinton, became key players in the important but unsuccessful attempts to bridge the gap between US interests and the interests of various Congolese factions.

In the sixty years leading up to independence in the Congo, American evangelical missionaries had gone about their humanitarian and spiritual work in blissful anonymity. However, when the Congo unexpectedly burst into the global spotlight in 1960, the relational, cultural, and political capital that they had accumulated suddenly assumed considerable Cold War significance. Accidental diplomats or not, American evangelical missionaries proved to be a pivotal factor in the Cold War conflict that was the Congo.

Notes

1. Larry Devlin, *Chief of Station Congo* (New York: Public Affairs, 2007), ix.
2. Ibid., 3.
3. Madeleine Kalb, *The Congo Cables* (New York: Macmillan, 1982); Michela Wrong, *In the Footsteps of Mr. Kurtz* (New York: Fourth Estate, 2002); Peter J. Schraeder, *United States Foreign Policy toward Africa* (Cambridge: Cambridge University Press, 1994); Peter Duignan and L. H. Gann, *The United States and Africa: A History* (Cambridge: Cambridge University Press, 1984).
4. Richard Pierard, "Pax Americana and the Evangelical Missionary Advance," in *Earthen Vessels: American Evangelicals and Foreign Missions, 1880–1980*, ed. Joel A. Carpenter and Wilbert R. Shenk (Grand Rapids, MI: Eerdmans, 1990), 158–169; Joel Carpenter, preface to Carpenter and Shenk, eds., *Earthen Vessels,* xii–xviii, xii; Paul E. Pierson, "The Rise of Christian Mission and Relief Agencies," in *The Influence of Faith: Religious Groups and U.S. Foreign Policy,* ed. Elliot Abrams (Lan-

ham, MD: Rowman & Littlefield, 2001), 153–74, 160–61; Walter Russell Mead, *Special Providence: American Foreign Policy and How It Changed the World* (New York: Knopf, 2002), 142.

5. For the best exploration of just how and why the Cold War became genuinely global, see Odd Arne Westad, *The Global Cold War: Third World Interventions and the Making of Our Times* (Cambridge: Cambridge University Press, 2005).

6. Pieter Lessing, *Africa's Red Harvest* (New York: Joseph, 1962), 26.

7. Ibid., 27, 32–35, 121–23. See also Ivan Potekhin, *Africa Looks to the Future* (n.p., n.d.).

8. Philip Dow, "Romance in a Marriage of Convenience: The Missionary Factor in U.S.-Ethiopian Early Cold War Relations, 1941–1960," *Diplomatic History* 35, no. 5 (November 2011): 859–95.

9. G. Mennen Williams, *Africa for the Africans* (Grand Rapids, MI: Eerdmans, 1969), 164; Devlin, *Chief of Station Congo,* 33.

10. Kalb, *The Congo Cables,* xxvi.

11. Beginning with the foundational period of King Leopold's dominance (1884–1908), the Congo witnessed almost unspeakable levels of violence that included state-sanctioned mass killings and kidnappings, conscripted labor, and a harsh quota system of rubber harvesting that included the liberal use of the chicotte (whip) for underperformance. Wrong, *In the Footsteps of Mr. Kurtz,* 47. The American Presbyterian missionary William Sheppard, who was among the first to bring the world's attention to the atrocities taking place in Leopold's Congo, was an eyewitness to the grisly aftermath of the Free Company's policies. Adam Hochschild, *King Leopold's Ghost* (New York: Pan, 1999), 164, 233. See also "Secret," *Geographical Intelligence Review,* no. 58, CIA/RR MR 59-2 (July 1959), 2. While the Congolese themselves were responsible for most of the violence, everyone involved knew who had planned, organized, and implemented the system—and they were white. "Secret," 1; interview with Carl and Gladys Becker, Minneola, FL, July 9, 2009.

12. Although there were limited local elections in some areas as early as 1957, the May 1960 national election was the first that would have included a large percentage of Congolese. Devlin, *Chief of Station Congo,* 7. In Kenya, e.g., the practice of selecting African leaders through democratic elections was well in place by the early 1950s. Andrew Morton, *Moi: The Making of an African Statesman* (London: Michael O'Mara, 1998), 71–73.

13. Williams, *Africa for the Africans,* 90–91.

14. William Attwood, *The Reds and the Blacks* (New York: Joanna Cotler, 1967), 191. Further, of the some five thousand management-level positions available in the civil service at independence, a total of five were filled by Africans. Hochschild, *King Leopold's Ghost,* 301. The lack of vested interest by the Congolese elite was a point first brought out in Crawford Young, *Politics in the Congo* (Princeton, NJ: Princeton University Press, 1965), 203; and Dwight Eisenhower, *Waging Peace: The White House Years, 1956–1961* (New York: Doubleday, 1965), 573.

15. Kalb, *The Congo Cables,* xxii. See also "Secret," 1–5.

16. "Secret," 6–8.

17. Larry Devlin, interview by Michela Wrong, quoted in Wrong, *In the Footsteps of Mr. Kurtz,* 68.

18. Quoted in Thomas Borstelmann, *The Cold War and the Color Line: American Race Relations in the Global Arena* (Cambridge, MA: Harvard University Press, 2003), 129. See also "Congo: Freedom at Last," *Time Magazine,* July 11, 1960.

19. This was especially true for members of the Congolese army, who could not claim a single black officer among their ranks and whose meager income was dwarfed by the relatively extravagant living set aside for their Belgian officers. Devlin, *Chief of Station Congo,* 113–15.

20. Distrust of Lumumba among the army rank and file—most of whom came from tribes hostile to Lumumba's—was also central to explaining the almost instantaneous mutiny. See Young, *Politics in the Congo,* 315.

21. This was certainly the view of the American policymaking establishment, which almost universally pushed for an end to the secession (despite the Katangan president's pro-Western positions). See Attwood, *The Reds and the Blacks,* 194–95; Devlin, *Chief of Station Congo,* 170; and Williams, *Africa for the Africans,* 89.

22. For the best moment-by-moment unfolding of this period in the Congo, see Kalb, *The Congo Cables.*

23. Devlin, interview by Wrong, cited in Wrong, *In the Footsteps of Mr. Kurtz,* 65–70.

24. This despite the fact that, as late as January 1960, a US National Security Council review of the Congo had concluded that Communist infiltration and influence there was "negligible." Quoted in Schraeder, *United States Foreign Policy toward Africa,* 52.

25. Devlin, *Chief of Station Congo,* 53.

26. Ibid.

27. Kalb, *The Congo Cables,* 15.

28. Devlin, interview by Wrong, cited in Wrong, *In the Footsteps of Mr. Kurtz,* 68.

29. Devlin, cable to Washington, quoted in Kalb, *The Congo Cables,* 53.

30. A survey of the online *Time* archives revealed a total of forty substantial articles on the Congo during 1960 and a further thirty-one during 1961.

31. Williams, *Africa for the Africans,* 86.

32. See Hochschild, *King Leopold's Ghost,* 102, 125, 165, 172–73, etc. There were significant financial as well as cultural and religious reasons for the loyalty of the Catholic Church to the Belgian colonial administration. For instance, in 1926, the de facto colonial support for Catholicism became de jure when a law sanctioning state support for religiously based native education prohibited funds from going to Protestant schools. American Presbyterian Congo Mission (APCM) Legal Representative to US Vice-Consul Harry Schwartz, February 7, 1945, 432/64/21, Presbyterian Historical Society (hereafter PHS), Philadelphia.

33. Presbyterian Missionary "Ray" to Rev. J. Morrison, September 8, 1944, and

Presbyterian Missionary Plummer Smith to Rev. J. Morrison, October 18, 1944, 432/64/20, PHS.

34. APCM Legal Representative Rev. J. Morrison to American Consul Patrick Mallon, November 24, 1943, 432/64/19, U.S. Consul General Robert Buell to Rev. J. Morrison, February 26, 1945, 432/64/21, Presbyterian Missionary "Ray" to Rev. J. Morrison, September 8, 1944, 432/64/20, APCM Legal Representative to US Vice-Consul Harry Schwartz, February 7, 1945, 432/64/21, Presbyterian Missionary "Ray" to Rev. J. Morrison, September 17, 1944, 432/64/20, Unsigned Letter to Rev. H. Coxill, October 5, 1944, 432/82/14, and Presbyterian Missionary Vernon Anderson to Rev. J. Morrison, October 17, 1944, 432/64/20, PHS.

35. US Consul General Robert Buell to Rev. J. Morrison, February 26, 1945, 432/64/21, PHS. For evidence of the improved relations between the Belgian community and the American missionary community, see letters exchanged between the Presbyterian Missionaries Plummer Smith and Vernon Anderson on April 29 and 30, 1952, 432/64/22, PHS; and Memo, US Consul General, Leopoldville, to Department of State, July 26, 1957, RG 84/350/C/60/1/box 21, National Archives II at College Park, MD (hereafter NARA).

36. Among other descriptions of the origins of the Kimbanguist movement, see Duignan and Gann, *The United States and Africa,* 245–46. One example of the many instances of the syncretism alive and well in Congolese Christianity is found in a 1944 American letter from southern Congo in which a missionary writes with marked concern of "our Baluba Bibles being misused by certain natives in a sort of secret cult." "Ray" to Rev. J. Morrison, September 8, 1944, 432/64/20, PHS. Another is found in American Presbyterian Congo Mission, "Annual Report," 1949, 432/40/34, PHS.

37. "A Biblical Prophecy of the Independence of the Congo," American Consul William C. Canup, February 26, 1960, RG 84/350/C/60/1/box 24, NARA.

38. Memo, Richard H. Sanger to Hugh S. Cumming Jr., "Secret," August 22, 1960, p. 11, RG 59/250/63/10/box 8, NARA. At exactly the same time, American Baptist missionaries closer to Leopoldville were assaulted by an angry mob and forced to flee. "Chronological Record," 432/14/6, PHS. In addition, African Inland Mission (AIM) internal documents during the latter part of 1960 show widespread antimissionary activity in the Lumumba strongholds of Stanleyville and Orientale and Kivu Provinces. Dr. Carl Becker to Sidney Langford, November 23, 1960, CN 81/10/32, Unsigned Letter, December 1960, CN 81/85/6, and Sidney Langford to "Dear Friends," November 28, 1960, CN 81/85/6, Billy Graham Center Archives (hereafter BGCA), Wheaton, IL. A further American missionary of the Evangelical Free Church was quoted in *World Vision Magazine* as saying: "Things got beyond all limit and description [around independence]. . . . White people beaten and put in jail, women abused, nobody was safe. . . . Bayonets were put to ribs, guns pointed at us from all sides, 'Doctor or missionary,' they said, 'it does not matter who you are or what you do. It is your skin." *World Vision Magazine,* "Facts of a Field: Congo Republic," September 1960, 21. See also Sanger to Cumming (n. 38 above).

39. Williams, *Africa for the Africans,* 94.

40. To the end of his protracted and violent fight for self-determination, the American-educated and Methodist president of Katanga, Moise Tshombe, could not understand why the United States had failed to support an ardently pro-West provincial government's pursuit of American-style federalism. As he said after the successful UN invasion of Katanga: "I sacrificed myself to Western values and the Westerners have betrayed me." Quoted in Anthony Bouscaren, *Tshombe* (New York: Twin Circle, 1967), 5.

41. In particular the Kivu and Orientale provinces, which were the home of several large American missionary groups. E. G. Schuit to Rev. Sidney Langford, February 11, 1961, CN 81/10/32, General Secretary of the AIM to Rev. Robert S. Wilson of the Church Center Press, February 28, 1961, CN 81/85/6, and E. G. Schuit to Rev. Sidney Langford, March 1961, CN 81/10/32, BFCA. It should also be noted that the word *perceived* is used quite intentionally here. While it seems to be clear that the United States had at one point considered, and perhaps even attempted, to assassinate Lumumba, the events that led to his death were not orchestrated by the CIA or any American government organization. Instead, all indicators point to the responsibility of Katangan soldiers with assistance from Belgian supporters. See Kalb, *The Congo Cables,* 189–96.

42. AIM General Secretary to Rev. Robert S. Wilson, "Confidential," February 28, 1961, CN 81/85/6, BGCA.

43. For instance, the CIA station chief for the Congo, Larry Devlin, recalled that, soon after independence, the Soviets attempted to distribute outdated and English versions of pro-Communist tracts among a Congolese army that was barely literate and, if literate, only in French. Devlin, interview by Wrong, cited in Wrong, *In the Footsteps of Mr. Kurtz,* 69; Memo, American Consul General, Leopoldville, James Green, to Department of State, n.d., RG 84/350/C/60/1/box 21, NARA.

44. Wrong, *In the Footsteps of Mr. Kurtz,* 69.

45. Unsigned Letter from AIM Missionary in Leopoldville, July 15, 1960, CN 81/85/6, BGCA. The perception that many missionaries had of a sudden wave of radio propaganda was not a product of hysterical anticommunism. The reality was that between 1956 and 1961 Soviet radio propaganda in Africa had grown from next to nothing to over 130 hours of programming a week. Lessing, *Africa's Red Harvest;* E. G. Schuit to Rev. Sidney Langford, February 15, 1961, CN 81/10/32, BGCA.

46. Peter J. Brashler, *Change: My Thirty-Five Years in Africa* (Wheaton, IL: Tyndale, 1979), 131.

47. See, e.g., Hochschild, *King Leopold's Ghost,* 79–84.

48. Jonathan Hildebrandt, *History of the Church in Africa: A Survey* (Achimota, Ghana: African Christian Press, 1990), 168.

49. See RG 84/350/49/18/box 2, folder 131, NARA.

50. According to John Crawford, the total number of Protestant missionaries in the Congo in 1959 was 2,608. If previous patterns apply, between 50 and 70 per-

cent of this number would have been Americans. John Crawford, "Protestant Missions in Congo, 1960–65," *International Review of Missions,* [1965?], 94. See also the list of Presbyterian missionaries prepared by the Presbyterian Legal Representative for American Consul, September 16, 1949, 432/64/22, PHS; and Memo to Wayne Fredericks, August 6, 1962, RG 59/250/63/10/box 5, NARA.

51. Interview with Carl Becker, Minneola, FL, 9 July 2009.

52. Gal. 3:28 (NIV).

53. Letter from Acting Area Secretary for Congo, APCM, Walter D. Shephard, January 1962, 432/80/16, PHS.

54. American Consul, Lewis Hoffacker, to Sheldon B. Vance, "Confidential," October 27, 1961, RG 59/250/63/10/box 6, NARA.

55. H. E. Griggs to the Vice Governor General of the Belgian-Congo, June 23, 1947, RG 84/350/49/18/2, NARA. Griggs was quoting Vernon Anderson, of the Congo Protestant Church, who in turn was quoting an interview he had had with Belgian Congo officials regarding Griggs.

56. Memo from the Congo Field, September 1957, CN 81/36/10, BGCA.

57. Ibid.; interview with retired Presbyterian missionary, David Miller, June 30, 2009, Montreat, NC. See also interview with retired AIM missionary to the Congo Carl Becker and son of Dr. Carl Becker AIM missionary to the Congo, July 9, 2009, Minneola, FL, and interview with retired Presbyterian missionary David Miller, June 30, 2009, Montreat, NC.

58. There is no more sophisticated analysis of the significant role that the infusion of the Protestant missionary worldview played in preindependence African cultures like those present in Congo than Lamin Sanneh, *Encountering the West: Christianity and the Global Cultural Process* (Maryknoll, NY: Orbis, 1993).

59. Smith Hempstone to Walter S. Rogers, Institute of Current World Affairs, January 22, 1958, RG 84/350/C/60/1/box 21, NARA.

60. Hildebrandt, *History of the Church in Africa,* 215–16.

61. This apparently minor point is of considerable significance, for it assumes an ultimate intellectual and spiritual independence that was present in neither the pre–Vatican II Catholic Church nor many traditional African tribal hierarchies. As Lamin Sanneh and others have noted, the quest to teach literacy and to translate the Bible into the local languages was, thus, near the heart of the movement toward political independence in Africa. See Sanneh, *Encountering the West,* 17.

62. Presbyterian Mission Treasurer to American Consul, Patrick Mallon, February 2, 1942, 432/64/19, PHS.

63. Informational Booklet Produced by the Council of Protestant Missions in Congo for 1946, RG 84/350/49/18/2/box 14, folder 360, NARA.

64. This estimate is a conservative one arrived at by taking the number of years that the Protestant missions had been involved in education by the time of independence, the increasing size of that program over the years, and the reality that most students would attend for only two or three years of primary-level education (grades 1–6). If, therefore, in 1951 there were 350,000 students in Protestant schools in the

Congo and in each year approximately one-fourth of those students would be new (85,000), over the fifteen years in which the Protestant educational push was at its peak, there would have been approximately 1.3 million. This does not include the large number of Congolese who had received some Protestant education prior to World War II. It should also be mentioned that, while American missionaries were widely successful in educating the Congolese at a primary level—i.e., in basic literacy—they were discouraged from training students beyond the secondary level. The handful of students who went to university prior to independence were, thus, forced to go outside the Congo for their postsecondary education.

65. William Peterson, *Another Hand on Mine: The Story of Dr. Carl K. Becker of the Africa Inland Mission* (Morgantown, PA: Masthof, 1967), 128. The complete Vera Hillis Papers, from which much of the Peterson biography was drawn, are available at the BGCA.

66. Peterson, *Another Hand on Mine,* 131–32, 159. The colony at Oicha included four thousand leprosy patients and six thousand additional family members who were self-supporting (having been given parcels of land to cultivate), making it the second largest leprosy colony in the world. Interview with retired missionary Vera Hillis, July 9, 2009, Minneola, FL.

67. Annual Statistical Report included in Vernon A. Anderson to Dr. C. Darby Fulton, Executive Secretary, Board of World Missions, February 12, 1959, 432/41/50, PHS.

68. Records of the normally understated AIM, e.g., claim that the mission treated over two million Congolese during 1961. AIM Congo Report 1961, CN 81/18/35, BGCA.

69. Statement by the Honorable Robert D. Murphy, Personal Representative of the President and Head of the American Delegation to the Independence Ceremonies of the Republic of the Congo, June 30, 1960, RG 84/350/C/60/1/box 24, NARA. See also Sanneh, *Encountering the West,* 16–19.

70. Protestant Council of Congo to American Supporters, July 26, 1960, CN 81/36/9, BGCA. See also Sanger to Cumming (n. 38 above).

71. AIM American Home Office to "the Relatives, Churches and Friends of Our Congo Missionaries," July 26, 1960, CN 81/3/25, BGCA

72. Carl Becker to Sidney Langford, February 17, 1961, CN 81/10/32, BGCA.

73. Mr. Stanfield from State Department, February 2, 1961, CN 81/85/6, BGCA.

74. AIM American Home Office to "the Relatives, Churches and Friends of Our Congo Missionaries," July 26, 1960, CN 81/3/25, BGCA. Other examples of Congolese officials supporting a missionary return include AIM Congo Field Council to "our Congo Missionaries everywhere," May 13, 1961, CN 81/85/2, BGCA.

75. Memo, Clyde W. Taylor, Evangelical Foreign Missions Association, to Evangelical Mission Executive, "Confidential," July 22, 1960, CN 81/85/6, BGCA.

76. AIM Congo Field Council to "our Congo Missionaries everywhere," May 13, 1961, CN 81/85/2, and Carl Becker to Sidney Langford, February 17, 1961, CN

81/10/32, BGCA; Memo, American Consul, Salisbury, to Secretary of State, August 5, 1960, RG 84/350/C/60/1/box 24, and Memorandum, American Consul General, Kampala, to Secretary of State, April 21, 1961, RG 84/350/C/60/1/box 27, NARA. By July 20, 1960, the State Department was reporting that roughly 70 percent of Americans (the vast majority missionaries) had been evacuated from the Congo. Memo, "Evacuation of Americans from the Republic of the Congo," July 20, 1960, RG 59/250/63/10/box 6, NARA. The AIM could report at the end of August that 75 percent of its missionaries had been evacuated. It appears, then, that the bulk of evacuations were completed by the end of July and that most of those missionaries remaining—around 25 percent—stayed throughout the crisis. Report from Dr. R. T. Davis, "Congo Turbulence," CN 81/85/6, BGCA.

77. Memo, American Embassy, Leopoldville, to Department of State, "Current Conditions in Stanleyville," February 24, 1961, RG 84/350/C/60/1/box 24, NARA.

78. Assistant Secretary Brooks Hays to Congressman L. C. Arends, March 9, 1961, RG 59/250/63/10/box 8, NARA.

79. American Consul Lewis Hoffacker to Congo Desk Officer Charles S. White-house, "Official-Informal Confidential," March 24, 1962, RG 59/250/63/10/box 5, NARA.

80. See, among many others, Letter from the Council of Protestants in Congo to "all readers of the Congo Mission News," July 26, 1960, CN 81/36/9, BGCA.

81. A particularly revealing description of American missionary identification with the Katangans comes in Lewis Hoffacker, American Consul, to Congo Desk Officer Sheldon Vance, October 27, 1961, RG 59/250/63/10/box 6, NARA. In it, Hoffacker claims that American missionaries there regularly referred to Katanga as "our country."

82. Memo to Governor Williams, "Confidential," January 18, 1962, RG 59/250/63/10/box 7, NARA.

83. Speech by Mr. Fred Lasse to the Keswick Convention in New Jersey, September 1960, CN 81/85/6, BGCA.

84. Senator Dodd entered many letters into the record, including one from Julia Hoel and James Brower. See *US Congressional Record—Senate,* December 6, 1961, and January 25, 1962, respectively.

85. See n. 84 above.

86. For information on Struelens, see "The Administration: An Abuse of Power," *Time,* December 28, 1962. For an excellent example of the impressive Katanga public relations machine and the use of American missionaries as sources for that effort, see the pamphlet written by Ernest Van Den Haag, RG 59/250/63/10/box 5, NARA.

87. A reference to a letter to Vice President Nixon by the American missionary P. D. Claar, even before the independence-era crisis, offering advice on Congo policy is seen in Memo to William Macomber Jr., February 29, 1960, RG 59/.855a/411.8-160, NARA. For letters to Dodd, see n. 84 above. See also Everett L. Woodcock to Mr. Adlai Stevenson, September 30, 1961, RG 59/250/63/10/box 6, and Mrs. Charles R. Johnson to Mr. Adlai Stevenson, November 15, 1961, RG 59/250/63/10/

box 9, NARA. In his memoirs, George McGhee relates: "I practically lived with Dodd during this period. . . . I then flew to Georgia to meet with Russell, who had come under the influence of missionaries from his state." George C. McGhee, *On the Frontline in the Cold War: An Ambassador Reports* (Westport, CT: Praeger, 1997), 154.

88. American Consul Lewis Hoffacker to Congo Desk Officer Sheldon Vance, "Confidential," October 27, 1961, RG 59/250/63/10/box 6, NARA.

89. Memos, Williams and Assistant Secretary of State George McGhee, "Confidential," December 21, 26, 1961, RG 59/250/63/10/box 5, NARA.

90. Memo, Williams to McGhee, January 9, 1962, "Confidential," RG 59/250/63/10/box 5, NARA.

91. Memo, "Congo Hearings," Sheldon Vance to Williams, January 30, 1962, RG 59/250/63/10/box 9, NARA.

92. Richard Mahoney, *JFK: Ordeal in Africa* (Oxford: Oxford University Press, 1983), 135. Mahoney's point here is simply that Dodd initiated the hearings and invited Tshombe, but, for some examples of the missionary letters to Dodd, see n. 84 above.

93. Memo, "Congo Hearings," Frederick Dutton to Williams, January 24, 1962, RG 59/250/63/10/box 9, NARA.

94. Memo, Sheldon Vance to Williams, "Confidential," January 18, 1962, RG 59/250/63/10/box 7, NARA.

95. The examples of friendships developing between US missionaries and diplomats in the Congo prior to independence are myriad. See, e.g., American Public Affairs Officer Gilbert E. Bursley to Rev. Vernon A. Anderson, December 4, 1956, 432/64/22, PHS, in which Bursley writes: "I've thought a lot about you and the very kind folks of the A.P.C.M. in the hectic weeks since my return to Leopoldville. Your kindness and hospitality are something I will never forget." Among many other examples, see J. A. Halverstadt to US Public Affairs Officer William M. Hart, October 30, 1959, 432/64/23, PHS. See also American Consul Patrick Mallon to the Legal Representative of the American Presbyterian Congo Mission, December 23, 1941, 432/64/19, PHS.

96. "Jack" to J. F. Watt, April 7, 1957, 432/14/5, PHS.

97. Interview with David Miller, June 30, 2009, Montreat, NC. See also Representant de Poste Mutoto to Vernon Anderson, April 29, 1952, and Burley to Anderson, December 4, 1956, 432/64/22, PHS; and a series of three lengthy memos from the American consul general: Leopoldville to State, July 26, September 21, and December 14, 1957, RG 84/350/c/60/1/box 21, NARA.

98. Memo, American Consul, Leopoldville, to State Department, June 3, 1960, RG 84/350/c/60/1/box 24, NARA.

99. Memo, American Consul, Salisbury, to Secretary of State, August 5, 1960, RG 84/350/c/60/1/box 24, NARA.

100. Memo, American Embassy, Leopoldville, to State Department, September 23, 1960, RG 84/350/c/60/1/box 24, NARA.

101. "Second Stated Mission Meeting, Luluabourg, 10–19 October 1961," 432/3/9, and draft of APCM to "Bulupe Folks," November 30, 1961, 432/9/34, PHS; "Situation in Kasai," Trip Report, March 3, 1962, RG 84/350/c/60/1/box 29, NARA.

102. Office Memo, American Consul, Leopoldville, June 15, 1960, RG 59/.855a/411.8-160, NARA.

103. Sanger to Cumming (n. 38 above).

104. Council of Protestants of Congo to "all readers of the Congo Mission News," July 26, 1960, CN 81/36/9, BGCA.

105. Acting General Field Secretary of the AIM to Mr. Thornberry, [ca. 1960], CN 81/36/9, and Transcription of Radio Message to AIM Headquarters in New York from Eddie Schuit, December 15, 1960, CN 81/3/25, BGCA.

106. Acting General Field Secretary to Rev. Sid Langford, December 18, 1962, CN 81/36/9, BGCA.

107. Dr. Carl Becker to Sid Langford, July 21, 1960, CN 81/10/32, and minutes of AIM Congo Field Council, December 13–19, 1960, CN 81/36/10, BGCA; *Inland Africa,* November–December 1960, 8–9. See also Memo, American Consul, Salisbury, to Secretary of State, August 5, 1960, and Telegram, US Consul Luanda to US Embassy, Leopoldville, July 30, 1960, RG 84/350/c/60/1/box 24, NARA; and Devlin, *Chief of Station Congo,* 3.

108. Telegram, American Ambassador Burden to Secretary of State, March 23, 1960, RG 59/.855a/411.8-160, NARA.

109. See, e.g., State Department Memo, January 20, 1962, "Confidential," RG 59/250/63/10/box 5, NARA, which quotes Kasavubu, Mobutu, and Adoula to confirm their already well-entrenched fears that an independent Katanga "would mean the end of moderate influence in the Congo." See also Williams, *Africa for the Africans,* 94; "Secret," 1; and Mrs. Charles R. Johnson to US Ambassador to the United Nations, Adlai Stevenson, November 15, 1961, RG 59/250/63/10/box 9, NARA. The latter refers to Congolese foreign minister Bomboko's speech to the United Nations stressing the critical importance of Katanga to the viability of the Congo.

110. State Department Memo, January 20, 1962, "Confidential," RG 59/250/63/10/box 5, NARA, quoting multiple Congolese leaders.

111. The anger of some Congolese toward Tshombe, which was fueled by Communist propaganda, was picked up by both independence-era African leaders from around Sub-Saharan Africa and the Africanists in the State Department led by Williams, Wayne Fredericks, and others. For instance, in his memoirs, G. Mennen Williams referred to Tshombe as "the devil" because of his apparently neocolonial perspective and policies. See Williams, *Africa for the Africans,* 87. According to US Ambassador William Attwood, later, in the Simba rebellion of 1964, President Kenyatta of Kenya's continuing animosity toward Tshombe was a critical hindrance to negotiations meant to free Western hostages in the rebel-held city of Stanleyville. According to Attwood, at one point, Kenyatta told the United States: "We can be

friends . . . only if you stop being friends with Tshombe." Attwood, *The Reds and the Blacks,* 215.

112. Memo, Sheldon Vance to G. Mennen Williams, "Confidential," January 18, 1962, RG 59/250/63/10/box 7, NARA.

113. Memo of Conversation Including Rev. Brinton, G. Mennen Williams, Robert Eisenberg, and Richard Sanger, January 19, 1962, RG 59/250/63/10/box 7, NARA.

114. Sheldon Vance to G. Mennen Williams, January 18, 1962, RG 59/250/63/10/box 7, NARA.

115. Memo of Conversation with Rev. Brinton, January 17, 1962, RG 59/250/63/10/box 7, NARA.

116. Memo of Conversation with Rev. Brinton, G. Mennen Williams, Robert Eisenberg, and Richard Sanger, January 19, 1962, RG 59/250/63/10/box 7, NARA.

117. Memo, Sheldon Vance to G. Mennen Williams, January 19, 1962, RG 59/250/63/10/box 7, NARA.

118. American Consul Lewis Hoffacker to Deputy Director at the Office of Central African Affairs Robert Eisenberg, "Confidential," March 7,1962, RG 59/250/63/10/box 6, NARA. See also Memo, Sheldon Vance to Governor Williams, January 19, 1962, Senator Thomas Dodd to Secretary of State Dean Rusk, July 11, 1962, and Memo, Wayne Fredericks to Secretary of State Dean Rusk, July 16, 1962, RG 59/250/63/10/box 7, NARA.

119. Memo, Sheldon Vance to Governor Williams, January 19, 1962, Senator Thomas Dodd to Secretary of State Dean Rusk, July 11, 1962, and Memo, Wayne Fredericks to Secretary of State Dean Rusk, July 16, 1962, RG 59/250/63/10/box 7, NARA.

120. Eisenhower, *Waging Peace,* 572.

121. Devlin, *Chief of Station Congo,* ix.

9

Structuring the Economy on the Periphery

The United States, the 1958 Argentine Stabilization Agreement, and the Evolution of Global Capitalism

Dustin Walcher

On December 19, 2001, protests erupted on the streets of Buenos Aires. People from all different walks of life converged to voice their opposition to the government of President Fernando de la Rúa, who had the misfortune of presiding over perhaps the most dramatic economic failure of the post–Cold War era to that date. Women who saw their savings wiped out emerged on the streets banging on pots and pans. People of all ages and socioeconomic classes directed their anger at de la Rúa, his predecessor, Carlos Menem, and Argentine bankers. But Argentine elites were not the only and in some ways not the most important targets of popular scorn; the International Monetary Fund (IMF) and the US government had supported Argentina's economic policies. Indeed, Argentina served as an often-cited example of a successful IMF intervention throughout the late 1990s. That point was not lost on the bankrupted masses, who believed that, in the course of the financial collapse, creditors from abroad would be protected at the expense of ordinary Argentines.[1]

Faced with massive debt and ever-increasing interest rates, which were demanded by investors fearful of a sovereign default, the de la Rúa government reached its breaking point. Having delayed what in retrospect appeared inevitable throughout the year, the IMF recalled its mission chief from Buenos Aires on December 3. Two days later, the IMF announced that it would not make available the latest tranche from an earlier agreement, effectively cutting off Buenos Aires from any outside capital. The international community lacked a mechanism or process for sovereign bankruptcy—yet bankruptcy was exactly the state in which Argentina found itself. A political crisis followed, albeit one that fortunately did not include the kind of military takeover that had been common before 1983.

Skepticism, if not hostility, toward international bankers, the United States, and the IMF was not new to Argentine political culture. Despite largely conforming to the contours of the global capitalist system after 1950, Argentine President Juan Perón refused to join the IMF and the World Bank. A military coup removed Perón from power in 1955, unleashing what its leaders dubbed the Liberating Revolution. Promising to purge the stain of Peronism from the Argentine body politic, the government of General Pedro Aramburu rolled back some Peronist reforms to the political economy. Aramburu also joined the IMF and the World Bank in 1956, beginning Argentina's formal participation in the Bretton Woods global capitalist system.

This chapter uses US and IMF policy toward Argentina as a case study to address many of the larger questions raised in this volume. In December 1958, the Arturo Frondizi government of Argentina concluded an agreement with the United States, the IMF, and eleven private banks through which it secured balance-of-payments and developmental assistance. In exchange, Frondizi pledged to liberalize important aspects of Argentina's economy and adopt fiscal austerity over the budget. Despite the agreement, economic growth was not sustained, the balance of payments returned to deficit, and social instability increased. Frondizi himself fell victim to a military coup in 1962, in large part because of his government's failure to produce economic growth and monetary stability.

The Argentine case serves as a useful measuring stick for understanding the extent to which US economic and strategic thinking about the global economic periphery changed between the height of the Cold War and the years following its conclusion. As in the early 1960s, in the wake of the 2001 economic collapse Argentine protesters assigned substantial blame to Washington and the IMF. As Frondizi pledged cooperation with Washington in 1958, successive Argentine governments embraced the Washington Consensus of the 1990s. Preached by US and IMF officials, the Washington Consensus advocated free markets, private property ownership, and minimal state intervention in the economy.

An examination of the 1958 agreement in light of Argentina's experience in the 1990s leads to two conclusions. First, it identifies an evolution in official US thinking about the proper relationship between the state and private enterprise in liberal economies. Although Frondizi liberalized many aspects of Argentina's economy, he secured public and private support for a limited strategy of import substitution industrialization (ISI). While the IMF was not a proponent of ISI, the Eisenhower administration was less rigidly orthodox in its economic thinking than US administrations of both political parties became after 1980. However, though US policy evolved in this respect, it did not undergo a radical transformation; the "self-help" preached by Washington policymakers during the 1950s and 1960s was quite similar to the fiscal austerity prescribed during the 1990s. Expanding private business while simultaneously decreasing the scope of the public sector was a priority in both eras but was pursued in a less compromising fashion under the Washington Consensus. Finally, the scale of the global economy was much larger after the collapse of the Bretton Woods currency regime. International capital flows and trade shot up, creating even greater stakes than existed in the mid-twentieth century.[2]

Second, the US conception of and economic engagement with the global economic periphery—including Argentina—remained remarkably consistent during and after the Cold War. In their pursuit of economic growth, Argentine elites have been compelled to operate within a structural and ideological framework largely defined in Washington. The structure of political and economic power both during and after the Cold War has had the effect of reinforcing the core-periphery dichotomy and with it an asymmetrical relationship between the Global North and the Global South. That is not to argue that Argentines—whether government officials, business or banking leaders, or ordinary citizens—lacked agency. Ordinary Argentines, during both the mid-twentieth century and the years after the Cold War, often strenuously objected to what they perceived as a loss of national sovereignty to transnational corporations and supranational institutions. Meanwhile, Argentine leaders often chose participation in the Washington-led global economic system because they perceived it to offer more advantages than disadvantages. Just as it would be incorrect to assign total power and influence to Washington, simply celebrating the agency of Argentines would not move us any closer to understanding the construction of power in the international system. Outcomes were ultimately the products of interactions between groups and individuals wielding asymmetrical levels of power and influence.

Frondizi understood the dynamics of power and, in light of his country's economic stagnation, prepared a new policy departure on his inauguration as president in 1958. His new job promised great challenges; Frondizi inherited a national economy in a chronic state of crisis, in large part because of structural deficiencies. Inflation was high, productivity was low, and the balance of payments was in deficit. Exports, which primarily consisted of agricultural goods, were stagnant. Inflation hovered around 32 percent. Argentina's balance-of-payments crisis dwarfed that confronted by the United States. When Perón came to power in 1946, Argentine reserves stood at $1.7 billion; by September 1958, they had dwindled to a meager $200 million. Moreover, Argentine officials estimated the country's 1958 deficit at $300 million, and US officials estimated total long-term external Argentine indebtedness at $1 billion. There were multiple reasons for Argentina's poor fiscal position. The nation's negative balance of trade contributed significantly to the balance-of-payments deficit. Low economic growth, a stagnant agricultural sector, inadequate capital investment, foreign exchange restrictions both foreign and domestic, international barriers to trade, and a lack of technological innovation in both the agricultural and the industrial sectors worked in tandem to contribute to the nation's deep economic crisis. Meanwhile, working-class residents of Argentina's cities, who had catapulted Frondizi to the presidency, enjoyed the benefits of the welfare state, subsidized meat purchases, and in many cases comfortable government jobs. But, in response to the spiraling rate of inflation, they also clamored for wage increases. Although the term would not be coined until the 1970s, in effect Argentina was mired in stagflation. Significantly, each component of the crisis contained a prominent transnational dimension. Somehow, Frondizi needed to balance the budget and the balance of payments, expand exports, and increase economic efficiency—all without prompting social revolution or some lesser political crisis.[3]

Given these challenges, Frondizi focused on the economic question from the beginning of his administration. In his inaugural address, he attempted to bring the country together to address the problem of under-development through a strategy that embraced important liberal ele-ments. However, he recognized that fixing the nation's ailing economy represented the most urgent task before the country and that his success in handling the crisis would ultimately define his presidency. To address the crisis, he affirmed his commitment to the international flow of invest-ment capital, emphasized the importance of private property, and called for a more limited state role in economic affairs. He argued that the state should coordinate economic activity to promote efficiency and industri-alization as a partner with private enterprise, rather than as a substitute. The rhetoric was strikingly different from the nationalistic positions that Frondizi had been known for, and it reflected his pragmatic assessment of his nation's economic crisis and the international environment.[4]

Together with his most trusted economic adviser, Rogelio Frigerio, Frondizi fleshed out the contours of his government's economic policy throughout the second half of 1958. The strategy that they crafted became known in Argentina simply as *desarrollismo* (developmentalism) and was designed to marshal all available resources domestically and internation-ally toward the objective of economic modernization. *Desarrollo* contained two key features: industrialization and national integration. Frondizi first wanted to expand the nation's industrial output for the domestic market, particularly in the nascent steel and automobile industries. The new gov-ernment further sought to integrate the domestic economy by directing scarce capital resources to regions that promised to make an immediate contribution to the national economy. To that end, Buenos Aires and Cór-doba were prized as industrial hubs. The Patagonian provinces, in addi-tion to Mendoza, Salta, and Santa Fe, were valued for their concentration of oil and coal. Together, these areas emerged as the favored regions that stood to gain under *desarrollismo*. Frondizi and Frigerio believed that, by diversifying its economy through the construction of modern industry, Argentina would become more self-sufficient and prosperous. Reflect-ing the scientific nature of developmentalist thinking, Frigerio posited a simple equation that would "develop integrated production through the transformation of the existing productive structure": "oil + meat = steel." Domestic oil production and agricultural exports, he argued, would drive the construction of a domestic steel industry and launch Argentina into modernity. Through *desarrollo,* Argentina could reclaim its past greatness on the international stage.[5]

Unsurprisingly, Frondizi's foreign economic policies were designed to serve his larger modernization strategy. The linkage between his domestic and his international visions was illustrated by his efforts to diversify Argentine exports, facilitate national industrialization, and escape the confines of export-oriented dependency while simultaneously expanding export earnings. Fundamentally, Frondizi and Frigerio attempted to finance a new ISI strategy with foreign capital in order to make Argentina self-sufficient in manufacturing and to correct the nation's structurally negative balance of payments. Under Perón's leadership, the country had employed an ISI strategy that used agricultural profits to underwrite the costs of industrialization, with devastating consequences for the underfunded agricultural sector. Perón's program had contributed to the polarization of the traditional agricultural elite and the working class. Frondizi sought to avoid that mistake by using international capital to finance *desarrollo.* He argued that Argentina would be able to break free of crippling underdevelopment only with US capital, technical assistance, and loan support. As a result, it became a strategic imperative for the Frondizi government to work closely with the United States and US-dominated supranational agencies, in particular the IMF. Although using the state to direct resources to critical areas was inherently questionable in the minds of international liberals, this eagerness to work cooperatively with private enterprise was consistent with the framework of the liberal international order. By adopting such an economic strategy, Frondizi would open the door to foreign private investment and international loans for both balance-of-payments stabilization and economic development, in that order. Given the nation's deep economic problems, it was a powerful incentive for Frondizi to cooperate with the Eisenhower administration.[6]

In order to salvage his own credibility, Frondizi needed to reframe the political discussion in a way that conceptually linked *desarrollismo* with nationalism. Since Argentines had long associated industrialization with modernity and progress, there was reason for Frondizi to believe that he might be successful. Having concluded that foreign investment capital and transnational corporations were essential partners if Argentina were to modernize, Frondizi and Frigerio publicly argued that Argentine nationalism demanded that the country take advantage of all available resources, regardless of their national origin. In his inaugural address, the new Argentine president asserted that domestic capital was "inefficient" to the task of modernization and proposed to substitute foreign capital in key sectors. He essentially argued that, because Argentine industrialization depended on the participation of transnational elites, any true nationalist would favor *desarrollo*. He went on to opine that "foreign capital is neither colonialist nor reactionary by its origin." He elaborated on this line of thought by drawing a distinction between "good" and "bad" foreign capital. Bad foreign capital, he argued, was directed strictly toward export-oriented enterprises that did not facilitate the modernization process and that were exploitative. On the other hand, good foreign capital financed an industrial infrastructure critical to advancement through the stages of growth. While bad foreign capital led to neocolonialism, good foreign capital would facilitate independent development and progress. Furthermore, Frigerio held that, by using foreign investment to construct a domestic manufacturing sector, the long-term "systematic transfer of wealth to foreign markets, which hampers national accumulation and so perpetrates underdevelopment," would be arrested. By making the case for the utility of foreign capital directed toward industrialization, Frondizi and Frigerio hoped to reappropriate the mantle of nationalism for their developmental strategy.[7]

Recognizing that political survival required that he deliver positive results quickly, Frondizi wasted little time implementing his agenda. Before the end of 1958, most key elements were put in place. He signed contracts with transnational petroleum corporations in the hope that they could more effectively exploit the nation's reserves and generate national self-sufficiency in energy production. He opened negotiations to conclude ongoing disputes with US and other foreign-owned steel, electric, and petroleum companies from which the Perón government had expropriated property. The most prominent outstanding dispute was with the American and Foreign Power Company (AFPC), a US-based transnational energy corporation with operations throughout Latin America. Since Perón's 1955 fall, US and Argentine officials had sought to secure appropriate compensation for the company's seized assets, without success. It had been a thorn in the side of the bilateral relationship that defied easy solution, primarily because the Argentines could scarcely afford either the financial or the political costs of compensation. Nevertheless, when the

Frondizi government took office, the negotiations took on a new urgency. On September 25, 1958, the Argentine government and the AFPC signed a new contract that guaranteed compensation for the company's expropriated assets and provided more evidence of Argentine liberalization.[8]

Although much of Frondizi's attention focused on stabilizing the economy and building Argentina's industrial base, primary products constituted the country's leading source of export earnings, and the sector could not be ignored. Moreover, the country's large landholders opposed Frondizi. The hostility was mutual. Frondizi characterized the landed elite as "enemies of development," arguing that they sought to return to the agricultural export-oriented economy that preceded World War I at the expense of industrial development and national progress. However, stagnant agricultural exports exerted a negative effect on the balance of payments. As a result, the president sought to stabilize the declining size of cattle herds by reinstituting price incentives for production. Meat producers had reduced the size of their herds as a result of Perón's policies that siphoned profits into industry. Increasing herd sizes, and subsequently the volume of exports, would boost revenues and thereby contribute to the eradication of the trade and balance-of-payments deficits, assuming price stability. Proposals to change the nature of the state's market intervention resulted in higher domestic beef prices, and domestic consumers in the heavily urbanized country scoffed at the resulting increase in the price of a dietary staple, especially during a time of economic crisis. In one of his frequent conversations with US ambassador Willard L. Beaulac, Frondizi insisted that "Argentines must eat less meat," a realistic but politically deaf statement given the central role of beef in the Argentine diet. While an increase in agricultural prices promised to help stabilize the balance of payments, it would join with inflation to further deteriorate consumer purchasing power.[9]

Austerity—particularly reductions in state employment and subsidies —was not a popular proposition for a majority of Argentines. But, by moving quickly to institute liberal reforms, Frondizi hoped to demonstrate concretely his liberal credentials. The strategy would be important to convince transnational business to invest in industrialization and to secure aid and stabilization loans from the United States and IMF. Frondizi created a record of accomplishment that he could showcase. With help from the global community, he hoped, the economy would turn the corner before voters returned to the polls to pass judgment on his administration.

US officials took note of Frondizi's policy departure. Washington's strategic objectives included both political and economic components best realized in a stable and prosperous Argentina. Politically, Washington sought Argentine alignment with the United States in the Cold War. Economically, as they did throughout the world, US officials encouraged their Argentine counterparts to institute a market-oriented economic system open to transnational capital and reliant primarily on the private sector. Doing so would create opportunities for US business overseas and, Eisenhower administration officials believed, usher in a more cooperative and prosperous world. Public and private American elites believed strongly that commitment to normal market mechanisms, liberal trade and investment policies, and currency convertibility offered unparalleled benefits for everybody involved—Americans and Argentines.[10]

The Eisenhower administration was serious about reform in Argentina. Although it switched from an approach of "trade not aid" to one of "trade and aid" throughout the Western Hemisphere during its second term, it also placed conditions on assistance. Before US tax dollars could be spent, Eisenhower demanded to see concrete reforms. Frondizi's liberal reform agenda went far in reassuring US officials. US ambassador Willard Beaulac explained that the administration "admired how [Frondizi] was solving problems one by one" and told the Argentine president that the Eisenhower administration was "impressed by reports of progress in Argentina, particularly in the economic field." NSC-5613/1, dated May 21, 1958, had identified Argentine resistance to the introduction of private capital in petroleum as an "important problem," on the grounds that Argentines "had neither the capital nor the know-how to develop their petroleum resources at a rate which would keep pace with their increasing needs for petroleum products." On the change in policy, US officials observed that it was now possible to direct additional public development money to Argentina. Beaulac grew increasingly optimistic about the prospects for US investments in the country, concluding that the improved climate for transnational businesses emerged *"because the Argentine Government* (and we hope the people) *wants them."* At the same time, the ambassador cautioned against giving the Argentines the perception that the US government was responsible for promoting investments for fear of inflaming Argentine nationalism and threatening existing American investments in the country. This note of caution was confined to the realm of public relations and not meant to suggest strict limits on the promotion of US business as a matter of policy. Beaulac was aware of the embassy's long-standing role as a promoter of free enterprise generally—and US business participation in Argentina specifically. However, he did not want to advertise his role in a way that would contribute negatively to the overall mission by stoking Argentine nationalism, a certain outcome if it were widely perceived that substantial power in Argentina was embedded in the US embassy. The balancing act between aiding the Frondizi government with conditional economic assistance, on the one hand, and not appearing as an overbearing imperial master, on the other, was a constant challenge. Nevertheless, in conversations with Frondizi, Beaulac observed that "the [Argentine] Central Bank needs dollars" and pledged that the United States "can be helpful in that regard." The Frondizi government's strategy of instituting liberal reform at home to secure capital from abroad appeared to be off to a promising start.[11]

The US government was not the only external body interested in Frondizi's reforms. To verify and enforce compliance with the tenants of international liberalism, the Eisenhower administration relied on the IMF. The director of the Office of International Financial and Development Affairs, Charles Adair, summarized the relationship most succinctly when he noted that US foreign economic policy was to make "balance-of-payments and stabilization assistance dependent on adequate financial programs worked out with the International Monetary Fund." Before the United States, the IMF, or private transnational banks would approve new lending to Argentina, the country would be required to demonstrate its creditworthiness to an IMF mission. Missions were composed of economists and other technical experts charged with probing into all aspects of a member country's economy. After examining the country's books, evaluating its economic health, and analyzing existing policy, the mission reported back to the IMF executive council with its analysis and recommendations. In general, missions mandated specific domestic reforms that must be instituted prior to the dispersal of IMF assistance. Since US policy was to follow IMF recommendations, the result of the field team's study was of paramount importance.[12]

The IMF mission visited Buenos Aires in July 1958, only two months into Frondizi's presidency, and issued its report in August. IMF officials identified inflation, the balance-of-payments deficit, the country's complicated exchange rate system, and the government's fiscal deficit as fundamental problems that needed to be corrected. Austerity, they agreed, was in order. Taxes must be raised and government spending reduced. The practice of featherbedding in key state-owned industries, particularly the railroads, must end. Layoffs were in order. The disadvantageous exchange rate system needed to be revised to promote primary product exports. The IMF called for greater realism from the Frondizi economic team in light of the high rate of inflation and the large budget deficits. Ominously, the IMF was not enthusiastic about the Frondizi government undertaking new development initiatives. "The investments in basic industries," the mission argued, "will either have to be reduced below present plans or substantial foreign sources of financing developed." The 60 percent wage increase that Frondizi granted labor and the continuation—as it turned out temporarily—of the multiple currency exchange system drew additional complaints. "In view of the extreme complexity of the existing restrictive system and the urgent need for further reform," the report read, "the staff does not recommend the approval of the Argentine multiple currency practices."[13]

The mission's analysis was important to the Frondizi government. Although representatives of governments sitting on the IMF board made final decisions on the dispersal of aid, they based those decisions in large part on the analysis and recommendations provided by the mission. Because US aid policy was conditioned on an agreement with the IMF, and because of its persistent balance-of-payments deficit, Argentina needed fund support. But that support was in turn conditioned on the initiation of specific economic reforms. From the IMF's point of view, applying conditionality on loans made sense. The organization was chartered for the specific purpose of maintaining balance-of-payments stability on a multilateral basis. Before tens of millions of dollars supplied by major country contributors including the United States would be allocated, fund officials demanded assurances that the loan would be repaid and that it was likely to shore up balance-of-payments disequilibrium.[14]

Understanding the IMF's position, Argentine minister of the economy Emilio Donato del Carril formally requested a stabilization agreement that included drawing rights of $75 million on December 4, 1958. In his letter to IMF managing director Per Jacobsson, del Carril emphasized his determination to attack inflation by containing the Central Bank's credit expansion, thereby limiting the money supply, and to reform the exchange system. The government's fiscal deficit would be tackled, he promised, by reducing expenditures and laying off public employees (including 15 percent of the maligned railroad workers). Public building projects would be delayed. Utility rates would increase. Consumer and producer subsidies would be rejected. In short, del Carril embraced the levels of austerity outlined in the IMF staff report. The Frondizi government was willing to take the steps necessary to earn a commitment from the liberal international community.[15]

In light of the reforms already implemented and those del Carril promised were forthcoming, the eighteen-member IMF board was disposed to sign off on the agreement. That disposition notwithstanding, some of the most penetrating questions directed toward del Carril centered on the potential social upheaval generated by austerity. One relatively optimistic board member noted the declining terms of trade and expressed his "hope that the social problems, which the plan may generate and the unavoidable unemployment in some activities which are overexpanded [*sic*] by inflation, will be of short duration." He went on to express his belief that "international public credits for economic development and a better environment for private investments, domestic and foreign, will undoubtedly help to smooth the process of adjustment." The British director, Guy Thorold, was even more buoyant, seconding del Carril's confidence that "the plan would be understood by the people, for such a large program would certainly need popular support." The Canadian director, A. B. Hockin, agreed, stressing that he had been "heartened" that the "Argentine Government seemed fully aware of the implications of what it proposed to do." Jean de Largentaye, the French director, displayed somewhat more realism—in addition to a penchant for understatement—when he noted: "The implementation of the program would be hard."[16]

Some concerns about the public reaction to the plan aside, the degree to which most of the board's questioning was friendly is informative. Members praised a new agreement with the Paris Club, the promise of a new system of exchange rates, the liberalized oil policy, and "a clear attack against inflation" that included "bold fiscal and credit policies and the elimination of subsidies which had threatened to destroy the major export industries of the country." They lauded the plan for being "bold" and "vigorous" and the Argentine authorities "for not having selected a half-way course which would have been much easier to implement."[17]

With the board's approval, both US and Argentine authorities were eager to complete the comprehensive stabilization and development package. The final agreement conformed to the public-private cooperative framework that was the hallmark of US foreign economic policy. As del Carril noted, if the program was to be successful, it would necessitate "the financial help of the International Monetary Fund, the United States Treasury, the Export-Import Bank, the Development Loan Fund, as well as commercial banks." Just such a series of loans were crafted to support balance-of-payments stabilization and the modernization of Argentine industry and infrastructure. On December 18, 1958, the Eisenhower administration, eleven private banks, and the IMF agreed on an economic-assistance package that totaled $329 million (the agreement was not announced by the IMF until December 29). Credits included the requested $75 million in drawing rights from the IMF, $54 million from the eleven banks, $125 million from the Export-Import Bank, $25 million from the Development Loan Fund, and $50 million from the US Treasury. To support the deal, members of the Paris Club agreed to allow Argentina to convert European currencies into dollars freely. Indeed, the agreement allowed it to devalue the peso. As the Argentine negotiator Roberto Alemann noted, the agreement did "away with every restriction on foreign exchange transactions." Frondizi announced the plan via a national radio broadcast that trumpeted his vision for liberal national development. The Argentine package aligned with Eisenhower's core principles as it ascribed a prominent role to private enterprise. It also provided a crucial example of the form that the administration's new policy of limited state support for Latin American modernization would take. Money was loaned, not granted, and the Frondizi government was expected to meet all its preexisting international commitments even as it attempted to expand its infrastructure radically. However limited, it was nevertheless an initiative that offered public US support for Argentine development and, in a larger sense, for the Argentine national project.[18]

The IMF's policy remedies for Argentina and other countries in similar economic straits draw attention to inconsistencies between US prescriptions offered for economic problems in the Global North and those

offered in the Global South. In pursuit of economic growth and max-
imum employment, US administrations of both political parties sub-
scribed to varieties of Keynesian economic theory during the postwar era.
But, rather than countercyclic responses to inflation or stagnation that
Keynesianism dictated, the IMF prescribed cyclic austerity policies for
Argentina. Designed to balance the government's budget and the balance
of payments, the IMF approach exacted a steep social cost. While transnational businesses and bondholders stood to benefit, costs were born dis-
proportionately by middle- and working-class Argentines.[19]

The 1958 stabilization agreement with Argentina also highlights
differences in the approaches that the Eisenhower administration took
to different parts of the world. Despite moving from a policy of "trade
not aid" to "trade and aid" toward Latin America, the administration
remained more tightfisted and fiscally orthodox in its approach toward
that region than it was toward other parts of the Third World. As the
historian Nick Cullather demonstrates in his study of Taiwanese development efforts, US officials were most successful when they adopted ideologically flexible policies and turned a blind eye when aid recipients did
not strictly adhere to IMF guidelines. The Eisenhower administration,
however, insisted on a high degree of liberal orthodoxy from Argentina as
a condition of assistance, and the structure of global power enforced the
administration's demands. Less economically developed countries, which
increasingly depended on the World Bank and the IMF for development
assistance and standby loans, were not well integrated into the governing
structures of those organizations. Instead, the IMF provided a mechanism whereby economically less developed countries seeking assistance
could secure the endorsement of their liberal credentials from economically developed countries.[20]

Stabilizing the Argentine economy through austerity was not Frondizi's ultimate objective; rather, the Argentine president sought to par-
lay his promised reforms into additional developmental assistance beyond
that included in the stabilization package. Following the December 1958
agreement, he requested additional US assistance to develop steel manufacturing and hydroelectric power as well as funding for transportation
and agricultural projects. The decision to prioritize steel in particular
was not arrived at by chance. The industrial development of the United
States had been punctuated by the late nineteenth-century emergence of

a dynamic steel industry centered in the Upper Midwest. As an age of big business emerged in the United States during the late nineteenth century, the steel industry surfaced as one of the largest and most important enterprises. Steel remained the masonry of modernity into the mid-twentieth century. With steel, a seemingly endless assortment of products could be manufactured, ranging from skyscrapers to cars to home appliances. Consequently, modernization theorists viewed the introduction of a domestic steel industry as a bellwether for industrial development. Moreover, there was precedent for US assistance for Latin American steel development; the Franklin Roosevelt administration provided assistance to Brazil to subsidize the construction of a domestic steel industry during World War II. More recently, the Eisenhower administration provided Export-Import Bank financing to Colombia for steel plant construction. Because the introduction of a national steel industry was widely viewed as a necessary precondition for the takeoff into modernity, and because other nations had successful track records securing international assistance, Frondizi hoped that he would be able to acquire funds from the United States.[21]

The availability of limited development assistance exposed subtle differences between the Bretton Woods liberal international order and the liberal orthodoxy of the late nineteenth century. Frondizi requested public funds to support a partnership between the Argentine government and private enterprise designed to enhance domestic production in both areas. Rather than dismiss the request out of hand on the grounds that it violated the principle of comparative advantage—as traditional nineteenth-century liberals would have done—Bretton Woods liberals quietly looked for ways to finance a limited ISI strategy that emphasized private ownership even as they emphasized fiscal austerity. Such an arrangement was precisely what Frondizi imagined when he argued that liberalism could serve as a component of Argentine nationalism because it provided a means to finance modernization efforts that most Argentines deemed critical to the success of the national project.[22]

For its part, the Frondizi government understood that liberal reform constituted the sine qua non of US-directed assistance. As a result, Argentine officials took pains to point out the progress that they had already made in the hopes of securing future credits. Minister-counselor of the US embassy Clare Hayes Timberlake reported that Frigerio emphasized:

"[The] Frondizi Government [was] firmly convinced [that] Argentina should align itself publicly and squarely with [the] US and free world in political and economic policy. [He] believes [the] Government has shown faith in [the] democratic process by acts already on record." The Frondizi government firmly declared its political and economic alignment with the United States. Frigerio hoped that the government's avowed commitment would translate into additional development loans.[23]

Ultimately, however, the strategy failed. That failure was in large measure the product of the insufficient attention all the principal actors paid to the conditions of working-class Argentines. As the economist Richard Ruggles commented in 1963: "The IMF can tell the Argentines to fire half of their nationalized railroad employees, but that might cause a strike that would do more long-run damage than an unbalanced budget." Despite del Carril's assurances, Frondizi never secured the support of the majority of Argentines for his policies. To the contrary, most saw his embrace of austerity and the international community as a sellout of Argentine sovereignty and their own interests. In light of the country's historic streak of populism and economic nationalism, the resulting anger should not have been a surprise. In that sense, the failure was the result of structural problems with the international approach to stabilization and development in the mid-twentieth century. Absent the intervention of an authoritarian government willing to pursue reforms without regard to the social consequences, for any policy to be successful, national and international leaders needed to win broad popular support. When sacrifices were necessary, they needed to be shared broadly and equitably. By contrast, in Argentina the working class sacrificed while bondholders were made whole and transnational corporations reported profits. It was a recipe for social unrest.[24]

As between 1958 and 1962, Argentine officials after 1983 were accountable to voters. The military coups that had occurred with the same frequency as elections between 1955 and 1976 ended following the disastrous Malvinas/Falklands War in 1982; on the return to democracy in 1983, military leaders dared not intervene in the political process. A positive development from the standpoint of democracy promotion, the anti-authoritarian direction of Argentine politics also made it more difficult for elected leaders to enforce austere spending measures. The predictable result of excessive spending, inadequate taxation, and a loose monetary policy was the soaring rate of inflation that incapacitated the country during the 1980s.

Inflation and economic stagnation continued to be a problem in 1989 when the Peronist Carlos Menem won the presidency. Unable to find a solution to the intractable problems, Menem named Domingo Cavallo economic minister in 1991. Cavallo arrived with a plan. He was convinced that the success of Argentina's economy during the first third of the twentieth century was attributable to the monetary stability that came with fidelity to the gold standard. Even though countries like Great Britain and the United States that had historically championed the gold standard abandoned it during the Great Depression, the US dollar emerged as the next best thing to gold in the years after World War II. Indeed, the Bretton Woods system was functionally a modified gold standard in which the US Treasury promised to exchange gold at $35.00 per ounce with other central banks. Even after the collapse of the Bretton Woods exchange system in 1971—a result of the structural US balance-of-payments deficit—international trade was routinely denominated in US dollars. The dollar also remained the most important reserve currency in the global economy. For Cavallo, the answer to rampant inflation appeared simple: link the value of the Argentine peso to the dollar. He did, guaranteeing dollar-peso convertibility at par. The dramatic move enforced monetary discipline by denying the state any control over the money supply. In order for this strategy to work, the Central Bank needed to maintain dollar reserves sufficient to honor the exchange rate. IMF officials were skeptical because the gambit eliminated options. As in 1958, they also insisted on drastic reforms to the domestic Argentine economy before stabilization assistance would be approved. Presidents Carlos Menem and Fernando de la Rúa embraced the Washington Consensus by rolling back the welfare state, privatizing government-owned corporations, and limiting the power of organized labor. The policies were all the more remarkable because of the political backgrounds of the protagonists: Menem was a Peronist and de la Rúa, like Frondizi, a Radical. Political bodies that had traditionally employed the language of social justice led Argentina down a neoliberal path. Yet, in light of Frondizi's reversal in 1958, Menem and de la Rúa's reversals appear ordinary—and certainly not unprecedented.[25]

Throughout the 1990s, however, the results of the currency board agreement appeared to vindicate Cavallo. The plan accomplished what he promised—it tamed inflation. At the same time, the Menem government presided over an era of significant economic growth. US and IMF officials heralded Argentina as the embodiment of the kind of success that other developing countries could enjoy through partnership with the IMF. Even the 1994–1995 Tequila Crisis failed to derail Argentina's prospects. Public support for economic policy usually accompanies positive results. Since the success was sustained for nearly a decade, it was easy for Argentines to conclude that they had finally turned a corner after having suffered economically since their country's pre–World War I heights. Unfortunately, structural problems caught up with policymakers by 1998. Exports remained insufficient to create a balance-of-payments equilibrium. In order to maintain prosperity, Argentina took on ever greater debt, becoming ever more overleveraged. Worse yet, most of the debt, both public and private, was dollar denominated. Consequently, devaluing the peso by abrogating the convertibility agreement would only exacerbate an already crushing debt burden, a political impossibility.[26]

Yet, by 2000, Argentina's foreign debt was unmanageable. In an effort to salvage the situation—after having supported Argentina throughout the past decade—the IMF cobbled together an emergency bailout package totaling nearly $40 billion in December 2000. Of that, the IMF pledged nearly $14 billion, with the rest coming from the World Bank, the Inter-American Development Bank, Spain, and a variety of private banks, both international and Argentine. In exchange, IMF officials mandated a new round of public spending cuts in an effort to bring the budget into balance. Other options were explored. Bondholders could take a haircut, but, because public Argentine banks held approximately one-quarter of their debt in government bonds, such a haircut would in part have shifted the crisis to another sector of the Argentine economy. Moreover, private transnational lenders were, as always, loath to accept such an outcome. In part because of the currency board, and in part because of the structure of international tariffs and agricultural supports, Argentine exports remained uncompetitive; there was no expansion.[27]

The crisis fully materialized only between November 28 and November 30, 2001. With the depth of the crisis clear to the public, individual depositors sought access to their funds. They were desperate to secure dollar-denominated assets before the government either froze or converted and devalued them. In effect, an old-fashioned bank run resulted. Depositors' fears were subsequently realized; in an effort to arrest capital flight, the Adolfo Rodríguez Saá government established *el corralito* in January 2002. The new policy restricted cash withdrawals to 250 pesos per week, scrapped the currency board, and revalued dollar-denominated Argentine bank deposits in pesos at the ratio of 1.4 pesos to the dollar. Fortunes were lost as the real value of the peso fell at an alarming rate. Real GDP declined 11 percent by the end of 2001 (and was down 20 percent since 1998). Meanwhile, the state's annual deficit stood at 10.5 percent of GDP. After the IMF withheld additional financing, Argentina defaulted on over $144 billion of sovereign debt in 2002.[28]

The global capitalist system evolved between 1958 and 2001. The Washington Consensus that frustrated Argentines at the beginning of the new millennium was not exactly the same as the Western policy consensus with which Frondizi dealt. Whereas in the 1950s IMF officials expressed annoyance at plans for state-led industrial development in strategic sectors, by the 1990s they would not tolerate any such deviation from liberal orthodoxy. Yet the changes were not as dramatic as they are sometimes characterized. Instead, ideological continuity was in many respects more pronounced than change in US and IMF engagement with Argentina.

US hegemony was limited in Argentina. In order to accomplish its objectives, Washington needed a cooperative government in Buenos Aires. Frondizi committed rhetorically to many priorities identified by the Eisenhower administration and the IMF and believed that integration with global capitalism offered the best opportunity for accomplishing his economic objectives. But, because of domestic political constraints, he did not always follow through. Cuts in public sector employees were not as steep as initially promised. Nor were welfare state cuts. Even while liberalizing important sectors of the economy, Frondizi provided a 60 percent wage increase to the nation's workers. Ultimately, he pursued austerity far enough to alienate the vast majority of Argentines but not so far as to accomplish his economic objectives. Although US officials remained supportive of his economic policies through the 1962 coup, they would not have pursued an identical course.

Despite the limited nature of US hegemony, efforts to decenter analysis of the US role in the world and highlight actors on the periphery ought not go too far. US and IMF officials were actively involved in Argentine affairs. During both the 1950s and the 1990s, they were confident that they had devised the ideal path to prosperity, social stability, and profits for transnational business. In both eras, they sought to export a system of market economics significantly more orthodox than that practiced in the United States. Therein lay the political problem. Austerity exacted steep social costs. Already high rates of unemployment were exacerbated. Welfare state measures designed to cushion economic distress were rolled back. The hand of the international community in these decisions was clear to Argentines in the streets. Washington was not an all-powerful force able to bend Argentina to its will. The Eisenhower and Kennedy administrations could not compel Frondizi to follow through on many of the austerity measures to which he had pledged. But the United States was not a passive onlooker. Rather, it was a complicit and powerful partner in bringing about the conditions that came to cripple Argentina.

Notes

1. The most detailed book to date on the relationship between Argentina and the IMF during the boom and bust of 1991–2001 is Paul Blustein, *And the Money Kept Rolling In (and Out): Wall Street, the IMF, and the Bankrupting of Argentina* (New York: Public Affairs, 2005). The IMF has produced its own postmortems. See Christina Daseking, Atish Ghosh, Timothy Land, and Alun Thomas, *Lessons from the Crisis in Argentina* (Washington, DC: International Monetary Fund, 2004); and Independent Evaluation Office of the IMF, *The IMF and Argentina, 1991–2001* (Washington, DC: International Monetary Fund, 2004). For a brief overview, see Russell Crandall, *The United States and Latin America After the Cold War* (Cambridge: Cambridge University Press, 2008), 70–73, 78–84. Claudia Kedar, *The International Monetary Fund and Latin America: The Argentine Puzzle in Context* (Philadelphia: Temple University Press, 2013), offers an important recent scholarly treatment. These works form the basis of the analysis in this and the following paragraph.

2. On the IMF's relationship with Argentina over time, see Kedar, *The International Monetary Fund and Latin America*. On the economic changes of the 1970s, see Niall Ferguson, Charles S. Maier, Erez Manela, and Daniel J. Sargent, eds., *The Shock of the Global: The 1970s in Perspective* (Cambridge, MA: Harvard University Press, 2010).

3. Paul H. Lewis, *The Crisis of Argentine Capitalism* (Chapel Hill: University of North Carolina Press, 1990); David Rock, *Argentina, 1516–1982: From Spanish*

Colonization to the Falklands War (Berkeley and Los Angeles: University of California Press, 1985), 321–31; Carlos F. Díaz Alejandro, *Essays on the Economic History of the Argentine Republic* (New Haven, CT: Yale University Press, 1970), 351–60, 528; Memorandum, Vaky to Bernbaum, August 22, 1958, RG 59, 735.00/8-22 58, National Archives II, College Park, MD (hereafter NARA).

4. Arturo Frondizi, "Mensaje inaugural," in Arturo Frondizi, *Mensajes presidenciales, 1958–1962,* 5 vols. (Buenos Aires: Centro de estudios nacionales, 1978), 1:9–57; Memorandum, Vaky to Snow and Sanders, May 9, 1958, RG 59, 735.11/5-958, NARA.

5. Celia Szusterman, *Frondizi and the Politics of Developmentalism in Argentina, 1955–1962* (Pittsburgh: University of Pittsburgh Press, 1993); Rogelio Frigerio, "Rogelio Frigerio," in *Argentina, 1946–83: The Economic Ministers Speak,* ed. Guido di Tella and Carlos Rodríguez Braun (New York: St. Martin's, 1990), 47–59, 48 (quotes); Álvaro Alsogaray, *Experiencias: De 50 años de política y economía Argentina* (Buenos Aires: Planeta, 1993), 41–57.

6. Carlos Florit, "Perfil internacional de un mundo en cambio, 1958–1962," in *La política exterior argentina y sus protagonistas, 1880–1995,* ed. Silva Ruth Jalabe (Buenos Aires: Grupo editor Latinoamericano S.R.L., 1996), 141–63, esp. 141; Felix Luna, *Dialogos con Frondizi* (Buenos Aires: Editorial desarrollo, 1963), 77; Rogelio Frigerio, *El desarrollo Argentino y la comunidad Americana* (Buenos Aires: Ediciones Gure, 1959). See also Frigerio, "Rogelio Frigerio."

7. Frondizi, "La batalla del petroleo," July 24, 1958, in Frondizi, *Mensajes presidenciales,* 1:133–49; Frondizi, "Mensaje inaugural"; Frondizi quoted in Andrés Cisneros and Cortes Escudé, *Historia general de las relaciones exteriores de la Republica Argentina,* vol. 11, *Las relaciones exteriores de la Argentina Subordinada, 1943–1989* (Buenos Aires: Centro de estudios de politica exterior, 1999), 66; Szusterman, *Frondizi and the Politics of Developmentism,* 126–29; Frigerio, "Rogelio Frigerio," 49.

8. Frondizi, "La batalla del petróleo"; Carl E. Solberg, *Oil and Nationalism in Argentina: A History* (Stanford, CA: Stanford University Press, 1979), 167–68; Dustin Walcher, "Petroleum Pitfalls: The United States, Argentine Nationalism, and the 1963 Oil Crisis," *Diplomatic History* 31, no. 1 (January 2013): 24–57; 1957 American and Foreign Power Company, Lot 59 D 73, NA, and 1958 American & Foreign Power Company, Lot 60 D 553, NARA; Memorandum of Conversation, October 13, 1958, *Foreign Relations of the United States, 1958–1960,* vol. 5, *American Republics* (Washington, DC: US Government Printing Office, 1991), 513–16 (hereafter, e.g., *FRUS, 1958–1960*). On the September 25 agreement, see *FRUS, 1958–1960,* vol. 5, *American Republics,* 513 n. 4.

9. Luna, *Dialogos con Frondizi,* 38–39; Memorandum of Conversation, October 18, 1958, *FRUS, 1958–1960,* vol. 5, *American Republics,* 516–18; Díaz Alejandro, *Essays on the Economic History of the Argentine Republic,* 528. On the significance of the meat industry, see Peter H. Smith, *Politics and Beef in Argentina: Patterns of Conflict and Change* (New York: Columbia University Press, 1969).

10. Burton I. Kaufman, *Trade and Aid: Eisenhower's Foreign Economic Policy, 1953–1961* (Baltimore: Johns Hopkins University Press, 1982).

11. Kaufman, *Trade and Aid;* NSC 5613/1, May 21, 1958, and Special Report on NSC 5613/1, November 25, 1958, *FRUS, 1958–1960,* vol. 5, *American Republics,* 2–19, 36–60; Szusterman, *Frondizi and the Politics of Developmentalism;* Memorandum of Conversation, October 13, 1958, *FRUS, 1958–1960,* vol. 5, *American Republics,* 513–16. On US investment, see Beaulac to Kearns, September 8, 1959, RG 59, 033.1135/9-859, NARA.

12. Memorandum, Adair to Mann, September 24, 1958, *FRUS, 1958–1960,* vol. 5, *American Republics,* 510–12. For a detailed evaluation of the state of the Argentine economy, see "Staff Report and Recommendations—1958 Consultations," August 20, 1958, SM/58/66, International Monetary Fund Archives (hereafter IMFA).

13. "Staff Report and Recommendations—1958 Consultations."

14. See, e.g., "The World Economy: Powerful IMF," *Time,* March 15, 1963.

15. "Argentina—Request for Stand-By Agreement," December 4, 1958, EBS/58/76, IMFA.

16. Minutes of the Executive Board, December 18, 1958, EBM/58/58, and Argentina—Stand-By Agreement, December 18, 1958, EBS/58/76, IMFA.

17. See the sources cited in the previous note.

18. Argentina—Stand-By Agreement; Memorandum of Conversation, October 13, 1958, *FRUS, 1958–1960,* vol. 5, *American Republics,* 513–16; Press Release no. 296, IMF, December 29, 1958, IMFA; Memorandum of Conversation, July 11, 1958, and Memorandum, Bernbaum to Rubottom, December 9, 1958, *FRUS, 1958–1960,* vol. 5, *American Republics,* 486–87, 521–23; Szusterman, *Frondizi and the Politics of Developmentalism,* 120–23; Roberto T. Alemann, "Roberto T. Alemann," in di Tella and Rodríguez Braun, eds., *Argentina, 1946–83,* 66–67; Arturo Frondizi, "Programa de estabilización para afirmar el plan de expansion de la economía Argentina," December 29, 1958, in Frondizi, *Mensajes presidenciales,* 1:227–53.

19. On Keynesianism in the United States, see Kevin Boyle, *The UAW and the Heyday of American Liberalism, 1945–1968* (Ithaca, NY: Cornell University Press, 1995); Alonzo L. Hamby, *Beyond the New Deal: Harry S. Truman and American Liberalism* (New York: Columbia University Press, 1973); Steve Fraser and Gary Gerstle, eds., *The Rise and Fall of the New Deal Order, 1930–1980* (Princeton, NJ: Princeton University Press, 1989); and Robert M. Collins, *The Business Response to Keynes, 1929–1964* (New York: Columbia University Press, 1981).

20. Nick Cullather, "'Fuel for the Good Dragon': The United States and Industrial Policy in Taiwan, 1950–1965," in *Empire and Revolution: The United States and the Third World since 1945,* ed. Peter L. Hahn and Mary Ann Heiss (Columbus: Ohio State University Press, 2001), 242–68.

21. Memorandum, Bernbaum to Rubottom, December 9, 1958, Memorandum

of Conversation, January 21, 1959, and Memorandum of Conversation, January 22, 1959, *FRUS, 1958–1960*, vol. 5, *American Republics*, 521–22, 531–33, 533–35.

22. On Frondizi's vision of his program, see Luna, *Diálogos con Frondizi*, esp. 67–80.

23. Telegram, Timberlake to Dulles, December 22, 1958, *FRUS, 1958–1960*, vol. 5, *American Republics*, 525–27.

24. "The World Economy: Powerful IMF."

25. Blustein, *And the Money Kept Rolling In (and Out)*; Daseking, Ghosh, Land, and Thomas, *Lessons from the Crisis in Argentina*; Independent Evaluation Office of the IMF, *The IMF and Argentina*; Barry Eichengreen, *Exorbitant Privilege: The Rise and Fall of the Dollar and the Future of the International Monetary System* (New York: Oxford University Press, 2012).

26. See the sources cited in the previous note.

27. See the sources cited in n. 25 above. See also "IMF Announces $39.7-Billion Rescue Package for Argentina," *Los Angeles Times*, December 19, 2000.

28. See esp. Daseking, Ghosh, Land, and Thomas, *Lessons from the Crisis in Argentina*, 37–38.

10

Dialogue or Détente

Henry Kissinger, Latin America, and the Prospects for a New Inter-American Understanding, 1973–1977

Tanya Harmer

On route to Panama in early February 1974, Secretary of State Henry Kissinger told a congressional group accompanying him that he was "serious about Latin America."[1] At first glance, such an assertion seems surprising. Kissinger had told Chile's foreign minister in 1969 that the axis of history excluded "the South."[2] With the exception of his efforts to exonerate himself of responsibility for the Chilean coup, Latin America is conspicuously absent from his first two voluminous sets of memoirs. It is also understandably the Middle East, Moscow, Beijing, and Europe that we think of in relation to Kissinger's jet-set travels rather than Latin America. Indeed, much to Latin American leaders' frustration, the visits he made to the region during his tenure at the State Department—he eventually visited Panama, Mexico, Venezuela, Peru, Brazil, Colombia, Costa Rica, Guatemala, the Dominican Republic, Bolivia, and Chile, mostly in 1976—were frequently postponed or canceled at the last minute owing to priorities elsewhere. As Kissinger later admitted, his "distorted geographic perspective" meant that South America seemed "beyond reach" compared to Europe.[3] Little wonder then that some scholars have suggested he was "indifferent to the fates of the countries in the Southern Hemisphere, regarding their internal affairs as mere subplots in the great superpower struggle."[4]

Kissinger nevertheless appears to have been more engaged with and interested in Latin America as secretary of state than is generally understood. Certainly, from 1973 to 1975, he believed that improving the US relationship with Latin America was important. In his view, Washington's ability to encourage a new inter-American understanding suddenly became a litmus test for what the United States could achieve more broadly around the world and particularly with regard to pressing North-South issues. "If we cannot do it with the countries with whom we have similar cultures and more or less the same political heritage," he warned those who were accompanying him to Panama, "we cannot do it anywhere."[5]

Beyond a vague idea of Pan-Americanism, it was the global role of the United States and its broader relationship with the periphery that drove US policy toward Latin America in the mid-1970s. In the context of the oil crisis and what US foreign policy analysts commonly referred to alarmingly as a shifting balance of power between the developed and the developing worlds—the "haves" and the "have-nots," as these groups were referred to by US officials at the time—Latin America increasingly mattered *precisely* because it was in the global South and had the potential to become a powerful group within it. Members of Nixon's beleaguered second administration desperately wanted to avert a situation in which Latin America lined up forcefully with the Third World against the United States in international forums and formed a powerful negotiating bloc on the world stage. As Kissinger's State Department analysts reasoned, it was not just that the region was the biggest US market outside Europe, Japan, and Canada, accounting for two-thirds of all US private investment in the developing world; the very legitimacy of the world system and the position of the United States in it were being challenged by a Third World agenda.

This agenda, in turn, had been significantly encouraged, if not shaped, by key Latin American countries. The global South's call for a new international economic order in 1973–1974 owed much to Chilean and Peruvian contributions within the UN Conference on Trade and Development, the Group of 77, and the nonaligned movement in the early 1970s. Between 1972 and December 1974, when it was adopted 115–6, with 10 abstentions (the United States voting against it), Mexico's president, Luis Echeverría, also proposed and championed the Charter on the Economic Rights and Duties of States at the United Nations to regulate international relations more equitably between North and South. Moreover, these collective demands—including the call for better terms of trade, preferential treatment for developing countries in international economic agreements, full national control over natural resources without the risk of discrimination or coercion, constraints on transnational corporations, and real resource transfers to developing nations—were ideas that emanated from the UN Economic Commission for Latin America (ECLA) and its director, the Argentine economist Raul Prebisch.[6] In the context of soaring oil prices and simultaneous rises in commodity values worldwide, ECLA had released a statement proclaiming the Arab OPEC nations' oil embargo as having proved "the vulnerability of the powerful and the strengthened position of the weak."[7]

In this context, US policymakers worried about the potential for Latin American countries to decouple themselves from the US sphere of influence and join forces with the South. The failure of the United States to respond meaningfully to regional demands was considered by the State Department as having the potential to encourage a "revolutionary transformation of the economic and political underpinnings of the international order."[8] Consumed as the United States was by a sense of panic, vulnerability, and despair in the context of the oil crisis, retreat from Vietnam, and Watergate, Kissinger therefore resolved to take action.

It was for these reasons that Kissinger was on route to Panama in early 1974. There, he signed a declaration of principles that would underpin subsequent negotiations to revise the Panama Canal Treaty and ultimately lead to the new 1977 Canal Treaties. However, as he later recalled, the aim of his trip was not simply related to bilateral US-Panamanian relations. Rather, it was a symbolic and carefully timed gesture aimed at improving inter-American relations. It was also his first official visit to Latin America as secretary of state, taking place two weeks before a major meeting of Western Hemispheric foreign ministers in Tlatelolco, Mexico City, in February 1974 at which he planned to commit the United States to a new era of inter-American solidarity.

Together, these visits to Panama and the inter-American meeting in Mexico underpinned what was known as Kissinger's "New Dialogue" for the Americas. Launched at a fancy luncheon for Latin American dignitaries at the Center for Inter-American Relations on Park Avenue in New York in October 1973, less than two weeks after Kissinger assumed the position of secretary of state, this dialogue promised to encourage new "understanding." Somewhat similar to Kissinger's proclamation of the "Year of Europe" in April 1973, this initiative, as the State Department conceived of it, was meant to "restore a sense of shared purpose" in an increasingly interdependent world.[9] Kissinger also waxed lyrical about "friendship based on equality and respect for the dignity of all."[10] Yet, as is so often the case with US initiatives in this part of its periphery, reaching a new understanding proved difficult. True, his new approach to Latin America was not helped by the fact that war broke out in the Middle East the day after Kissinger lunched with the Latin Americans, thereby diverting his attention. But there were also other fundamental challenges to the very concept of the New Dialogue that came to undermine it. These included a lack of empathy between US and Latin American policymakers, regional sensitivities to economic coercion and pressure from Washington, acute divisions between Latin American countries themselves, Kissinger's inability to devote enough time to the region, and, last but by no means least, his ineffectiveness in fully harnessing the instruments of US foreign relations to support his efforts. Consequently, at the beginning of 1975, the New Dialogue was effectively pronounced dead. Although select Latin American governments and US policymakers tried to revive it, the initiative struggled to come back to life.

So why bother to examine the New Dialogue? Despite being pronounced a failure, it offers an intriguing window through which to study US relations with the periphery at a time of perceived crisis. It allows us to examine how US policymakers—and especially Kissinger, who is widely regarded as not caring about the South—conceived of the Third World through an examination of Washington's relations with one particular part of it. US conceptualizations of Latin America's place in the world and US national interests in the region appear to have changed during this period. Traditionally viewed by US policymakers as separate from other parts of the Third World—and generally examined by historians of US foreign relations as such—Latin America was significant to Washington in the mid-1970s because it suddenly appeared to be an integral part of the Third World. And this was not something US policymakers wanted. Keeping Latin America beholden to the idea of a special relationship with the United States—anchored in the Western Hemisphere as opposed to the global South—was perceived as being the key to stopping the global South as a whole from challenging the North and forcing substantial changes to the international system.

This was admittedly a unique moment in postwar twentieth-century US foreign relations. Washington's leaders faced the prospect of global change from a position of self-perceived weakness. The New Dialogue tells us about this sense of vulnerability. That the actual balance of power in the Western Hemisphere had not actually changed as substantially as US policymakers feared, and that concerns regarding the Third World's potency to affect such change later proved vastly exaggerated, is not the point. What is interesting is that, for over a year, fears of an upheaval in international relations were taken seriously enough to launch an initiative in Latin America consisting of major international conferences, bilateral consultations, and interagency coordinating groups in Washington to shore up US power. As declassified US documents show, the significance of Latin America and the Third World therefore grew briefly in the mid-1970s: these areas no longer lay on the outskirts of global events but appeared to be threatening to move up the agenda and derail foreign policy priorities elsewhere. Issues such as Third World development and economic security, previously dismissed as peripheral concerns by the Nixon administration, therefore came into view. And it was for this reason that Kissinger decided to get serious about Latin America. In order to ensure that these issues remained peripheral, he had to engage with Latin American governments, he believed, and reassert the idea of a special inter-American relationship.

How the New Dialogue related to the Nixon administration's pursuit of détente was relatively ambiguous. The very concept of détente in a Latin American context was problematic. The first Nixon administration had rejected the idea that negotiations with Moscow and Beijing would automatically extend to Havana. And, as it continued to battle ideological enemies in the region, the Soviet Union distanced itself from its Latin American allies, fearing they might undermine superpower relations. Détente was also rejected by some Latin Americans as a dangerous compromise and a distraction from their primary goal of fighting either for communism or against it, depending on where they stood on the region's polarized political spectrum. While Fidel Castro worried that his country's future might be negotiated over his head, Pinochet argued that détente was misguided and perilous. "Communism advances during periods of détente," the Chilean dictatorship's representative at the United Nations told his US counterpart.[11] Nevertheless, in 1975, the United States accepted the end of multilateral sanctions against Cuba, at least in part because of the New Dialogue, while Kissinger engaged in highly secret and tentative discussions with Castro. All of this, however, begs the question as to how Kissinger's initiative—and concerns regarding North-South issues—related to détente.

This chapter also addresses more specific issues relating to the history and periodization of US–Latin American relations. It argues that the mid-1970s were transformative years that laid important foundations for what are commonly regarded as having been President Carter's policy innovations rather than having been years of neglect. Carter's renegotiation of the Panama Canal Treaty and his openings to Cuba, for example, would not have occurred without the New Dialogue. It is also now clear that Nixon and Kissinger's intervention in Chile and the continued support for right-wing dictators in the Southern Cone during Ford's presidency were not the sum of their policies toward Latin America, however important (and distasteful) these were. As Daniel Sargent notes, the mid-1970s have thus far tended to be missing years in histories of Kissinger's influence over US foreign policy.[12] Examining them from a US perspective, this chapter therefore helps fill that gap.

The New Dialogue in Theory

When Kissinger arrived at the State Department in September 1973, US relations with Latin America were no longer at the low point that they had been at when President Nixon took office. Neither were they particularly good. Armed with a hubristic belief in his power to remake international relations, Kissinger therefore set about trying to improve them. Getting on with the "Latins," as he and his team of policymakers referred to those south of the Rio Grande, was considered something one *should* do. However, in the specific context of late 1973 and early 1974, it was also increasingly perceived as something the United States *had* to do if it was to ward off the Third World challenge and survive as a predominant global power.

The fact that Kissinger was now in charge of the State Department had a lot to do with his decision and his willingness to pay closer attention to Latin America. While under attack during his confirmation hearings over alleged US involvement in the Chilean coup, he had told Foreign Minister Emilio Rabasa that he wanted to make US policy toward Latin America "more active."[13] First, however, he had to come to grips with regional affairs. According to Jack Kubisch, Kissinger's hand-picked assistant secretary for Latin American affairs, the new secretary "confessed he didn't know much about Latin America" when he arrived at Foggy Bottom. He therefore set up a series of lunch meetings two to three times a week to learn about the region. The fact that Kubisch and Kissinger knew each other well was important for facilitating a new approach to the hemisphere given the new secretary's long-held skepticism of and disdain for most other Foreign Service officers. In late 1973 and early 1974, the two of them worked closely together over "hours and days and weeks" on Latin America. Kubisch recalled that Kissinger "really did his utmost to learn as much as he could" and "learned a tremendous amount."[14]

The way in which the New Dialogue was conceptualized placed the reins of US–Latin American relations firmly in the secretary of state's hands and called on foreign ministers from Latin America and the Caribbean to engage with him. Nixon had ultimately been in control of Latin American policy during his first administration. However, with the president distracted by Watergate, Kissinger now took control. As Matias Spektor argues, the new secretary made a specific point of transferring hemispheric relations "from the presidential palaces to the foreign ministries."[15] In terms of multilateral regional negotiations, the so-called dialogue was also to be explicitly conducted outside the "rigidity" of the Organization of American States (OAS), a forum not only in crisis at the time but also considered "plodding" and "over-formalized."[16] While many Latin American representatives were skeptical about sidestepping legally binding OAS structures, they were encouraged that this would bring them into direct contact with Kissinger, the man widely recognized throughout the hemisphere—and the world—as determining US foreign policy.

Another factor that encouraged Kissinger and his team to rethink policy toward Latin America was the diminished threat of revolution in South America. True, Cold War warriors in the Southern Cone believed that World War III against international communism was on the horizon.[17] But, as Latin America was seen from Washington, Salvador Allende's government had been overthrown, and left-wing parties throughout the region were on the run from severe repression. Intelligence sources also concluded that Cuba's support for revolution had sharply declined. In fact, a State Department policy paper from the beginning of 1974 argued against bilateral rapprochement with Cuba on the grounds that this "would exaggerate the importance we attach to [it]." Castro's regime (or something similar) was permanent, this group advised; the United States also had "no vital interests" related to Cuba that warranted special concern or a separate détente process.[18]

Beyond Cuba, Peru's military government was considered the most radical challenge to US influence in the hemisphere. Yet it was never identified as being a Cold War ideological foe. Even Lima's recent Soviet tank purchase was interpreted in Washington as having been an assertion of independence rather than a Cold War challenge. As the CIA observed: "Most Peruvian leaders remain suspicious of Soviet motives and are reluctant to allow more than a minimal number of advisers and technicians into the country."[19] Moreover, CIA sources indicated that the Peruvians wanted to keep the door open when it came to relations with Washington and that they needed foreign loans and investment despite the government's Third World and nationalist rhetoric.[20]

When it came to the Soviet Union's interests in Latin America more generally, the director of the CIA briefed the Senate Armed Services Committee at the beginning of 1974 that détente may not have implied a "change of heart" on the part of the Kremlin but that it had forced it to weigh its priorities and adjust its foreign policy behavior accordingly.[21] As a State Department briefing for Kissinger put it in early February: "We can accept as a tenet of policy that Latin America has not yet become a 'legitimate' field of exploitation by the Soviets and other powers."[22] The Monroe Doctrine, in other words, still held firm as far as the Soviet Union was concerned, and by 1974 there was slim prospect of socialist revolution within Latin America.

Nonetheless, the United States still had reason to be on guard when it came to its relationship with the region. As the State Department advised President Nixon in mid-February 1974, there was a "multilateral dimension" to US relations with Latin American countries that tended to be "characterized . . . by a spirit of confrontation."[23] Development, sovereignty, nonintervention, and economic relations—the very issues that were central to the Global North-South debate—determined this dynamic. As

US intelligence sources emphasized, it had become increasingly possible that Third World nations previously divided by geography and the Cold War would develop an "identity of interest" that would result in "collaboration against both superpower complexes."[24] Third World–leaning forces in the hemisphere therefore had to be contained. "Attempts by Latins to challenge the international order with new concepts are evidence of the struggles between the old and new values and ties [in world affairs]," an internal State Department strategy paper noted. "[It] would be a blow to U.S. interests outside the region as well as within it if sizeable areas of Latin America were to identify their interests more closely with the Third World."[25]

By 1974, hemispheric problems were therefore looked at in a world context at a time when Cold War concerns had diminished. Although superpower relations had improved, a CIA report noted, "new developments have increased the number and nature of challenges to world stability": "Relationships among countries are no longer clear cut. . . . Among the main reasons for the less well defined relationships that exist now are: the era of détente; oil producers; shifts in the communist world; and the emergence of the so-called third world. . . . [The] general outlook is for continuing stress and disruptions. . . . [Our] ability to exert decisive political influence is being challenged. This is true in multilateral organizations such as the United Nations and the Organization of American States as well as in bilateral relations."[26] In this context, Kissinger emphasized the need to find new solutions for dealing with inter-American tensions. "Maybe we are in the position of the ancient Greeks with the Macedonians and Romans, who saw what their danger was but couldn't get it together. If so, we have had it," he mused as he explained his new regional approach to congressional leaders.[27]

To Kissinger and members of the State Department, getting it together meant reinvigorating Latin America's allegiance to the United States. "We . . . want a special relationship," Deputy Secretary of State Kenneth Rush outlined, "in which the tone of our relations is generally friendly and cooperative, thus promoting a favorable environment for our security and economic interests in the region, and in which the Latins operate generally on our side in the global arena." While Rush underscored that the United States could not go as far as the Latin Americans might want to on certain issues, he suggested that it could at least respond partially and "more importantly" "fold them into a larger picture of Hemispheric cooperation in meeting some important problems in our era, such as the need to reform the international economic system and to build a more peaceful, cooperative world order. . . . [T]he question is no longer what the United States can do *for* Latin America but what the United States and Latin America can do together in an interdependent world. . . . [The task is] to try to begin at least to evoke a greater sense of reciprocal obligations and common purposes which go beyond a North-South regional relationship and extend into a global arena."[28] Kissinger echoed these hopes when he met Peru's foreign minister, Miguel Ángel de la Flor, in early 1974. The United States was moving "from domination to cooperation," he explained, "not as a favor, but out of enlightened self interest."[29] Cooperating with Latin America, in other words, was about rescuing and upholding US hegemony.[30]

Prior to Kissinger's departure for Mexico to meet Latin America's foreign ministers, the State Department put forward a new "Agenda for the Americas" that spelled out this aim. At its core were a number of quid pro quos: Latin Americans would support US positions in pending international trade negotiations in return for high-level consultation and coordination of US trade policies; the United States and Latin America would offer each other mutual support vis-à-vis Europe and Japan in multilateral forums; and the United States would encourage regional leaders to accept "principles on matters of special interest to the U.S., such as access to scarce commodities and the treatment of foreign enterprises" in return for US briefings and participation in hemispheric efforts to alleviate those suffering from the energy crisis. The deal on the table might not have been generous as far as Latin American rewards for this kind of support were concerned. But this was not an "exercise to satisfy Latin demands." It was about the standing of the United States in the world.[31]

The New Dialogue was therefore essentially defensive. Publicly, the State Department emphasized that it was underpinned by a "political will to cooperate in promoting development and working out problems . . . [and by] good faith, solidarity, social justice and economic cooperation."[32] Privately, it was designed to "diminish confrontation, provide an alternative to Third Worldism, slow down trend towards a Latin American bloc."[33] As State Department officials acknowledged on the eve of Tlatelolco, there was a "disparity between Latin American aspirations and our ability to satisfy them."[34] If the Latin Americans gathered in Mexico to meet Kissinger in February 1974 had yet to discover this disjuncture, the secretary of state would also soon find out that manipulating Latin Americans was not as easy as simply flying south to meet them.

The New Dialogue in Practice

Latin America's leaders had enthusiastically embraced the concept of the New Dialogue. As the director of the CIA noted, having "felt excluded" from high-level diplomacy in previous years, they were hopeful that their interests were poised to take center stage.[35] Kissinger appears to have been optimistic too. "I like them personally," he mused. Unlike the Europeans, who had rejected his Year of Europe initiative, Latin Americans had seized on his "overture" and immediately "agreed to get together": "They are excited."[36] However, they had had their own agenda. As John Crimmins, US ambassador in Brasilia, reflected, Latin America saw the New Dialogue as a "vehicle for getting their demands."[37]

After the New Dialogue had been launched in New York in October 1973, Latin American foreign ministers had devised their own framework for the Mexico meeting with what the CIA depicted as "unusual consensus."[38] In what became known as the "Declaration of Bogotá," following a meeting in Colombia in mid-November 1973, Latin American and Caribbean foreign ministers tabled eight priority topics that they wanted to discuss with Kissinger: (1) development cooperation (including measures to ensure collective economic security and free access for Latin American products to US markets), (2) protection against economic coercion, (3) the restructuring of the inter-American system, (4) settlement of the Panama Canal negotiations (a "high priority"), (5) Latin American participation in discussions related to the structure of international trade and the international monetary system, (6) a review of transnational corporations and their threat to state sovereignty, (7) technology transfer, and, finally, (8) political problems in the hemisphere related to regional and world contexts. On the whole, the declaration's language was combative: development cooperation should no longer be "subject to unilateral conditions imposed by the country lending assistance or be discriminatory in nature." The Latin Americans wanted to emphasize their "solidarity" with Panama, and they accused transnational corporations of having "meddled in the internal affairs of sovereign nations" and demanded that it was imperative for the United States to "share Latin American aspirations and to join in Latin American efforts to achieve radical changes" in the inter-American system.[39] As State Department analysts noted, Latin Americans believed that the time had come for the United States to "make atonement" for past sins.[40]

The Venezuelan foreign minister's reference to being on the cusp of eradicating "slavery" in the international system on arriving in Mexico City added to this impression. "This is what worries the rich countries," Arístides Calvani continued. "For the first time in history, the underdeveloped countries have taken the initiative and are changing the hour of history."[41] The Mexicans also put forward what US delegates perceived as being a confrontational draft communiqué prior to the conference. As the US ambassador in Mexico City, Joseph Jova, told Mexico's representative to the OAS, Rafael de la Colina, its language was like a "shower of cold water."[42] What is more, US diplomats increasingly worried that Echeverría could use the event to assume the position of "pre-eminent spokesman for Latin America—if not all of the Third World." As Jova warned, Echeverría seemed to be "convinced that if the poor are to get richer, the rich must get poorer."[43]

To counter this kind of view, US diplomats worked bilaterally to limit Latin America's collective scope for maneuver and spell out its preferred language for the final communiqué. Jova visited Latin American delegations in Mexico to express the American "disappointment" with the "tone" of the Mexican draft communiqué and to emphasize "constructive" goals. The Nixon administration was hoping for a declaration that incorporated "nobler, more elevated terms" and stressed "common aims, mutuality of interests and principles."[44] In the end, Jova did not have to work too hard. Despite public rhetoric from Venezuelan and Mexican participants, the majority of delegations emphasized their desire to work with the United States and their understanding that the conference was unlikely to produce "miracles."[45] What is more, Jova's conversations with Latin American diplomats and the preliminary proceedings of the conference revealed that the apparent unity underpinning the Declaration of Bogotá was fragile.[46] All of this made it unlikely that Latin American foreign ministers could use their collective strength to make comprehensive demands on the United States. As Echeverría himself lamented, the "Disunited States of the South" faced an uphill struggle in their dialogue with the *United* States of America.[47]

The conference proved this true. Public pledges for a new spirit of consultation and cooperation followed. However, in concrete terms, only the promise of future discussions was heralded. True, the United States pledged to "avoid as far as possible, the implementation of any new measures that would restrict access to the United States market" and "maintain as a minimum, present aid." The conference's attendees also welcomed US-Panamanian negotiations on a new Canal treaty and Kissinger's recent trip to Panama. Yet the final communiqué was an unbinding statement of intent rather than a firm commitment to rewriting the rules of inter-American relations. With respect to concerns regarding transnational corporations, it postponed discussion to "a later meeting." On the question of reforming the inter-American system, it underlined the "need for intensifying work." When it came to US calls for protecting private investment, the Latin Americans "took note" and agreed to consider the matter further, and the question of establishing an Inter-American commission of science and technology was "left over for later decision."[48] As Kubisch recalled, it was "more appearance than substance that was given away."[49]

Kissinger's mere presence in Mexico City, his willingness to talk to Latin American foreign ministers, and his apparent attention to Latin American issues had nevertheless been significant. As Rabasa stated: "To have convinced the US Secretary of State to come and engage in dialogue with us, in frank and open manner, with mutual respect, on basis of coordination and never, never (*jamas, nunca*) of subordination, constitutes, I believe, another advance in [the] history of this continent."[50] Summing up the conference's results, the State Department similarly reflected: "The Latins were extremely pleased that the Secretary of State, after the impasse in drafting the communiqué, was willing to get down to face-to-face negotiations with them and hammer out a mutually acceptable final version of the declaration. This action bespoke more than 100 speeches."[51] As one US ambassador sycophantically explained to Kissinger, the New Dialogue was a way for Latin Americans "to engage [his] prestige, [his] magicianly qualities, and [his] standing in the administration, with the congress and with the American people in an effort to obtain a rapid and positive response to the litany of their demands."[52] Indeed, vague resolutions aside, Kissinger's physical presence in Mexico seemed enough to keep Latin Americans buoyed by the New Dialogue. His preemptive visit to Panama two weeks before the conference was also regarded as an indication that Kissinger was willing to respond personally to Latin American demands. The important thing, as Torrijos had told him in Panama, was to create an "atmosphere of faith."[53]

In an effort to do just that, the secretary sent individual letters to the region's foreign ministers after Tlatelolco hailing it as having been "enormously useful and productive." The conference had been "one of the most important inter-American conferences in recent years" on account of the "spirit of frankness and openness," he underlined.[54] Yet his reference to being on route to resuming work to bring peace to the Middle East implied that his engagement with Latin America was transient. No matter how special and important Kissinger told his counterparts Latin America was, the truth of the matter was that it remained a secondary concern in an otherwise overcrowded agenda. And this is exactly where the secretary ultimately wanted it to remain. Indeed, one of the New Dialogue's principal objectives all along had been to stop the region from becoming a major headache for Washington. Kissinger's personal engagement had therefore been designed to assuage Latin Americans just enough to make sure that the region remained a peripheral problem. Yet there was an obvious flaw in this strategy: keeping Latin America *off* the agenda so as to concentrate on détente or bringing peace to the Middle East required keeping *up* the effort to engage seriously and sincerely with its leaders.

The New Dialogue's future was also dependent on keeping the divisive issue of Cuba off the agenda. And US policymakers had left Cuba off its agenda. As Kissinger told Argentina's foreign minister when they met in Mexico, it had to "be kept apart from the current effort to improve Hemispheric relations, otherwise both problems would be more difficult to solve."[55] At Bogotá, differences between those who wanted to review increasingly untenable OAS sanctions against Cuba and those who did not had led to the inclusion of a vague reference to political problems in the hemisphere (point 8). Consequently, Cuba, the continuation of collective sanctions, and the island's place within the "Western Hemispheric community" that Kissinger sought to promote were left precipitously hanging in midair.

Moreover, a number of Latin American leaders indicated that they regarded the attitude of the United States toward Cuba as a test of Kissinger's sincerity in charting a new path for inter-American affairs. For the Peronist administration in Argentina, which had unilaterally reestablished relations with Cuba in 1973, granted a $200 million credit to the island, and wanted Argentine subsidiaries of US companies to trade with the island, it was particularly important. Argentina's foreign minister asked Kissinger directly how the Americas could be unified if Cuba was "frozen out." As State Department analysts admitted: "In spite of *détente,* doubts remain about the willingness of the U.S. to accept fully the Latins' right to ideological diversity, or in the new Latin lexicon, 'ideological pluralism.' These doubts are nourished by continued U.S. intransigence regarding the OAS sanctions against Cuba and skepticism that the U.S. assistance boycott of Allende was caused solely by expropriation disputes."[56] Conversely, other foreign ministers personally urged Kissinger to ensure that there would be no change on Cuba. In private, Brazil's outgoing foreign minister, Gibson Barbosa, stressed his government's fears that the United States was avoiding discussing the issue because it was about to make a unilateral move toward some kind of détente. (Kissinger found himself reassuring the Brazilian that the Nixon administration had no "surprises" in store and would consult the Brazilians if anything changed.)[57] Prior to Tlatelolco, the new Chilean dictatorship's foreign minister, Admiral Ismael Huerta, had also told Kubisch that Santiago "would oppose discussion of Cuba and submit resolution against Cuban intervention if Cuba was discussed." Contrary to US calculations about Cuba's diminishing Cold War threat, Huerta insisted that the inter-American system had to "be more alert than ever."[58]

Even if it was formally kept off the agenda, Cuba was thus a simmering issue. Despite frequent, repeated US references to what "the Latins" thought and wanted, it also unmasked the fallacy of a single Latin voice. This boded well as far as Washington's fear of a powerful Latin American bloc on North-South issues was concerned. Despite recognizing these divisions, however, US policymakers were not reassured. With a special UN General Assembly session to debate the global South's agenda for a new international economic order scheduled to take place in May 1974, efforts to keep up the New Dialogue therefore continued.

The New Dialogue Tested

Tlatelolco had raised expectations in Washington and Latin America as to what the New Dialogue could achieve. US policymakers seem to have been genuinely encouraged by the proceedings, which in turn boosted their commitment to making the initiative more concrete than they had perhaps envisaged at the outset. A number of Latin American foreign ministers also emphasized the need for substantive progress on the Declaration of Bogotá. As Colombia's foreign minister, Alfredo Vazquez Carrizosa, put it, what was needed were "more precise" steps. The next meeting of the New Dialogue in Washington at the end of April 1974 had to be a "conference of decisions."[59]

For decisions to be made, however, the thorny questions of Cuba, Latin American access to US markets, the role of transnational corporations in Latin America, the future of the inter-American system, and collective economic security would have to be addressed. And, in this respect, the Washington conference merely nudged the New Dialogue along. In response to Latin Americans stressing the urgency of access to US markets, Kissinger reassured foreign ministers that as much as possible was being done. The issue of transnational enterprises was deferred to a working group and further discussion in March 1975, when foreign ministers were next due to meet in Buenos Aires under the New Dialogue framework. Latin Americans also voiced their concerns over "the problems of economic coercion and the desirability of their elimination from relations among the countries of the Americas," without any apparent response from Kissinger.[60]

Even so, all was not lost. The US-Panamanian negotiations continued to elicit praise, and Kissinger at least pledged close consultation with Latin Americans on trade negotiations and the formation of a new international monetary system, something that foreign ministers "noted with satisfaction."[61] Writing to Nixon, Kissinger argued that it was "appropriate to take advantage" of the "real impetus" the New Dialogue had given "[US] multilateral relations with Latin American countries." On June 10, 1974, the secretary subsequently signed National Security Decision Memorandum 257 (NSDM 257) on behalf of the president to "give full and prompt effect to the initiatives" underscored by the New Dialogue. As well as committing the administration to resolving fisheries disputes with Ecuador and Peru and giving "close attention to negotiations with Panama," NSDM 257 also outlined measures to prevent new disputes from arising. These included "pursuing agreement in the UN on an acceptable Charter of Economic Rights and Duties of States," being willing to discuss the concepts of "collective economic security" and "integral development," and participating in talks to agree on the regulation of transnational enterprises. The most concrete aspect of the new directive revolved around plans for "high level" consultations "in order to adjust and coordinate U.S. positions with those of Latin America . . . to the greatest extent feasible" in multilateral trade negotiations and on issues such as access to markets and raw materials and international monetary reform. NSDM 257 underlined "supporting as a minimum the current level of bilateral and multilateral assistance to Latin America."[62] The following month, Kissinger endorsed proposals while simultaneously working toward protecting Latin American interests within the US Trade Reform Act, which was then being ironed out in Congress. Over August and September, the administration subsequently established an interagency mechanism for dealing with trade aspects of the New Dialogue under the overall purview of the National Security Council.[63]

These measures notwithstanding, skepticism about the New Dialogue persisted. As the CIA noted toward the end of 1974, there were still serious regional concerns regarding forthcoming trade restrictions and the role of US private companies in Latin America. Regional leaders also expressed growing impatience with Washington's willingness to deal meaningfully with priorities laid down in the Declaration of Bogotá such as the question of transnational corporations, technology transfers, and economic development goals central to Global North-South dialogue.[64]

Alongside these already substantive issues was Cuba. As a State Department briefing paper put it in the run-up to the OAS General Assembly's meeting in Atlanta shortly after the Washington conference, US policymakers were hoping to "keep this issue in a minor key and to avoid a vote on a resolution."[65] However, they could no longer avoid the prospect of it flaring up within the OAS and affecting the New Dialogue. In April 1974, while still holding out hope for "talk but no action," the

State Department therefore began exploring options. On the one hand, the administration gave special permission to Argentine subsidiaries of Ford, General Motors, and Chrysler to sell cars to Cuba.[66] On the other, it hunkered down and advocated rounding up no votes and trying to "get as many Latin supporters of the sanctions, e.g. Brazil, Bolivia, Chile, Nicaragua, to take a public lead" if the Cuba issue came to a vote.[67] True, by this point, Kissinger and Nixon were privately willing to countenance a situation whereby a simple majority instead of two-thirds of OAS members could terminate sanctions.[68] However, when the Atlanta meeting did not come to a vote, this option was kept quiet. So, too, were the tentative, highly secret back-channel contacts with the Cubans that Kissinger authorized in June 1974. Despite having told the Brazilians that he would consult them before making any move in this regard, it appears that the secretary's initiative was a unilateral venture. Even Presidents Nixon and Ford do not appear to have been fully briefed.[69] And, as very preliminary contacts got under way, US officials formally rejected any move that would end hemispheric sanctions against the island.[70]

When, at the Washington New Dialogue meeting, the Mexican, Argentine, and Peruvian foreign ministers had formally raised the issue of Cuban participation at the Buenos Aires meeting in March 1975, the Cuba question gained momentum. In late 1974, there was a strong possibility of Venezuela and Colombia following Mexico, Chile (until 1973), Peru, Argentina, and four Caribbean nations (Barbados, Guyana, Jamaica, and Trinidad and Tobago) in unilaterally reestablishing relations with Cuba regardless of continued OAS sanctions. Together with Costa Rica, they therefore tabled a resolution that would give the OAS the opportunity to overturn collective sanctions with a requisite two-thirds majority. In September 1974, OAS foreign ministers consequently agreed to meet in Quito in November to respond.[71]

In planning for the Quito OAS foreign ministers' conference, State Department officials and CIA analysts seem to have been unsure of how to play their cards. First and foremost, they were wary that Cuba could wreck the New Dialogue. The problems of keeping up hemispheric sanctions against Cuba were that they were "increasingly difficult to enforce" and served as "irritants" in US relations with countries like Argentina, Peru, Venezuela, Panama, and Mexico. However, to actively vote for an end to collective sanctions against the island would antagonize allies like

Chile and Uruguay. The strategy the US representatives in Quito opted for was therefore to hold the majority option in reserve and assume a position of "strict neutrality, making certain that [the United States] could not be accused of exerting influence on the outcome."[72] Kissinger appears to have been more willing to accept that the United States would have to change its position on Cuba within the OAS so as not to lose the initiative to Latin Americans and Castro himself. But, as he later recalled, Ford, like Nixon, was resistant to pushing for change.[73] The hope was therefore that the Latin Americans themselves would resolve the question of Cuba's place within the inter-American system and that the secondary issue of Cuba would not spiral into a broader US–Latin American confrontation that derailed the New Dialogue.[74]

When they met in Quito, the majority of Latin American foreign ministers appear to have shared the view that resolving the Cuba problem was a means to an end rather than an end in itself. As Ecuador's foreign minister put it, the "entire Inter-American system" was "at stake."[75] The problem was that Latin American foreign ministers could not resolve it. When those seeking to overturn the 1964 sanctions failed to get the necessary fourteen votes, the conference ended in gridlock, which, because the two issues had been linked at the Washington meeting, in turn undermined the New Dialogue.

As important for the New Dialogue—if not more so—was the impact that the Quito conference had on Latin American opinions of Kissinger and the US commitment to improving inter-American relations. Although a major US–Latin American confrontation had been avoided, foreign ministers visited the main US representative at the conference, Rush's successor as deputy secretary of state, Robert S. Ingersoll, to ask the United States to intervene. As Ecuador's foreign minister had underlined, the US position was "decisive."[76] With a divided region looking for leadership, the secretary's absence had also been acutely felt. Prior to the conference, the CIA reported that Latin Americans regarded it as an "affront."[77] Mexico's foreign minister, Emilio Rabasa, one of the key architects in helping get the New Dialogue off the ground, warned Ingersoll that Kissinger's nonattendance would cause "resentment." Would Kissinger please consider flying down to Quito to vote? he asked.[78] In reality, as Brazilian foreign minister Silveira lamented, the conference had been "badly prepared," and those tabling the motion to remove sanctions should have been surer of getting the necessary fourteen votes before it opened. While Silveira expressed private satisfaction with the outcome—it forced "Castro to negotiate instead of handing him what he wants on a silver platter"—there was no mistaking that the United States was blamed by the majority of delegates for not doing something to resolve the issue. The next meeting of the New Dialogue would now also have to broach the Cuba issue directly and move beyond it.

To be sure, progress continued to be made in other areas of the New Dialogue. In November 1974, the subgroup on US–Latin American trade congratulated itself that it had done its best since the Washington meeting to avoid trade restrictions with Latin America and had "tried to take Latin American trade interests into account." "Generally . . . our record . . . has been good," it concluded.[79] Ingersoll's report for Ford on NSDM 257 at the end of 1974 similarly noted that the New Dialogue had been a success in terms of its "immediate objective of checking the erosion which had begun to take hold in U.S.–Latin American relations." Yet he acknowledged that progress still rested on "high level attention" and deeds following words. And, in this respect, the report underlined the problems that the forthcoming US Trade Reform Act might bring.[80]

The New Dialogue Pronounced Dead

Ingersoll's fears were not groundless. To an even greater extent than feared, the US 1974 Trade Reform Act, passed by the Senate on December 13, 1974, and coming into effect on January 5, 1975, accelerated the New Dialogue's demise. At issue was Ecuador and Venezuela's exclusion from the Generalized System of Preferences (GSP) owing to their OPEC membership. As the US ambassador in Quito recorded Ecuador's foreign minister as having argued: "The basis for the New Dialogue had been destroyed. . . . Many Latin American countries were disturbed by the U.S Trade Bill because, while it excluded OPEC members today, its provisions would exclude any other countries which tried to protect their export prices in a concerted manner tomorrow."[81] Within the OAS, Venezuela led complaints against what its leaders perceived as the trade act's discriminatory character; Ecuador's representative said that it was "impossible to conduct a dialogue under threats of coercion"; Mexico's representative "vigorously denounced" the exclusion of Venezuela and Ecuador from the GSP; Brazil's representative pronounced the law a "code of restriction"; and Argentina's representative "deplored" the trade bill, specifically stating that it went against Kissinger's reassurances.[82] On January 23, 1975, the OAS council voted 20–1 (with the United States abstaining and two member states absent) against what it called "discriminatory and coercive" measures. Ensuing recriminations on all sides also did much to undermine the relatively improved understanding and trust that the previous year had seen. Indeed, Latin American leaders, one by one, quickly gave up on the New Dialogue as a means to resolve hemispheric problems. As Kissinger recalled in his memoirs, in late 1974, US policy toward Latin America therefore subsequently moved back "from the multilateral to the bilateral."[83]

The key problem with the Trade Act is that it seemingly attacked core principles of the Declaration of Bogotá and the new international economic order, such as freedom from economic coercion and discrimination on the basis of ideology and full control over national resources. It also undid the US policymakers' commitment to consult and cooperate with Latin Americans specifically on trade. Ecuador and Venezuela had not participated in the OPEC Arab members' oil embargo but were punished by association. Furthermore, punishing OPEC was not popular in Latin America, where oil producers' moves had been widely celebrated despite many of the region's countries being likely to suffer from rising oil prices. Indeed, the US ambassador in Brasilia, John Crimmins, explained to Kissinger "the fallacy of trusting to the cold-blooded calculation of economic interest as a reliable guide to Latin American conduct": "Sovereignty, national dignity, pride and honor are not to be lightly dismissed as shibboleths empty of operative meaning."[84] As Ecuador's foreign minister, Lucio Paredes, saw it, the trade bill had undermined Latin Americans' "dignity" and unmasked the US attitude as that of a "school teacher toward a student."[85] Meanwhile, Venezuelan newspapers quoted the country's representative to the OAS as saying: "Venezuela will not kneel before Kissinger at [the forthcoming inter-American foreign ministers meeting in] Buenos Aires." Indeed, US diplomats reported pessimism with regards to the future of the New Dialogue.[86] Although Brazil's new foreign minister since March 1974 and Kissinger's principal ally in the region, Antonio Francisco Azeredo da Silveira, was reluctant to weigh in on the argument, other Brazilian diplomats were more direct. Beyond

Venezuela and Ecuador, every Latin American country had a grievance with the United States, Silveira's chief of cabinet told Crimmins. These grievances had been "exacerbated by the Trade Act" and would continue to grow until the United States "accepts politically the distributionist concept that wealthy industrialized nations should support the development of poorer nations."[87]

The New Dialogue was officially put on ice when Venezuela and Ecuador refused to attend the forthcoming Buenos Aires meeting and Argentina then announced that it was postponing it indefinitely. As Argentina's foreign minister explained in a letter to Kissinger, his decision to postpone the conference reflected "a divergence within the [inter-American] family which will be overcome when the North American government can produce adjustments and clarifications to the aspects which now are little comprehensible to Latin America."[88] As far as he saw it, he had little choice, given the widespread sympathy for Venezuela and Ecuador throughout Latin America. To do otherwise, he privately told the US ambassador in Buenos Aires, would have been to risk being labeled a US "stooge."[89]

Although the State Department insisted that "the United States has renounced any method of pressure as obsolete," pledged continued "friendship" and "conciliation," and tried to counter charges of "coercion" by pointing out that the trade act also offered benefits for the region, it was clear that the empathy between US policymakers and their Latin American counterparts had broken down.[90] Kissinger quite simply hit back at Latin American recrimination and cancellation of the Buenos Aires conference by stating: "Pressure from the South is as inappropriate as pressure from the North." Argentina's decision to cancel the Buenos Aires meeting, he stated publicly, was "substantively unjust."[91] Meanwhile, a State Department report simply lamented "the dominant political fact . . . that the United States remains the one country in the hemisphere able to evoke regional unity—against itself."[92]

As well as dealing a blow to Latin American interests, the Trade Reform Act also revealed Kissinger to be powerless to act on the personalized style of dialogue that he had instigated with the region. In public, the State Department and President Ford repeatedly underlined the executive branch opposition to the exclusion of Venezuela and Ecuador from the GSP.[93] Yet, as Ecuador's foreign minister put it, Latin America had "no choice but to deal with the U.S. as a single national unit."[94] Panama's representative to the OAS similarly lamented: "It was not possible to know with whom in the U.S. G[overnment] one could negotiate."[95] While in the spring of 1975 the administration tried unsuccessfully to distance itself from and amend the trade act, the New Dialogue floundered. This was not the only initiative of Kissinger's to be undermined by a lack of congressional support. Whether limiting his ability to support Latin American dictators or placing conditions on superpower détente, Congress effectively pulled the rug out from under him when it came to his pursuing his own particular brand of unilateral, centralized foreign policy, revealing the New Dialogue to have been toothless in the process.

Relying on Kissinger's personal involvement was also detrimental as he could not be everywhere at once. His last-minute decision to postpone his scheduled trip to seven Latin American countries in early February 1975—owing to the situation in the Middle East—severely undermined the chances of rescuing the New Dialogue. For Latin American foreign ministers who had staked part of their political reputation on having a direct line to the secretary, the implications were also substantial. As Argentina's foreign minister explained, if a visit did not take place soon, this would mean a "serious reverse" to the relatively "favorable atmosphere in Argentina for closer relations and understanding." "If Secretary Kissinger does not come," he added, "I am dead politically."[96] When Kissinger was again forced to postpone his trip at the last minute in April 1975, this time as a result of the collapse of South Vietnam, Argentine officials reacted with "dismay" that Latin America always seemed to take "second place to another area of the globe." While understanding for such a cancellation was expressed publicly, the message behind closed doors from across Latin America was that the New Dialogue was now dead. As the US ambassador in Buenos Aires reported: "Efforts to convince [Argentine foreign ministry officials] otherwise draw only sardonic smiles."[97] Indeed, the New Dialogue's original strength and impetus—Kissinger's personal engagement with it—turned out to be one of its main downfalls. As the initiative had been grounded on the secretary's personality, status, and willingness to consult with his Latin American counterparts, his absence irrefutably damaged it. Such was the disappointment with Kissinger's lackluster attention to the region by 1976 that, when he eventually visited many of the countries in the region, one Brazilian lead editorial simply called Latin America Kissinger's "Last Frontier."[98]

The New Dialogue therefore essentially ended in early 1975. True, US and Latin American diplomats continued to refer vaguely to continuing it, but no substantial progress was made toward cohesive multilateral negotiations along the lines begun at Tlatelolco. Nonetheless, there were tangential consequences to the initiative's evolution over the previous year. For example, the OAS voted to change the style of debating within its General Assembly in 1975 so that it would be less formal and more "conversational," in line with the spirit and practices of Tlatelolco and Washington.[99] In July 1975, the United States also joined the majority of Latin American and Caribbean nations in voting to allow OAS member states to decide for themselves what relations, if any, they wished to have with Cuba at a meeting of the organization's foreign ministers in San José, Costa Rica. By this point, nearly half of OAS members had broken sanctions unilaterally already.[100] The US decision to support the majority vote was therefore bowing to the inevitable. However, it did not come out of the blue. By supporting a simple majority vote rescinding the 1964 sanctions, the Ford administration carried out what had essentially already been agreed to over a year earlier as part of the New Dialogue's efforts to stop the secondary issue of Cuba interfering with the New Dialogue process—namely, accepting any resolution agreed to by Latin Americans themselves.

Other points tabled by the Latin Americans in the Declaration of Bogotá nevertheless stalemated. US-Panamanian negotiations came to a halt during the run-up to the 1976 US presidential election. Kissinger had told Torrijos back in February 1974 that the "basic problem" was that "most Americans don't give a damn": "A small minority is violently opposed to the agreement, but no group is really for it."[101] Challenged by Ronald Reagan on Panama in the Republican primaries, and fearing the domestic political consequences of moving ahead with negotiations, Ford therefore decided to delay signing a new Canal Treaty until after the election.

The quest for an improved level of US–Latin American understanding and an improvement of North-South relations also proved elusive. Even Kissinger's ally in Latin America Foreign Minister Silveira felt it necessary to spell out irrevocable differences between the United States and the global South in his correspondence with the secretary of state. "The exasperation with which some industrialized countries view the demagogic behavior of some developing countries," he wrote to "My dear Henry" in late August 1975, "is but the same feeling of exasperation these less developed countries harbor against what they see as a lack of understanding on the part of the developed countries towards problems originating in an inequitable economic order on the international level."[102] And, as long as this order persisted, US–Latin America tensions persisted even as the potency of the global South's mid-1970s challenge receded from view.

The New Dialogue's immediate failure is probably why we do not know more about Kissinger's interest in trying to reach a new inter-American understanding. When he finally got round to writing his third set of memoirs at the end of the 1990s, Kissinger seems to have belatedly remembered Latin America and the crucial importance it had to him as secretary of state. As he recalled, the region was "the principal focus of that part of our foreign policy not driven by immediate crises": "I devoted an enormous amount of time and effort to the Western Hemisphere."[103] Writing these sentences in the context of a post–Cold War world and in the shadow of the then still-blossoming "Washington Consensus," Kissinger now aimed to show that his vision for the New Dialogue had been ahead of its time and a precursor to the relative inter-American harmony of the 1990s. As he explained in his memoirs, his approach could also well have borne fruit were it not for what he described as having been the "bloodcurdling rhetoric" of the Mariachi loving, confrontational, ungrateful, emotional, and uncooperative Latin Americans.[104]

The blame Kissinger heaped on his Latin American counterparts was obviously a distorted explanation for what had gone wrong when it came to the New Dialogue. However, his condescending attitude also went a long way toward explaining why the New Dialogue failed. There was, in short, never any real empathy or understanding between US policymakers and their Latin American counterparts. True, as secretary of state, Kissinger took Latin America far more seriously than has previously been understood. However, the seriousness with which he approached the region was born of temporary necessity in a moment of vulnerability—a way of engaging the periphery in the hope that it might ultimately remain peripheral to US foreign policy priorities—rather than the result of any significant change when it came to how policymakers perceived their counterparts in Latin America. Reflecting on superpower détente, Kissinger would later write that the US "adversary . . . became in a sense a partner in the avoidance of nuclear war."[105] Yet he never regarded Latin Americans collectively as partners in inter-American or world affairs. And herein lay the problem when it came to dealing effectively with the periphery and reaching a new level of understanding with it. Although for two years Kissinger perceived Latin America as being much closer to, if not on, the axis of history, he dismissed the majority of its leaders—and those pertaining to the global South beyond the Western Hemisphere— as being unworthy of the respect needed to forge a new inter-American community of interest and reciprocity.

Even so, the New Dialogue, and the way it played out, helps us understand Washington policymakers' concerns about the US position in the world in the mid-1970s. Perceiving the US position in Latin America as weak, and finding the United States increasingly isolated within the hemisphere on questions such as Panama, Kissinger endorsed significant concessions and shifts in US foreign policy. In an "age of global anti-colonialism," he later wrote, it would have been "too costly to insist on the status quo of extraterritorial rights bisecting a sovereign country."[106] As we have seen, keeping Cuba indefinitely isolated was also considered secondary to the larger prize of keeping Latin America firmly in the Western Hemisphere in the context of the North-South dialogue. And this in turn tells us something about US policymakers' conceptualization of the region's significance for world affairs in the mid-1970s (as part of the global South and no longer a theater of the Cold War). This nevertheless brought the United States into conflict with ideologically driven dictatorships in the Southern Cone and provoked recriminations of its having given up its leadership role in the battle against communism. Ironically, the fact that the United States tried to take more of a backseat role on the issue in response to complaints over its past role in restricting change also resulted in pleas from Cold Warriors and left-wing nationalists alike to take responsibility for resolving the problem, albeit in different directions.

It was impossible for the United States to lead and please all Latin Americans at once. Cuba demonstrated that the New Dialogue's failure was just as much the result of divisions *within* Latin America as it was of divisions between the United States and its neighbors to the south. The very idea of a Latin bloc—so feared in 1973–1974 by US policymakers as the embodiment of a surging periphery—quite simply proved ephemeral.[107] And, as it did, the New Dialogue between the United States and Latin America in the mid-1970s gave way to increasing reliance on bilateral—as opposed to multilateral—dealings between individual countries in the region and Washington. On the eve of Carter's inauguration, all Latin America and the Caribbean countries, except Cuba, remained firmly in the Western Hemisphere, even if US–Latin American relations remained beleaguered.

Latin American leaders did not decouple themselves decisively and realign their countries within the global South. To the contrary, many continued to rely heavily on the United States in the late 1970s, and the South's hoped-for changes in the international economic system also did not materialize. Regardless of complaints that its countries had, Latin America continued to need the United States for the purposes of trade, aid, markets, and supplies. The Soviet Union, Europe, and the Third World—with the exception of Havana's relationship with Moscow—simply could not compete with US hegemony or offer comprehensive alternatives for the region. Mexico, for example, remained acutely reliant on good relations (in 1974, 70 percent of exports went to the United States).[108] The bonds that tied the region to the United States became greater in the context of mounting debt burdens. By 1975, the oil crisis and the subsequent rise in prices had cost the Third World $40 billion, amounting to 60 percent of its joint balance-of-payments deficit.[109] And, aside from the region's oil producers, Latin America was by no means immune. Peru's debt in 1976, for example, was five times what it had been in 1970 as a result of borrowing and rising oil costs, meaning that the country's leaders found themselves accepting an International Monetary Fund stabilization package the following year. As Hal Brands writes, these constraints "undermined the autonomy of independent-minded governments" while the "North-South stratification remained firmly intact."[110]

Indeed, with hindsight, the brief, hopeful interregnum in 1973–1975, when US policymakers took the global South's agenda—and Latin America's contribution to it—seriously enough to arrange consultations and conferences, reconceptualize world affairs, and contemplate the redrawing of international relations, was fleeting. Given how transient it was, the scale of US policymakers concerns at the time is what is intriguing. It is of course easy to look back in retrospect and proclaim their fears as foolish, exaggerated, and easily forgettable. But, as we have seen, from 1973 to 1975, even the most steadfast proponents of a world in which the axis of history was located firmly in the North took them seriously enough to countenance a different future. Latin America's geographic fatalism in the world was also questioned not because its leaders were being attacked from outside but because there was a chance they might redraw the globe in North-South terms. The result was admittedly a knee-jerk reaction on Kissinger's part that was probably never needed in the first place. If it succeeded, it also did so by default. Meanwhile, the multilateral New Dialogue is interesting as having been one of the few times that US policy toward Latin America was premised on the region's potential to alter the global balance of power and the US position in it. For a brief moment, because of Latin America's association with the Third World and the peculiar context of the mid-1970s, this part of the US periphery promised to become central to US international priorities in a way that it had not been before (and arguably has not been since).

Notes

1. Memorandum of Conversation, Kissinger et al., Aboard the Secretary's Aircraft, February 7, 1974, box 1028, Presidential/HAK MemCons, National Security Council Institutional Files, Nixon Presidential Materials Project (hereafter Mem-Cons/NSCIF/NPMP), National Archives, College Park, MD.

2. Mark Atwood Lawrence, "Containing Globalism: The United States and the Developing World in the 1970s," in *The Shock of the Global: The 1970s in Perspective,* ed. Niall Ferguson, Charles S. Maier, Erez Manela, and Daniel J. Sargent (Cambridge, MA: Belknap Press of Harvard University Press, 2011), 205–22, 208.

3. Henry Kissinger, *Years of Renewal* (New York: Simon & Schuster, 1999), 706, 737–38.

4. Niall Ferguson, "Crisis, What Crisis? The 1970s and the Shock of the Global," in Ferguson, Maier, Manela, and Sargent, eds., *The Shock of the Global,* 1–24, 15.

5. MemCon, Kissinger et al., February 7, 1974.

6. "Resolution Adopted by the General Assembly: 3201 (S-VI) Declaration on the Establishment of a New International Economic Order," May 1, 1974, http://www.un-documents.net/s6r3201.htm.

7. Hal Brands, *Latin America's Cold War* (Cambridge, MA: Harvard University Press, 2010), 133.

8. Briefing Paper, Department of State, "The Panorama of U.S.–Latin American Relations," February 1974, box 196, Office of the Secretary Executive Secretariat, Record Group 59, National Archives, College Park, Maryland (hereafter ExecSec/RG59/NARA).

9. Memorandum for the President from Kenneth Rush, "The Secretary's Meeting with the Latin American Foreign Ministers in Mexico City, February 20–23," February 12, 1974, box 48, HAK Trip Files, HAK Office Files, National Security Council Files, NPMP (hereafter HAKTF/HAKOF/NSCF/NPMP).

10. Kissinger, October 5, 1973, New York, as quoted in "Agenda for the Mexico Meeting as Proposed by the Latin American Foreign Ministers," Enclosure, Memorandum Kissinger for the President, February 16, 1974, box 48, HAKTF/HAKOF/NSC/NPMP.

11. Admiral Ismael Huerta as quoted in Telegram, US Mission USUN to SecState, September 25, 1974, State Department Central Foreign Policy Files (1973–1977) (hereafter: DOS/CFP), http://aad.archives.gov/aad/series-description.jsp?s=4073.

12. Daniel J. Sargent, "The United States and Globalization in the 1970s," in Ferguson, Maier, Manela, and Sargent, eds., *Shock of the Global,* 49–64, 50.

13. TelCon, Rabasa/HAK, September 18, 1973, box 22, HAK TelCons/NSC/NPMP.

14. Interview with Jack B. Kubisch, January 6, 1989, Frontline Diplomacy: The Foreign Affairs Oral History Collection of the Association for Diplomatic Studies and Training, Library of Congress, http://memory.loc.gov/ammem/collections/diplomacy/index.html.

15. Matias Spektor, "Equivocal Engagement: Kissinger, Silveira and the Politics of U.S.-Brazil Relations (1969–1983)" (Ph.D. diss., Oxford University, 2006), 146.

16. Intelligence Memorandum, "Quito: Not Just Another Conference," November 4, 1974, Central Intelligence Agency Records Search Tool (hereafter CREST), National Archives, College Park, MD.

17. ARA Monthly Report, Shlaudeman to the Secretary, August 3, 1976, in Peter Kornbluh, *The Pinochet File: A Declassified Dossier on Atrocity and Accountability* (New York: New Press, 2003), 383–84. See also Brands, *Latin America's Cold War,* 115.

18. Paper, S/PC Ad Hoc Study Group, "U.S.-Cuban Policy: Effects of Sanctions on Our Third Country Relations," Enclosure, Memorandum, Rush to Kubisch, January 21, 1974, box 196, ExecSec/RG59/NARA. See also CIA Report, "The Limits of Cuban Subversion in Latin America," August 28, 1974, CREST.

19. CIA Weekly Summary Special Report, "Peru: The Revolution Moves On," September 6, 1974, CREST.

20. Ibid.

21. DCI Briefing, January 24, 1974, CREST.

22. "The Panorama of U.S.–Latin American Relations."

23. "The Secretary's Meeting with the Latin American Foreign Ministers in Mexico City."

24. Memorandum for US Intelligence Board Principals and Intelligence Resources Advisory Committee, "Perspectives on Intelligence," June 18, 1974, CREST.

25. "The Panorama of U.S.–Latin American Relations."

26. CIA Memorandum, "Conceptual Framework," November 1974, CREST.

27. MemCon, Kissinger et al., February 7, 1974.

28. "The Secretary's Meeting with the Latin American Foreign Ministers in Mexico City."

29. Telegram, AmEmbassy Mexico to SecState, "Secretary's Bilateral Discussions with Peruvian Foreign Minister," February 20, 1974, box 196, ExecSec/RG59/NARA.

30. This tallies with Kissinger's "Year of Europe" initiative. See Andrew Scott, *Allies Apart: Heath, Nixon and the Anglo-American Relationship* (Basingstoke: Palgrave Macmillan, 2011), 165.

31. "Agenda for the Americas," Enclosure, Memorandum for the President, February 16, 1974.

32. Briefing Paper, "The Secretary's Trip to Panama," January 1974, box 136, ExecSec/RG59/NARA.

33. Draft Briefing Paper, "Washington Meeting of Foreign Ministers April 17–18, 1974: Objectives and Strategy," March 22, 1974, box 202, ExecSec/RG59/NARA.

34. "The Panorama of U.S.–Latin American Relations."

35. DCI Briefing, January 24, 1974.

36. MemCon, Kissinger et al., February 7, 1974. On Europe's rejection of Kissinger's Year of Europe, see Scott, *Allies Apart,* 140–65.

37. Telegram, John Crimmins, AmEmbassy Brasilia to SecState, February 27, 1975, DOS/CFP.

38. DCI Briefing, January 24, 1974.

39. "Agenda for the Mexico Meeting as Proposed by the Latin American Foreign Ministers."

40. "The Panorama of U.S.–Latin American Relations."

41. Foreign Minister Arístides Calvani as quoted in Telegram, Joseph Jova, AmEmbassy Mexico to SecState, "MFM: Arrival Statements of LA Foreign Ministers," February 17, 1974, box 48, HAKTF/HAKOF/NSCF/NPMP.

42. Telegram, Jova to SecState, "Current Experts Group Thinking on Structure of MFM on Final Document," February 15, 1974, box 48, HAKTF/HAKOF/NSCF/NPMP.

43. Telegram, Jova to SecState, "Possible Character of President Echeverria's Speech at Inauguration of MFM," February 16, 1974, box 48, HAKTF/HAKOF/NSCF/NPMP.

44. Telegram, Jova to SecState, "Mexican 'Suggestions' for a Document to Be Drawn Up by Conference of Tlatelolco," February 15, 1974, box 48, HAKTF/HAKOF/NSCF/NPMP.

45. Telegram, Jova to SecState, "Preliminary Meeting for MFM," February 13, 1974, box 196, ExecSec/RG59/NARA; Comments by Argentina's ambassador to the OAS, Raul Quijano, in Telegram, Jova to SecState, "Preparatory Meeting for MFM," February 16, 1974, Comments by Nicaraguan and Guatemalan Delegations in Telegram, Jova to SecState, "MFM: Arrival Statements of LA Foreign Ministers," February 17,1974, and Telegram, Jova to SecState, "MFM: Further Conversations with Fonmins and Other Delegates," February 19, 1974, box 48, HAKTF/HAKOF/NSCF/NPMP.

46. Telegram, Jova to SecState, "MFM: Further Conversations with Fonmins and Other Delegates," February 19, 1974.

47. Echeverría as quoted in Telegram, Jova to SecState, "Echeverria Remarks about Meeting of Foreign Ministers," February 16, 1974, box 48, HAKTF/HAKOF/NSCF/NPMP.

48. Tlatelolco Conference Final Communiqué, 1974, in *The Encyclopedia of the United Nations and International Agreements,* ed., Edmund Jan Osmańczyk (Philadelphia: Taylor & Francis, 1985), 803.

49. Kubisch Interview.

50. Telegram, Jova to SecState, "Rabasa's Remarks to Press on Meeting of Foreign Ministers," February 16, 1974, box 48, HAKTF/HAKOF/NSCF/NPMP.

51. Telegram, SecState to All American Diplomatic Republics, "Preliminary Latin American Reaction to the Conference of Tlatelolco," February 26, 1974, box 196, ExecSec/RG59/NARA.

52. Telegram, Crimmins to SecState, February 27, 1975, DOS/CFP.

53. Draft Memorandum of Conversation, Kissinger and General Torrijos et al., February 7, 1974, box 1028, MemCons/NSCIF/NPMP.

54. See Telegrams, SecState to AmEmbassy Brasilia, AmEmbassy Buenos Aires, AmEmbassy Santiago, and AmEmbassy Lima, February 27, 1974, box 48, HAKTF/HAKOF/NSCF/NPMP.

55. Telegram, Jova to SecState, "Bilateral Talk: Secretary Kissinger and Foreign Minister Vignes," February 20, 1974, box 196, ExecSec/RG59/NARA. On Rabasa's help in keeping the issue off the Tlatelolco agenda, see Kissinger, *Years of Renewal,* 727.

56. "The Panorama of U.S.–Latin American Relations."

57. Telegram, Jova to SecState, "Secretary's Bilateral Discussion with Brazilian Foreign Minister," February 20, 1974, box 196, ExecSec/RG59/NARA.

58. Telegram, Hill, AmEmbassy Buenos Aires, to SecState, "MemCon of Kubisch Conversation with Chilean Fonmin Huerta on Mexico MFM," February 11, 1974, box 48, HAKTF/HAKOF/NSCF/NPMP.

59. Telegram, White, AmEmbassy Bogota, to SecState, March 13, 1974, DOS/CFP.

60. Telegram, SecState to All American Republic Diplomatic Posts, "Text MFM Communique," April 19, 1974, DOS/CFP.

61. Ibid.

62. National Security Decision Memorandum 257, "Latin American Initiatives," June 19, 1974, http://www.fas.org/irp/offdocs/nsdm-nixon/nsdm_257.pdf.

63. Memorandum, W. D. Eberle for Kissinger, "Trade Policy Management in Light of New Dialogue with Latin America," July 12, 1974, Memorandum, Kissinger to Bill [Eberle], July 20, 1974, Memorandum for the Secretary of the Treasury et al. from Eberle, "Latin American Initiatives in the Trade Field," August 2, 1974, and Memorandum for Secretaries, "Latin American Initiatives in the Trade Field," August 1974, box H248, Policy Papers (1969–1974) NSDMs, NSDM 256–259, NSCIF/NPMP.

64. "Quito: Not Just Another Conference."

65. DOS Briefing Paper, "OAS General Assembly, April 19–May 1, 1974," n.d., box 202, ExecSec/RG59/NARA.

66. Lars Schoultz, *That Infernal Little Cuban Republic: The United States and the Cuban Revolution* (Chapel Hill: University of North Carolina Press, 2009), 272.

67. DOS Briefing Paper, "OAS General Assembly April 19–May 1, 1974: Cuba and the OASGA—Contingencies and Tactics," n.d., box 202, Exec/Sec/RG59/NARA.

68. See "Talking Points for Your Opening Statement at Washington MFM, April 17–18, 1974 (Second Draft)," March 21, 1974, box 202, ExecSec/RG59/NARA; Telegram, Ingersoll, AmEmbassy Quito, to SecState, November 9, 1974, box 211, ExecSec/RG59/NARA. In his telegram, Ingersoll referred to Kissinger's recommendation of a majority option to Nixon on March 23, 1974, and Nixon's approval on April 5, 1974.

69. Peter Kornbluh and James G. Blight, "Dialogue with Castro: A Hidden History," *New York Review of Books* 41, no. 16 (1994): 45–49.

70. Kissinger, *Years of Renewal*, 770–87; Kornbluh and Blight, "Dialogue with Castro."

71. "Quito: Not Just Another Conference."

72. Briefing Paper, "Cuba," November 1974, box 210, and Telegram, Ingersoll to SecState, November 8, 1974, box 211, ExecSec/RG59/NARA.

73. Kissinger, *Years of Renewal*, 774; Schoultz, *Infernal Little Cuban Republic*, 262.

74. "Quito: Not Just Another Conference."

75. Telegrams, Ingersoll to SecState, November 10, 11, 1974, box 211, ExecSec/RG59/NARA.

76. Telegrams, Ingersoll to SecState, November 8, 10, 11, 1974, box 211, ExecSec/RG59/NARA.

77. "Quito: Not Just Another Conference."

78. Telegram, Ingersoll to SecState, November 10, 1974.

79. Memorandum, Sub-Group on United States–Latin American Trade to the NSC Under Secretaries Committee and the Executive Secretariat of the CIEP, "U.S. Actions Affecting Latin American Trade and NSDM 257," November 14,

1974, Enclosure, Memorandum, Wreatham E. Gathright (Staff) to the Assistant to the President for National Security Affairs et al., December 6, 1974, box H248, NSDMs/NSCIF/NPMP.

80. Memorandum for the President from Ingersoll, Chairman, NSC Interdepartmental Group on Inter-American Affairs, "U.S. Government Initiatives toward Latin America," November 21, 1974, box H248, NSDMs/NSCIF/NPMP.

81. Lucio Paredes, as quoted in Telegram, Brewster, AmEmbassy Quito, to SecState, January 3, 1975, DOS/CFP. On Latin American reaction beyond Ecuador, see Telegrams, White to SecState, January 7, 1975, Barnebey, AmEmbassy Lima, to SecState, January 22, 1975, and Mulligan, AmEmbassy Port au Spain, to SecState, January 27, 1975, DOS/CFP.

82. Telegrams, SecState to All American Republics, January 22, 25, 1975, DOS/CFP.

83. Kissinger, *Years of Renewal,* 736–37.

84. Telegram, Crimmins to SecState, February 27, 1975, DOS/CFP.

85. Telegram, Brewster to SecState, January 3, 1975.

86. Telegram, McClintock, AmEmbassy Caracas, to SecState, January 23, 1975, DOS/CFP.

87. Telegram, Crimmins to SecState, January 31, 1975, DOS/CFP.

88. Letter, Vignes to Kissinger, February 7, 1975, and Telegram, Hill to SecState, "Text of Vignes Letter to Secretary Kissinger," February 9, 1975, DOS/CFP.

89. Telegram, Hill to SecState, "Vignes on Postponement of BA MFM and Secretary Kissinger's Trip," February 9, 1975, DOS/CFP.

90. The State Department emphasized the reduction of tariffs on 30 percent of exports to the United States (valued at more than $750 million) and authorization to embark on multilateral trade negotiations in Geneva.

91. Telegram, SecState to All American Republics, January 28, 1975, DOS/CFP.

92. Kissinger, *Years of Renewal,* 729–30.

93. Telegram, SecState to All American Republics, January 28, 1975.

94. Telegram, Brewster to SecState, January 3, 1975.

95. Telegram, SecState to All American Republics, January 25, 1975.

96. Telegram, Hill to SecState, "Vignes on Postponement of BA MFM," February 9, 1975.

97. Telegram, Hill to SecState, April 25, 1975, DOS/CFP. See also Kissinger, *Years of Renewal,* 737.

98. Telegram, AmConsul Rio to USINFO WASHDC, June 18, 1976, DOS/CFP.

99. Telegrams, SecState to All American Republics, March 19, April 5, 1975, DOS/CFP.

100. Schoultz, *Infernal Little Cuban Republic,* 262.

101. Draft MemCon, Kissinger, Torrijos et al., February 7, 1974.

102. Silveira to Kissinger, August 22, 1975, transcribed in Telegram, SecState (Ingersoll) to NAVFAC ELEUTHERA (Naval Facility Eleuthera, Bahamas), August 25, 1975, DOS/CFP.

103. Kissinger, *Years of Renewal,* 731, 733.

104. Ibid., 722, 730, 745.

105. Henry A. Kissinger, *Years of Upheaval* (London: Weidenfeld & Nicolson, 1982), 981.

106. Kissinger, *Years of Renewal,* 712.

107. Brands, *Latin America's Cold War,* 160.

108. DCI Briefing, January 24, 1974.

109. Bernard D Nossiter, *The Global Struggle for More: Third World Conflicts with Rich Nations* (New York: Harper & Row, 1987), 66.

110. Brands, *Latin America's Cold War,* 131, 152–55.

11

Uncertainty Rising

Oil Money and International Terrorism in the 1970s

Christopher R. W. Dietrich

Shots rang out in the foyer of the Vienna headquarters of OPEC on Sunday morning, December 20, 1975. The petroleum minister of Saudi Arabia, Ahmed Zaki Yamani, rushed for cover underneath the conference table. Yamani later told a Saudi television host that his first thought was that "European terrorists" had come "to avenge themselves" for the havoc high oil prices had wrought on the international economy. After further shots and an explosion, two masked gunmen burst into the room. "Have you found Yamani?" one asked in English. On seeing the oil minister, the invader saluted sarcastically and roughly separated him from his colleagues.[1]

Yamani "became yellow to the extent that no one could have imagined that there was any blood in his face," the Libyan oil minister recounted. The still-unidentified intruders divided their hostages into three groups. The ministers from Iran, Qatar, and the United Arab Emirates joined Yamani in the "criminals" group. In the "liberals and semi-liberals group" stood the representatives from Iraq, Libya, Algeria, and Kuwait. The non-Arab members, except Iran, joined the "neutralist group." The leader of the assailants then told the ministers in Arabic that they were Palestinian commandos.[2]

The leader of the raid began a "kindly" conversation in Spanish with the Venezuelan minister after transmitting demands for an airplane. The

discovery that he was "the well-known leftist terrorist" Ilich Ramírez Sánchez, better known as Carlos the Jackal, unnerved Yamani. The French
government had unearthed a detailed plan for Yamani's assassination in a
raid on his Paris hideaway the previous summer. Carlos took Yamani aside
that evening and confided that he had already arranged a refueling stopover in Tripoli and a final landing in Damascus. There he would execute
Yamani and the Iranian finance minister, Jamshid Amouzegar. Yamani
spent the next thirty-six hours expecting death, as his captors' DC-9 shuttled from Vienna to Algiers to Tripoli and finally back to Algiers.[3]

The OPEC kidnapping raises a number of questions about the international history of the 1970s. Why did Yamani first believe that the
intruders were Europeans? What defined the link between oil prices and
the international, pro-Palestine position of Carlos? More broadly, how did
the kidnapping reflect contemporary understandings of the international
politics of energy and security? To offer some exploratory answers, this
chapter examines the historical intersection of two important concepts:
oil power and international terrorism.[4] Together, the two ideas elucidate
the increasingly central position of formerly peripheral concerns in global
politics. That is, diplomats, policymakers, and other observers began to
see international economics and security blend together in a pyretic mix,
one that inaugurated a sense of uncertainty characteristic of the earliest
days of modern globalization.[5] One common theme of insecurity linked
oil power and international terrorism in their minds: the growing power
of the Arab oil producers led to the circumscription of meaningful action
against nonstate violence by supporters of an independent Palestine.

Power on the Periphery

To understand that dynamic, it is important to discuss the changing
political economy of oil prices after the Second World War. The use of
petroleum exploded, and the presence of petroleum was pervasive—"the
world's main source of power" and "the life-blood of progress," according to a series of Shell advertisements from the 1950s.[6] Progress was "its
own taskmaster, generating new and changing demands," Shell reminded
its consumers, and oil analysts consistently noted that consumption out-
paced their annual predictions throughout the 1960s.[7] Energy-intensive
production was central to the success of liberal capitalism, and the vora-

cious appetite of the West grew. A decade-long advertising campaign by Mobil in the 1970s made the message clear. "The energy we market helps alleviate problems and nurture hopes," one advertisement said. "Energy use and living standards go hand in hand," held another.[8]

Yet, as oil became the engine of the global economy, demand began to outpace supply.[9] When the economic terms of the world oil trade shifted in their favor, the oil-producing nations began to take control of production. A mutual vision of an imperial economic hangover resonated broadly with nationalists across the Third World of former colonies and other poor nations, including the members of OPEC.[10] The shared history of imperial exploitation, formal or informal, left a backlogged legacy. "Economic emancipation," in the words of the fifty-four heads of state attending the 1964 nonaligned summit in Cairo, became essential to the ongoing "struggle for the elimination of political domination."[11]

The West owed the rest a debt, it was felt. When OPEC successfully increased oil prices fourfold between October 1973 and January 1974, its most vocal leaders framed higher prices in the language of liberation. The shah of Iran opined from the steps of OPEC headquarters: "It is only equitable and just that the oil producing countries" had ended the era in which oil sold "at ridiculously low prices."[12] Algerian president Houari Boumediène emphasized the "new equilibrium between developed and developing states" and the possibility for "non-aligned [countries] to assert greater control over their natural resources."[13] The Third World could not allow the First "to establish a protectorate" over the postcrisis petroleum order, he told *Le monde*.[14]

The rise in oil prices simultaneously fed a perspective of decline among the leaders of the industrialized West. No country could be immune from oil power. In a "solemn speech to a hushed Bundestag," German economic minister Helmut Schmidt conceded that high oil prices would have immediate employment consequences.[15] French president Georges Pompidou nostalgically likened the advent of expensive oil to "waking up from a too beautiful dream" in a national television address.[16] The price increases were "so large" that they "must be regarded as a qualitative as well as a quantitative change," the Secretariat of the Organization of Economic Cooperation and Development informed its members in December 1973.[17]

Dwight Eisenhower had famously written off OPEC in 1960. "Anyone could break up the Organization by offering five cents more per barrel [to] one of the countries," he told a meeting of the National Security Council. Allen Dulles was not so sure, noting that the five founders of OPEC held more than 80 percent of global reserves.[18] Eisenhower's interpretation outweighed that of Dulles in the following decade, and the belief that the OPEC nations could not form a viable collective unit held sway, even as the producing nations slowly gained an advantage in the following decade. Richard Nixon, George Shultz, and Kissinger all dismissed concerns about oil power as "overly alarmist" months before the energy crisis despite warnings from experts inside and outside government.[19] Such disregard was impossible afterward.[20] The change was so great that Gerald Ford would link the potential for energy independence to the American Revolution in his bicentennial State of the Union address.[21]

Other commentators also saw energy dependence as an affront to American sovereignty in the early 1970s. A pseudonymous Miles Ignotus described oil power as inverted colonialism in *Harper's* magazine. OPEC now held the rest of the world in its thrall. "A somewhat impoverished America would be surrounded by a world turned into a slum" if the United States did not invade Saudi Arabia. American citizens would be "forced to finance the executive jets of the sheiks."[22] Henry Kissinger did not engage in such extreme rhetorical acrobatics, but he was no less mordant. (The ambassador to Saudi Arabia, James Akins, later contended that Kissinger gave the background briefing that led to the Ignotus story.)[23] In one candid moment, Kissinger complained to the heir apparent to Francisco Franco in Spain, Luis Carrero Blanco, who hours later would be assassinated by Basque nationalists. "It is really an unbelievable situation," he grumbled. "If some small country had tried in the 19th Century to do what the Arabs are doing, it would have been occupied."[24] Kissinger was not the only one who pined for the more orderly days of his beloved Metternich. Popular discussion added to the sense that the tables had been turned. Robert Tucker called for "the threat of force" in *Commentary*.[25] Daniel Yergin's lament in the *New York Times Magazine* was more deliberate but no less preoccupied—a "hostage constituency" to OPEC within the US foreign affairs establishment might undermine the independence of foreign policymaking.[26]

The conflicted responses to oil power reveal that the energy crisis did not occur in a political vacuum but became a doubt-inducing additive to a number of different national and international political contexts. For the purposes of this chapter, oil power also factored in Western considerations of *international terrorism,* a catchall phrase that analysts began to use to describe Palestinian activities outside the Middle East, especially following the passage of UN General Assembly Resolution 3034 in December 1972.[27] Transnational networks of militants—including the December 1975 team of the polyglot Carlos, which included two German anarchists, a Lebanese, and two Palestinians—became characteristic of the politics of national liberation in a new age of global interdependence.

If oil power cut in different directions, its polyvalence made it a potentially useful lever for the Palestinian cause. More broadly, oil power provided a critical context from which to interpret the spread of violence by nonstate actors in the 1970s. However, it is important to note that it was not a principle cause of the "revolutionary cosmopolitan worldview" of the Palestinian movement or other causes that turned to nonstate violence.[28] Yet oil power mattered to a wide cross section of commentators and policymakers concerned with international terrorism.

"A Sword of Damocles"

It is difficult to track the direct effect of oil money on individual violent acts.[29] But it is easy to see that a number of Western actors posited an advantageous setting for pro-Palestinian activity in the 1970s. At the same time, many saw the international politics of insecurity through the prism of oil power. In particular, the sense of uncertainty felt in the capitalist world put a brake on how far Western European nations, and oil producers for that matter, were willing to part ways with the supporters of Palestine. A number of cases of nonprosecution of pro-Palestine fighters provided sharp examples of this pattern.

When Carlos planned the fate of Yamani and the criminals group in December 1975, the link between oil and the Arab-Israeli problem was not startlingly new. As the producing nations became richer, their expendable income had long been part of Pan-Arab strategic thought. The association first raised serious concern for the West in the months before the June 1967 Arab-Israeli War. Gamal Abdel Nasser, the president of Egypt, explicitly linked petroleum to Pan-Arabism as tension mounted in late May, telling a Kuwaiti correspondent: "All weapons must be used in this battle; whether by governments or by the people."[30] The leaders of Arab labor unions called on their workers to "destroy the oil sources, pipe-lines and installations from which the enemy could benefit."[31] The implicit and explicit threats effectively dragooned the oil-producing monarchies of Saudi Arabia, Kuwait, and Libya into support. Each understood that their population would tolerate no actions short of oil withdrawal in the case of war.[32] "Any Arab leader who refused to do so would risk literal as well as political assassination," the American ambassador in Cairo wrote.[33]

During the subsequent three-month embargo, a public debate about the use of oil power took place across Arab airwaves and in the printed press. Yamani argued that the flow of oil needed to recommence promptly. If it did not, Iran and Venezuela would take over Arab-dominated markets. His counterparts in Iraq accused Saudi Arabia of abandoning the Arab cause.[34] The August 29, 1967, Arab heads-of-state meeting in Khartoum settled the rift. The resultant communiqué is most famous for its "three noes"—no peace, no recognition, and no negotiation with Israel—but it had other consequences. Saudi Arabia, Libya, and Kuwait would pay $378 million in reconstruction aid per year to Egypt and Jordan. In return, the producers received approval to resume oil shipments to the West without accusations of betrayal. The August 1967 communiqué also noted: "Arab oil . . . is an Arab asset which can be put to use in the service of Arab aims."[35] The Khartoum payments soon began to go directly to the Palestinian groups and became their central means of financial support, according to reports from American embassies, the CIA, and the Near East Desk of the State Department.[36]

Oil production and armed conflict continued to intersect in the following years, but often in countervailing ways. For example, despite the fact that a sizable proportion of the Khartoum payments reached Palestinian nationalists acting in Jordan and Syria, the Popular Front for the Liberation of Palestine announced a sabotage policy on the Trans-Arabian Pipeline, which was scheduled to resume production in late 1969 even though a small section of it traversed the Israeli-controlled Golan Heights.[37] The pipeline was sabotaged four times in the second half of 1969 before Syria finally closed it in early 1970.[38] Palestinian activities, especially the pipeline sabotages, "made it clear that the future of U.S. oil interests was bound up with U.S. Middle East policy," the chairman of Aramco told the British ambassador in Jidda.[39]

American analysts agreed on that broad issue. Arab oil and the politics of Palestinian liberation had become deeply intertwined. Palestinian guerrillas had become the "popular symbols of defiance of Israel" throughout the Arab world, the authors of an April 1968 National Intelligence Estimate wrote. Moreover, the "new breed" of guerrillas subsisted not just on the Khartoum money but also on the "heavy financial support . . . from well-to-do Palestinians and other Arabs in the oil-rich states."[40] Arab oil-producing states—led by Iraq and Libya but followed by Saudi Arabia and Kuwait—expanded their funding. American officials believed that the increased petroleum receipts of the Arab world would counteract their attempts to marginalize pro-Palestine radicals. The State Department concluded that it was likely that official and unofficial Saudi subsidies would increase despite the new turn toward hijackings and kidnappings. "The exploits of the fedayeen . . . remain the favorite topic of the Saudi media," the US embassy reported. "There was no noticeable slackening in public support for the commando cause."[41] Prince Fahd, the Saudi defense minister, announced a fifty-thousand-riyal personal gift to the "families of the martyrs cause" in June 1970.[42] The international strategies of pro-Palestinian groups were the objects of widespread sympathy.

Yet financial support was often given begrudgingly. Carlos had not been the first actor to identify Saudi Arabia as an enemy of a free Palestine, nor would he be the last. The conservative Saudi monarchy was constantly ridiculed for its lukewarm support of Palestinian nationalism, resented especially for its attempts to counter what the American ambassador to Jordan called "leftist and ideological trends among the fedayeen."[43] The September 1973 taking of hostages in the Saudi embassy in Paris evinced the boldness of nationalists acting outside the region as well as placing on display the often contradictory relationship between oil power and the movement for an independent Palestine. After the intervention of the Kuwaiti ambassador, the French decided to provide safe conduct for the hijackers and hostages to an Arab country, where it would be "more difficult for the feddayin [sic] to perpetrate a massacre."[44]

The group left France for Kuwait, a decision roundly attacked in the French press. On arrival in Kuwait, armored vehicles surrounded the plane, and the captors surrendered.[45] The commandos identified themselves as members of Fatah and were transported to Beirut. According to secret sources of the British embassy, the Kuwaiti government provided safe passage with the goal of maintaining good relations with the resistance movement.[46] They did so because they "had second thoughts about risking a row with the Palestinians." The problem of civilian attacks remained a "hot potato," the ambassador continued. Prudence was well advised given support for the Palestinians, especially among trade unions.[47]

The hot potato extended into Italy. Italian police apprehended "a group of five Arab terrorists" operating underneath the flight path of the Rome airport on September 5, 1973. Captured weapons included two portable, ground-to-air-missile launchers of Soviet origin.[48] The Israeli defense minister, Moshe Dayan, stated: "The Rome discovery underscores the necessity for Israel to go outside international law to defend itself."[49] Italian leaders sought to wipe their hands of the problem, releasing the men on provisional liberty, and losing "no time in getting them out of the country."[50] After a stopover in Malta, the Italian air force transmitted the terrorists to Libya. Maltese leaders, used as intermediaries, were told that the transfer was to be made with "the minimum of fuss."[51]

American embassy officials in Cairo noted the "dim prospects" for the prosecution of Palestinian nationalists who resorted to acts of violence because of the pervasive support for their activities.[52] A 1972 American initiative seeking a unified official demarche against the "foreign involvement of Fedayeen" in the Middle East and Europe—including "hijacking, sheltering of criminals, and training of terrorists"—failed completely. European governments did not want to denounce pro-Palestine activity publicly for fear of reprisal. The Dutch, Swiss, Greek, and West German governments were all "extremely cautious." The Dutch expressed concern that their "oil interests" would become the object of "Fedayeen terrorism."[53] Conversations with the French government neatly summarized the broader view. Its own "pro-Arab stance" had "insured the immunity of French interests."[54]

The primary financial supporters of Palestinian insurgents agreed. The Saudi government found the public relations of Palestinian violence vexing, but the need to maintain an "escape valve on the Arab pressure cooker" was greater than the irritant.[55] Any international "anti-Palestinianism" would be counterproductive, the Kuwaiti minister of defense told the American ambassador.[56] The embassy in Jidda reported that Saudi Arabia would continue to pay the Khartoum "insurance policy" for this reason.[57] Some intelligence reports discussed temporary suspensions of the subsidies for what the Saudi monarchy deemed "bad ideas and practices." However, an October 1973 report from Beirut on the future of state support for the Palestine cause predicted the continuation of funding.[58] At the height of the oil price increases that December, the minister of foreign affairs of Algeria, Abdelaziz Bouteflika, noted to Henry Kissinger that Palestinian international violence—"the affair of Lufthansa, the affair of Rome"— had become "a sword of Damocles" for the oil-dependent West.[59]

"A Very Thin Veneer"

Debates about arms sales also revealed the extent to which oil power complicated the response to international terrorism. The absence of consensus on regional disarmament left a void in the post-1967 Middle East. Persistent sales efforts by Soviet bloc and Western companies stepped in to fill it. The change in the scale of arms sales to oil-rich, anti-Western Libya presents another study of the prevalent uncertainty regarding the concurrent rise in oil prices and international political violence.

The imminent peril that Bouteflika referred to was clearly evident when, in 1977, Parisian police intercepted Abu Daoud, the alleged mastermind of the 1972 murders at the Munich Olympics. He had entered France using a false Iraqi passport, and now the French government faced an extradition request from West Germany. Diplomatic notes from Israel and the United States supported the West Germans, but the Palestine Liberation Organization, Iraq, and Libya claimed that Daoud should receive diplomatic immunity because he was traveling to the funeral of a fellow guerrilla. The French government refused the German extradition request on the grounds that forms had been filled out improperly. To the shock of the international community, Daoud was placed on a plane to Algeria.[60] The British Foreign and Commonwealth Office (FCO) and other critics quickly drew a connection between the release and French interests in the sale of fighter planes to Libya.[61]

The Libyan-French arms connection was less than a decade old. When the British and the Americans put unfulfilled contracts in abeyance after the 1969 revolution, Muammar Gaddafi and the Libyan Revolutionary Command Council turned to France.[62] Buoyed by successful negotiations with different oil companies, the new government more than tripled its defense budget in 1970. Paris entered the military assistance picture with "high drama and great initial impact" that year when officials announced the conclusion of a multiyear, $400 million contract that included the eventual sale of 110 Mirage aircraft.[63] The sale had "a very thin veneer," Henry Kissinger told the US secretary of state, William Rogers. What he meant was that the aircraft and other arms ultimately would likely go to Egypt and other Arab frontline states.[64]

Policymakers in the State Department were even more fearful that the arms sales would encourage Libyan sponsorship of Palestinian groups. Gaddafi already had announced that Libya would increase the Khartoum payments agreed to by the previous "puppet regime" and direct them more pointedly toward arms purchases for Palestinian groups.[65] As the rumors of the French sale circulated in late 1969, the State Department worried that the Revolutionary Command Council would disobey customary "no-transfer" clauses and send arms directly to Palestinian guerrillas.[66] Libya remained highly suspected of what William Bundy called "money for mischief" throughout the following decade.[67] Its "support for liberation movements" was owed to the fact that "it [could] do more than most," the North Africa Department of the British FCO wrote in 1979.[68]

Some British and American officials criticized the French sales, but others understood that the new arms deals represented a profitable opportunity.[69] A British study of French defense sales in 1975 emphasized the financial benefits to be reaped by imitating the French "pragmatic attitude . . . regardless of political objections."[70] Still, the government continued its post-1969 policy of sharply curtailed sales, consistently denying export licenses to national companies. In one example, the Defense Ministry refused an export license for a £150,000 sale of .38-caliber revolver spare parts in 1977. The reason was clear: one-third of illegally held handguns in Northern Ireland were of the same caliber, and a number of these were out of commission owing to a lack of spare parts.[71]

The link between oil power and nonstate violence shaped the cabinet debate. The British secretary of industry argued for the sale. The company applying for the export license, Webley and Scott, had "in recent years lost a lot of ground to their overseas competitors." Worse, the license refusal damaged their and others' prospects of future business throughout the Middle East. But the government did not approve the sale. The reasoning was clear: Libya had provided support to the Irish Republican

Army since 1970. Although Libya claimed to have stopped sending arms, the Revolutionary Command Council still supported other organizations with which the separatists had contacts. If the "spare parts were to find their way into the wrong hands," the risk of the politically embarrassing result outweighed the profits.[72]

Even though British arms could find their way into Irish nationalist holsters via Tripoli, the desire to increase defense sales led the British government to reconsider its policy after 1975. British officials argued then—despite the brazen attempt to ship weapons to the Irish Republican Army on the SS *Claudia* two years earlier and the fact that Gaddafi had "almost certainly provided" the missiles discovered near the Rome airport—that a marked change had transpired in Libyan foreign policy.[73] The argument of a reformed Gaddafi became more and more prevalent. "It has now become habitual outside Libya to see a Libyan hand behind every terrorist incident," one FCO analyst wrote. Governments found the country "a convenient scapegoat for every subversive plot, whether real or imagined." Moreover, the politicized category of terrorism needed to be considered, he said, turning to the cliché that "one man's terrorist is another man's freedom fighter."[74]

The basic question, according to this view, was one of whether the British single Libya out when many other members of the Third World expressly supported national liberation and patriotic fronts. There were compelling reasons, it was said, for discontinuing the sales ban. For one, as the French had argued since Gaddafi came to power, sweetened relations could "make a worthwhile contribution towards lessening Libyan dependence on Soviet military training." More importantly, the French example was yet another demonstration that the post-1971 influx of oil money into Libya had changed the scale of sales. Arms-sale relationships were far more profitable by middecade. The implications for potential Libyan contracts were "considerable," several companies wrote to the Defense Ministry when urging a policy revision in 1977.[75]

After "extensive Ministerial correspondence," a special committee recommended relaxed restrictions that year. Their main justification was that once-dominant British arms makers had begun to "lag well behind the Germans, French and Italians." Curtailing arms deliveries would do nothing to enhance the prospects of peace. Continued restraint meant abandoning a traditional commercial advantage.[76]

The British army fought the decision. Libyan support for Irish nationalists "completely overshadowed" all other considerations. "[Given that] soldiers are being killed and wounded daily by the IRA, it would be indefensible, besides being inexplicable . . . to supply equipment to the Libyans or worse to be seen to train them," one official warned.[77] But, as opposed to its handling of the 1975 decision, the Defense Ministry now disregarded that and other complaints. Defense secretary Fred Mulley believed that the British willingness to supply defense equipment could be a "key factor" in improving bilateral relations. The sales not only benefited the military industry, he told Foreign and Commonwealth secretary David Owen; they would also help other firms secure civil contracts in the emerging petro economy.[78]

Owen expressed his concern about Libyan sales to Mulley. "Political acceptability" was questionable in the face of "American and Egyptian anxieties" over Libyan procurements. The State Department already had made a formal representation to the FCO urging the denial of equipment that "would augment Libya's ability to work against peace and foment terrorism."[79] Nevertheless, Owen did not press the cabinet to suppress the suggestions of the Defense Ministry. He wrote Mulley later privately, agreeing with the sales: "Our aim should be to keep the Libyans in play."[80] Like Owen, Prime Minister James Callaghan expressed his concerns but approved the sales.[81] The secretary of state for industry noted that the approval was "most welcome to British Aerospace" and "a much needed fillip to British Shipbuilders."[82]

The British perspective had shifted for mostly economic reasons that resulted from the 1973–1974 oil price increases. The Ministry of Defense noted in a 1977 review that international arms sales had "expanded beyond recognition" since the price increases. Half the production of the Royal Ordnance Factories was exported, and the volume of overseas sales had a sizable impact on the domestic economy. Official estimates placed employment in the defense industry between seventy and eighty thousand, but most analysts believed that the number was much greater.[83]

The US government may have disapproved of the renewed British-Libyan sales relationship, but the broad direction of internal discussions in Washington was similar. The Nixon administration had spoken out strongly against the new trend of nonstate violence, spearheading the work of both the 1970 Hague hijacking commission and the 1971 Montreal sabotage commission of the United Nations. After the Munich assassinations, the American ambassador, George H. W. Bush, repeated the official US policy contrasting "the senseless act of terrorism" to "a climate of reasonableness and realism" to the UN Security Council.[84]

Yet a yawning gap existed between public representation and intercabinet debate. The secretary of defense, Melvin Laird, discussed the possibility of future sales to Libya in a December 1971 letter to the secretary of state, William Rogers. Laird recommended that the State Department permit a Spanish firm to sell five F-5 fighters to Libya in order to relieve pressure on American oil companies. Rogers declined to do so, even though he understood Laird's concern for "maintaining our considerable interests in Libya."[85] Libya had shown no signs of "moderation in Middle Eastern affairs," he wrote. The Revolutionary Command Council not only espoused armed conflict as the only means of settling Arab-Israeli problems; it also had just nationalized the holdings of British Petroleum. Funds had been thrown behind Palestinian guerrillas. Qaddafi had supported the recent coup in Morocco and stretched his diplomacy toward Chad and Eritrea.[86] Rogers repeated the sentiments to the foreign affairs minister of Spain in April 1972.[87]

Oil power mixed with Cold War anxieties to complicate the American stance. In a sense, because the Soviet Union and the United States—as well as France, Great Britain, and other European nations—armed regional states so heavily, superpower détente never arrived in the Middle East. In the case of Libya, although official policy was to remain neutral in the Cold War, "ready, willing, and able" Soviet ships began to unload tanks and artillery in 1970. According to the US ambassador, the Soviet Union hoped to establish in Libya "an area for the maintenance of strategic reserves of weapons and a training sanctuary for all the Arab confrontation states." In this context, the US government supported Western arms sales to the Revolutionary Command Council. Weapons transfers kept open the lines to clients within Soviet clutches while providing important benefits to the increasingly embattled Western economies. On learning of the 1970 French sale, the State Department approved the reasoning behind it. If the French did not fill the vacuum left by the cancellation of American and British sales, "the Soviets would."[88]

Qaddafi was a ready student of other nonaligned powers, and the Libyan government appreciated the benefits of Cold War competition for its hand. In one example, Libyan prime minister Abdel Salam Jallud told oil executives that their refusal to accede to Libyan production terms would cause Libyan concessions and business to be "pushed into the arms of the eager Soviets."[89] That rationale was enough to convince the State Department, which continued to deny direct sales, to reconsider its policy on third-party deals between American companies and the Revolutionary Command Council. The US ambassador in Rome reviewed the rationale in a May 1972 cable about Libyan pressure on the Italian national oil company to link the export of oil directly to an arms deal. "The question is not whether the Libyans will get the equipment," he wrote. "The question is from where they will get it."[90]

The Saudi oil minister, Ahmed Zaki Yamani, was released in exchange for an undisclosed ransom in December 1975. He said in his interview that Carlos the Jackal rested "on the throne of a terroristic organization which has an international structure." For this reason, he continued, "it would be an offense and a sin to lay the blame on Palestinian commandos."[91] The reticence Yamani felt in associating the Palestinian movement with Ramírez Sánchez pointed toward a broader desire to dissociate the virulent international politics of Palestine from oil power as well as to distinguish Palestinian nationalism from broader networks of nonstate violence.

Much contemporary commentary was less discriminating, as is some current discussion of the historical antecedents of terrorism. It remains common to relate the Palestinian insurgency of the 1970s to the terrorism of the present, for example. A number of analysts have drawn a direct line between oil power and international terrorism in the 1970s and the financing of groups like al-Qaeda in the present. According to this position, the post-1973 oil bonanza left the Arab regimes with "more money than they could possibly absorb internally . . . which contributed to the establishment of terrorism as a permanent feature of international politics."[92] A more recent argument compares the belief in religious inevitability in the "modern terrorist mindset" to the secular struggle for an independent Palestine.[93] Such straightforward connections between the 1970s secular movements for national liberation and the religious lens of groups like al-Qaeda are anachronistic. The global insurgency of Palestinian nationalism "was at most a precursor" to al-Qaeda, its historian writes, because of the use of international networks and a willingness to exercise violence on behalf of its goals.[94]

The problem of conflation may also be a broader one, deeply rooted in the psyche of US foreign policy. US secretary of state Hillary Rodham Clinton instructed the ambassador to the United Nations to support the new Comprehensive Convention on International Terrorism in October 2009. In particular, she urged her to voice American disapproval of the exemption of national liberation movements from the language covering the definition of *terrorism*. The convention could not provide a national-ist "pretext for terrorist groups." Rather, it should reinforce the principle that "no cause or grievance," including national liberation and resistance to foreign occupation, "justifies terrorism in any form."[95]

Supporters and critics of this view both understand that the separation of the international politics of national liberation from the ideology of global jihad cannot be entirely clean. This is true because of another shared context, that of oil power. Two months after her telegram to the United Nations, Clinton wrote to her ambassadors in Saudi Arabia, Kuwait, and Afghanistan about the need to hold the oil-backed financiers of al-Qaeda publicly accountable.[96] The connection between oil money and international insecurity began a decade before Saudi aid to the muja-hideen in Afghanistan and almost three before Osama bin Laden began to invoke images of "oil-stealing infidels."[97] The events described in this chapter—each unique—fit into a more general rethinking of the relation-ship between the politics of expensive oil and international security in the 1970s. The price of oil moved from a peripheral concern to a central one, and the influx of money to the Arab world created an astounding admix-ture of interests and fears. The link between oil power and nonstate vio-lence would have different iterations, but anxiety about such a connection would be neither casual nor short-lived.

Notes

1. "Yamani Relates the Story of His Severe Suffering at the Hands of the Ter-rorist Gang Which Assaulted OPEC's Headquarters in Vienna," January 4, 1976, Records of the Foreign and Commonwealth Office, ser. 96, folder 518, National Archives of the United Kingdom (hereafter, e.g., FCO 96/518, UKNA).

2. Libyan Press Service, "Mabrouk in Vienna Operation," December 29, 1975, FCO 93/739, UKNA.

3. "Yamani Relates the Story of His Severe Suffering."

4. Historians and other scholars have examined the link between oil production and international political uncertainty in different ways. See, e.g., Tyler Priest, "The Dilemmas of Oil Empire," *Journal of American History* 99, no. 1 (2012): 236–51; Steve A. Yetiv, *The Petroleum Triangle: Oil, Globalization, and Terror* (Ithaca, NY: Cornell University Press, 2011); Michael T. Klare, *Rising Powers, Shrinking Planet: The New Geopolitics of Energy* (New York: Holt, 2009); and Vaclav Smil, *Energy at the Crossroads: Global Perspectives and Uncertainties* (Cambridge, MA: MIT Press, 2005). The influential consultant Walter Levy discussed oil power as the ability of the OPEC nations to threaten Western supply for political reasons. See Walter J. Levy, "Oil Power," *Foreign Affairs* 49, no. 4 (July 1971): 662–63. This chapter employs a revisionist definition of *power* as the ability to set the agenda on a particular topic. See Steven Lukes, *Power: A Radical View* (1974), 2nd ed. (New York: Palgrave Macmillan, 2004); and Michel Foucault, *Discipline and Punish: The Birth of the Prison,* trans. Alan Sheridan (New York: Pantheon, 1977), 24–38. On the difficulty of defining *power* in the dynamic 1970s, see Stanley Hoffmann, "Notes on the Elusiveness of Modern Power," *International Journal* 30, no. 2 (1975): 183–206.

5. The notion of energy security is a useful one. See Rüdiger Graf, "Between *National* and *Human* Security: Energy Security in the United States and Western Europe in the 1970s," *Historical Social Research* 35, no. 4 (2010): 329–48.

6. Shell, "Routes of Progress," *The Arab World: The Journal of the Anglo-Arab Association,* no. 27 (July 1956): 19, and "Power for Progress," *The Arab World: The Journal of the Anglo-Arab Association,* no. 31 (April 1957): 13.

7. *Petroleum: Journal of the European Oil Industry* 29, no. 6 (1966): 258, and 31, no. 1 (1968): 295.

8. Mobil, "Our Product Is Prehistoric. We Try Not To Be," *New York Times,* January 13, 1972, 2.207/E85, and "More Power to the People," *New York Times,* January 27, 1972, 2.207/E85, Exxon-Mobil Historical Collection (EMHC), Austin, TX.

9. David S. Painter, "Oil and the American Century," *Journal of American History* 99, no. 1 (2012): 24–39; Daniel Yergin, *The Prize: The Epic Quest for Oil, Money and Power* (New York: Simon & Schuster, 2008), 543–69.

10. United Nations, Economic and Social Council, Thirty-Ninth Session, Official Records, June 30, 1965, E/SR.1365 and July 8, 1965, E/SR.1373.

11. For characteristic expressions, see "Cairo Declaration of Non-Aligned Countries," "Charter of Algiers, Adopted at the Ministerial Meeting of the Group of 77," and "Lusaka Declaration on Peace, Independence, Development, Co-Operation and Democratisation of International Relations," in *A New International Economic Order, Selected Documents, 1945–1975: Volume I* (New York: UN Institute for Training and Research, 1975), October 10, 1964, October 24, 1967, and September 10, 1970. See also Giuliano Garavini, "The Colonies Strike Back: The Impact of the

Third World on Western Europe, 1968–1975," *Contemporary European History* 16, no. 3 (2007): 299–319.

12. AmEmbassy Vienna to SecState, "Shah's Press Conference," December 29, 1973, National Archives of the United States, Record Group 59, Central Foreign Policy Files, 1973–1976, Electronic Telegrams (hereafter, e.g., NARA, RG 59, CFP 73–76, ET).

13. AmEmbassy Algiers to SecState, January 31, 1974, box 321, National Security File, Richard Nixon Presidential Materials (RNPM); *Yearbook of the United Nations, 1974* (New York: United Nations, 1975), 305. On the importance of Algerian foreign policy, see Jeffrey James Byrne, "Our Own Special Brand of Socialism: Algeria and the Contest of Modernities in the 1960s," *Diplomatic History* 33, no. 3 (2009): 427–47; and Matthew Connelly, *A Diplomatic Revolution: Algeria's Fight for Independence and the Origins of the Post–Cold War Era* (New York: Oxford University Press, 2002), 68–116. For an interpretation of modernization in the Arab world emphasizing similar assumptions between Arab and Western visions of societal change, see Nathan J. Citino, "The 'Crush' of Ideologies: The United States, the Arab World, and Cold War Modernisation," *Cold War History* 12, no. 1 (2012): 89–110.

14. AmInt Algiers to SecState, "President Boumediene's [*sic*] Le Monde Interview," February 5, 1974, NARA, RG 59, CFP 73–63, ET.

15. AmEmbassy Bonn to SecState, "German Government Considering New Oil Related Economic Measures," December 14, 1973, NARA, RG 59, CFP 73–76, ET.

16. AmEmbassy Paris to SecState, "President Pompidou's Interview," December 21, 1973, NARA, RG 59, CFP 73–76, ET.

17. OECD Paris to SecState, "OECD Secretariat Assessment of Oil Situation's Economic Consequences," December 31, 1973, NARA, RG 59, CFP 73–76, ET.

18. Memorandum of Discussion at the 460th Meeting of the National Security Council, September 21, 1960, *Foreign Relations of the United States, 1958–1960*, vol. 4, *Foreign Economic Policy* (Washington, DC: US Government Printing Office, 1992), doc. 309 (hereafter, e.g., *FRUS, 1958–1960*). On the founding of OPEC as a conservative coalition to counteract Nasserism, see Nathan J. Citino, *From Arab Nationalism to OPEC: Eisenhower, King Sa'ud, and the Making of US-Saudi Relations* (Bloomington: Indiana University Press, 2002).

19. George Shultz, "Remarks at OECD Ministerial Meeting," June 6, 1973, box 43, Papers of Herbert Stein, RNPM; MemCon, "Meeting with Oil Company Executives," October 26, 1973, NARA, RG 59, CFP 70–73, PET 6; Memorandum of Conversation, August 8, 1973, *FRUS, 1969–1976*, vol. 36, *The Energy Crisis, 1969–1974* (Washington, DC: US Government Printing Office, 2014), doc. 190; Richard Nixon, "News Conference," September 5, 1973, in John Woolley and Gerhard Peters, eds., *The American Presidency Project* (hereafter *APP*), http://www.presidency.ucsb.edu/ws/index.php?pid=3948; James E. Akins, "The Oil Crisis: This Time the Wolf Is Here," *Foreign Affairs* 51, no. 3 (April 1973): 462–90.

20. For a skeptical perspective on the reality of the energy crisis, see Maurice A.

Adelman, "Politics, Economics, and World Oil," *American Economic Review* 64, no. 2 (May 1974): 58–67; and Timothy Mitchell, "The Resources of Economics: Making the 1973 Oil Crisis," *Journal of Cultural Economy* 3, no. 2 (2010): 189–204. On the contested relationship between higher oil prices and the 1970s recession, see Robert Barsky and Lutz Kilian, "Oil and the Macroeconomy since the 1970s," *Journal of Economic Perspectives* 18, no. 4 (Fall 2004): 115–34. Whether the energy crisis was contrived or not, policymakers in the 1970s uniformly viewed higher oil prices as a root cause of the global recession.

21. Gerald Ford, "Address Before a Joint Session of the Congress Reporting on the State of the Union," January 19, 1976, *APP,* http://www.presidency.ucsb.edu/ws/index.php?pid=5677.

22. Miles Ignotus, "Seizing Arab Oil," *Harper's* 250, no. 1498 (March 1975): 45, 62.

23. Akins responded on television that "anyone who would propose that is either a madman, a criminal, or an agent of the Soviet Union." See Robert Dreyfuss, "The Thirty Year Itch," *Mother Jones,* March/April 2003, http://www.motherjones.com/politics/2003/03/thirty-year-itch.

24. MemCon, "Secretary's Call on Carrero-Blanco," December 19, 1973, NARA, RG 59, CFP 70–73, POL 27 ARAB-ISR.

25. Robert W. Tucker, "Oil: The Issue of American Intervention," *Commentary,* January 1975, 21–31.

26. Daniel Yergin, "The Economic-Political-Military Solution," *New York Times Magazine,* February 16, 1975.

27. This chapter uses *international terrorism* as a historical concept rather than an analytic one, following Paul Thomas Chamberlin, *The Global Offensive: The United States, the Palestine Liberation Organization, and the Making of the Post–Cold War Order* (New York: Oxford University Press, 2012), 7–10, 178–83. For the early use of the phrase to describe violence by pro-Palestinian forces, see Ali A. Mazrui, "The Contemporary Case for Violence," *Adelphi Papers* 11, no. 82 (1971): 17–27. The most sophisticated theorists argue that terrorism is primarily a form of political violence. See, e.g., Peter Kurrild-Klitgaard, Mogens K. Justesen, and Robert Klemmensen, "The Political Economy of Freedom, Democracy and Transnational Terrorism," in "The Political Economy of Terrorism," special issue, *Public Choice* 128, nos. 1/2 (July 2006): 289–315. Scholars also note the use of *terrorism* as a pejorative to denigrate a cause rather than describe behavior. See, e.g., Isabelle Duyvesteyn, "How New Is the New Terrorism?" *Studies in Conflict and Terrorism* 27, no. 5 (2004): 439–54.

28. For a thorough discussion, see Chamberlin, *The Global Offensive.*

29. Michael Levi, "Combating the Financing of Terrorism: A History and Assessment of the Control of 'Threat Finance,'" *British Journal of Criminology* 50, no. 4 (2010): 650–69.

30. Memorandum by Nathaniel Davis, May 26, 1967, Lyndon Baines Johnson

Presidential Library, National Security File, box 106 (hereafter, e.g., LBJL, NSF 106).

31. Memorandum of Conversation, June 12, 1967, and Memorandum from Solomon to Katzenbach, June 12, 1967, *FRUS, 1964–1968,* vol. 34, *Energy Diplomacy and Global Issues* (Washington, DC: US Government Printing Office, 2004), docs. 240, 242.

32. Harold Saunders, "Memorandum for the Record," May 31, 1967, LBJL NSF 106.

33. Nolte to DOS, June 2, 1967, LBJL NSF 106.

34. "Saudi Minister Urges Arabs to Reconsider," *Financial Times,* July 1, 1967; Nicholas Herbert, "More Moderation on Arab Oil," *The Times* (London), July 1, 1967; *Middle East Economic Digest: Weekly Report* 11, no. 27 (July 13, 1967): 481–82.

35. Telegram from the Embassy in Saudi Arabia to the Department of State, August 27, 1967, Telegram from the Embassy in Saudi Arabia to the Department of State, September 7, 1967, and Intelligence Note from the Director of the Bureau of Intelligence and Research (Hughes) to Secretary of State Rusk, September 1, 1967, *FRUS, 1964–1968,* vol. 21, *Near East Region: Arabian Peninsula* (Washington, DC: US Government Printing Office, 2000), docs. 300, 301, 458.

36. National Intelligence Estimate, "The Outlook on Saudi Arabia," April 7, 1970, National Intelligence Estimate, November 14, 1970, Telegram from the Department of State to the Embassies in Saudi Arabia, Kuwait, and Libya, "Arab Governments Financial Support for Fedayeen," April 23, 1969, Intelligence Memorandum Prepared in the Central Intelligence Agency, March 1971, and Memorandum from the Assistant Secretary of State for Near Eastern and South Asian Affairs (Sisco) to Secretary of State Rogers, January 6, 1970, *FRUS, 1969–1976,* vol. 24, *Middle East Region and Arabian Peninsula* (Washington, DC: US Government Printing Office, 2015), docs. 140, 61, 7, 94, 18.

37. "PFLP Claims Responsibility for Sabotage," *Middle East Economic Survey* 13, no. 3 (November 14, 1969): 17.

38. "Tapline Sabotaged for Third Time," *Middle East Economic Survey* 13, no. 2 (November 7, 1969): 6.

39. British Embassy, Jedda, "Aramco and U.S. Middle East Policy," November 5, 1969, UKNA, FCO 67/247.

40. Special National Intelligence Estimate, "Terrorism and Internal Security in Israel and Jordan," April 18, 1968, *FRUS, 1964–1968,* vol. 20, *Arab-Israeli Dispute, 1967–68* (Washington, DC: US Government Printing Office, 2001), doc. 148.

41. A-181 from Jidda, "Monthly Commentary for Saudi Arabia," August 3, 1970, NARA, RG 59, CFP 70–73, 2584, POL 2 SAUD.

42. A-157 from Jidda, "Monthly Commentary for Saudi Arabia," July 6, 1970, NARA, RG 59, CFP 70–73, 2584, POL 2 SAUD.

43. AmEmbassy Amman to SecState, "Changing Saudi View on Yasir Arafat," October 10, 1970, NARA, RG 59, CFP 70–73, 2043, POL 13–10 ARAB.

44. Renwick to Craig, "Attack on the Saudi Embassy in Paris," September 12, 1973, FCO 93/178, UKNA.

45. Telegram 801, Kuwait to FCO, "Hijacking," September 9, 1973, FCO 93/178, UKNA.

46. Kealey to Young, "Attack on the Saudi Embassy in Paris," September 19, 1973, FCO 93/178, UKNA.

47. Telegram 883, Kuwait to FCO, "Paris Hi-Jackers," October 13, 1973, FCO 93/178, UKNA.

48. Intelligram, Secretary of State to American Embassy, London, "Terrorist Possession of Soviet Origin Ground-to-Air Missiles," September 20, 1973, FCO 93/178, UKNA; D. A. Gore-Booth, "The Ostia Incident," September 10, 1973, FCO 93/178, UKNA.

49. "United Nations General, A/9173, Letter from the Permanent Representatives of Egypt, Iraq and the Syrian Arab Republic to the Secretary General," September 25, 1973, FCO 93/178, UKNA.

50. Telegram 783, Rome to FCO, "Arab Terrorists," November 14, 1973, FCO 93/178, UKNA.

51. Telegram 530, Valletta to FCO, November 12, 1973, FCO 93/178, UKNA.

52. USINT Cairo to SecState, "PAA Hijacking," October 15, 1970, NARA, RG 59, CFP 70–73, 2043, POL 13–10 ARAB 10/1/70.

53. Outgoing Telegram, Department of State 070888, "Foreign Involvement of Fedayeen," April 25, 1972, NARA, RG 59, CFP 70–73, 2044, POL 13–10 ARAB, 3/7/72.

54. AmEmbassy Paris to SecState, "Foreign Involvement of Fedayeen," April 10, 1972, NARA, RG 59, CFP 70–73, 2044, POL 13–10 ARAB, 3/7/72.

55. AmEmbassy Jidda to SecState, "Foreign Involvement of Fedayeen," April 20, 1972, NARA, RG 59, CFP 70–73, 2044, POL 13–10 ARAB, 3/7/72.

56. AmEmbassy Kuwait to SecState, "Foreign Involvement of Fedayeen," April 15, 1972, NARA, RG 59, CFP 70–73, 2044, POL 13–10 ARAB, 3/7/72.

57. AmEmbassy Jidda to SecState, "Possible Approach to King Faisal Re Fedayeen," March 8, 1972, NARA, RG 59, CFP 70–73, 2044, POL 13–10 ARAB, 3/7/72.

58. State Department, Intelligence Brief, "Arab World: Fatah Gets Back into Faysal's Good Graces," June 12, 1973, NARA, RG 59, CFP 70–73, 2047, POL 13–10 ARAB, 6/1/73; A-181, AmEmbassy Beirut, "Future Evolution of the Fedayeen Movement," October 5, 1973, NARA, RG 59, CFP 70–73, 2047, POL 13–10 ARAB, 6/1/73.

59. MemCon, Bouteflika and Kissinger, December 20, 1973, NARA, RG 59, CFP 70–73, 2082, POL 27–14 ARAB-ISR, 12/6/73. In December 1973, terrorists killed thirty-two people in the Rome airport and then hijacked a Lufthansa aircraft to Kuwait. There, they told Kuwaiti authorities that Muammar Gaddafi had financed their operation. See Lamb to Nixon, Draft, "Libyan Support for Terrorism," March 23, 1979, FCO 93/1881, UKNA.

60. "*L'Affaire* Daoud: Too Hot to Handle," *Time* 109, no. 4 (1977): 32; James F. Clarity, "Abu Daoud Release Sets Off an Uproar," *New York Times,* January 13, 1977.

61. Graham to Whitney, "Abu Daoud," January 31, 1977, FCO 93/1137, UKNA; Reeve to Wheeler, Attachment, "Legal Aspects of the 'Abu Daoud Affair,'" January 31, 1977, FCO 93/1137, UKNA.

62. NSC Interdepartmental Memo on Libyan Arms Sales, April 1969, NARA, RG 59, CFP 67–69, 1574, DEF 12-5 LIBYA, 1/1/69.

63. Intelligence Memorandum 531/70, "Libyan Arms Supplies since the 1969 Revolution," July 31, 1970, *FRUS, 1969–1976,* vol. E-5, no. 2, *Documents on North Africa, 1969–1972* (Washington, DC: US Government Printing Office, 2007), doc. 63.

64. Telephone Conversation, Rogers and Kissinger, January 14, 1970, National Security Archive, Kissinger Telephone Transcripts, KA01924.

65. AmEmbassy Tripoli to SecState, "Threat to Withdraw Reserves Deposited UK," November 4, 1969, NARA, RG 59, CFP 67–69, 1574, DEF 12-5 LIBYA, 1/1/69.

66. Department of State, Intelligence Note 829, "Reported French Arms Sale Agreement with Libya," November 26, 1969, RG 59, SNF 67–69, 1574, DEF 12-5 LIBYA, 1/1/69, NARA; SecState to AmEmbassy Paris, "Soviet Reply to US Formulations: French-Libyan Arms Talks," December 27, 1969, NARA, RG 59, CFP 67–69, 1574, DEF 12-5 LIBYA, 1/1/69.

67. William P. Bundy, "Elements of Power," *Foreign Affairs* 56, no. 1 (October 1977): 5.

68. C. D. Powell, "Libyan Training for Patriotic Front Guerrillas," May 22, 1979, FCO 93/1881, UKNA.

69. State Department, Bureau of Intelligence and Research, RSGS-14, "Arms Transfers: New Opportunities for France in the Middle East," December 14, 1973, NARA, RG 59, CFP 70–73, 2082, POL 27–14 ARAB-ISR, 12/6/73.

70. D/MAO/51/52, March 5, 1976, DEFE 68/174, UKNA.

71. Of these, according to British intelligence, 141 of 380 were on the Protestant side and 172 of 430 on the Catholic side. Mulley to Mason, July 13, 1977, DEFE 13/1322, UKNA.

72. "Hill to Owen, Defence Sales to Libya: Revolver Spares," July 5, 1977, DEFE 13/1322, UKNA.

73. On the *Claudia,* see "Irish Links with Western Europe and the Middle East," December 3, 1979, FCO 93/1881, UKNA. On the Rome missiles, see Lamb to Nixon, Draft, "Libyan Support for Terrorism," March 23, 1979, FCO 93/1881, UKNA.

74. Nixon to Jenner, "Libya's Policies towards Liberation Movements, Subversion, and Terrorism," March 31, 1978, FCO 93/1881, UKNA.

75. Minute, B. M. Nordbury, "Libya: Sales of Arms and Provision of Training," April 28, 1977, DEFE 13/1322, UKNA.

76. "Defence and Overseas Policy Committee, Draft Paper, Libyan Defence Sales," July 22, 1977, DEFE 13/1322, UKNA.

77. Loose Minute, "Anglo-Libyan Relations," April 19, 1977, DEFE 13/1322, UKNA.

78. Mulley to Owen, "Defence Sales to Libya," April 7, 1978, DEFE 13/1322, UKNA.

79. Owen to Mulley, "Defence Sales to Libya," April 23, 1978, DEFE 13/1322, UKNA.

80. Owen to Mulley, "Libyan Defense Sales," December 7, 1978, DEFE 13/1322, UKNA.

81. Healey to Owen, "Libyan Defense Sales," December 8, 1978, DEFE 13/1322, UKNA.

82. Eric to Owen, "Defense Sales to Libya," December 1, 1978, DEFE 13/1322, UKNA.

83. Attachment 1 to COS 1136/124, "Defense Sales," April 1, 1977, DEFE 23/172, UKNA; AUS(D Staff)/BF.8/1, Defense Relations Policy Group, April 18, 1977, DEFE 23/172, UKNA.

84. White House 164994, September 10, 1972, CFP 70–73, 2044, POL 13–10 ARAB, 9-10-72, NARA.

85. Laird to Rogers, December 2, 1971, RG 59, CFP 70–73, 1767, DEF 12-5 LIBYA, NARA.

86. Rogers to Laird, December 15, 1971, RG 59, CFP 70–73, 1767, DEF 12-5 LIBYA, NARA; Department of State, Information Memorandum, "Sale of Military Equipment to Libya," November 1, 1971, RG 59, CFP 70–73, 1767, DEF 12-5 LIBYA, NARA.

87. Rogers to Lopez Bravo, April 13, 1972, RG 59, CFP 70–73, 1767, DEF 12-5 LIBYA, NARA.

88. Intelligence Memorandum 531/70, "Libyan Arms Supplies since the 1969 Revolution," Washington, July 31, 1970, *FRUS, 1969–1976,* vol. E-5, part 2, *Documents on North Africa, 1969–1972,* doc. 63.

89. AmEmbassy Tripoli to SecState, "Jallud Demarche to Oil Companies," June 16, 1972, NARA, RG 59, CFP 70–73, 1507, PET 6 LIBYA, 5/1/72.

90. AmEmbassy Rome to SecState, "Military Sales to Libya," May 2, 1972, NARA, RG 59, CFP 70–73, 1767, DEF 12-5 LIBYA; AmEmbassy Tripoli to SecState, "Military Sales to Libya," May 4, 1972, NARA, RG 59, CFP 70–73, 1767, DEF 12-5 LIBYA.

91. "Yamani Relates the Story of His Severe Suffering."

92. James Adams, *The Financing of Terror* (London: New English Library, 1986), 53.

93. Bruce Hoffman, *Inside Terror* (New York: Columbia University Press, 2006), 240–41.

94. Chamberlin, *The Global Offensive,* 269. See also Yevgeny Primakov, *Russia*

and the Arabs: Behind the Scenes in the Middle East from the Cold War to the Present, trans. Paul Gould (New York: Basic, 2009), 16–17.

95. Cable 104391, Secretary of State, "Statement for Sixth Committee on UN Counterterrorism Issues," October 7, 2009, http://wikileaks.org/cable/2009//09STATE104391.html.

96. Cable 1381801, Secretary of State, "Terrorist Finance: Action Request for Senior Level Engagement on Terrorism Finance," December 30, 2009, http://wikileaks.org/cable/2009/12/09STATE131801.html.

97. Yetiv, *The Petroleum Triangle,* 63–73; Rachel Bronson, *Thicker Than Oil: America's Uneasy Partnership with Saudi Arabia* (New York: Oxford University Press, 2008), 168–77; Giles Kepel, *Jihad: The Trail of Political Islam* (Cambridge, MA: Harvard University Press, 2003), 66–74.

12

The Peripheral Center

Nicaragua in US Policy and the US Imagination at the End of the Cold War

David Ryan

From the "Strategic Rear" to the "Backburner"

"We have a vital interest, a moral duty, and a solemn responsibility." In April 1983, with these words, President Ronald Reagan attempted to wrest further funding out of an inconsistent and divided Congress. The Boland Amendment had in 1982 restricted aid to the contras and the regional actors: Mexico, Venezuela, Colombia, and Panama had initiated the Contadora process to search for a negotiated solution to the Central American crisis. Reagan's address to a joint session of Congress was an extraordinary feat of rhetorical positioning in a faltering attempt to win bipartisan support for his controversial policies. The gambit included a plea to recognize the geostrategic importance of the region and the attendant risks to US credibility. Central America was contiguous to the Caribbean, "our lifeline to the outside world"—which was pivotal to the sea lines of communication that carried large proportions of US trade— and, in "a European crisis," Reagan asserted, "at least half of our supplies for NATO would go through these areas by sea." The Nazis during the Second World War and the Soviets during the Cold War years recognized the importance of the region. "Shouldn't we also?" Reagan beseeched his divided and partially skeptical audience. He quoted an extended passage from the Truman Doctrine, denied the applicability of the Vietnam analogy, exaggerated the Soviet-Cuban-Nicaraguan military challenge, and concluded with the costs to US credibility should his modest request be rejected: "If we cannot defend ourselves there, we cannot expect to prevail elsewhere. Our credibility would collapse, our alliances would crumble, and the safety of our homeland would be put at jeopardy."[1] These vital interests were constructed from ideological illusions that prevailed on this issue in a divided administration coupled with an attempt to restore US credibility in the wake of the Vietnam War. These goals were set against the backdrop of ongoing Soviet activity in the Third World but also, and more importantly, the Reagan administration's perception of Soviet-supported activity in Central America in 1981 and 1982. Nicaragua was the testing ground, and, therefore, failure there presented a challenge to the Reagan administration's credibility. When President George H. W. Bush entered the White House in 1989, one of the immediate concerns was to place US-Nicaraguan policy on the proverbial back burner at Foggy Bottom. A tilt toward a more realist approach to the region recognized the relative unimportance of the country, the regime, and the region to the United States; they certainly did not deserve the limelight as a test case of US resolve. True, the desire to remove the Sandinistas remained, but it was pushed down the agenda (eclipsed by events in Central Europe), and, within thirteen months, in February 1990, democratic choices in Nicaragua ousted the Sandinistas, but not before the Bush administration conducted tentative explorations to normalize relations with the regime.

This chapter examines the transition from Reagan to Bush. It seeks to explain why the Reagan administration constructed the Nicaraguan revolution as a vital national security issue. It does so by examining the place of the periphery in the US imagination after the Vietnam War. In that regard, Nicaragua provided an opportunity to centralize the peripheral; here was the new test case after the catastrophe of Vietnam and the debacle in Angola to demonstrate US resolve and credibility. Yet the American memory of the Vietnam War and geopolitical vision simultaneously kicked against the Reagan worldview. Opponents of Reagan, frequently citing the lessons of Vietnam, urged the administration to consider the regional and national dimensions of the Sandinista revolution and the Salvadoran resistance, that is, to truly see the peripheral as peripheral. Division on the issue played out within the administration, between the administration and elements of Congress, in public opinion, and in elite discourse.

Constructing the Vital Interest:
Nicaragua in the Reagan Mind

Reagan wanted US power to reengage with world affairs. He sought to move out of the shadow of Vietnam.[2] His ability to do so was heavily constrained by concerns with public opinion, especially on Central America, yet the ideologues in his administration believed that they had to check Soviet expansionism in the Third World. Nicaragua provided an opportunity, a place—geographically proximate to Washington, strategically redundant to the Soviets—where the Reagan administration might win the "battle for the American soul" after Vietnam.[3]

The alarmist advice that Reagan received first on the campaign trail and then when in office forged links between the success of revolutionary nationalist movements throughout the Third World and Soviet designs. For instance, in 1980, the Committee of Santa Fe argued: "Survival demands a new US foreign policy. America must seize the initiative or perish. For World War III is almost over." "The crisis," it contended, "is metaphysical. America's inability or unwillingness either to protect or project its basic values and beliefs has led to the present nadir of indecision and impotence and has placed the very existence of the Republic in peril." The supposed Soviet penetration of Central America threatened US interests. Cuban aid throughout the isthmus presented numerous problems for the United States and "in turn . . . great opportunities for both Cuba and the Soviet Union in Mexico with its oil and Panama with its canal."[4]

Not all within the administration shared these extreme fears. Still, there was the perception that something had to be done to reverse the malaise of the late 1970s. Years later, Robert McFarlane, the former national security adviser, outlined to Congress that the Soviets had supported guerrilla movements throughout the world and that they had tremendous success in the 1970s. He contended: "If we could not muster an effective counter to Cuban-Sandinista strategy in our own backyard, it was far less likely that we could do so in the years ahead in more distant locations. . . . We had to win this one."[5] Whether or not Nicaragua was that bound up with Cuban and/or Soviet designs was largely immaterial to some of the thinking in the executive branch.[6] There was intelligence on and discussion of the arms flow into Nicaragua, from a variety of countries, and discussion of the arms transferred from Nicaragua to the

Farabundo Martí National Liberation Front (FMLN) in El Salvador. The Cubans were cautious and constrained by agreement with Moscow not to transfer Soviet weapons to third parties, but weapons from other sources, including American weapons from Vietnam, were transferred early in the early revolutionary period;[7] moreover, from late 1982, Moscow increased its supply of weapons to the Sandinistas *after* the initiation of the contra operations. Soviet bloc deliveries amounted to $45 million in 1981, $90 million in 1982, $115 million in 1983, and $250 million in 1984 but then fell to $75 million in 1985.[8] The often-repeated lines that Nicaragua was closer to Texas than the latter was to Washington supposedly made the threat appear all the more proximate when augmented by a discourse on dominoes and depictions of cartographic illusions. Yet, repeatedly in congressional testimony and State Department commissioned reports, the evidence belied the administration's rhetoric. Lieutenant Colonel John H. Buchanan, appearing before the House Subcommittee on Inter-American Affairs, broke with protocol and violated the "rules of military briefers" when he testified: "I brought with me a detailed map of the region. This is the sort of map men engaged in mortal combat use—not the sort used in budget battles." The Soviet tanks could use only one route out of Nicaragua, the Pan American Highway; the T-55 would have to travel a route of 290 miles and in one stretch climb from five hundred to five thousand feet, a gradient that Buchanan did not think the tank could achieve, given its maximum ability to climb gradients of thirty degrees. The journey would take ten hours, and US satellites and/or Honduran reconnaissance could detect such movement, and the Honduran air force could then eliminate the threat. These tanks and the HIND helicopters were principally useful for domestic control and defense; the Sandinista military did not have the capacity for offensive operations.[9] What it did have by then was a significant capacity for the defense of the revolution, at least in the conventional military sense, and the ability to increase the costs of any potential US invasion.[10] The threat was made during a number of diplomatic exchanges. Moreover, Sandinista diplomacy involved frequent contact with Democrats on the Hill to convey the folly of a potential intervention. The concern for probable US casualties was considerable. By 1985, State Department officials indicated that the rest of the decade would involve "damage control" and the pursuit of low-intensity conflict (LIC) in Nicaragua. An interviewee informed Lars Schoultz that a critical change had occurred: "They've learned to operate their helicopters." From late 1982, the Sandinistas acquired sophisticated Soviet military supplies. Though not a security threat to the United States, access to these Soviet weapons was sufficient to repel some contra attacks. The willingness of Nicaraguans to fight to defend the initial gains of the revolution assisted in the strategic defeat of the contras but also quieted administration officials who contemplated invasion.[11]

The State Department–sponsored report, authored by Carl Jacobsen, argued that "all-too-many US claims proved open to question." Evidence corroborating the numerous assertions by administration officials in congressional testimony, media commentary, and official reports could not be found. Where administration officials referred to particular weapons and quantities, local and regional reporting identified very different types of equipment and more limited numbers of trainers. While Reagan referenced the Libyan delivery of equipment in his congressional speech, the Brazilian paper *O estado de S. Paulo* reported: "Nothing of what was found is capable of changing the balance of forces in Central America."[12] Indeed, the 1983 Presidential Finding on Nicaragua concluded: "The USSR is not likely to take an active direct military role in Central America."[13] It is also worth noting that, despite the lack of attention drawn to it by Reagan, France provided the Sandinistas with one hundred missile launchers and seven thousand missiles in 1982 and 1983 and with mine-sweeping equipment after the CIA mined the Nicaraguan ports in early 1984. The Netherlands provided for port defense improvements.[14]

The issue of Sandinista shipment of weapons and materials to the FMLN remained a staple rationale for the Reagan administration and was maintained by the Bush administration in 1989 as a tool when bargaining with Gorbachev. When it became clear that the Reagan administration could not fund the contras for *the purpose* of overthrowing the Sandinistas, the rationale for the funding focused on the assertion that the contras were supposed to interdict the flow of weapons to El Salvador.[15] Again, it is difficult to reconcile the evidence with the rhetoric. Clearly, the Sandinistas did support the FMLN in the period between the 1979 revolution and January 1981. The US ambassador, Lawrence Pezzullo, indicated that there should be no real surprise about this in an area with permeable borders, especially when "a revolutionary regime sat cheek to jowl with a revolutionary guerrilla movement." The real issue for him was whether the quantity of weapons was *substantial*. He held talks with the Sandinistas from January to March 1981 to impress on them the changed nature of the regime in Washington, and he believed that his talks bore fruit. An "intelligence windfall" had clearly indicated that the Sandinistas were supporting the FMLN, but there were also reports "indicat[ing] they were closing off the channels and telling the FMLN that it was due to US pressure."[16] Contra leaders later testified that they did not intend to pursue interdiction; they were more interested in the Sandinista regime. Moreover, the US intelligence analyst David McMichael eventually testified before the International Court of Justice (ICJ) that there was no detection of an arms shipment during his employment at the CIA. He began work in March 1981 but reviewed earlier materials. In 1986 the ICJ established: "An intermittent flow of arms was routed via the territory of Nicaragua. . . . [T]he evidence is insufficient to satisfy the court that, since the early months of 1981, assistance has continued to reach the Salvadoran armed opposition from the territory of Nicaragua on any significant scale, or that the Government of Nicaragua was responsible for any flow of arms at either period."[17] It was relatively clear from an early date that the principal source of FMLN weapons was those captured from the Salvadoran forces.[18] The interdiction rationale ultimately gave way to that of applying pressure on the regime to enhance the prospects of democracy in Nicaragua and to enter meaningful negotiations.[19] The official rationale of the Reagan administration changed as circumstances required.

Reagan's geopolitical vision conflated an ideology with a spatial dimension. The outlook was uncomplicated. From the beginning of Reagan's presidency, his rhetoric on the Sandinistas was strident. Given his commitment to the contras, it was inconceivable that he temper his support for them, especially after the Vietnam War. Through the Manichaean prism Reagan adopted to describe the world, the Soviet Union lay behind all "the unrest that is going on": "If they weren't engaged in this game of dominoes, there wouldn't be any hot spots in the world."[20] The complexities of regional conflict were reduced, at least at the highest level, to conform to his geostrategic, East-West vision. The regional experts who had served the Carter and earlier administrations in Central America were removed from office, replaced by ambassadors who had largely gained experience in Southeast Asia.[21] Their reporting replaced the regional with the global, transforming the Sandinista revolution from a nationalist revolt against the inter-American system to a central prong of a Soviet strategic design.[22] The effect was to simplify the reporting on the situation in El Salvador and Nicaragua and to focus on communism and Cuba rather than on poverty as the principal source of instability.[23] The Reagan administration wanted to reengage US power, restore the nation's credibility after Vietnam, and roll back the gains made by the Soviet Union under Ford and Carter. Reagan considered Central America *the* vital center.[24]

There was an urge to demonstrate that the United States had overcome its Vietnam experience. Alexander Haig, Reagan's first secretary of state, was intent on capitalizing on the opportunity created in Central America. He talked about "going to the source," meaning Cuba, and drawing a line past which communism could not advance.[25] Yet he had established with the Soviet ambassador in Washington, Anatoly Dobrynin, that Cuban adventures in Central America were a matter between Washington and Havana; Soviet interests were limited.[26] Haig later wrote: "Castro had fallen between two superpowers. The way was open to solve the problem in Central America, and solve it quickly, through the unequivocal application of pressure. The question was, had we the will to do it promptly, while the President still enjoyed the freedom of action he had won at the polls?"[27]

The Vision of the Periphery in the Emerging Reagan Doctrine

The American visions of the Asian periphery that Hilfrich offers is instructive here because first he compares the visions of Vietnam in the mid-1960s with the US acquisition of the Philippines in 1898, concluding that, though important, the Cold War did not solely determine US views of the periphery. Second, the rhetorical construct that became the domino theory was important because it was built on a geographic premise coupled with a psychological injunction that moved from the local to the regional and on to the universal. Therefore, Hilfrich illustrates, the movement in thought passed through concentric circles that related, not to the importance of the country in question, but to the US vision of itself within the orbit. That is, the fear of losing Vietnam (through the narratives of geography, credibility, commitment, and US leadership) passed through the concentric circles to the regional concerns with Southeast Asia and the Pacific. Through the logic of the domino theory: "In the outer circle, the psychological domino theory extended the significance of a defeat in South Vietnam to the world, for it spelled the loss of confidence in the United States and, by encouraging the enemies of the United States, the onset of a wider war." Thus, ultimately, the construction suggested that the US worldview "remained anchored in the monumental conflict between barbarism and civilization, much as the domino theory relied on the binary opposition of democracy and communism."[28]

It was this construction that created the problem. However, more than that, it was a combination of the binary construction of the world—and Nicaragua's location in that construction—with the politics of perception and illusion. Militarily, politically, or economically, there was little in the Central American crises that *actually* threatened the vital interests of the United States. In and of itself, Nicaragua was unimportant to US security. The export of the revolution to El Salvador was not significant after January 1981; Soviet weapons were limited and defensive in nature.[29] But, once the symbol was created, there was no turning back: "Rhetorical commitment served *to create* a vital interest, an interest in not having to back down and suffer a loss of credibility." It also created significant opposition because it mirrored a ghost of an earlier symbol.[30] Reagan could not abandon Nicaragua or the contras. The administration believed that the consequences would be too serious. By May 1985, Reagan signed a national emergency because the Sandinistas "posed an *unusual and extraordinary threat* to US foreign policy."[31]

The wording in the US declaration is instructive. Neither Nicaragua nor the Sandinistas posed a security threat to the United States. Instead, the difficulty related to the symbolic threat that they posed to US foreign policy. This condition had little to do with the actualities in Nicaragua, relating instead more directly to the psychology of American leaders and to the geostrategic vision they constructed. This vision necessitated a revival of the US spirit and strategic identity after Vietnam.

Such concern with credibility had been a frequent point of discussion during the Cold War, especially after the distinction between vital and peripheral US interests had been eroded. While some might locate this in the differences between Kennan and Nitze's conception of containment, that is, the differences between asymmetrical and symmetrical containment, others reference the so-called period of Cold War consensus, when most regional conflicts were read through global prisms.[32] Despite Kennan's five "vital regions," even his realism initially extended to a concern with US credibility in South East Asia. "No one can question the thesis that a precipitate withdrawal representing the total capitulation of our entire proposition in that region, would be one of the worst alternatives before us," he argued in December 1965. However, he also recognized that Vietnam might distract and distort US policy elsewhere and that the war might undermine US relations with its allies, who still feared withdrawal. While Kennan had advocated containment on the perimeter to shore up the confidence of regional allies and recognized that the Chinese and North Vietnamese would "exploit mercilessly" a defeat in Vietnam, he also recognized that these repercussions would last only a few months.[33]

Much to the dismay of the Sandinistas, large segments of the US public, Congress, the United Nations, the European Community, and the Contadora countries, Nicaragua became a symbol demonstrating that the United States had overcome Vietnam, that it was serious about containment (as they perceived it), that it sought to limit the "proliferation of Cuba-model states."[34] The United States sought to demonstrate that it was not in terminal decline and could assert its power. "To arrive at a crisis calling for U.S. intervention, it becomes necessary to inflate the concept of vital interests—to argue, for instance, that U.S. interests are compromised by such ineffables as blows to our prestige or possible doubts abroad about our resolve to act decisively," Kenworthy argued as early as 1983.[35] Most analysts at the time agreed that a Soviet satellite in Central America would be detrimental to US interests. The puzzle at the time centered on why, then, the Reagan administration did not pursue negotiations to reduce such a prospect and why it could not see that, while accepting all the help they could get, the Sandinistas did not represent a Soviet beachhead on the American mainland. Of course, one can point to the lack of expertise on the region among those who designed policy (Jeane Kirkpatrick, William Clark, William Casey, and Elliot Abrams); one can also examine the divisions between the ideologues and the pragmatists in the administration. Negotiations, properly verified, would have addressed most of the Reagan administration concerns, but mutually acceptable resolutions would also have placed severe limits on what the United States

could do in El Salvador or Guatemala. The Sandinistas pursued negotiations with the objective of ensuring their continuance. As the Reagan
administration either added issues to invoke Sandinista rejection or moved
from multilateral to bilateral talks, the Sandinistas adopted a strategy of
concessions to ensure that, if talks collapsed completely, they would not
be to blame.[36] Moreover, as the Reagan administration persisted with the
evasion of conclusive negotiations and stepped up the military maneuvers
and the LIC operated by the contras, it rarely considered the costs to its
credibility among US allies in Latin America and Europe. Most governments did not accept the Reagan administration position. Regional allies
spearheaded the Contadora diplomacy to seek satisfactory solution; when
that effectively collapsed, the isthmian countries picked up the pieces and
eventually concluded the Arias Plan. Transatlantic allies were, with a few
exceptions, wary, and France and Spain in particular were very sympathetic to the Sandinista position.[37] That said, Congress and public opinion
most effectively, yet inconsistently, set the limits of Reagan's power.

The Reagan Doctrine accommodated the realities of US *military*
power: realism and restraint. In essence, it did not require direct US intervention in the Third World, which was deemed impossible given opposition within the administration, within Congress, and among the public.
It proposed to challenge the Soviet Union on the periphery, where direct
engagement was unlikely.[38] It amounted to US funding indigenous movements ostensibly to defend "freedom and democracy [on] every continent,
from Afghanistan to Nicaragua."[39] Clearly, the fundamental or strategic
lessons of Vietnam had not been learned; the administration focused on
instrumental opportunities and tactical considerations. Nevertheless, the
doctrine, coupled with Reagan's outlook and hyperbolic rhetoric, created
a central dilemma for the administration. If the problem in Nicaragua was
as acute as Reagan asserted, how could proxy forces—the contras—solve
it? Despite his functional use as head of the 1983 Bipartisan Commission
on Central America, Henry Kissinger later captured the dilemma while
privately expressing doubts about the administration's policy. Both sides
in the debate on Nicaragua were "spouting nonsense," he argued in what
he thought was a private meeting in the Library of Congress. "It cannot
be that it is such a vital interest and it can be solved with $100 million."[40]

Despite the unusual and "extraordinary threat," Reagan was bound
up in what Brands has called the "Doolittle Lemma."[41] He wanted to get

rid of the Sandinistas, the contras were largely ineffective except at sabotage, yet he could not use US troops. He was stuck between the analogous lessons: no more Munichs, no more Cubas, no more Vietnams (or no appeasement, no revolution, no defeat). A few months before the outbreak of the Iran-Contra scandal, and after years of devastating consequences in the region, the *New York Times* captured the dilemma. It noted: "Where then does the president stand? For 'no more Vietnams, no more Cubas.' With a war he can't win and a negotiation he can't abide. He lets the contras fight and the diplomats talk, to no discernible end."[42]

These dilemmas arose from the administration's ambitious agenda coupled with the constraints of Vietnam. After that war, it seemed imperative that the US reassert its leadership and its confidence throughout the world. Among a number of goals, a 1982 US National Security Strategy paper spoke of bringing about "a fundamentally different East-West relationship by the end of the decade." More specifically, it sought to "contain and reverse the expansion of Soviet control and military presence throughout the world." It argued that direct confrontation with the Soviets was unlikely but that the Soviets were less averse to taking risks in support of proxy forces to confront the United States in regional conflict. Vietnam was not far beneath the surface of US planning. The paper continued: "They may expect that the burden of avoiding such a confrontation is shifting to the U.S." It suggested a combination of the Nixon Doctrine with the emerging Reagan Doctrine: "In contingencies not involving direct Soviet aggression our strategy is to rely on regional states to the extent possible." In addition: "The U.S. will rely primarily upon indigenous forces to protect mutual interests, with U.S. assistance as appropriate." Such proxy warfare became the norm under the Reagan Doctrine: "Where quick termination of conflict cannot be assured, the U.S. must confront adversaries with the prospect of a prolonged, costly, and ultimately unwinnable war."[43]

The National Security Council was well aware of the dilemmas it faced even if its reasoning on Soviet intentions in Nicaragua was overstated. Still, as it pointed out: "Moscow has perceived the US as politically constrained not only by the trauma of Vietnam but by an inability to achieve domestic consensus on foreign policy. In turn, the Soviets have probed US resolve in the Third World." Nicaragua had been lost. Still, a leftist victory in El Salvador would encourage revolutionaries in Guatemala and elsewhere in the region.[44] Assistance from international communism to the insurgencies would "make Central America a battleground over the next few years which would distract, weaken, and undermine the United States in other parts of the world." The NSC was also aware that Latin American states or European allies, "except for the British, have been opposed to our policy in Central America." In the absence of such support, US forces remained an "essential back-up" to local forces. The preferred option was to pursue LIC by "providing, if necessary, US combat forces to supplement the capabilities of indigenous forces when other menas [sic] are ineffective, in the context of a statement of clear US political objectives and national will."[45]

In essence, Nicaragua had become a vital location because the administration incorrectly perceived it as a place where the United States could prevail and thus demonstrate its capabilities, commitment, and resolve. It was not of geostrategic importance; the Sandinistas did not threaten the oil fields of Mexico, the Panama Canal, or the sea lines of communication across the Caribbean, nor did they have the capability to do so. The Sandinistas did not present a strategic threat to the credibility of the United States. Despite the Reagan administration's characterization of the threat, their agendas were national and *initially* regional. The advent and prospect of revolutionary success in Nicaragua, El Salvador, and Guatemala did pose a potential embarrassment because it represented a rejection of the inter-American system and more broadly the world system, yet even the Sandinistas maintained a mixed economy and attempted to run two sets of democratic elections.[46]

The Reagan Commitment

Reagan's commitment to the contras and to Nicaragua as *the* symbolic and constituent part of the Reagan Doctrine was, in 1985, belatedly identified by Charles Krauthammer as the effort to support "those who are risking their lives on every continent from Afghanistan to Nicaragua to defy Soviet-supported aggression and secure rights which have been ours from birth."[47] In the early stages of the engagement, the Sandinistas outmaneuvered the contras, who soon turned to soft targets. In contrast to the FMLN, they did not occupy any Nicaraguan village or town on an ongoing basis. They moved through the hinterland and retreated into the safety of Honduras or Costa Rica. Their targets focused on the peasantry and the infrastructure: oil facilities, schools, hospitals, medical facilities, and villages.[48] The human toll amounted to approximately forty thousand.

By 1984, the CIA and UCLA (Unilaterally Controlled Latino Assets) mined the harbors of Nicaragua. In 1986, the ICJ found the United States in breach of customary international law, violating the sovereignty of Nicaragua on sixteen counts, including using force, authorizing overflights, mining harbors, disseminating manuals on guerrilla warfare, imposing a trade embargo, and unlawful aggression.[49] By then, and in the face of congressional inconsistency, the administration had turned to private donors and other nations willing to do its bidding and, most famously, engaged in diverting profits from weapons sold to the Khomeini regime in Iran to the contras.[50]

Early in his second term, Reagan described the contras as "our brothers, these freedom fighters, . . . the moral equivalent of the Founding Fathers and the brave men and women of the French Resistance." They could not be abandoned because this was an issue of, not "right versus left, but right versus wrong."[51] Thereafter, and despite the appropriation of $100 million in June 1986, the contra war persisted, with devastating effects on the people and the economy, but soon after unraveled with the Iran-Contra revelations in late 1986, hearings in 1987, and lawsuits thereafter.[52]

Congressional opponents rejected the geopolitical interpretation. Senator Christopher Dodd's response to Reagan's 1983 speech argued that there would be no revolution were it not for the poverty and inequality in the region.[53] Members of the Bipartisan Commission on Central America threatened to resign unless US military aid to El Salvador was conditioned on improvements in the army's human rights record. Despite Kissinger's assertions and conclusions, the commission "admitted that the revolutions and pressures for change were indigenous and therefore no danger to hemispheric security."[54] Still, the final report in January 1984 concluded: "The triumph of hostile forces in what the Soviets call the 'strategic rear' of the United States would be read as a sign of U.S. impotence. It would signify our inability to manage our policy or exercise our power."[55] The editors of the *New York Times* decried the administration's inability to learn from the past, noting: "The same fears about impotence and credibility were the stuff of a thousand speeches justifying American involvement for a generation in the lost war in Indochina."[56]

Most European allies disparaged the Reagan outlook and by 1984 set up the San Jose process to provide economic aid to the region as a whole, despite Reagan administration pressure to exclude Nicaragua. The first statement of the Contadora group expressed "deep concern regarding foreign intervention—direct or indirect—in Central American conflicts," advised that it was "highly undesirable to classify such conflicts in the context of an East-West confrontation," and agreed on "the need to eliminate the external factors which make [those conflicts] worse."[57] Even the Central American governments did not share the Reagan administration's fear of the Sandinistas.

Bush and the Backburner

The Reagan attempt to roll back the Sandinista revolution had effectively ended by February 1988. The contras were no longer an effective fighting force, and Congress yet again suspended military aid. A congressional report concluded that the "lame duck" presidency no longer significantly influenced events in Nicaragua as regional actors asserted themselves in the field and at the negotiating table.[58] Gorbachev's "New Thinking," an attempt to remove ideology from foreign policy and address the Soviet Union's *real* interests, had initiated a reduction in commitment to regional issues. The disengagement was becoming apparent, much to the chagrin of Fidel Castro, who was celebrating the thirtieth anniversary of the faltering revolution. In Washington, Congress became more involved, and the Bush administration's *realism* altered the temperament of policy on Nicaragua. Secretary of State James Baker's *moderate* approach urged a bipartisan effort at cooperation with Congress. Aides to the Bush transition team made it clear that the "ideological zeal" of the Reagan-Abrams years were over. The Bush administration recognized the limits of its power and understood that Congress would not fund military aid to the contras; it was not going to make that request. As LeoGrande argues: "Bush . . . seemed to regard Central America's problems as the troublesome bequest of his predecessor rather than as issues of intrinsic significance."[59]

Recognizing that, to secure consistent congressional funding, requests had, until the February 1990 elections, to be limited to humanitarian assistance, the Bush administration moved to defuse the acrimonious relationship with Congress by advancing the Bipartisan Accord on Central America. Certainly, it could not be seen to abandon the contras, but it resolved to make the Esquipulas Process work to its advantage by focusing on Nicaragua's responsibilities in terms of democratization, "an end to subversion," and "Soviet bloc military ties that threaten U.S. and regional security."[60] Crucially, the administration was not willing to waste political capital on Nicaragua. By 1989, events in El Salvador—the FMLN's final offensive—and Panama—Noriega's electoral fraud and defiance of the United States—took precedence; events in China and Eastern Europe also commanded attention. Further pursuit of and investment in the failed Reagan agenda was simply not worth it. Moreover, the presidency and the executive branch were at that stage only one among several influential protagonists affecting Nicaragua; Congress and the isthmian countries were more assertive.[61]

Shortly after the 1988 US elections, it was apparent that the last of Reagan's Central American architects, Assistant Secretary of State for Inter-American Affairs Elliot Abrams, would be replaced by a more moderate figure. James Baker and Bush worked more closely with Congress and regional allies to ensure a democratic election in 1990. They geared continued aid for the contras to that end and the promotion of talks between the contras and the Sandinistas. If diplomacy failed, they reasoned, they would have a better chance of securing military aid at a later stage, but, for now, the military option was off the table.[62]

The Bipartisan Accord, struck between James Baker and Speaker of the House Jim Wright, provided sufficient funds to keep the contras intact, if not militarily effective, until after the scheduled February 1990 elections.[63] Bush and Baker had little choice. The Democrats controlled both Houses of Congress, and Wright indicated that his intention was to back the Esquipulas Peace Process that had begun in 1987. If Congress blocked the military option, the contras were also a spent force. Sol Linowitz, the former US ambassador to the Organization of American States, recognized that "the possibility of a military solution using the contras simply does not exist anymore."[64] The immediate Nicaraguan retort, delivered by Manuel Espinoza Enríquez, argued that Washington could not have it both ways. It could not support the maintenance of the contras and assert support for the peace process, which called for their demobilization. The Foreign Ministry conceded that the process did not put a time scale on demobilization, but Managua had signed the Tesoro Beach Accord of February 14, 1989, under that assumption.[65] Though the Nicaraguans argued that such provision violated the accord, Washington asserted that it supported contra demobilization toward the end of a *democratic* Nicaragua. At minimum, the Bush administration did not want to abandon the contras and suffer the political costs of doing so. It had also concluded that it would have to learn to live with the Sandinistas.

Still, Bush demanded that Moscow demonstrate its New Thinking in Central America, insisting that the Soviet Union and Cuba had an obligation to support the Esquipulas process by ceasing aid to regional regimes or forces.[66] Washington expressed incredulity at Gorbachev's May 1989 statement in Havana that the Soviet Union had stopped shipping arms to Managua. Instead, it heaped on the rhetorical pressure, calling for Moscow to "decouple from Nicaragua," and holding Moscow "accountable for the consequences of its intervention."[67] They maintained that the policy should be one of preventing the "Soviet strategic use of Nicaragua," including pushing for the withdrawal of the Soviet military presence. Moreover, the Bush administration sought to "reduce the threat posed by Nicaragua to its neighbors and other countries in Latin America by ending Nicaraguan subversion." Yet the immediate priority was to "engage in active diplomacy" to enhance the democratic opening in Nicaragua.[68]

By August 1989, shortly after the tenth anniversary of the revolution, the belatedly appointed assistant secretary of state, Bernard Aronson, held discussions with Victor Tinoco, the Nicaraguan vice minister of foreign affairs, "about a step-by-step process for normalising relations between the two countries after the anticipated Sandinista victory."[69] James Baker had told his Soviet counterpart that Washington would recognize the legitimacy of the Sandinistas if the elections were fair. Moscow urged the Sandinistas to conduct free elections.[70] Former president Jimmy Carter, acting as an elections observer, met with Ortega and was convinced that the process was fair; he also determined that "Ortega wants to see tension with the U.S. relieved."[71]

Nicaragua then became a bargaining chip at the November 1989 Malta summit between Bush and Gorbachev. The Bush White House saw the summit as an "excellent opportunity to add momentum to the political changes sweeping Eastern Europe" rather than letting it become an "arms control summit."[72] While Gorbachev sought face-saving initiatives and reciprocity at Malta, Bush intended to use Central America as a caveat to improved superpower relations.[73] Gorbachev understood that Washington intended to berate him for continued Soviet support for Nicaragua and purported ongoing arms transfers from Cuba to the FMLN in El Salvador. Moscow attempted to co-opt the issue in October 1989. After his visit to Washington, Eduard Shevardnadze flew straight to Managua to publicize an agreement struck between Gorbachev and Ortega on October 7 in East Germany. In Managua, he emphasized the need for a regional military balance of forces for defensive purposes. Of course, this implied cuts on the part of US allies. By late October, US intelligence acknowledged that Soviet aid had been reduced by 20 percent since 1988, and Shevardnadze indicated that all direct shipments had ceased. Soviet economic aid, estimated at $465 million a year, would continue, but the $500 million in military aid was coming to an end.[74] Bush's strategists also thought that "in keeping with his 'new thinking,' [Gorbachev] is likely to stress the latility [*sic*] of regional conflicts and their potential for escalation and the need for political rather than military solutions." On regional issues at the Malta summit, Douglas Mulholland, the director of the US Bureau of Intelligence and Research, informed Baker that, on the one hand, Gorbachev anticipated "heavy flak on Central America" owing to the Sandinista suspension of the cease-fire, the FMLN "final offensive," and the delivery of MIGs to Cuba but that, on the other hand, he was likely to argue that the Bush people ought to accept "political realities in the region," namely, the "survival of the Sandinista regime." Though he was not "consulted" about or "pleased" with the Sandinista termination of the cease-fire with the contras, Gorbachev was likely to argue that ongoing contra activity necessitated the decision. Finally, he might suggest that the United States and Moscow act as coguarantors of a regional peace scheme working together to control the arms flow.[75]

Still, US objectives included pointing out to Gorbachev the "contradiction" between the Soviets' support for peaceful settlements and their actual conduct. Baker advised Bush to take advantage of Soviet economic difficulties: "Indeed, you might even indicate that our ability to move beyond 'technical cooperation' in our economic relationship will depend

on better performance on regional issues, particularly Central America."
Moreover: "You should stress that Soviet credibility is on the line in ensuring a free and fair election in Nicaragua and tell Gorbachev flatly that the
Soviets cannot escape responsibility for Cuba's actions."[76] Even though
the briefing book for Bush linked Soviet, Cuban, and Nicaraguan support
for the FMLN and sought to press the advantage in negotiations through
such a linkage, despite the Soviets' assertions that they had ceased arms
shipments to Nicaragua,[77] the Bush administration did not privilege
Nicaragua in its internal policy discussions.

Moreover, at this stage it was highly unlikely that Gorbachev could
control Castro. The meeting of the two in Havana in April 1989 was acrimonious. Castro had made clear his disagreements with Gorbachev's New
Thinking. He distanced himself from perestroika and made overtures to
a number of Latin American governments because of Soviet unreliability.
In 1987, Moscow had already made overtures to Reagan on a mutual cut-
off of military aid to the region. Any new proposal would require recip-
rocation. "How can we talk about cutting the Nicaraguan defenses when
you have the 82d Airborne sitting in Honduras?" Komplektov asked.[78]
Yet Moscow did ultimately move unilaterally. It had done so in a range
of other regional conflicts; in those places—Afghanistan, Cambodia,
Angola—Soviet interests were far more extensive.[79] In Nicaragua, ironically, it was in part about Moscow's credibility and Gorbachev's credibility among the hard-liners in the Politburo.

Ultimately, when Gorbachev and Bush did meet at the first plenary session on Central America on December 2, 1989, Gorbachev was
forthright:

> We see how you perceive the situation in Latin America. But it
> is not quite clear to us what you want from Nicaragua. There is
> political pluralism in that country, there are more parties there
> than in the United States. And the Sandinistas—what kind of
> Marxists are they?! This is laughable. Where are the roots of the
> problem? At the core are economic and social issues. Why does
> the U.S. fail to see them? You say that the main problem in Nica-
> ragua is the question of power. Well, there will be elections there.
> Let the United Nations monitor them. Frankly speaking, it is not
> our business. Let this process go where it will.

Gorbachev then distanced himself from Castro, indicating that no one could "lord themselves over" him. And finally: "I want to emphasize again: we are not pursuing any goals in Central America."[80]

In their subsequent private conversation, Bush responded that he now agreed with Gorbachev on the Sandinista Marxist characteristics, yet he emphasized that the Sandinistas still exported arms to El Salvador and added his concerns about the ongoing Soviet shipment of helicopters to Nicaragua. Gorbachev played the disingenuous card, indicating that US arms were in the region too. Bush suggested that they should look to remove this source of tension in their relationship; free elections were the road forward. Gorbachev agreed. Bush did hope that Ortega would not cling to power with the help of the army, but he also indicated: "If there are really free elections certified by a group of foreign observers, then the United States will accept their results and will in no way attempt to influence or sabotage their outcome." He eventually urged a termination of aid to Cuba and added: "It would be very good to find a way to halt assistance to Cuba and to certain forces in Central America so that we do not stand divided on such issues as Panama, Nicaragua, and Cuba." Gorbachev replied: "The Soviet Union has no plans with regard to spheres of influence in Latin America. This was and will continue to be the case."[81]

Ritualistic Invocation

In his study of credibility, McMahon opens the section on Vietnam with an observation on the frequency with which US policy had relied on credibility as an explanatory framework for the importance of the war. He writes: "American leaders explained, justified, and defended the U.S. commitment to South Vietnam so frequently in terms of the need to prove U.S. credibility that their statements *resemble ritualistic incantations.*" In the case of Reagan's Nicaraguan policies, it seems that a slight adjustment of the phrase might be apt. A "ritualistic invocation" of the credibility framework and the attendant expectations of behavior in terms of demonstrating "resolve, reliability, believability, and decisiveness," coupled with an "ability to convince adversaries and allies alike of its firmness, determination, and dependability," represented the desired agenda for Reagan. Though some advisers tried to ascribe geopolitical significance to their arguments, these were questioned extensively as plausible explanatory features. The credibility argument soon became more attractive, and, in that sense, this seemingly peripheral part of the world, so thoroughly embedded in the US sphere of influence, became vital (as was the case in several earlier Cold War conflicts). The problem was that this was not a straightforward Cold War conflict. In the aftermath of the so-called Cold War consensus, Reagan's rhetoric and the policy framework advanced by his team thoroughly lacked credibility. Allies throughout Latin America, Europe, and elsewhere did not share the sense of danger and foreboding advanced by Reagan's people, and, hence, his stance appeared implausible. McMahon (citing Jervis) captured the problem: "Small issues will often loom large, not because of their intrinsic importance, but because they are taken as tests of resolve." But he had an equally important point when he observed: "Only other states can validate the credibility of any power's words or actions."[82] It was quite apparent from early on that the Reagan administration suffered in this regard. Its allies and its adversaries did not read the situation in the same stark terms, they did not share the global Manichaean zero-sum framework advanced by the administration, and they frequently advanced policies and actions to counter US moves on Nicaragua. Moreover, significant numbers of congressional representatives objected to the framework, and US public opinion largely was wary of the hyperbolic rhetoric and questioned the centrality of the area and the need for a muscular US response there. US adversaries sometimes disparaged Washington's duplicity on the combination of covert operations and LIC with its hyperbolic rhetoric and begrudging diplomacy. Alternatively, they relished the sight of US overinvestment in and overcommitment to such an area. (Indeed, in that sense, Kennan's criticism of symmetrical containment—that it provided adversaries with the opportunity to define the initiative—had come full circle: the Reagan administration overreacted to peripheral Soviet interests.) Vladimir Stanchenko once observed that, whatever the scenario, the Soviets were going to take advantage. If Reagan's militarism was successful, they could point to US aggressive tendencies (again); if the situation stalemated, they could use it as a public relations counterweight to Afghanistan; if Washington failed (again), they could play up its weaknesses and its inability to deal with minor revolutions. When the Bush administration entered the White House in 1989, it was not just that it recognized that, in realist terms, the region was of little importance; it also recognized that the Reagan administration had expended too much credibility on the region and that it was time to move on before more damage was done. What distinguishes the policies and perceptions of the Reagan administration from those of the Bush administration is that sufficient Reagan advisers linked US credibility with a military solution (albeit within constrained circumstances). Nevertheless, the demonstration that the United States could act was important. The Bush people, however, realized that the military option was not viable and, moreover, that it undermined US credibility.

Notes

1. President Ronald Reagan, "Central America: Defending Our Vital Interests," Address Before a Joint Session of Congress, April 27, 1983, *Department of State Bulletin* 83, no. 2075 (June 1983): 1–5. See also *New York Times,* April 28, 1983.

2. Alexander Haig explained as much to the Cuban vice premier, Carlos R. Rodriguez, at their secret meeting in November 1981. He noted that the US "national spirit has significantly strengthened," and, while he maintained that the situation in Nicaragua was of geopolitical concern, Rodriguez retorted that Haig would be "committing a serious error in allowing a geopolitical mirage to impel you toward a mistaken interpretation." Secretary of State Alexander Haig Meeting with Cuban Vice Premier Carlos R. Rodriguez, Mexico City, Transcript, November 23, 1981, US-Cuban Relations, Cold War International History Project (CWIHP), Woodrow Wilson International Center for Scholars, Washington, DC.

3. Robert Kagan cited in Odd Arne Westad, *The Global Cold War: Third World Interventions and the Making of Our Times* (Cambridge: Cambridge University Press, 2005), 345.

4. The Committee of Santa Fe, L. Francis Bouchey, Roger Fontaine, David C. Jordan, Gordon Sumner, and Lewis Tambs, *A New Inter-American Policy for the Eighties* (Washington, DC: Council for Inter-American Security, 1980), 1, 3, 46, 52.

5. Peter Kornbluh, "The US Role in the Counterrevolution," in *Revolution and Counterrevolution in Nicaragua,* ed. Thomas W. Walker (Boulder: Westview, 1991), 323–49, 325.

6. The *and/or* is important at least in terms of the historiography because, despite the Reagan administration treating them as a part of a concerted attempt to subvert the Central American isthmus, there were considerable differences between Moscow and Havana, certainly Moscow and Managua, and, if anything, Castro played a cautious game in the early Reagan years. See Wayne S. Smith, *The Closest of Enemies: A Personal and Diplomatic Account of US-Cuban Relations since 1957* (New York: Norton, 1987); Carl G. Jacobsen, *Soviet Attitudes towards Aid to and Contacts with Central American Revolutionaries* (Washington, DC: US Department

of State, 1984); Vladimir I. Stanchenko, "United States—USSR—Latin America: Soviet Role in Central America" (paper delivered at the Jean Donovan Conference, University College Cork, January 26–27, 1990); Nicola Miller, *Soviet Relations with Latin America, 1959–1987* (Cambridge: Cambridge University Press, 1989); and Wayne S. Smith, ed., *The Russians Aren't Coming: New Soviet Policy in Latin America* (Boulder, CO: Lynne Reinner, 1992).

7. Memorandum of Todor Zhivkov–Fidel Castro Conversation, Havana, April 9, 1979, Bulgaria in the Cold War, CWIHP. Moreover, in November 1981, Carlos Rodriguez challenged Haig to identify the purported amount of weaponry that Cuba had been sending and challenged the content of the State Department White Paper on arms transfers. Secretary of State, Alexander Haig Meeting with Cuban Vice Premier, Carlos R. Rodriguez, Mexico City, Transcript, November 23, 1981, US-Cuban Relations, CWIHP.

8. "Soviet Geopolitical Momentum: Myth or Menace?" *Defense Monitor* (Center for Defense Information, Washington, DC) 15, no. 5 (1986): 30; Department of State and Department of Defense, *The Sandinista Military Buildup: An Update,* Publication no. 9432 (Washington, DC: Department of State, 1987), 16; Democratic Policy Committee, *Foreign Aid to Central America, FY 1981–1987* (Washington, DC: Senate Democratic Policy Committee, February 12, 1987), 79–80.

9. Lieutenant Colonel John H. Buchanan USMC (Ret.), Prepared Statement, Subcommittee on Inter-American Affairs, Committee on Foreign Affairs, US House of Representatives, on US Aid to Honduras, Washington, DC, September 21, 1982, https://babel.hathitrust.org/cgi/pt?id=purl.32754076917768;view=1up;seq=1.

10. Westad, *The Global Cold War,* 344, citing Danuta Paszyn, *The Soviet Attitude to Political and Social Change in Central America, 1979–1990: Case Studies on Nicaragua, El Salvador and Guatemala* (Basingstoke: Macmillan, 2000), 39–55.

11. Lars Schoultz, *National Security and United States Policy toward Latin America* (Princeton, NJ: Princeton University Press, 1987), 323; David Ryan, *US-Sandinista Diplomatic Relations: Voice of Intolerance* (London: Macmillan, 1995), 27–29.

12. Jacobsen, *Soviet Attitudes,* 15 (citing *O estado de S. Paulo,* May 3, 1983).

13. Finding on Nicaragua, September 19, 1983, Senate, House Joint Committees, *Iran-Contra Investigation,* app. A, vol. 2, Source Documents, November 13, 1987, and doc. 00203, fiche 32, *The Iran-Contra Affair: The Making of US Policy* (Washington, DC: National Security Archive, 1990) (hereafter *Iran-Contra,* NSA).

14. Jacobsen, *Soviet Attitudes,* 19.

15. See Presidential Findings Pursuant to Section 662, Foreign Assistance Act of 1961, from February 1981, Attached to Robert C. McFarlane to the Secretary, Memorandum, Covert Action Proposal for Central America, February 27, 1981, US Congress, Senate, House, Select Committee on Secret Military Assistance to Iran and the Nicaraguan Opposition and House Select Committee to Investigate Covert Arms Transactions with Iran, *Iran-Contra Investigation,* 100th Cong., 1st sess., 100–101, app. A, vol. 1, Source Documents, November 13, 1987; and Ronald

Reagan, Presidential Finding on Central America, December 1, 1981, and Finding on Nicaragua, September 19, 1983, *Iran-Contra Investigation,* app. A, vol. 2, Source Documents, November 13, 1987, and doc. 00203, fiche 32, *Iran-Contra,* NSA.

16. Lawrence A. Pezzullo to author, September 18, 1990.

17. Edgar Chamorro, Affidavit, September 5, 1985, Washington, DC; *Nicaragua v. The United States of America* (The Hague: International Court of Justice, June 27, 1986), 63, 75. See also Ryan, *US-Sandinista Diplomatic Relations,* 15.

18. Clarence Long, Chairman of the House Appropriations Sub-Committee Responsible for US Aid Programs, cited in Jacobsen, *Soviet Attitudes,* 17.

19. Ryan, *US-Sandinista Diplomatic Relations.*

20. Ronald Reagan cited in *Wall Street Journal,* June 3, 1980. See also Walter LaFeber, *America, Russia, and the Cold War, 1945–1990* (New York: McGraw-Hill, 1991), 302.

21. Thomas O. Enders was appointed assistant secretary of state for inter-American affairs; he had no Latin American experience, having previously served Kissinger on Cambodia. Langhorne Motley replaced Enders in 1983. Elliot Abrams served Jeane Kirkpatrick at the United Nations and eventually filled the post of assistant secretary for inter-American affairs in 1985. Robert White, the ambassador to San Salvador, who had served every administration since Eisenhower, was "retired" by Haig. His replacement, Deane Hinton, had four years' experience in Latin America. Jack R. Binns was replaced as ambassador in Tegucigalpa by John D. Negroponte, who had one year's experience in Ecuador but worked for Kissinger on Vietnam. Lawrence Pezzullo remained ambassador in Managua until August 1981; his replacement, Anthony E. Quainton, had no Latin American experience and did not speak Spanish.

22. See Elizabeth Dore and John Weeks, "The Red and the Black: The Sandinistas and the Nicaraguan Revolution," Research Paper 28 (London: Institute of Latin American Studies, 1992).

23. Raymond Bonner, *Weakness and Deceit: US Policy and El Salvador* (London: Hamish Hamilton, 1985), 244–54; Schoultz, *National Security and United States Policy,* 9–10, 63; Ryan, *US-Sandinista Diplomatic Relations,* 8–9; William M. LeoGrande, *Our Own Backyard: The United States in Central America, 1977–1992* (Chapel Hill: University of North Carolina Press, 1998), 75–80.

24. LeoGrande, *Our Own Backyard,* 126, 348; John A. Booth and Mitchell A. Seligson, eds., *Elections and Democracy in Central America* (Chapel Hill: University of North Carolina Press, 1989); Ryan, *US-Sandinista Diplomatic Relations,* 88–106.

25. Juan de Onis, "State Department Says Salvador Rebels Get Fewer Arms," *New York Times,* February 24, 1981; John Goshko and Don Oberdorfer, "Haig Calls Arms Smuggling to El Salvador 'No Longer Acceptable,'" *Washington Post,* February 28, 1981.

26. See Jacobsen, *Soviet Attitudes;* Stanchenko, "United States—USSR—Latin America"; and Miller, *Soviet Relations with Latin America.*

27. Alexander M. Haig, *Caveat: Realism, Reagan, and Foreign Policy* (London: Weidenfeld & Nicolson, 1984), 131.

28. Fabian Hilfrich, "Visions of the Asian Periphery: Vietnam (1964–1968) and the Philippines (1898–1900)," in *America, the Vietnam War, and the World,* ed. Andreas W. Daum, Lloyd C. Gardner, and Wilfried Mausbach (Cambridge: Cambridge University Press, 2003), 53–54, 57.

29. Buchanan, Prepared Statement (n. 9 above).

30. Schoultz, *National Security and United States Policy,* 279–80.

31. Ronald Reagan, Executive Order 12513, "Prohibiting Trade and Certain Other Transactions Involving Nicaragua," May 1, 1985, Public Papers of Ronald Reagan, 1985, Reagan Library, http://www.reagan.utexas.edu/archives/speeches/1985/50185a.htm.

32. John Lewis Gaddis, *Strategies of Containment: A Critical Appraisal of Postwar National Security Policy* (Oxford: Oxford University Press, 1982), 25–88.

33. Walter L. Hixon, "Containment on the Perimeter: George F. Kennan and Vietnam," *Diplomatic History* 12, no. 2 (April 1988): 149–64, 154, 157.

34. Oliver L. North, Constantine Menges, Memorandum for Robert C. McFarlane, Special Activities in Nicaragua, March 2, 1984, on file, National Security Archive, Washington, DC.

35. Eldon Kenworthy, "Central America: Beyond the Credibility Trap," *World Policy Journal* 1, no. 1 (Fall 1983): 181–200, 182.

36. Ryan, *US-Sandinista Diplomatic Relations,* passim.

37. Sally-Ann Treharne, *Reagan and Thatcher's Special Relationship: Latin America and Anglo-American Relations* (Edinburgh: Edinburgh University Press, 2015).

38. James M. Scott, *Deciding to Intervene: The Reagan Doctrine and American Foreign Policy* (Durham, NC: Duke University Press, 1996), 217.

39. David Ryan, *US Foreign Policy in World History* (London: Routledge, 2000), 173.

40. AP, "'Off Record' Kissinger Talk Isn't," *New York Times,* April 20, 1986.

41. H. W. Brands, *The Devil We Knew: Americans and the Cold War* (New York: Oxford University Press, 1993), 170.

42. Editorial, "It Takes Two to Contadora," *New York Times,* May 22, 1986.

43. US National Security Strategy and Accompanying Papers, April 1982, doc. 8290283 (NSDD 32) System II, NSC Records, Ronald Reagan Presidential Library, Simi Valley, CA.

44. Just as in 1954, Reagan's administration, like Eisenhower's, worried about the demonstration effects of successful revolutions. Draft Policy Paper Prepared in the Bureau of Inter-American Affairs, NSC Guatemala, August 19, 1953, *Foreign Relations of the United States, 1952–1954,* vol. 4, *The American Republics* (Washington, DC: US Government Printing Office, 1952–1954), 1074–79.

45. US National Security Strategy (n. 43 above).

46. Booth and Seligson, *Elections and Democracy in Central America;* The Report

of the Latin American Studies Association, Delegation to Observe the Nicaraguan General Election of November 4, 1984, in *The Electoral Process in Nicaragua: Domestic and International Influences* (Pittsburgh: Latin American Studies Association, November 19, 1984); Council of Freely Elected Heads of Government, *Observing Nicaragua's Elections, 1989–1990* (Atlanta: Carter Center, 1990).

47. *New York Times,* February 24, 1985, cited by Norman A. Graebner, Richard Dean Burns, and Joseph M. Siracusa, *Reagan, Bush, Gorbachev: Revisiting the End of the Cold War* (Westport, CT: Praeger Security International, 2008), 76; Charles Krauthammer, "The Reagan Doctrine," *Time,* April 1, 1985.

48. See Peter Kornbluh, *Nicaragua: The Price of Intervention* (Washington, DC: Institute of Policy Studies, 1987), and "The Covert War," in *Reagan versus the Sandinistas: The Undeclared War on Nicaragua,* ed. Thomas W. Walker (Boulder, CO: Westview, 1987), 21–38.

49. *Nicaragua v. The United States of America,* 137–41.

50. See Theodore Draper, *A Very Thin Line: The Iran-Contra Affairs* (New York: Hill & Wang, 1991).

51. Ronald Reagan, Remarks at the Dinner of the Conservative Political Action Conference, March 1, 1985, Public Papers of Ronald Reagan, https://www.reaganlibrary.archives.gov/archives/speeches/1985/30185f.htm.

52. John Tower, Edmund Muskie, and Brent Scowcroft, *The Tower Commission Report: Full Text of the President's Special Review Board* (New York: Bantam, 1987); US Senate Select Committee on Secret Military Assistance to Iran and the Nicaraguan Opposition, US House of Representatives, Select Committee to Investigate Covert Arms Transactions with Iran, *Iran-Contra Affair,* 100th Cong., 1st sess., SP 100-216/HR 100-433 (Washington, DC: US Government Printing Office, November 17, 1987); Lawrence E. Walsh, *Final Report of the Independent Counsel for Iran/ Contra Matters,* 3 vols. (Washington, DC: US Court of Appeals, August 4, 1993).

53. Senator Christopher J. Dodd, "Text of Democratic Response to Reagan Speech to Congress," April 27, 1983, *Congressional Quarterly Weekly Report* 41, no. 17 (April 30, 1983): 856–57.

54. Graebner, Burns, and Siracusa, *Reagan, Bush, Gorbachev,* 70; US Congress, Senate Committee on Foreign Relations, *National Bipartisan Report on Central America: Hearing before the Committee on Foreign Relations,* 98th Cong., 2nd sess., February 7–8, 1984.

55. Graebner, Burns, and Siracusa, *Reagan, Bush, Gorbachev,* 71.

56. Editorial, *New York Times,* January 23, 1984, cited in Graebner, Burns, and Siracusa, *Reagan, Bush, Gorbachev,* 72.

57. Foreign Ministers of Colombia, Mexico, Panama, and Venezuela, Information Bulletin, Contadora Island, Mexico, January 9, 1983, in *Contadora and the Central American Peace Process: Selected Documents,* ed. Bruce Michael Bagley, Roberto Alvarez, and Katherine J. Hagedorn (Boulder, CO: Westview, 1985), 164.

58. Ryan, *US-Sandinista Diplomatic Relations,* 149.

59. LeoGrande, *Our Own Backyard,* 578. See also Robert Pear, "Bush Aides

Speak of New Policy of Diplomacy in Central America," *New York Times,* November 20, 1988, and "Baker at the State Dept: Pragmatism over Zeal," *New York Times,* November 15, 1988.

60. G. Philip Hughes, Memorandum for David Demarest, Talking Points on Bipartisan Accord on Central America, March 24, 1989, NSC, David Pacelli Files, CF 01576-014, Nicaragua, January 1989–April 1989 (1), George H. W. Bush Presidential Library, College Station, TX.

61. Gaddis Smith, *The Last Years of the Monroe Doctrine, 1945–1993* (New York: Hill & Wang, 1994).

62. Pear, "Bush Aides Speak of New Policy." When Elliot Abrams was replaced in January 1989, he argued that he had had no regrets. The one major error in his mind was that the administration had not been "tougher": "When you look back eight years, a mistake was made in 1981 in the approach to this problem, which was to try to put it on a middle burner or a back burner." Doyle McManus, "Abrams Says Goodbye with 'No Regrets,'" *International Herald Tribune,* January 24, 1989.

63. Chris Norton, "Contras Seek Democracy Before Demobilisation," *The Independent* (London), February 16, 1989.

64. Thomas L. Friedman, "The Biggest Diplomatic Openings for Baker," *New York Times,* January 29, 1989.

65. Mark A. Uhlig, "Sandinistas Assail Renewed Rebel Aid," *New York Times,* March 25, 1989.

66. President George Bush, Statement, March 24, 1989, *New York Times,* March 25, 1989.

67. Martin Walker, "Bush Beefs Up Monroe Doctrine," *The Guardian* (London), May 3, 1989, and "Bush Doubts Soviet Pledge on Managua," *The Guardian* (London), May 17, 1989; Alexander M. Sullivan, "U.S. Finds Gorbachev's Havana Speech 'Hard to Fathom,'" USIA, April, 5, 1989, text link 88026 (copy in author's possession); Thomas L. Friedman, "U.S. Asks Soviets to Aid Latin Peace on Gorbachev Trip," *New York Times,* March 30, 1989.

68. President George Bush, Memorandum for the Vice President and Other Principals, U.S. Policy toward Nicaragua and the Nicaraguan Resistance, May 1, 1989, NSC, H Files, 90003–9, NSD May 8, 1989, George H. W. Bush Presidential Library.

69. William M. LeoGrande, "From Reagan to Bush: The Transition in US Policy towards Central America," *Journal of Latin American Studies* 22, no. 3 (September 1990): 595–621, 605; author discussion with Victor Tinoco, Washington, DC, July 19, 1989.

70. Raymond Garthoff, *The Great Transition: American-Soviet Relations and the End of the Cold War* (Washington, DC: Brookings Institution, 1994), 742–43.

71. President Carter, President Bush, et al., Memorandum of Conversation, September 21, 1989, NSC, Daniel Levin Files, CF 00940-016, Nicaragua (2), George H. W. Bush Presidential Library.

72. E. Rowny, ART, to the Secretary, Malta Meeting, November 17, 1989, Bush and Gorbachev at Malta, National Security Archive (hereafter NSA).

73. Garthoff, *The Great Transition,* 404–9.

74. Mark A. Uhlig, "Soviets Reducing Arms for Managua," *New York Times,* October 16, 1989.

75. Douglas P. Mulholland, INR, to the Secretary, Regional Issues at Malta: Gorbachev's Agenda, November 17, 1989, Bush and Gorbachev at Malta, NSA.

76. James A. Baker III to the President, Your December Meeting with Gorbachev, November 29, 1989, Bush and Gorbachev at Malta, NSA.

77. The President's Meeting with Soviet President Gorbachev, December 2–3, 1989, bk. II, Bush and Gorbachev at Malta, NSA.

78. Joshua Muravchik, "Summit Goals: Nicaragua's Election," *New York Times,* November 29, 1989; Larry Rohter, "A Caribbean Communist Seeks New Friends," *New York Times,* April 2, 1989; Bill Keller, "Gorbachev-Castro Face-Off: A Clash of Style and Policies," *New York Times,* April 2, 1989 (quote).

79. S. Neil MacFarlane, "Bush's Missing Link in Nicaragua," *New York Times,* April 6, 1989.

80. Mikhail Gorbachev and George Bush, First Plenary Session, December 2, 1989, Soviet Transcript of the Malta Summit, December 2–3, 1989, Bush and Gorbachev at Malta, NSA.

81. Record of Conversation between General Secretary Mikhail Gorbachev and President George Bush (One-on-One), December 2, 1989, Bush and Gorbachev at Malta, NSA.

82. Robert McMahon, "Credibility and World Power: Exploring the Psychological Dimension in Postwar American Diplomacy," *Diplomatic History* 15, no. 4 (Fall 1991): 455–72, 466 (emphasis added), 455, 457.

13

Enlargement and Its Discontents

Core and Periphery in Clinton-Era Foreign Policy

Hal Brands

The end of the Cold War created new vistas for US policy toward the global periphery. If one conceptualizes the periphery as those areas outside the economically developed, democratic West—in other words, those areas outside the Cold War–era First World—then, during the 1990s, the periphery looked both larger and more inviting than ever before.[1] The demise of the Soviet Union eliminated Washington's major competitor for the loyalties and emulation of the late-developing countries, while the collapse of the Cold War order opened up new geographic areas like Russia and Eastern Europe to American influence. "The end of history" indeed seemed to be at hand; American values and institutions could now be promoted with greater confidence and ease than ever before.

The resulting sense of opportunity was at the heart of the Clinton administration's national security strategy during the 1990s. That strategy was premised on the idea of "enlargement," or the notion that America's key geopolitical interest lay in the energetic promotion of democracy and free market economics not just in the First and Third Worlds but in the former Second World as well. At a time when American power was unmatched and Cold War divisions had disappeared, the United States would use its influence to make an expanded global periphery look ever more like the Western core while simultaneously containing or defeating challenges to this transformational project. America's "cherished goal," Clinton announced in 1995, was "a more secure world where democracy and free markets know no borders." It was a highly ambitious vision and one whose implementation would often prove difficult indeed.[2]

The early 1990s were a time of great promise and uncertainty in American foreign policy. The end of the Cold War had removed the major geopolitical threat to US security and vanquished the most important ideological challenge to American global leadership. Washington's military power and diplomatic influence were unrivaled, and American values seemed to be on the march. Democracy was blossoming in Latin America and Eastern Europe; free market economics was spreading throughout the Third World and the former Soviet bloc as well. The resulting sense of power and optimism was evident from the catchphrases that animated public discourse on the shape of the post–Cold War world: *the end of history, the democratic peace, the New World Order.* In the phrasing of the neoconservative commentator Charles Krauthammer, the world had reached a "unipolar moment," with the United States reigning supreme.[3]

In other respects, however, the end of the Cold War left the United States facing a more ambiguous situation. By the time the Clinton administration took office in January 1993, the post–Cold War world had already seen its share of disorder. The Iraqi invasion of Kuwait in 1990, murderous internal violence in Africa and Southern Europe, the prospect of nuclear proliferation, the specter of chaos or renewed authoritarianism in the former Soviet Union: these and other issues raised fears of an emerging era of global turmoil. "We should expect continuing change and upheaval around the world," noted CIA director Robert Gates in 1992. The United States would have to live with "the reality of an unstable, unpredictable, dangerously overarmed, and still transforming world."[4]

Looming over all this uncertainty was the question of what American grand strategy should be now that containment had been rendered irrelevant by its own success. "We've got to begin to lay an intellectual base for US involvement in the world, a rationale that people understand and support and around which you can build a consensus, as was done with containment," commented House Foreign Affairs Committee chair Lee Hamilton in 1991.[5] The Bush administration, which was so often consumed by crisis management, had only begun to provide a persuasive response to this challenge when the president left office in early 1993, giving Clinton and his aides the opportunity to articulate an enduring conception of American purpose in the post–Cold War world.[6]

In many respects, Bill Clinton himself seemed ill suited to the task. He had minimal experience with or expertise in international affairs, and early in his presidency he derided the entire concept of grand strategy. As his adviser Strobe Talbott recalled: "Clinton had been reading biographies of Roosevelt and Truman that convinced him that neither had grand strategies for how to exert American leadership against the global threats posed by Hitler and Stalin. Rather, they had 'powerful instincts about what had to be done, and they just made it up as they went along.' Strategic coherence, he said, was largely imposed after the fact by scholars, memoirists and 'the chattering classes.'"[7]

For all this skepticism, however, there were also powerful factors pushing the new president to set forth a compelling and cohesive narrative about America's role in the world. From a political perspective, Clinton instinctively understood that doing so was necessary if his administration was to maintain domestic support for a global foreign policy of any sort. "You've still got to be able to crystallize complexity in a way people get right away," he said. "The operative problem of the moment is that a bunch of smart people haven't been able to come up with a new slogan, and saying that there aren't any good slogans isn't a slogan either."[8] In the same vein, key advisers like National Security Adviser Anthony Lake and Secretary of State Warren Christopher argued that the administration needed to provide an overall sense of direction for US policy, lest the complexity of the international environment render American diplomacy confused and ineffective. "We cannot afford to careen from crisis to crisis," remarked Christopher in early 1993.[9]

The policy that thus emerged during Clinton's first year in office was anchored in a belief that the international environment had arrived at a crucial tipping point. As Lake explained in a major address at Johns Hopkins University in September 1993, the end of the Cold War had left the United States with unchallenged global power and cleared the way for a fairer, richer, and safer international order. "America's core concepts—democracy and market economics—are more broadly accepted than ever," he noted. Insofar as these trends could be encouraged and the world made to look more like the United States, American interests would inevitably be advanced. At the same time, while there was no "near-term threat to America's existence," there was no shortage of lesser challenges that might derail this progress and perhaps even lead to a new era of international upheaval. The United States, Lake announced, had reached a "historic crossroads" in its approach to a changing world.[10]

This situation offered a new and attractive purpose for American power. "We have the world's strongest military, its largest economy and its most dynamic, multiethnic society," Lake declared. The United States must use this position of post–Cold War preponderance to promote democratization and market reform while holding back the challenges to these trends. As Lake put it: "The successor to a doctrine of containment must be a strategy of enlargement—enlargement of the world's free community of market democracies." "To the extent democracy and market economics hold sway in other nations," he argued, "our own nation will be more secure, prosperous and influential, while the broader world will be more humane and peaceful." The United States, in other words, would do good by doing well: its exertions would advance the well-being of all humanity while also forging a global order in which America would be rich and secure.

Enlargement, as Lake explained it, had four components. First, the United States would strengthen "the core from which enlargement is proceeding" by deepening economic ties with its traditional Western allies and acting as a guarantor of regional stability in Europe and the Far East. Second, the United States should use financial assistance, political support, and other tools to encourage the emergence of new democracies and market economies in key strategic regions, most notably Central and Eastern Europe and the former Soviet Union. "If we can support and help consolidate democratic and market reforms in Russia and the other newly independent states," Lake commented, "we can help turn a former threat into a region of valued diplomatic and economic partners." Third, America must use its military and political influence to contain aggressive authoritarian regimes and prevent them from impeding global progress. "We should expect the advance of democracy and markets to trigger forceful reactions from those whose power is not popularly derived," Lake warned. Fourth, and finally, the United States should consider using military force to address human rights violations, civil wars, and other threats to democracy in places like Bosnia and Somalia. "Where we can make a difference . . . we should not oppose using our military forces for humanitarian purposes."

As Lake acknowledged, enlargement represented an attempt to provide direction to the domestic debate on foreign policy: "It is time for those who see the value of American engagement to steady our ranks; to define our purpose; and to rally the American people." Yet that policy was also rooted in core-periphery dynamics and the immense confidence that characterized the early post–Cold War era. Enlargement was infused with a belief that the global scene was pliant and malleable and that the historical currents were running in America's direction. The United States could thus go beyond its Cold War mission of defending the First and Third Worlds against the Second. At a time of no existential threats and unmatched American power, the United States could use its influence to strengthen the Western core and foster positive change throughout an expanded global periphery. "We have the blessing of living in the world's most powerful and respected nation at a time when the world is embracing our ideals as never before," Lake argued; the United States would not let the opportunity pass. Notwithstanding Clinton's aversion to grand strategy, this was an expansive vision of American purpose. As it turned out, however, the dilemmas of enlargement were not long to appear.

Those dilemmas were first apparent when it came to the issue of how and when to use military force. At the outset, many of Clinton's top civilian advisers believed that the selective use of force could be an essential tool for promoting democratic values and righting moral outrages. "What's the point of having this superb military you're always talking about if we can't use it?" Ambassador to the United Nations (and later Secretary of State) Madeleine Albright asked Joint Chiefs of Staff chair Colin Powell in one early meeting.[11] Lake put the same point rather less confrontationally. "I want to work to end every conflict," he remarked at an early press briefing. "I want to work to save every child."[12]

The proving ground for these sentiments was Somalia. Bush had committed US troops to that country in late 1992 in an effort to ease a massive famine caused by rampant internal strife. This narrow task was accomplished by early 1993, and Clinton withdrew more than half of the US contingent in May of that year. Notably, however, he left several thousand American soldiers there as part of an expanded UN mission to reconcile warring clans and build longer-term stability. American involvement, he announced, would enable the Somalis "to complete the work of rebuilding and recreating a peaceful, self-sustaining, and democratic civil society."[13]

The rhetoric was firmly in concert with the major themes of enlargement and the humanitarian instincts within the administration. Unfortunately, the policy results were disastrous. The expanded mission quickly drew the United States and its UN partners deeper into Somalia's internal politics and made them enemies of certain of the competing factions in that country. A raid in early October 1993 meant to capture one prominent warlord—Mohammed Farah Aideed—backfired disastrously, causing nineteen American deaths and a hailstorm of criticism at home. "The president had better get his foreign policy act together before Somalia becomes another Vietnam," one congressman declared. Stung by the attacks, Clinton quickly wound down the US mission, made preparations to withdraw all American troops, and explicitly disavowed his formerly expansive aims. "It is not our job to rebuild Somalia's society, or even to create a political process that can allow Somalia's clans to live and work in peace," he announced.[14]

Clinton's misadventure in Somalia demonstrated two key problems with the administration's conception of enlargement. First, it showed that there was a strategy deficit in the administration's new grand strategy. In his September 1993 address, Lake had pledged that the United States would focus its efforts on areas of key geopolitical significance, but Somalia came nowhere close to meeting this criterion. Moreover, the course of US involvement in that country showed a troubling inattention to the relationship between means and ends as Clinton had withdrawn the majority of American troops at precisely the time he was embracing an expanded mandate. In effect, he had weakened US forces in Somalia while simultaneously directing them to execute a more challenging task. The results were costly, in human and political terms alike.

This political fallout touched on the second and deeper problem, which was that humanitarian intervention and armed democracy promotion were in 1993 policies in search of a constituency. The idea of saving lives and spreading the democratic gospel was pleasing to Americans in an abstract sense, but not once it became clear that US troops would be bleeding and dying in missions with no obvious link to the nation's security. After the "Blackhawk down" incident in October, public opinion turned sharply against an American military role in Somalia, and the notion of humanitarian intervention as a whole came under fierce attack. "Right now the average American doesn't see our interests threatened to the point where we should sacrifice one American life," Clinton acknowledged.[15]

Indeed, Clinton's experience in Somalia was so painful that he hastened to junk this military component of enlargement altogether. "Peacekeeping is not at the center of our foreign or defense policy," Lake announced in early 1994. The implications of this statement became clear just a few weeks later. Amid furious ethnic violence in Rwanda that ultimately claimed 800,000 lives, Clinton and his advisers never so much as considered intervening to stop the killing. Wary of any entanglement whatsoever, the administration even refused to use the word *genocide* to describe events in Rwanda, a move that Lake later called "shameful."[16] Clinton had overreached in Somalia, and he and his advisers now sat silent amid a much greater humanitarian catastrophe.

During Clinton's remaining years in office, however, the problems of humanitarian intervention would not go away. This was most notably the case in Southeastern Europe, where the Balkan Wars set off by the breakup of Yugoslavia had tragic and destabilizing results. During the mid-1990s, Serbian atrocities in Bosnia garnered worldwide media attention and outrage; in 1998–1999, Serbian repression in Kosovo horrified consciences around the globe. These latter two conflicts mocked the promise of a new and more humane global order, and they called into question both the utility of NATO and the credibility of American leadership in that organization. If left unchecked, the Balkan Wars might even threaten the stability of the democratic core itself. "We need a Europe that is prosperous, secure, undivided, and free," Clinton declared in 1999. "Let a fire burn here in this area, and the flames will spread."[17]

The administration thus found itself gradually pulled toward intervention, launching two separate air wars against Slobodan Milošević's Serbian forces. The first of these interventions helped bring about the peace deal that ended the war in Bosnia in 1996; the second eventually forced Milošević's troops to withdraw from Kosovo in 1999. Clinton rightly took pride in his role in dousing the fires in the Balkans, and he invoked the Kosovo War as proof of his commitment to the principles of enlargement. "Whether you live in Africa or Central Europe or any other place," he announced in June 1999, "if somebody comes after civilians and tries to kill them *en masse* because of their race, their ethnic background, or their religion, and it is within our power to stop it, we will stop it."[18]

The rhetoric was partially misleading, however, for there was always something hesitant and halfhearted about Clinton's wars. When the president ultimately committed to intervention in Bosnia and Kosovo, he did so for reasons that had as much to do with the core—NATO and Europe—as they did with the principle of humanitarian intervention in the periphery. And, in both cases, the administration resolved to use force only after a long (and, for the victims, costly) period of vacillation and delay. As one critic observed, Clinton had a penchant for "doing as little as possible as late as possible in place after place."[19] During the Balkan Wars, in fact, Clinton remained so scarred by Somalia that he explicitly ruled out using US ground troops in combat situations, instead relying solely on airpower and local forces—Kosovar Albanians, Bosnian Muslims, and Croats—to get the job done. The restrictions were most pronounced in Kosovo, where the president publicly declared at the outset that ground forces would not be used and largely restricted bombing missions to high-altitude attacks meant to keep American pilots safe from antiaircraft fire. The strategy made sense in terms of minimizing casualties, but it also compromised the effectiveness of the air offensive, encouraged Milošević to think that he could simply outlast the United States, and occasioned criticism from pundits and even officials within the administration. "If you're going to use military force," army chief of staff Dennis Reimer argued during the Kosovo War, "using the total military force available is the right way to go."[20]

Some of this derision was surely overblown, in light of the results that Clinton obtained in the end. Nonetheless, the president's experience with humanitarian intervention testified to a key tension within the idea of enlargement. That policy was originally premised, in part, on using American military power to secure positive change along an inviting but potentially unstable periphery. At a time when there seemed no overriding threat to American security, however, the domestic audience—and thus Clinton himself—hesitated to pay the costs of such a policy. From Somalia to Kosovo, Clinton struggled to resolve these conflicting imperatives, and the military side of enlargement took on a distinctly halting quality as a result.

The limits of enlargement were also prominent in Clinton's dealings with Russia. Few issues seemed more important during the early 1990s than the success of the political transition in Moscow. Russia remained in economic and political turmoil in 1992–1993, and the fate of its nascent democracy hung in the balance. If the United States could help the reform faction, led by Boris Yeltsin, emerge triumphant, it would be a major victory for democratization and a step toward integrating Russia into an expanded Western community. "We must say to the democratic reformers in Russia that the democratic nations stand with them," Christopher argued in early 1993. During the Cold War, Moscow had been the subject of containment; during the 1990s, it would be enlargement's greatest challenge.[21]

The early years of Clinton's presidency saw deep American involvement in Russian affairs. US economists pushed the Russian government to embrace "shock therapy," or the drastic liberalization of the country's economy, while the Clinton administration, the World Bank, and the Group of 7 sweetened the pill with billions of dollars in aid. "We want the Russian people to understand that the world stands with them as they make the transition from communism to free markets," Talbott announced.[22] Clinton's team also intervened heavily in Russian politics, putting its full support and prestige behind Yeltsin despite his sometimes antidemocratic tendencies. "Knock it off," Clinton told one aide who suggested that the president distance himself from Yeltsin after he had the Russian parliament shelled in late 1993. "We're in this thing for keeps."[23] The extent of the US role in Russia during this period was related in a dispatch by the journalist Stephen Cohen: "American economists, notably the Harvard team headed by Professor Jeffrey Sachs, sit as official advisers to the Russian government. U.S. political organizations, some with federal funds, reward favored political factions. The AFL-CIO is deeply involved in Russian trade union politics. Proposals are even afloat to put a resident corps of Western 'experts' in Russia's governing bureaucracies, to assign NATO advisers the job of reshaping Russia's armed forces, and to make the dollar an official Russian currency." Cohen added: "Americans need only imagine their own reaction if Russians were playing such roles in our government and political life."[24]

Clinton's support for Yeltsin helped guard against a Communist revival and other nightmare scenarios during the early 1990s, which was itself a victory for the United States. Yet the hope of transforming Russia into a democratic, free market, Western-oriented regime was simply too ambitious. The structural obstacles—the history of authoritarian rule, the lack of a democratic political culture, the massive traumas inherent in promoting drastic reform—were just too great. In some ways, in fact, US policies actually exacerbated those traumas. The rapid liberalization of the Russian economy led to the looting of government assets, extreme concentrations of wealth, and severe hardship for the poor and the middle class. "As a result of the U.S.-backed 'shock therapy,' millions of Russian families have lost their life savings and fallen below the poverty line," wrote Cohen. "To many of those citizens, their misery seems to be 'made in the U.S.A.'"[25] By the mid-1990s, Russia was evolving into something approximating a mafiocracy, with key institutions in thrall to organized crime or corrupt political elites. When Russian forces attacked Chechnya in December 1994, the growing doubts about the country's future were amplified all the more.

Clinton's aims vis-à-vis Russia were also complicated by another aspect of his agenda—the expansion of NATO into Central and Eastern Europe. The administration had not initially seemed interested in this initiative; in 1993, Christopher commented that expansion was "not on the agenda."[26] By the end of the year, however, the president had reconsidered. NATO expansion seemed to fit perfectly with the key concepts of enlargement. It would reassert the US commitment to Europe, ease concerns about a potential German or Russian revival, and thereby provide a climate of security that would allow the nations of Eastern Europe to focus their energies on democratization and economic development. At one stroke, expansion would solidify the core and promote reform in the periphery. Following a meeting with Czech president Vaclav Havel and Polish leader Lech Walesa in 1993, Clinton declared that NATO expansion was only a question of "when and how."[27] Over the next half decade, the United States gradually moved toward bringing Poland, Hungary, and the Czech Republic into the alliance.

Judged solely on its own merits, NATO expansion lived up to expectations. It eased fears of resurgent instability in Central and Eastern Europe and extended American influence deeper into these regions than ever before. The drawback, of course, was that expansion threatened to undercut Clinton's policy toward Russia. NATO, as Undersecretary of Defense

Walter Slocombe pointed out, "began historically as an alliance against the Soviet Union." Now that alliance was expanding into a region that US leaders viewed as part of the democratizing periphery but that Kremlin officials had long seen as part of their country's security core. NATO expansion thus seemed certain to inflame Russian nationalism and likely to put Yeltsin and other reformers on the defensive. Yevgeny Primakov, the head of Russian intelligence, said that, if NATO moved eastward, "irritation in military circles might emerge that is not in the interests of the political or military leadership of Russia or the country in general." One Russian reformer put it similarly: "Frankly, the politicians who support this decision believe Russia is a country that should be put aside, a country that should not be included in the civilized world—ever."[28] By promoting enlargement in Eastern Europe, in other words, Clinton might compromise that same goal in Russia.

This was a real dilemma and one that Clinton and his diplomats spent much of the mid- and late 1990s trying to manage. At times, the president did quite well. The US-NATO intervention in Bosnia—traditionally a Russian sphere of influence—in 1995 elicited angry condemnations from legislators in the Duma and provoked talk of a crisis with Moscow. Clinton used his close personal ties to Yeltsin to smooth over the dispute, persuading the Russian leader to support the US-sponsored peace settlement in Bosnia by committing two battalions of troops to the NATO contingent. Indeed, with Russia effectively a ward of the international financial institutions, there was little Yeltsin could do but swallow hard and go along with the proposal.[29]

Yet Clinton's balancing act could not last forever. In early 1998, before the first round of NATO expansion was even complete, US officials announced that Latvia, Lithuania, and Estonia—all former Soviet republics—would eventually become members of the alliance as well. This decision to push a historically anti-Soviet alliance up to Russia's borders was difficult to square with Clinton's desire to integrate Moscow into an expanded Western community, and it added to the growing undercurrent of tension in the relationship. Those tensions burst into the open in 1999 when Clinton again overrode Russian objections in leading US and NATO intervention in Kosovo. The airstrikes provoked a virulent Russian response, with Yeltsin even hinting that war might result. The immediate crisis passed, and Clinton won Russian participation in the postconflict peacekeeping mission. Tensions soon flared again, however, as the Russians preemptively deployed into Kosovo, leading to a race (won by Moscow) to seize the airport in the capital as well as close calls between Russian and NATO troops. As the 1990s came to a close, US-Russian relations were at a post–Cold War nadir. And, far from aligning with the Western core, Kremlin leaders were increasingly courting a variety of nondemocratic powers—Iraq, Iran, even China—in hopes of balancing American global influence.[30]

By this point, the Russian reform agenda had also collapsed. A massive financial crisis in August 1998 inflicted severe damage on the Russian economy and effectively foreclosed further attempts at economic liberalization. Authoritarian tendencies reasserted themselves as the resumption of the Chechen War in 1999 led to a massive crackdown on media freedoms and civil rights more broadly. At the turn of the millennium, Yeltsin handed over the presidency to a former KGB agent, Vladimir Putin, who over the next several years would return Russia to a barely veiled authoritarian regime. By the time Clinton left office, his administration was dogged with the question, Who lost Russia?[31]

The question was more than a little unfair. It ignored the real achievements of NATO expansion and US intervention in the Balkans, and it implied that Clinton had it in his power to decisively affect the internal evolution of a massive country on the other side of the globe. Yet it nonetheless testified to the frustrated ambition of enlargement. Clinton and his advisers had initially sought to promote a democratic, Western-oriented Russia as a key pillar of their global policy. The inherent difficulty of that task and the contradictions within their own strategy ensured that this aspiration went wanting.

Clinton found it little easier to deal with those authoritarian states that stood athwart his global vision. Lake termed these governments *backlash states,* the notion being that bellicose, dictatorial regimes—Saddam's Iraq, Khamenei's Iran, the Kim dynasty's North Korea—represented a dangerous but ultimately transitory backlash against the inevitable march of human progress. If the United States could just contain the threat and prevent damage to the democratic core and the democratizing periphery, these regimes would eventually be left by the wayside. "Slowly but surely,"

Lake argued in 1994, "they are coming to understand that there is a price to pay for their recalcitrant commitment to remain on the wrong side of history." If the United States remained patient and purposeful in dealing with this "band of outlaws," it would be "still very much within our power to prevail."[32]

This was a sensible policy given the alternatives, yet it was often difficult and frustrating to execute. Governments in Tehran, Pyongyang, and Baghdad refused to passively accept their containment or slip quietly into history. Instead, they caused problems for Clinton at every turn. Iran, the Pentagon commented in 1995, remained "both a serious immediate and an important long-term threat to the security of the Gulf." The Iranian government counterattacked against the US containment policy through terrorism and other means, the bloodiest example being its support of a bombing attack that killed nineteen American servicemen in Saudi Arabia in 1996.[33] In the Far East, North Korean progress toward a nuclear weapon brought Washington and Pyongyang to the brink of war in 1993–1994 and constituted a source of recurring tension for years thereafter. Isolated from the world community, these regimes also increased cooperation with one another, trading in missiles, advanced technology, and other commodities.

Then there was Iraq. For the Clinton administration, Iraq was the very exemplar of a backlash state. Saddam Hussein's forces had been thrashed during the Persian Gulf War in 1990–1991, but the dictator remained unbowed and unrepentant. His regime apparently sought to have former president Bush assassinated in 1993, and it massed eighty thousand troops on the Kuwaiti border a year later. It also interfered with UN weapons inspections, supported a variety of international terrorist groups, and remained as brutal as ever in dealing with its own population.

Clinton and his advisers took a three-pronged approach to confronting Saddam. First, they sought to weaken Iraq economically by holding UN sanctions in place. Second, they contained the regime militarily by stationing substantial US forces in the Gulf and rushing reinforcements to the region during the 1994 Kuwait crisis. Finally, Clinton ordered periodic airstrikes against Iraqi targets to punish Saddam's outrages, weaken his military base, protect opposition groups like the Kurds in northern Iraq, and convince other Baathist officials that, as one US adviser put it, "following this man is not good for your health."[34] (Indeed, while the Clinton administration was not actively seeking a coup in Iraq during the early 1990s, it made no secret that it would welcome one should it occur.)

In a narrow sense, the containment policy did its job. Confronted by American diplomatic and military power, Iraq could not seriously disrupt the regional order. Saddam remained "trapped in a strategic box," as Albright put it in 1997.[35]

Yet containment also had serious drawbacks, which became increasingly clear as the 1990s wore on. The policy was costly because it required continuous military vigilance, and it was diplomatically problematic because it necessitated the indefinite stationing of US troops in Saudi Arabia. It was also difficult to sustain over time. The international coalition that had confronted Saddam in 1990–1991 frayed as countries like France and Russia sought to once again do business with oil-rich Baghdad, and, by 1998–1999, the sanctions and inspections regime was on the verge of collapse. Above all, containment was frustrating because it offered no quick means of removing the source of the problem altogether. "Containment doesn't bring about a decisive resolution quickly," commented one official. "It's unsatisfying and ungratifying by its nature."[36] Just when America's power to transform the global order seemed greatest, its energies were being absorbed by a seemingly endless duel with a tinpot tyrant.

Clinton attempted to break free of these dilemmas by sponsoring covert action to topple Saddam in 1995–1996, but this undertaking collapsed amid last-minute indecision in Washington and infighting among the Iraqi opposition.[37] And, as the headaches of containment piled up, so did domestic criticism of the policy. Republicans assailed Clinton with charges of weakness and hesitation, and, in 1998, the House and Senate broke with the administration by passing the Iraqi Liberation Act. The law called for "regime change" and pledged US support to various Iraqi dissident groups. "Give the Iraqi National Congress a base, protected from Saddam's tanks," said one Iraqi exile, "give us the temporary support we need to feed and house and care for the liberated population, and we will give you a free Iraq, an Iraq free of weapons of mass destruction and a free market Iraq."[38] The rhetoric was inspiring, and it channeled the very ideas that animated enlargement. Given Saddam's firm grip on power, however, the actual measures contained in the law were more symbolic than anything else. As the 1990s came to a close, America's Iraq policy was in disarray, and Saddam remained a defiant reminder of enlargement's limits.

So did the Communist rulers of China. In the early days of the Clinton administration, the president and his advisers had seen US-Chinese relations as a key test of enlargement. During the 1992 presidential campaign, Clinton had severely criticized Bush's restrained reaction to the Tiananmen Square massacre in 1989. "I believe that our nation has a higher purpose than to coddle dictators and stand aside from the global movement toward democracy," he said. Once in office, he pledged to reevaluate Beijing's most-favored-nation (MFN) status in light of its human rights violations. "Americans cannot forget Tiananmen Square," the State Department official Winston Lord told Congress; US-Chinese relations would remain circumscribed "until a more humane system emerges."[39]

The use of economic means to promote internal reform was a favored tactic during the Clinton years. "Our economic strength gives us a position of strength on almost every global issue," the president wrote in 1995.[40] By offering incentives for cooperation and punishments for recalcitrance, the United States could thus tip the balance in favor of liberalization in countries where the outcome was in doubt. During the 1990s, Clinton used economic aid to assist democratization in places like South Africa and Cambodia. He also used the threat of trade sanctions to help thwart a coup in Guatemala in 1993. These were the quiet successes of enlargement—the cases in which American economic leverage was sufficient to support a preexisting movement toward democracy or to deter disruptions to the democratic process.

US-Chinese relations, by contrast, quickly turned into a case study in the limits of American power. American economic leverage was simply insufficient to compel internal reform in Beijing. Chinese officials were especially sensitive on this count after the upheaval of 1989, and they dismissed calls for liberalization as attempts "to undermine the unity and racial harmony of other countries under the pretext of 'freedom,' 'democracy,' and 'human rights.'" "China will never accept the US human rights concept," one official declared in 1993. It soon became clear that a slowdown in bilateral commerce would hurt the United States as much as Beijing, and Clinton quietly delinked Chinese human rights practices from MFN renewal. From 1994 onward, he essentially put the human rights issue aside in seeking "comprehensive engagement" on trade, security, and diplomatic issues. The policy shift represented a realistic recognition of Beijing's growing power, but it was also morally discomfiting to those who had hoped for greater change within the Chinese system. "There is no moral or practical difference between trading with the PRC dictatorship and trading with the Nazis," argued one Republican congressman.[41]

US officials could console themselves by hoping that China's economic liberalization would eventually lead to political reform as well. The idea that economic and political openness went hand in hand was a key tenet of administration thinking, and, during his presidency, Clinton was an energetic proponent of freer trade. In 1993, the United States, Mexico, and Canada concluded the North American Free Trade Agreement, creating the largest trade bloc in the world. Clinton's negotiators then helped bring about the conclusion of the Uruguay Round of the General Agreement on Tariffs and Trade, which provided for broad global tariff reductions and led to the founding of the World Trade Organization (WTO). Bilateral trade deals also proliferated during the Clinton years; by one count, the administration signed some five hundred such accords. As one author has noted, the administration behaved as if it were riding a sort of free trade bicycle—it feared that, if it stopped pedaling, it would lose momentum and fall over.[42]

This frenetic activity drew on some of the core tenets of Clinton's worldview. It reflected the widespread sense that globalization was inevitable and that the United States must participate in and shape this process. "Efforts to resist the powerful technological and economic forces behind globalization . . . are misguided and, in the long run, futile," argued Undersecretary of State Joan Spero. The activity also reflected a desire to link the United States ever more closely to core and periphery and to ensure that economic openness prevailed in both. As one commentator put it in 1996, the administration's aim was that Latin America, Europe, and the Asian Pacific should "all have one thing in common: Clinton's America was locking itself into the heart of each." And, of course, Clinton's free trade enthusiasm represented a firm belief that all nations, Western and developing alike, would benefit from the inexorable progression toward global interconnectedness.[43]

In the end, however, the economic side of enlargement proved both rewarding and frustrating. Clinton frequently touted his trade diplomacy as one of his greatest strengths, and there was much evidence to back up this assertion. The sheer number of agreements he signed was impressive. On balance, these deals benefited a booming American economy during the 1990s, and they employed the lure of the US market to promote unprecedented global openness. "The dynamism of the global economy is transforming commerce, culture, communications and global relations," stated the administration's final version of the *National Security Strategy* in 1999, "creating new jobs and opportunities for Americans."[44]

Yet globalization and free trade also engendered resistance as the decade progressed. Global integration could be a constructive force that brought prosperity and innovation, but it could also be a destructive phenomenon that tore down existing customs, privileges, and arrangements. In countries around the world, the resulting insecurities gave rise to a growing antiglobalization movement. Labor unions and blue-collar workers in Latin America railed against the loss of job security that came with lower tariffs and free trade. Community leaders in India led boycotts of foreign goods and resisted the intrusion of outside ideas. Pious Muslims denounced the increasing accessibility of Internet pornography and the advance of Western cultural mores. In France and Germany, anti-immigrant riots broke out as citizens sought to shield their societies and economies from foreign influence. The dangers of globalization were perhaps best illustrated in 1997–1998 when a financial crisis spread uncontrollably from East Asia to Russia and Latin America. The contagion wiped out the savings of many working- and middle-class individuals; it also forced countries like Thailand, Indonesia, and Brazil to seek International Monetary Fund (IMF) bailouts that came with stringent and deeply unpopular conditions attached. By 1999, one *Financial Times* commentator was warning that there was a "powerful backlash against globalization" at work.[45]

This backlash was also evident in the United States. Organized labor, environmental groups, and other constituencies worried that the administration's trade agenda would impinge on their interests. Free trade and globalization also came under fire from a growing number of conservative Republicans, who argued that, by linking itself more firmly to the international economy, the United States was also exposing itself to instability caused by economic crises abroad. This sentiment was fueled by the Mexican peso crisis of 1994, which necessitated a $20 billion bailout to the Mexican government, and by the Asian crisis in 1997–1998, which required extensive US and IMF intervention. Patrick Buchanan, a self-styled "economic nationalist," argued: "We are running into bailouts without end because of this global economy." As Undersecretary of Commerce David Aaron admitted in 1999: "The proven contribution of trade to our current prosperity has . . . not convinced most Americans of the value of trade."[46]

These sentiments made it more and more difficult for Clinton to advance his trade agenda as his presidency progressed. In 1997 and 1998, legislators denied the administration fast-track trade authority, thereby making it virtually impossible to conduct another round of multilateral trade negotiations or proceed with the much-touted Free Trade Area of the Americas. In 1999, anarchists rioted at the WTO Summit in Seattle while an array of peaceful demonstrators—from the Sierra Club, the Teamsters, the AFL-CIO, and other organizations—protested the proceedings. Clinton acknowledged the dislocations caused by globalization, saying: "If we're going to have an open trading system, we have got to make it work for ordinary folks." He sought to accommodate such concerns by proposing stricter WTO sanctions on countries with insufficient labor protections, but the proposal was anathema to developing countries. The Seattle summit meeting ended in deadlock, with the *New York Times* commenting that the episode represented "a sharp setback, and perhaps a fatal blow," to Clinton's trade liberalization plans.[47] As subsequent post–Cold War administrations worked to reinvigorate that agenda, they too would discover that globalization and free trade were issues that were indeed difficult to reconcile.

The Clinton years were a time of great optimism in US foreign policy. Cold War divisions had disappeared; democracy and markets were advancing; American power was unchallenged. The goal of enlargement was to capitalize on these conditions to solidify the core, integrate the periphery, and make the global environment ever more conducive to US interests. As Lake put it in 1993, no longer was America's mission one of merely "trying to contain the creeping expansion of that big, red blob"; that mission now revolved around driving the progressive expansion of the "'blue areas' of market democracies."[48]

The ambition was inspiring. The implementation could be quite difficult. Clinton and his advisers achieved several notable successes during the 1990s—expanding NATO, ending (eventually) the Balkan Wars, concluding hundreds of trade agreements, and others—that advanced the vision of a more open, democratic world where core and periphery looked ever more alike. Yet enlargement also occasioned dilemmas that the administration was hard-pressed to resolve. Clinton continually struggled to reconcile the dictates of humanitarian intervention and armed democracy promotion with the cost-averse nature of the domestic audience, and containing states like Iraq proved problematic in both political and geopolitical terms. Efforts to promote reform in Russia stumbled on the pure enormity of the challenge and the contradictions within US policy, and the early attempt to pressure China on human rights was less successful still. Finally, the promotion of global openness worked well during Clinton's first term, but it eventually ran up against a backlash in both periphery and core. Even at a time of unparalleled US power, transformative visions were not easily realized.

In retrospect, of course, Clinton's greatest failure came, not in any of these areas, but in his inability to deal effectively with the one rising threat that would soon rupture the self-assured mood of the post–Cold War years. Osama bin Laden's al-Qaeda movement was a reaction against a number of concrete US policies in the Middle East. Yet, in a broader sense, it was also a rejection of precisely the open, democratic, US-led world order that enlargement envisioned. "We are seeking to drive them out of our Islamic nations and prevent them from dominating us," bin Laden declared.[49] Clinton's airpower-only template for military intervention had worked in the Balkans, but it was woefully insufficient for dealing with this challenge, and the threat continued to metastasize as a result.

The terrorist attacks of September 11, 2001, had a paradoxical effect on US views of the global periphery. The attacks shattered the optimism of the 1990s and cast the nation into a new climate of anxiety and fear. But fear, too, can be a powerful motivator, and the post-9/11 period saw, not the decline, but the intensification of the missionary impulse in US foreign policy. The Bush administration was soon using massive military force to counter threats and bring democracy to Afghanistan and Iraq; top officials spoke purposefully of spreading freedom and free markets throughout the Middle East and, eventually, "to every corner of the world." In a new era of danger, the United States would find safety by remaking the global security environment, starting with some of the most inhospitable political terrain on earth. America would "seek and support the growth of democratic movements and institutions in every nation and culture," Bush declared in his 2005 inaugural address, "with the ultimate goal of ending tyranny in our world."[50]

Yet, if the desire to reshape the periphery in the American image did not abate after 9/11, neither did the difficulties inherent in that task. The wars in Iraq and Afghanistan demonstrated the awesome capabilities of the American military to destroy hostile regimes, but, in both cases, the aftermath also illustrated the limits of the country's ability to implant its own institutions on foreign soil. When Bush left office (and for several years thereafter), it was not yet clear whether the new Iraq and Afghanistan would eventually emerge as democratic beacons in a troubled part of the world or ultimately serve as examples of the hubris of American power. What was clear was that, when it came to the transformative impulse in US foreign policy, there remained an undeniable tension between grand visions and stubborn reality.

Notes

1. There are, of course, other ways to conceptualize the periphery, but this is perhaps the simplest and the one that seems to fit most closely with the themes of US foreign policy during the Clinton years.

2. *A National Security Strategy of Engagement and Enlargement* (Washington, DC: White House, 1995), iii.

3. Charles Krauthammer, "The Unipolar Moment," *Foreign Affairs* 70, no. 1 (Winter 1991): 5–17.

4. Testimony before the House Committee on Foreign Affairs, Federal News Service Transcript, February 25, 1992, accessed at lexisnexis.com.

5. Michael Putzel, "U.S. Searches for Stability in New World's Disorder," *Boston Globe,* September 29, 1991; Andrew Rosenthal, "Farewell, Red Menace," *New York Times,* September 1, 1991.

6. On this subject, see Hal Brands, *From Berlin to Baghdad: America's Search for Purpose in the Post–Cold War World* (Lexington: University Press of Kentucky, 2008), chaps. 1–3.

7. Strobe Talbott, *The Russia Hand: A Memoir of Presidential Diplomacy* (New York: Random House, 2002), 133.

8. Ibid., 133–34.

9. Senate Foreign Relations Committee, *Nomination of Warren M. Christopher to Be Secretary of State* (Washington, DC: US Government Printing Office, 1993), 19–21.

10. The quotations in this paragraph and the next three come from Anthony Lake, "From Containment to Enlargement" (remarks at the School of Advanced International Affairs, Johns Hopkins University, September 21, 1993), http://www.mtholyoke.edu/acad/intrel/lakedoc.html.

11. Michael Dobbs, *Madeleine Albright: A Twentieth-Century Odyssey* (New York: Macmillan, 2000), 360.

12. Quoted in James Goldgeier, *Not Whether but When: The U.S. Decision to Enlarge NATO* (Washington, DC: Brookings Institution, 1999), 21.

13. *Public Papers of the Presidents of the United States, William J. Clinton, 1993* (Washington, DC: US Government Printing Office, 1994), 565–66.

14. "Withdraw United States Troops from Somalia Now," House of Representatives, October 5, 1993, *Congressional Record* 139, no. 133 (1993): H7382; *Public Papers . . . 1993,* 713. See also Brands, *From Berlin to Baghdad,* 130–35.

15. George Stephanopoulos, *All Too Human: A Political Education* (Boston: Little, Brown, 1999), 214.

16. Anthony Lake, "The Limits of Peacekeeping," *New York Times,* February 6, 1994; John Darnton, "Revisiting Rwanda's Horrors with a Former National Security Adviser," *New York Times,* December 14, 2004.

17. *Public Papers of the Presidents of the United States, William J. Clinton, 1999* (Washington, DC: US Government Printing Office, 2000), 451–54.

18. John Dumbrell, *Clinton's Foreign Policy: Between the Bushes, 1992–2000* (New York: Routledge, 2009), 44.

19. Quoted in George Herring, *From Colony to Superpower: U.S. Foreign Relations since 1776* (New York: Oxford University Press, 2008), 936.

20. On these issues, see Jane Perlez, "Clinton and the Joint Chiefs to Discuss Ground Invasion," *New York Times,* June 2, 1999; John Harris, "Clinton Says He Might Send Ground Troops," *Washington Post,* May 19, 1999; and Steven Erlanger, "Allies Were Nearing Kosovo Ground War," *New York Times,* November 7, 1999.

21. Quoted in Senate Foreign Relations Committee, *Nomination of Warren M. Christopher,* 26.

22. Statement by Strobe Talbott before the Subcommittee on Foreign Operations of the House Appropriations Committee, April 19, 1993, US Department of State, *Dispatch,* 4, May 1993, 20–24 (quote 21).

23. Talbott, *The Russia Hand,* 102.

24. Stephen Cohen, *Failed Crusade: America and the Tragedy of Post-Communist Russia* (New York: Norton, 2001), 117–18.

25. Cohen, *Failed Crusade,* 118.

26. Elaine Sciolino, "U.S. to Offer Plan," *New York Times,* October 21, 1993.

27. The quote is in *Public Papers of the Presidents of the United States, William J. Clinton, 1994* (Washington, DC: US Government Printing Office, 1995), 40. See also Goldgeier, *Not Whether but When,* 19–20.

28. The quotes are from Senate Armed Services Committee, *Department of*

Defense Authorization for Appropriations for Fiscal Year 1994 and the Future Years Defense Program, Part IV (Washington, DC: US Government Printing Office, 1994), 80, 97. See also Steven Erlanger, "Russia Warns NATO on Expanding East," *New York Times,* November 26, 1993; and James Goldgeier and Michael McFaul, *Power and Purpose: U.S. Policy toward Russia after the Cold War* (Washington, DC: Brookings Institution, 2003), 184.

29. Talbott, *The Russia Hand,* 180.

30. These issues are covered in Michael Gordon, "Kremlin versus Its Army," *New York Times,* June 12, 1999; Talbott, *The Russia Hand,* 344–47; Michael Dobbs, "NATO Occupies Tense Kosovo Capital," *Washington Post,* June 13, 1999; Thomas Ambrosio, *Challenging America's Global Preeminence: Russia's Quest for Multipolarity* (Burlington, VT: Ashgate, 2005), 89–93; J. L. Black, *Vladimir Putin and the New World Order* (New York: Rowman & Littlefield, 2004), 303–10.

31. See Goldgeier and McFaul, *Power and Purpose,* chaps. 9–12.

32. Anthony Lake, "Confronting Backlash States," *Foreign Affairs* 73, no. 2 (March–April 1994): 45–55, 55.

33. Quoted in House Committee on International Relations, *U.S. Policy toward Iran* (Washington, DC: US Government Printing Office, 1996), 10. See also Kenneth Pollack, *The Persian Puzzle: The Conflict between Iran and America* (New York: Random House, 2004), 255–61.

34. See James Collins, "Striking Back," *Time,* July 5, 1993, 20–21; Kenneth Pollack, *The Threatening Storm: The Case for Invading Iraq* (New York: Random House, 2002), 68–85.

35. US Department of State, *Dispatch,* March–April 1997, 5–8.

36. Quoted in Tim Weiner, "U.S. Long View on Iraq," *New York Times,* January 3, 1999. See also Walter Slocombe's testimony in Senate Armed Services Committee, *U.S. Policy on Iraq* (Washington, DC: US Government Printing Office, 1999), esp. 5.

37. See Jim Hoagland, "How CIA's Secret War on Saddam Hussein Collapsed," *Washington Post,* June 26, 1997.

38. Quoted in Senate Foreign Relations Committee, *Iraq: Can Saddam Be Overthrown?* (Washington, DC: US Government Printing Office, 1998), 8, 25.

39. Quoted in Edward Walsh, "Clinton Indicts Bush's World Leadership," *Washington Post,* October 2, 1992; US Department of State, *Dispatch,* April 5, 1993, 218.

40. *A National Security Strategy of Engagement and Enlargement,* ii.

41. The quotes in this paragraph are from *Congressional Record,* 104th Cong., 1st sess., 141 (1995): H7277, H7289. See also Elaine Sciolino, "China Rejects Call from Christopher for Rights Gains," *New York Times,* March 13, 1994.

42. Dumbrell, *Clinton's Foreign Policy,* 48–49.

43. See US Department of State, *Dispatch,* September 30, 1996, 483, and September 1997, 5–6. See also Dumbrell, *Clinton's Foreign Policy,* 50.

44. *A National Security Strategy for a New Century* (Washington, DC: White House, 1999), 1.

45. Martin Wolf, "In Defence of Global Capitalism," *Financial Times*, December 8, 1999. Good introductions to the resistance caused by globalization include William Greider, *One World, Ready or Not: The Manic Logic of Global Capitalism* (New York: Simon & Schuster, 1997); and David Held and Anthony McGrew, eds., *The Global Transformations Reader: An Introduction to the Globalization Debate* (Oxford: Blackwell, 2000).

46. Quoted in House Committee on International Relations, *Fast Track: On Course or Derailed? Necessary or Not? Part III* (Washington, DC: US Government Printing Office, 1998), 15; Senate Finance Committee, *Managing Global and Regional Trade Policy without Fast Track Negotiating Authority* (Washington, DC: US Government Printing Office, 1999), 8.

47. Bob Deans, "With Nod to Protests, Clinton Chides WTO," *Atlanta Journal and Constitution,* December 2, 1999; Steven Greenhouse and Joseph Kahn, "U.S. Effort to Add Labor Standards to Agenda Fails," *New York Times,* December 3, 1999.

48. Lake, "From Containment to Enlargement."

49. Quoted in Barry Rubin and Judith Colp Rubin, *Anti-American Terrorism and the Middle East: A Documentary Reader* (New York: Oxford University Press, 2002), 154.

50. The quotes are from *The National Security Strategy of the United States of America* (Washington, DC: White House, 2002), 4. See also Bush, "Inaugural Address," January 20, 2005, American Presidency Project, University of California at Santa Barbara, http://www.presidency.ucsb.edu/ws/index.php?pid=58745&st=&st1=. On this aspect of Bush's foreign policy, see esp. Benjamin Miller, "Explaining Changes in U.S. Grand Strategy: 9/11, the Rise of Offensive Liberalism, and the War in Iraq," *Security Studies* 19, no. 1 (January 2010): 26–65.

14

The War on Terror and the New Periphery

Maria Ryan

In late 2001, as the world focused on the US invasion of Afghanistan, the Bush administration began to plan the next campaign in the so-called War on Terror. However, it was not just Iraq that was on the administration's radar. In November 2001, President Bush came to an agreement with the president of the Philippines, Gloria Macapagal Arroyo, to arm the Philippine military and send US Special Operations Forces (SOF) to the southern Philippines to assist in a counterinsurgency campaign against the Islamist separatist group the Abu Sayyaf. This campaign, named after its larger counterpart in Afghanistan, was known as Operation Enduring Freedom—the Philippines (OEF-P); an effort is still ongoing at the time of writing, over a decade later.

The same month that US forces were deployed to the Philippines, SOF was also sent to Georgia, where Islamist extremists with alleged links to international terrorism were rumored to be hiding—and where the Georgian government sought to exert control over the Pankisi Gorge, an area known to shelter Islamist Chechen rebels. By the end of 2002, the Bush administration had opened up a fourth front in the War on Terror: Africa. Beginning in late 2002, under the auspices of the Pan-Sahel Initiative (PSI), SOF was deployed across the continent—from the Horn in the East, across the Sahel (or Sahara region), to the Gulf of Guinea in the West—in an attempt to prevent the emergence of terrorism across Africa and confront existing terrorist groups in Somalia, Algeria, Mali, and Mauritania. This campaign was known as Operation Enduring Free-dom—Trans-Sahara (OEF-TS).[1]

These interventions were smaller in scale than their counterparts in Afghanistan and Iraq but nonetheless conceptualized as integral compo-nents of a war on terror that was potentially global in scope. The two cen-tral theaters of the War on Terror—Afghanistan and Iraq (though the latter's connection to terrorism was virtually nonexistent)—undoubtedly received the greatest political, financial, and military commitments from Washington. This focus is reflected in the emerging scholarship in this field, which focuses overwhelmingly on the wars in Iraq and Afghani-stan.[2] To these early histories of the War on Terror we can already add another dimension: its peripheral theaters in the Philippines, Africa, and the Caspian Sea region.[3] After the uncertainty over what constituted the *periphery* during the Clinton years and what US objectives there were, the War on Terror offered an attractive—though fundamentally flawed—strategic paradigm out of which there emerged a new approach to the periphery premised on a securitized narrative of global counterterrorism. This resulted in the emergence of a new strategic *core*, the principal the-aters in Afghanistan and Iraq, and a new periphery, the secondary fronts of what was ostensibly a global counterterrorist campaign, though, as we shall see, the emergence of these regions as fronts in that campaign was also influenced by evolving perceptions of material and other strategic interests in these regions. All the while, the ultimate global objective of the United States remained the maintenance of its position as the world's sole superpower—a goal that signaled continuity with both the Clinton and the George H. W. Bush administrations. This chapter will examine how and why certain countries and regions emerged as secondary fronts in the War on Terror, how the United States engaged with these regions, and what it sought to achieve in the new periphery.

A Global War

As Hal Brands demonstrates in his contribution to this collection, the American periphery was an expansive construct during the Clinton years. Depending on how it was defined, almost anywhere could be included: from the fringes of Europe to the oil-rich states of the Middle East. In the months prior to the 9/11 attacks, and indeed during the 2000 election campaign, George W. Bush and his advisers outlined the contours of an expansive global strategy designed to prevent the emergence of rival powers, but prior to 9/11 there were few hints of which regions would be at the periphery of the administration's hegemonic project and which would be at the core. The approach taken from early 2001 resonated in many respects with the infamous 1992 Defense Planning Guidance document produced by Paul Wolfowitz and Zalmay Khalilzad at the request of then secretary of defense Dick Cheney.[4] In the first seven months of its term, the policies followed by the Bush administration clearly prioritized strategic interests—both tangible and intangible—over high ideals. In this sense, it reflected a realist sensibility; however, this was not a narrow definition of the national interest based on balance-of-power calculations. For the Bush administration, *the national interest* was synonymous with *global hegemony.* Prior to 9/11, this manifested in a number of ways: withdrawal from the Anti-Ballistic Missile Treaty and the deployment of a national missile defense (NMD) system were prioritized. Though NMD was framed as a *defensive* system, it would also facilitate greater *offensive* action by immunizing the United States from retaliation in the form of ballistic missiles. In April 2001, the administration also took a hawkish stance toward China, refusing to give a full apology when a US military plane strayed into Chinese airspace and its crew was taken hostage. At the same time, the administration increased its annual arms sales to Taiwan.[5] Iraq, too, was on the administration's radar: regime change was the first item on the agenda at the first meeting of the National Security Council in February 2001. According to Rumsfeld, ousting Saddam would "change everything in the region and beyond": "It would demonstrate what U.S. policy is all about."[6] US interests were therefore global in scope, but prior to 9/11 the core regions—and, by extension, the peripheral ones—had not been clearly identified.

In the aftermath of the 9/11 attacks, the Bush administration also defined the parameters of its new War on Terror as global in scope. Though it did not explicitly define which regions of the world would be core and which peripheral in its new schema, the war was defined in expansive terms. From its inception, policymakers discussed the possibility of multiple fronts and within months were ordering actions that would see the establishment of the peripheral theaters of the War on Terror. Almost immediately after the 9/11 attacks, members of the administration began to discuss ways in which their response to the attacks could be framed in as broad a way as possible. Douglas Feith, the undersecretary of defense for policy, later described how the War on Terror was defined from the very beginning as global in scope: "Identifying the perpetrators was not the same as deciding how to define the enemy." (However, Feith also candidly acknowledged that the United States could not target every state that supported or tolerated terrorism: "It . . . complicated matters that the U.S. considered some of these states important friends.") According to Condoleezza Rice, the national security adviser, the terrorists constituted a broad network, and the response to 9/11 would be a broad war: "We're not just going to do something once," she said. Two days after the attacks, Feith noted, "the President, Rice and Rumsfeld were already discussing the war as an effort against not only al Qaida but the terrorists' network broadly conceived."[7] Rumsfeld had also mused on the importance of surprising the enemy. Surprise was "a crucial operational value," and, accordingly, striking Afghanistan first might not be the best option. Instead, it might be better "for the initial strike to be directed someplace else and preferably someplace like South America or South East Asia."[8] Ultimately, the president did not support beginning the War on Terror with strikes outside Afghanistan, but the congressional Authorization for the Use of Military Force (AUMF), passed on September 18, gave the Bush administration a mandate that was more expansive than the blank check of the 1964 Tonkin Gulf Resolution. The president was granted permission to use "all necessary and appropriate force" against unspecified "nations, organizations, or persons [the president] determines planned, authorized, committed, or aided the terrorist attacks that occurred on September 11, 2001, or harbored such organizations or persons, in order to prevent any future acts of terrorism against the United States." The resolution thus not only sanctioned the use of force against those thought responsible for 9/11 but also permitted the administration to take preventive action against individuals or entities thought to be involved in future acts of terrorism anywhere in the world.[9] In other words, it permitted action in more than one theater. Though this by no means signaled a developed conception of a counterterrorist periphery, it did provide the administration with the opportunity to broaden the scope of the War on Terror beyond just Afghanistan and, later, Iraq and open up multiple fronts under the auspices of preventing future acts of terrorism.

On September 19, 2001, the day after the passage of the congressional resolution, Rumsfeld wrote a memo of guidance to the heads of *all* the Combatant Commands (i.e., covering *every region of the world,* not just the US Central Command (CENTCOM), which presides over the Middle East) to help them draft war plans for the counterterrorist campaign to fulfill the president's directives. Rumsfeld told the commanders to plan for "targets worldwide, such as U[sama] B[in] L[aden] Al Qaida cells in regions outside Afghanistan and even outside the Middle East": "It will be important to indicate early on that our field of action is much wider than Afghanistan."[10] He went on to state: "The President has stressed that we are not defining our fight narrowly and are not focused only on those directly responsible for the September 11 attacks."[11] On September 24, Bush reported to Congress that he had already deployed US forces to "a number of foreign nations in the Central and Pacific Command areas of operations," that he might find it necessary to deploy additional forces into other areas of the world, and that he could not predict the scope and duration of these deployments.[12] While none of this suggests that the scope and rationale for the global War on Terror came fully formed, the embryonic outlines of an expansive campaign, which were consistent with the scope and duration of the operations that were soon to begin in peripheral regions, had been sketched. The congressional AUMF permitted the establishment of multiple fronts in the War on Terror, and policymakers were already discussing options beyond Afghanistan.

Nevertheless, the administration did not, at this stage, provide a formal statement of policy or doctrine that outlined in explicit terms its intention to pursue a *global* war on terror. Currently available evidence suggests that operations in the secondary fronts of the new war appeared to anticipate the formalization of strategy. Whereas operations on the periphery originated in late 2001–2002, it was not until 2003 that the phrase Global War on Terror (GWOT) came into usage, though there was still no formal public justification of a *global* war on terror.[13] It was not until 2006 that the most comprehensive public articulation of the rationale for these global operations came in the Pentagon's Quadrennial Defense Review (QDR). According to the 2006 QDR, the GWOT "extends far beyond the borders of Iraq and Afghanistan," and "actions must occur on many continents in countries with which the United States is not at war"—actions pithily described as "war in countries we are not at war with."[14]

The QDR also described the GWOT as an "irregular" war, a struggle that was not solely military in nature and "cannot be won by force alone."[15] By this stage, the Bush administration had concluded that terrorism was less likely to be state sponsored than it was to manifest in the form of transnational networks.[16] "The enemies we face are not nation states" the QDR stated, "but rather dispersed non-state networks." The unconventional nature of the terrorist threat meant that success in the GWOT would require "multiple, irregular asymmetric operations" such as counterinsurgency, psychological operations, and unconventional warfare.[17] On the grounds that irregular warfare (IW) tactics would be integral to the War on Terror, Rumsfeld had in July 2002 directed the head of Special Operations Command (SOCOM), General Charles R. Holland, to develop a plan for SOCOM to act as the lead unified military command for planning and synchronizing the GWOT. This resulted in the 2004 Unified Command Plan, which designated the head of SOCOM as "the lead combatant commander for planning, synchronizing, and as directed, executing global operations against terrorist networks in coordination with combatant commanders."[18] It was in the peripheral theaters that these IW tactics were first used in the War on Terror. This is significant. The use of counterinsurgency techniques in Iraq and Afghanistan from 2005 on and the publication in December 2006 of the US Army's first field manual on counterinsurgency since Vietnam attracted a good deal of publicity and much attention from scholars, but it was in the peripheral theaters that these techniques were first used as part of the War on Terror.[19] The use of counterinsurgency and foreign internal defense (FID)—both variants of classic IW—in the Philippines, across Africa, and in the Caspian Sea region anticipated the use of IW in the core theaters of the GWOT from 2005–2006 on and also anticipated the formalization of new military doctrine on IW—a method of warfare that had been deliberately neglected by the US military after its disastrous attempt at counterinsurgency in Vietnam.[20] Thus, the peripheral theaters of the GWOT are important, not just because of what they tell us about the geographic scope of the War on Terror and the historical evolution of the idea of the periphery, but also because of the character of the US intervention in these regions. There is much to be said about the way in which the United States conducted the War on Terror on the periphery; for now, suffice it to say that it was not Iraq—as is commonly assumed—that catalyzed the first major US IW campaign since Vietnam; rather, it was in the peripheral theaters of the War on Terror that the US military began to grapple in a meaningful way, for the first time since Vietnam, with the challenges of IR and conducting "war in countries we are not at war with."[21]

Two final caveats are necessary before we briefly examine the peripheral theaters of the War on Terror. The first concerns non-American agency. The post-9/11 periphery emerged only partly by design. US interactions were shaped considerably by the responses of local elites, some of whom invited and even welcomed the United States, while others offered only partial or minimal cooperation. Though this chapter focuses primarily on what drove the US interest in these regions, it is an analysis that is informed by an awareness that local actors were able to facilitate, block, or otherwise shape the US presence in their region in various ways. In other words, the United States was not and is not omnipotent.

The second caveat concerns preexisting or emerging US strategic interests in these peripheral regions. The reason that the potential for terrorism around the Caspian Sea, across Africa, and in the Philippines concerned US policymakers was, not just because of the possibility of further terrorist attacks inside the United States, but also because of preexisting and newly emerging US strategic interests in these regions. As a former American colony, the Philippines had been the site of key long-term US military bases until the Filipino Congress closed them in 1992. As we shall see, Manila's receptivity to the War on Terror gave Washington the opportunity to reassert its strategic presence in the Philippines. Africa and the Caspian Sea region had been identified in the early months of the Bush administration as areas with underexploited energy reserves that could lessen US dependence on the Middle East and minimize the impact of a supply disruption.[22] Terrorism in these two regions could potentially imperil vital energy reserves. Thus, the periphery of the War on Terror emerged from a confluence of counterterrorism, strategic interests, and the local response to US initiatives.

Into the Periphery

The Philippines

As Richard Swain observes, operations in the Philippines anticipated the formalization of US IW doctrine perhaps more than any other part of the War on Terror did.[23] Reportedly, they also represented a campaign that pleased Rumsfeld; when he received responses from the regional combatant commanders to his September 19 request that they draft war plans for their areas of responsibility, only that of the Pacific Command (PACOM) met with his approval, the rest being dismissed as narrow and unimaginative.[24] This may have been because of PACOM's familiarity with counterterrorist and train-and-equip operations in the Philippines, for its involvement in training Philippine security forces predated 9/11. In response to a request from Manila, the Bush administration sent an SOF unit to the Philippines from March to July 2001 to help train Philippine counterterrorist forces fighting against Muslim separatists on the southern islands of Mindanao, Jolo, and Basilan. After 9/11, this cooperation was stepped up and recast as OEF-P.[25]

The separatist conflict in the southern Philippines dates back to the fifteenth century, when Spanish invaders failed to conquer and Christianize the whole of the archipelago, resulting in the southern islands' rejection of rule from Manila, which continues to this day.[26] The fact that the southern islands are mostly Muslim has given the conflict a sectarian dimension, although the driving force is the regional nationalism of the Bangsamoro people. Of the three separatist groups—the Moro National Liberation Front (MNLF), the Moro Islamic Liberation Front (MILF) and the Abu Sayyaf Group (ASG)—the latter was, in the early twenty-first century, the only one not engaged in tentative but ongoing peace negotiations with the Manila government. The ASG, though much smaller than the MILF and the MNLF, was also an extreme Islamist group, though it had no direct links with al-Qaeda.[27] As such, it became the focus of the Philippine counterinsurgency campaign supported by the United States. The United States engaged in FID: it did not take part in combat operations, instead training and equipping the Filipino forces and conducting civil affairs and psychological warfare of its own.

Given the sectarian overlay of the conflict, it was easy for Philippine president Gloria Macapagal Arroyo to utilize the discourse of the War on Terror after 9/11 and easy for Washington to accept this, even though the contemporaneous links between ASG and al-Qaeda were very minimal, if they existed at all. Arroyo was happy to exploit and encourage the inauguration of the War on Terror in the Philippines; the Armed Forces of the Philippines (AFP) were underfunded, undertrained, and struggling to maintain the peace in the south and to cope with the ASG's kidnapping-for-ransom activities. As Arroyo commented in October 2001: "Every dark cloud has a silver lining and this (U.S. support) is the silver lining. . . . We expect to have more international co-operation in our efforts [now]."[28] US intervention in the Philippines therefore had the full cooperation and encouragement of the Philippine ruling elite, though it remained unpopular with large sections of the public and the political Left.[29]

In October 2001, PACOM deployed an SOF assessment team to the southern Philippines to conduct detailed area assessments down to the village level and collect information about ASG activities, army training requirements, local demographics, infrastructure, and socioeconomic conditions. The ultimate objective was to "build a map of the disenfranchised to ascertain where active and passive support [for the ASG] would likely blossom."[30] In November, Arroyo visited Washington and secured $100 million in US military assistance, $4.6 billion in economic aid, and an agreement that US special forces would train and equip their Filipino counterparts. In February 2002, under the guise of the annual US-AFP training exercise, "Balikatan" (the Tagalog translates as *shoulder to shoulder*), 650 US troops were deployed to the southern islands of Basilan and Mindanao: 500 support and maintenance personnel and 150 special forces for advisory and training purposes. Together, they formed Joint Task Force–510 (JTF-510). In April 2002, an additional 340 US troops were dispatched to Basilan, including 280 military engineers to engage in civil works projects. It was also announced that the US mission would continue beyond the initial six-month period.[31] In July 2002, JTF-510 was replaced by the Joint Special Operations Task Force—Philippines (JSOTF-P) based in Zamboanga City, which continues to this day.[32] Every year thereafter, the annual six-month-long Balikatan exercises, held in different locations, formed the cornerstone of the US train-and-equip effort, though there have been so many additional exercises that the training effectively continues all year round.[33]

The military component has been complemented by a vigorous civil affairs effort. As Admiral Dennis Blair, then PACOM commander in chief, said in his 2002 testimony before the Senate: "The war against the ASG will not be won by military operations alone."[34] As part of Balikatan 2002, Washington agreed to cooperate with the Filipino Department of Social Welfare and Development and help fund and repair the dilapidated infrastructure of Basilan. Special forces were involved with building roads, wells, bridges, a port, and an airstrip and the renovation of schools. These operations have continued as an integral part of the SOF campaign.[35] In an effort to enhance these activities, SOF also engaged in information operations (IO) in the Philippines, though far less is known of these at present. According to Command Sergeant Major William Eckert of the JSOTF-P, these operations were about "'influencing others' in a positive and effective manner": "Through the public-affairs efforts, the task force is constantly telling people what it is going to be doing, how it is going to do it, and how it will benefit them. The goal is to ensure that people are not surprised or caught off guard by anything the teams are accomplishing."[36]

In addition, IO specialists produced propaganda based on their analysis of the cultures and subcultures of each area of operation. One example of this was a ten-part graphic novel series containing local culture and real-world correlations. Titles, names, attire, scenery, dialect, and historical context were all designed to appeal to the targeted community.[37] In 2005, this work was expanded with the introduction of military information support teams to improve the production and printing of media products. IO personnel also began to develop combined products with the AFP Civilian Relations Group, products that were approved through both the US and the AFP chains of command.[38]

The US presence in the Philippines also led to the full reestablishment of the military ties between the two countries that had been partially severed in 1992 after the closure of the valued US bases at Clark Air Field and Subic Bay. After the pro-American Marcos regime was deposed in 1986, limits were placed on the presence of foreign military forces, and the unpopular American bases were shut down completely by the Filipino Congress in 1992. Seeking to reestablish a hegemonic presence in the country (and to hedge against emerging Chinese influence in the Philippines and the South China Sea),[39] Washington was able to negotiate the Visiting Forces Agreement (VFA) of 1999, which permitted it to station forces on the islands for forward military operations.[40] For both Manila and Washington, 9/11 and the War on Terror catalyzed a full reassertion of the US military presence in the Philippines, an objective both sides had been working toward, both for their own reasons. Arroyo was the first Asian leader to endorse the War on Terror. She quickly established an All Agency Terrorism Task Force and visited Washington within two months of the attacks. While the VFA of 1999 had provided the legal basis for US troops to operate in the Philippines, it did not provide for the transfer of materials and supplies from the United States to the Philippines. This logistic omission was addressed in the controversial 2002 Mutual Logistics and Support Agreement (MLSA). The two agreements combined effectively allowed the Philippines to become a permanent site of US military activities.[41] The MLSA generated a great deal of resentment as well as a heated debate over whether it violated the 1987 constitution—which imposed restrictions on the presence of foreign military forces—and therefore required ratification by the Philippine Senate. After several months of debate, the MLSA was eventually signed in a secretive late-night meeting on November 21, 2002, between US and Filipino military representatives after being shown to just five senior members of the Philippine Congress.[42] The net result was that the United States regained the privileges it had enjoyed in the pre-1992 period under the auspices of the War on Terror and with the consent of the Philippine elite.

Overall, however, the US presence in Southeast Asia received a mixed reception. This was demonstrated by the failure of Washington's Regional Maritime Security Initiative (RMSI), which was designed to secure the Malacca Strait, a vital choke point for global shipping and oil supplies located mainly within the territorial waters of Indonesia, Malaysia, and Singapore. In 2005, the strait carried a quarter of the world's maritime trade; it also had the highest rate of piracy in the world, and the lack of cross-border maritime patrols fed fears that terrorists could target it.[43] According to Admiral Thomas Fargo, head of PACOM from 2002 to 2005: "The ungoverned littoral regions of Southeast Asia are fertile ground for exploitation by transnational threats like proliferation, terrorism, trafficking in humans or drugs, and piracy." Established in 2004, the RMSI was designed, according to Fargo, "to assess and then provide detailed plans to build and synchronize interagency and international capacity to fight threats that use the maritime space to facilitate their illicit activity."[44]

Before long, however, the RMSI was quietly abandoned by PACOM owing to opposition from Indonesia and Malaysia. In congressional testimony in 2004, Fargo announced that PACOM was considering placing SOF on high-speed vessels used for interdiction operations. When it was reported in Indonesia that PACOM planned to station SOF in the Malacca Strait, the governments in Jakarta and Kuala Lumpur condemned the RMSI as a violation of their sovereignty and warned that the presence of US forces in the strait would only fuel Islamic radicalism. Although Rumsfeld stated that the United States did not seek to station forces in the strait permanently, the damage to the reputation of the RMSI was too great, and the initiative was dropped.[45] However, the intent of the program survived: shortly after, the Indonesian government suggested naval patrols with Singapore and Malaysia, which began in July 2004. (Thailand joined in 2008.) Since the participants were sensitive to issues of national sovereignty, each country controlled its own waters, and there were no joint naval patrols. Each country also conducted two aircraft patrols per week. These exercises formed the basis for the Malacca Strait Patrols initiative. As a result, the instances of piracy declined from thirty-eight in 2004 to eleven in 2006 and seven in 2007.[46] This was not entirely without assistance from the United States, however. Indonesia and Malaysia were opposed to nonnationals patrolling their waters, but they were prepared to accept other forms of assistance from Washington: in fiscal years 2006 and 2007, the United States gave Indonesia $47.1 million in maritime security equipment, while Malaysia received $16.3 million.[47] This was given minimal publicity owing to the RMSI controversy. As Victor Huang notes, enduring postcolonial nationalism and popular antagonism toward the United States meant that it could assist local maritime security activities only within highly circumscribed limits.[48] Ultimately, security initiatives similar to those suggested by PACOM were implemented, but the United States could not play the leading role, as PACOM had originally envisioned. In the Southeast Asian front of the War on Terror, Washington did not have everything its own way.

Africa, East to West

When Bush ran for office, there was no sign that he would substantially alter existing US strategy toward Africa by engaging with the continent through a geopolitical lens. His two keynote foreign policy speeches did not mention Africa, while the Republican platform offered only faint support for "international organizations and non-governmental organizations that can improve the daily lives of Africans."[49] The only hint toward Africa's future importance to the Bush administration came in May 2001 with the publication of the report of the National Energy Policy Development Group, led by Vice President Dick Cheney. The ultimate objective of the report's recommendations was to diversify US energy supplies so as to avoid excessive dependency on a single country or region. (Almost three decades on, US energy policy remained deeply affected by the experience of the 1973 oil embargo.) The Cheney report recommended "that the President make energy security a priority of our trade and foreign policy," with a particular focus on the Western Hemisphere, Africa, and the Caspian region. In particular, West Africa and the Caspian were areas that, if fully exploited, could lessen the impact of a supply disruption. West Africa was destined to be "one of our fastest-growing sources of oil and gas for the American market": "African oil tends to be of high quality and low in sulphur making it suitable for stringent refined product requirements, and giving it a growing market share for refining centers on the East Coast of the United States."[50]

Accordingly, the report called for the President to direct the secretaries of state, energy, and commerce to reinvigorate the US-Africa Trade and Economic Co-Operation Forum and the US-African Energy Ministerial process, to deepen bilateral and multilateral engagement to promote a more receptive environment for US oil and gas trade, investment, and operations in Africa, and to promote geographic diversification of energy supplies, addressing such issues as transparency, sanctity of contracts, and security. In addition, policymakers should revive the Joint Economic Partnership Committee with Nigeria to improve the climate for US oil and gas trade, investment, and operations and to advance shared energy interests.[51] (In July 2002, Assistant Secretary of State for Africa Walter Kansteiner visited Nigeria and Angola and stated US concerns explicitly: "African oil is a strategic interest to us and it will increase and become more important as we go forward.")[52]

This represented a significant shift in the administration's view of Africa. During the campaign, Bush had virtually renounced the continent on the grounds that it was home only to intractable humanitarian problems, but Cheney's energy report identified vital material interests there that could serve the geopolitical imperative of diversifying America's foreign energy sources. Thus, in the months prior to 9/11, the administration had signaled that, unlike during the Clinton years, Africa might now be considered in strategic rather than humanitarian terms.

The 9/11 attacks strengthened the emerging view of Africa as a location of strategic importance, not only because of its oil, but also because of its weak and failing states, which could potentially be exploited by terrorists. In the aftermath of 9/11, Bush administration officials became concerned about what General James L. Jones referred to as the "large uncontrolled, ungoverned areas" of Africa, which might offer sanctuary to terrorists.[53] In particular, the administration's initial fear was that, after being chased out of Afghanistan, terrorists would move west to East Africa. Somalia became the key country of concern on the grounds that it lacked a stable central government. (Indeed, it served as the base for the 2002 attacks on Mombasa, Kenya.)[54] Colonel Victor Nelson, who would later oversee a major counterterrorism program in Africa, commented: "We have said for a long time that if you squeeze terrorists in Afghanistan, Pakistan Iraq and other places, they will find new places to operate and one of those is the Sahel-Maghreb."[55] The prevention of terrorism thus became the rationale for a continentwide campaign of FID.

On November 19, 2001, Assistant Secretary of Defense Mike Westphal arrived in Djibouti for talks on bilateral relations with President Ismael Guelleh.[56] For Guelleh, the prospect of hosting a US military presence was an attractive one. As a former French colony, Djibouti had been supported financially by Paris since its independence in 1977 and was, in fact, the largest per capita recipient of French overseas aid. But, despite this, aid levels were still relatively low, and the country was poor. The Djiboutian government wanted to find a wealthier patron and rent its military base out for a higher premium.[57] The US defense attaché there had been withdrawn when the US military presence in the Horn of Africa declined after the deaths of the American service members in Somalia in October 1993. Between 1994 and 2000, the United States provided less than half a million dollars per year to Djibouti in aid.[58] The War on Terror not only brought Djibouti to the attention of the United States; it allowed Guelleh to bargain with Washington, which now believed that a presence in the Horn of Africa was a strategic imperative.[59]

Indeed, Djibouti was not the only country in the Horn that actively sought a US presence. By mid-2002, the Eritrean government had made it clear that it would welcome a US military base on its soil. Later in the year, it hired a Washington lobbying firm, Greenberg Traurig LLC, to make the case for a US presence in the country.[60] General Tommy Franks, then CENTCOM commander, reportedly visited both Eritrea and Djibouti four times in 2002, but it was Djibouti that would eventually host the American-led Combined Joint Task Force–Horn of Africa (CJFT-HOA), established in October 2002.[61] This regional task force encompassed seven countries in addition to the United States: Kenya, Somalia, Sudan, Eritrea, Ethiopia, Djibouti, and Yemen. Its original mandate included "detecting, disrupting and ultimately defeating transnational terrorist groups operating in the region" and training the region's security forces in counterterrorism and intelligence collection. Task force personnel would serve as advisers to peace operations, conduct activities to maintain critical maritime access to Red Sea routes, and oversee and support humanitarian assistance efforts. Civil-military operations throughout East Africa would be an integral part of the effort in an attempt to "win hearts and minds" and enhance the "long-term stability of the region."[62] The perception at CENTCOM was one of success; General John Abizaid believed: "Dollar for dollar, person for person, our return on our investment out here [in the Horn of Africa] is better than it is anywhere in the CENTCOM area of responsibility."[63] The task force is ongoing at the time of writing.

Also in late 2002, the State Department established the PSI, an interagency security program with Mali, Niger, Chad, and Mauritania. Its purpose was twofold: "waging the war on terrorism in Africa and enhancing regional peace and security." This would come in the form of training, material support, and local capacity building.[64] The military component of the PSI, overseen by the Pentagon, was OEF-TS. This was a train-and-equip program designed to boost the border capabilities of Chad, Niger, Mali, and Mauritania against arms smuggling, drug trafficking, and transnational terrorism.[65]

The PSI was a small program, however; it had a start-up budget of just $8.4 million. Notwithstanding the perception that small investments in such programs yielded disproportionate results, the PSI was expanded in 2004 into the much larger Trans-Sahara Counter-Terrorism Initiative (TSCTI), again led by the State Department. Probably referring to the kidnapping activities of the Algerian Groupe Salafiste pour la prédication et le combat (Salafist Group for Preaching and Combat [GSPC]), General Jones claimed that the need for the TSCTI "stems from concern over the expansion of operations of Islamic terrorist organizations in the Sahel region." The program would be expanded from four nations to nine (Algeria, Chad, Mali, Mauritania, Morocco, Niger, Senegal, Nigeria, and Tunisia), and it would also use "a full range of political, economic, development and security tools."[66] According to Theresa Whelan, deputy assistant secretary of defense for African affairs, the PSI was "a step in the right direction" but, given its limited funding, "just a drop in the bucket" given the needs of the region. The TSCTI was "a broader package" that went beyond a train-and-equip approach to encompass civil affairs and IO.[67] According to the State Department, the initiative was envisioned as "a five-year program based on counterterrorism, democratic governance assistance, a public diplomacy component, and military assistance."[68] With a budget of $100 million over five years, the TSCTI included the Departments of State, Defense, and Treasury and USAID. (In 2005, USAID established the Office of Military Affairs to facilitate its work with the Defense Department.)[69]

Paralleling the civil affairs operations in the Philippines, SOF teams in Africa also engaged in what the 2006 QDR called "humanitarian and early preventive measures." These included public works projects and medical assistance projects, including the construction of health clinics, water wells, and schools that were marked by so-called grand openings attended by representatives from the US embassy, local and national governments, and the local press.[70] Media projects designed to present a relatively pro-US perspective included the establishment of the Magharebia news Web site, aimed at audiences across Africa, and run by the Anteon International Corps.[71] The Pentagon's OEF-TS train-and-equip program was also expanded to include five more nations (Morocco, Algeria, Tunisia, Senegal, and Nigeria) in addition to the original four. (A tenth, Burkina Faso, joined later.)[72] The programs were an implicit testimony to the importance of bilateralism and multilateralism in the GWOT. As Theresa Whelan said at the TSCTI launch, the notion that the United States could confront global terrorism alone was "just a physical impossibility": "You have to build the capacity of like-minded states to be able to help you confront the threat. And that's what [the TSCTI] represents."[73]

This approach to Africa culminated in the establishment of Africa Command (AFRICOM), the first US military unified combatant command structure for the continent. The command was created by presidential order in February 2007, was activated on October 1, 2007, and became fully operational on October 1, 2008, when it took over all the existing programs of the US European Command (EUCOM) in Africa as well as the CJTF-HOA (which had been under CENTCOM's control, all of which continue at the time of writing). Counterterrorism was an integral part of the command's purpose, but its rationale also transcended this: "U.S. Africa Command protects and defends the national security interests of the United States by strengthening the defense capabilities of African states and regional organizations and, when directed, conducts military operations, in order to deter and defeat transnational threats and to provide a security environment conducive to good governance and development."[74]

What made AFRICOM slightly different from the other combatant commands was that its focus transcended the purely military; some Defense Department officials referred to it as a combatant command "plus" with a broader "soft power" mandate, including civil affairs activities in addition to military operations.[75] As well as taking on the civil-military activities of the CJTF-HOA, the command was mandated to "work with other elements of the US government and others to achieve a more stable environment where political and economic growth can take place." There was a major emphasis on interagency cooperation and building African capacity "through military-to-military programs, military-sponsored activities, and other military operations as directed to promote a stable and secure African environment."[76] The command was not popular with Africans, however. It had been established without consultation, and, by the end of Barack Obama's first term in office, it was still headquartered at a US base in Stuttgart, Germany, because, even five years after its founding, no African nation would agree to host it. This made it the only US geographic combatant command that was not based in its area of operations.[77]

Georgia and the Pankisi Gorge

A similar pattern of action emerged in the former Soviet republic of Georgia: the building up of pro-American forces to conduct counterterrorism operations and support broader US objectives in the region, although, relative to the size of this theater, operations there were by far the smallest in comparison to the other peripheral fronts of the War on Terror, with the main component being the train-and-equip programs, which were accompanied by a small public diplomacy element.

US fears that terrorism could thrive in the lawless regions of this area—specifically in Georgia's Pankisi Gorge—were bolstered by Tbilisi's own acknowledgment that Islamist Chechen separatists were using the gorge as a base. In 1999, thousands of Chechen refugees fled to the Pankisi region and were followed there by armed fighters. Moscow accused the Georgians of harboring terrorists and longed to attack the Chechens on the Georgian side of the border.[78] The Tbilisi government struggled to assert control over the gorge, and, after 9/11, President Eduard Shevardnadze was quick to condemn the attacks, pledge allegiance to the United States, and frame Georgia's problems in the gorge as part of the global struggle against terrorism. This narrative resonated with the Bush administration; in October 2001, when Shevardnadze visited Washington, Bush responded affirmatively to his request for assistance to enhance Georgia's counterterrorism capabilities.[79]

The Georgia Train and Equip Program (GTEP) was announced in February 2002. Though it was presented as part of a global war on terror, US officials provided scant evidence that international terrorists were present in the Pankisi Gorge.[80] Torie Clarke, the assistant secretary of defense for public affairs, and General Peter Pace, vice chair of the Joint Chiefs of Staff, spoke only of vague "linkages" with international terrorism and of "indications of connections . . . of Al Qaeda in that country." Further detail was deemed inappropriate. Still they noted: "We have said repeatedly, it is important to go after the terrorists wherever they are."[81] Strengthening Georgia's counterterrorism capabilities and its control over its own territory would, in theory, prevent terrorists from harboring in the Pankisi. According to Lieutenant Colonel Robert Waltemeyer, commander of the GTEP, the purpose of the mission was to help the Georgians "maintain sovereignty in this region, which would obviously deny safe haven to any of those type of terrorist organizations that would seek to transit through this region."[82] In a broader sense, the train-and-equip program would promote stability in an important location. In his meeting with the acting Georgian president, Nino Burjanadze, in December 2003, Rumsfeld stressed his commitment to a stable Georgia, which was strategically important, not just in the War on Terror, but also for overflight permissions and in terms of energy pipelines from the Caspian Sea.[83] This corresponded with Cheney's National Energy Task Force report, which had recommended that the new administration continue its predecessor's policy by "work[ing] closely with private companies and countries in the region to develop commercially viable export routes such as the Baku-Tbilisi-Ceyhan and Caspian Pipeline Consortium oil pipelines."[84]

The GTEP was modest in size and inexpensive in comparison to conventional operations; its initial two-year budget was $64 million, and there would never be more than 150 US trainers in Georgia at any one time. However, the program would train approximately two thousand Georgians out of an army of just twenty thousand.[85] According to Waltemeyer, his team was training the Georgians to conduct "light infantry operations as they would in a counterinsurgency environment—specifically Pankisi." US forces would not set foot in the Pankisi, but they would train the Georgians in infantry techniques under "Pankisi-like conditions."[86] Subsequent Georgian raids into the Pankisi were based on training undertaken with US troops.[87]

The GTEP also had a small IO component. All its activities were favorably reported by the GTEP Public Affairs Office as well as by the American Forces Press Service (owned by the Pentagon and staffed by the military).[88] The perceived success of the eighteen-month GTEP led to the inauguration of a follow-on program: the Georgia Sustainment and Stability Operations Program (GSSOP), which ran from April 2005 to March 2006. This program, which would train and equip a further twelve hundred Georgians, had a dual purpose: the training would boost internal security and also facilitate the deployment of two Georgian battalions to Iraq to assist with stability operations there. Lieutenant Colonel Chuck Hensley, chief of EUCOM Operations Division's international cell, explained the program as follows: "In the short term, Georgia provides two battalions to Iraq that the U.S. doesn't have to provide. . . . In the long term, Georgia gets a better trained total force." According to Major Doug Peterson, the Georgia desk officer for EUCOM policy and assessments: "A strong Georgian military lends itself to stability in the region. Where you have stability in a country . . . that's one less place that the U.S. has to concern itself."[89]

The GSSOP also had its own Public Affairs Office, which provided positive news stories about the personal bonds between American and Georgian soldiers and the good relations between the marines and the Georgian people, including a marriage between an American trainer and a Georgian woman working at the GSSOP base. Also publicized was the Americans' whistle-stop tour of famous Georgian tourist sites and their admiration for all the "remarkable things they saw during their trip." The GSSOP Medical Detachment conducted a half-day outreach program for the minority Gachiani community and arranged for follow-up care to be provided by the American nongovernment organization A Call to Serve. Members of the US team also volunteered to help renovate the grounds of the Waldorf Free School in Tbilisi.[90]

Conclusions (and More Questions)

The origins of the War on Terror on the periphery lie in the Bush administration's belief that US interests were truly global in scope and that Islamist terrorism, wherever it existed, might pose a threat to long-standing or newly emerging strategic or material interests. In addition to the two principle theaters of the War on Terror, we can now identify a further three: the Philippines, Africa, and Georgia. What remains unknown, however, is just how much farther the periphery of the GWOT and its successor operations might have extended. In a testimony to the Senate, Admiral Eric Olson of SOCOM, stated that, as of 2008, SOF was active in "about sixty" countries.[91] The gradual move toward drone warfare—which began in the Bush administration but was dramatically stepped up during Obama's first term—may account for US intervention in Pakistan, Yemen, and other parts of East Africa but not for the presence of SOF forces.[92] Given the difficulty of complete secrecy in the age of the Internet, and given the breakdown of the Pentagon's budget requests, it seems unlikely that there are or have been additional operations of a scope and a size similar to the ones outlined above. Nevertheless, in 2007, Assistant Secretary of

Defense for Special Operations Michael Vickers told the *Washington Post* that SOCOM's global counterterrorism plan focused on a list of twenty "high-priority" countries, a further twenty-nine "priority" countries, as well as "other countries" that were not named. "It's not just the Middle East. It's not just the developing world. It's not just non-democratic countries— it's a global problem," Vickers said. "Threats can emanate from Denmark, the United Kingdom, you name it."[93] There is, then, a covert side to the GWOT that is not visible and not currently knowable in the absence of whistle-blowers, leaks, or things going wrong.[94] For now, these are what Rumsfeld might call *the unknown unknowns* of the War on Terror that will occupy historians of the future.

Notes

1. The most well-known strand of Operation Enduring Freedom was, of course, in Iraq.

2. Some of the best examples of this scholarship include Nick Ritchie and Paul Rogers, *The Political Road to the War with Iraq: Bush, 9/11 and the Drive to Overthrow Saddam* (London: Routledge, 2007); Tony Smith, *A Pact with the Devil: Washington's Bid for World Supremacy and the Betrayal of the American Promise* (New York: Routledge, 2007); Michael Gordon and Bernard Trainor, *Cobra II: The Inside Story of the Invasion and Occupations of Iraq* (London: Atlantic, 2007); Peter W. Galbraith, *The End of Iraq: How American Incompetence Created a War without End* (New York: Pocket, 2007); Andrew Bacevich, *American Empire: The Realities and Consequences of U.S. Diplomacy* (Cambridge, MA: Harvard University Press, 2002); David Ryan and Patrick Kiely, eds., *America and Iraq: Policy-Making, Intervention and Regional Politics since 1958* (London: Routledge, 2008); and David Ryan, *Frustrated Empire: U.S. Foreign Policy, 9/11 to Iraq* (London: Pluto, 2007).

3. There is no single monograph or collection that focuses on the *global* War on Terror with all its different fronts rather than just on Iraq and/or Afghanistan. There are a small number of books that focus on single regions of the War on Terror, but these are presented in isolation rather than as part of a broader campaign with multiple fronts. These include Jeremy Keenan, *The Dark Sahara: America's War on Terror in Africa* (London: Pluto, 2009); Robert I. Rotberg, ed., *Battling Terrorism in the Horn of Africa* (New York: Brookings Institution, 2005); John David, ed., *Africa and the War on Terrorism* (Aldershot: Ashgate, 2007); Patricio N. Abinales and Nathan Gilbert Quimpo, eds., *The U.S. and the War on Terror in the Philippines* (Manila: Anvil, 2008); Zachary Abuza, *Militant Islam in Southeast Asia* (Boulder: Lynne Rienner, 2003); Rommel C. Banlaoi, *Philippine Security in the Age of Terror: National, Regional, and Global Challenges in the Post-9/11 World* (Boca Raton, FL: CRC, 2010); George Baylon Radics, "Terrorism in Southeast Asia: Balikatan Exer-

cises in the Philippines and the U.S. 'War against Terrorism,'" *Stanford Journal of East Asia Affairs* 4, no. 2 (Summer 2004): 115–27; and Minton F. Goldman, *Rivalry in Eurasia: Russia, the United States, and the War on Terror* (Santa Barbara, CA: Praeger Security International, 2009).

4. Condoleezza Rice, "Promoting the National Interest," *Foreign Affairs* 79, no. 1 (January/February 2000): 45–62. See also Bush's main campaign speeches on foreign affairs: "A Period of Consequences," September 23, 1999, http://www3.citadel.edu/pao/addresses/pres_bush.html; and "A Distinctly American Internationalism," November 19, 1999, https://www.mtholyoke.edu/acad/intrel/bush/wspeech.htm. See as well the 2000 Republican Party platform at http://www.presidency.ucsb.edu/ws/index.php?pid=25849. On the Defense Planning Guidance, see "Excerpts from the Pentagon's Plan: 'Prevent the Re-Emergence of a New Rival,'" *New York Times,* March 8, 1992.

5. President Bush Speech on National Missile Defense, May 1, 2001, http://www.fas.org//nuke/control/abmt/news/010501bush.html. On the pre-9/11 period in office, see Scott Lucas and Maria Ryan, "Against Everyone and No-One: The Failure of the 'Unipolar' in Iraq and Beyond," in Ryan and Kiely, eds., *America and Iraq,* 154–80.

6. Cited in Ron Suskind, *The Price of Loyalty: George W. Bush, the White House and the Education of Paul O'Neill* (London: Free Press, 2004), 85.

7. Douglas J. Feith, *War and Decision: Inside the Pentagon at the Dawn of the War on Terrorism* (New York: HarperCollins, 2006), 6, 8, 13, 17. See also Tim Weiner, "A Nation Challenged: Global Links; Other Fronts Seen," *New York Times,* October 10, 2001.

8. Feith, *War and Decision,* 66. For the Pentagon's preference for targeting "the entire network of states, non-state entities, and organizations that engage in or support terrorism," see ibid., 50.

9. Authorization for Use of Military Force, September 18, 2001, Public Law 107-40, https://www.congress.gov/107/plaws/publ40/PLAW-107publ40.pdf.

10. Rumsfeld Memo to General Hugh Shelton (Chair, Joint Chiefs of Staff), "Some Thoughts for CINC's as They Prepare Plans," September 19, 2001, cited in Feith, *War and Decision,* 55.

11. Feith, *War and Decision,* 66.

12. Lauren Ploch, "Africa Command: U.S. Strategic Interests and the Role of the U.S. Military in Africa," Congressional Research Service Report for Congress, July 22, 2011, 36, http://www.fas.org/sgp/crs/natsec/RL34003.pdf.

13. One of the earliest references came in Donald Rumsfeld's speech of May 27, 2003, in New York. See http://www.guardian.co.uk/world/2003/may/28/iraq.iran. For full details of the evolution in strategy, see Maria Ryan, "'Full Spectrum Dominance': Donald Rumsfeld, the Department of Defense, and U.S. Irregular Warfare Strategy, 2001–2008," *Small Wars and Insurgencies* 25, no. 1 (February 2014): 41–68.

14. QDR 06, US Quadrennial Defense Review Report, February 6, 2006 (here-

after QDR 06), 9, 11, vi, http://www.defense.gov/Portals/1/features/defenseRe-
views/QDR/QDR_as_of_29JAN10_1600.pdf.

15. Ibid., i, vi, 9.

16. See "National Strategy for Combating Terrorism," February 2003, https://
www.cia.gov/news-information/cia-the-war-on-terrorism/Counter_Terrorism_
Strategy.pdf. In this strategy, terrorism is described as *both* state sponsored and
transnational. In the updated 2006 version of this strategy, transnational networks
were the clear focus. See "National Strategy for Combating Terrorism," September
2006, http://georgewbush-whitehouse.archives.gov/nsc/nsct/2006.

17. QDR 06, 9 (quote), vii. For more on these themes, see Capstone Concept for
Special Operations, US Special Operations Command, 2006, http://www.dtic.mil/
cgi-bin/GetTRDoc?AD=ADA458268&Location=U2&doc=GetTRDoc.pdf; and
USSOCOM Posture Statement 2007 (hereafter SOCOM 2007), http://www.fas
.org/irp/agency/dod/socom/posture2007.pdf.

18. US Special Operations Command, *History: 1987–2007* (hereafter SOCOM
History), 14–16 (quote 16), http://www.fas.org/irp/agency/dod/socom/2007history
.pdf.

19. *The U.S. Army/Marine Corps Counterinsurgency Manual* (Chicago: University
of Chicago Press, 2007), 3–24.

20. On the post-Vietnam neglect of IW, see David Fitzgerald, "Vietnam, Iraq
and the Rebirth of Counter-Insurgency," *Irish Studies in International Affairs* 21
(2010): 149–59; Robert M. Cassidy, *Counterinsurgency and the Global War on Terror: Military Culture and Irregular Warfare* (Stanford, CA: Stanford University
Press, 2008), 99–126; and Richard Lock-Pullan, *U.S. Intervention Policy and Army
Innovation: From Vietnam to Iraq* (London: Routledge, 2005).

21. On Iraq and the rebirth of counterinsurgency, see Steven Metz, *Iraq and
the Evolution of American Strategy* (Washington, DC: Potomac, 2008); Thomas
R. Mockaitis, *Iraq and the Challenge of Counterinsurgency* (Westport, CT: Praeger Security International, 2008); Carter Malkasian, "Counterinsurgency in Iraq,
May 2003–January 2007," in *Counterinsurgency in Modern Warfare,* ed. Daniel
Marston and Carter Malkasian (Oxford: Osprey, 2008), 241–59; and Brian Burton and John Nagl, "Learning as We Go: The U.S. Army Adapts to Counterinsurgency in Iraq, July 2004–December 2006," *Small Wars and Insurgencies* 19, no. 3
(2008): 303–27.

22. *National Energy Policy,* Report of the National Energy Policy Development
Group (hereafter NEP Report), May 2001, esp. chap. 8, http://www.wtrg.com/
EnergyReport/National-Energy-Policy.pdf.

23. "Case Study: Operation Enduring Freedom Philippines," by Richard Swain,
Ph.D., Booz Allen Hamilton, under Contract to US Army Counterinsurgency Center, October 2010, 1, http://www.dtic.mil/dtic/tr/fulltext/u2/a532988.pdf.

24. "Pacific Plan Seeks Clues to Al Qaeda Contacts," *Washington Post,* November 4, 2001; "Somalia Draws Anti-Terrorist Focus," *Washington Post,* November 4,
2001.

25. SOCOM History, 129–30. See also "ARSOF in the Philippines," special issue, *Special Warfare: The Professional Bulletin of the John F. Kennedy Special Warfare Center and School,* vol. 17, no. 1 (September 2004), http://www.dvidshub.net/publication/issues/8225.

26. For background on the Philippines, see Steven Rogers, "Beyond the Abu Sayyaf," *Foreign Affairs* 83, no. 1 (January/February 2004): 15–20.

27. Jason Burke, *Al Qaeda: The True Story of Radical Islam* (London: Penguin, 2004), 107, 110–11.

28. "U.S. Advisors May Aid Philippine Antiterror Effort," *New York Times,* October 11, 2001.

29. See Ben Reid, "Bush and the Philippines after September 11: Hegemony, Mutual Opportunism and Democratic Retreat," in *Bush and Asia: America's Evolving Relations with East Asia,* ed. Mark Beeson (New York: Routledge, 2006), 145–61; and Renato Cruz De Castro, "The U.S.-Philippine Alliance: An Evolving Hedge against an Emerging China Challenge," *Contemporary Southeast Asia* 31, no. 3 (2009): 399–423.

30. Gregory Wilson, "Anatomy of a Successful COIN Operation: OEF-Philippines and the Indirect Approach," *Military Review,* November–December 2006, http://cgsc.contentdm.oclc.org/cdm/ref/collection/p124201coll1/id/415. Wilson was a participant in the operations he describes. For further detail, see Christopher A. Parrinello, "Enduring Freedom, Phase II: The Philippines, Islamic Insurgency, and Abu Sayyaf," *Military Intelligence,* April–June 2002, 39–44. See also Swain, "Case Study: Operation Enduring Freedom Philippines," 18.

31. Abuza, *Militant Islam in South East Asia,* 204

32. The Public Affairs component of this task force keeps a blog of its activities at http://jsotf-p.blogspot.co.uk.

33. There were also many additional exercises: two more in 2002, two in 2003, four in 2004, nine in 2005, and seven in 2006. For a full list, see "Joint Exercises between U.S. and Filipino Troops, 1992–2006," in Abinales and Quimpo, eds., *U.S. and the War on Terror in the Philippines,* 77–80.

34. "Statement of Admiral Dennis C. Blair, U.S. Navy, Commander in Chief, U.S. Pacific Command, Before the Senate Armed Services Committee on U.S. Pacific Command Posture," March 5, 2002, 19, http://www.globalsecurity.org/military/library/congress/2002_hr/blair0305.pdf.

35. Radics, "Terrorism in Southeast Asia," 124–25; William Eckert, "Defeating the Idea: Unconventional Warfare in the Southern Philippines," *Special Warfare* 19, no. 6 (November/December 2006): 16–22; Brian Petit, "OEF-Philippines: Thinking COIN, Practicing FID," *Special Warfare* 23, no. 1 (January/February 2010): 10–15; Wilson, "Anatomy of a Successful COIN Operation"; Swain, "Case Study: Operation Enduring Freedom—Philippines," 19–21; Larry Niksch, "Abu Sayyaf: Target of Philippine-U.S. Anti-Terrorism Cooperation," Congressional Research Service Report for Congress, January 24, 2007, 14, http://www.fas.org/sgp/crs/terror/RL31265.pdf.

36. Eckert, "Defeating the Idea," 21.

37. Ibid., 22.

38. Wilson, "Anatomy of a Successful COIN Operation."

39. On China's attempt to influence Philippine foreign policy and diminish US influence, see Cruz De Castro, "The U.S.-Philippine Alliance."

40. Radics, "Terrorism in South East Asia," 117–19; Reid, "Bush and the Philippines after September 11," 154.

41. Radics, "Terrorism in South East Asia," 121.

42. Ibid., 119–21; Reid, "Bush and the Philippines after September 11," 156.

43. Tammy M. Sittnick, "State Responsibility and Maritime Terrorism in the Strait of Malacca: Persuading Indonesia and Malaysia to Take Additional Steps to Secure the Strait," *Pacific Rim Law and Policy Journal* 14, no. 3 (June 2005): 743–69, 744–45; Rommel C. Banlaoi, "Maritime Terrorism in Southeast Asia: The Abu Sayyaf Threat," *Naval War College Review* 58, no. 4 (Autumn 2005): 63–80, 63–64.

44. "Testimony of Admiral Thomas B. Fargo, United States Navy Commander, U.S. Pacific Command, before the House Armed Services Committee, United States House of Representatives, Regarding U.S. Pacific Command Posture," March 31, 2004, http://www.globalsecurity.org/military/library/congress/2004_hr/040331housearmedsvcscomm.htm.

45. All from Ian Storey, "Maritime Security in Southeast Asia: Two Cheers for Regional Cooperation," *Southeast Asian Affairs,* January 2009, 36–58, 40.

46. "Factsheet: Milestones of Malacca Strait Patrols," Ministry of Defense, Singapore, March 28, 2008, http://www.mindef.gov.sg/imindef/news_and_events/nr/2008/mar/28mar08_nr/28mar08_fs.html (link inactive; copy in author's possession).

47. Storey, "Maritime Security in Southeast Asia," 44.

48. Victor Huang, "Building Maritime Security in Southeast Asia: Outsiders Not Welcome?" *Naval War College Review* 61, no. 1 (Winter 2008): 87–105, 96, 99.

49. 2000 Republican Party platform (n. 4 above).

50. NEP Report, 8-3–8-4, 8-7, 8-11 (quote).

51. Ibid., 8-11.

52. See Daniel Volman, "The Bush Administration and African Oil: The Security Implications of US Energy Policy," *Review of African Political Economy* 30, no. 98 (December 2003): 573–84, 573, 578.

53. Jones cited in Eric Schmitt, "Pentagon Seeking New Access Pacts for Africa Bases," *New York Times,* July 5, 2003. See also "Statement of General James L. Jones, U.S.M.C., Commander, United States European Command, before the Senate Foreign Relations Committee," September 28, 2005, 9, http://web.archive.org/web/20070110031318/http://www.senate.gov/~foreign/testimony/2005/JonesTestimony050928.pdf.

54. Princeton N. Lyman and J. Stephen Morrison, "The Terrorist Threat in Africa," *Foreign Affairs* 83, no. 1 (January/February 2004): 75–86, 76–77.

55. Nelson cited in Pierre Abramovici, "The United States: The New Scram-

ble for Africa," *Le monde diplomatique,* July 7, 2004, http://mondediplo.com/2004/07/07usinafrica.

56. "President in Talks with Visiting US Official," November 20, 2001, IRIN, a service of the UN Office for the Co-Ordination of Humanitarian Affairs, http://www.irinnews.org/Report/28405/DJIBOUTI-President-in-talks-with-visiting-U.S.-official.

57. See Amedee Bollee, "Djibouti: From French Outpost to US Base," *Review of African Political Economy* 30, no. 97 (September 2003): 481–84.

58. See *Terrorism in the Horn of Africa,* Special Report 113 (Washington, DC: US Institute of Peace, January 2004), 9.

59. See, e.g., Cable, US Embassy Djibouti, "President Guelleh and U.S-Djibouti Bilateral Relations," December 3, 2004, http://www.cablegatesearch.net/cable.php?id=04DJIBOUTI1541.

60. "Eritrea Eager for U.S. Military Partnership," *Daily Yomiuri* (Tokyo), July 5, 2002; "Tiny Desert Nation Bids to Host Troops; Hires D.C. PR Firm to Press Its Case," *Washington Times,* December 12, 2002.

61. Bollee, "Djibouti," 483; *Economist Intelligence Unit,* Country Report, Eritrea, March 2003, 21, cited in Adekeye Adebajo, "Africa and America in an Age of Terror," *Journal of Asian and African Studies* 38, nos. 2–3 (June 2002): 175–91, 181.

62. Quotations and summary taken from the original CJTF-HOA Web site cited in Ploch, "Africa Command," 18. For the updated (though similar) mission, see http://www.africom.mil/about-the-command/our-team/combined-joint-task-force-horn-of-africa. For an overview of the program, see John Davis, "The Bush Model—U.S. Special Forces, Africa and the War on Terror," in David, ed., *Africa and the War on Terrorism,* 143–62, 144–50.

63. Quoted in Hans Sholley, "U.S. African Command: Shaping Africa for the Future," October 23, 2006, 11, http://www.dtic.mil/cgi-bin/GetTRDoc?AD=ADA463683.

64. The original PSI Web site is cited in Davis, "The Bush Model," 151.

65. "The Trans-Sahara Counterterrorism Partnership: Program Overview," http://www.africom.mil/tsctp.asp (no longer active; copy in author's possession); Jim Fisher-Thompson, "U.S.-African Partnership Helps Counter Terrorists in Sahel Region," March 23, 2004, America.gov, http://iipdigital.usembassy.gov/st/english/article/2004/03/20040323170343r1ejrehsif0.1366693.html#axzz4EsxDqb2e; Robert G. Berschinski, *Africom's Dilemma: The "Global War on Terrorism," "Capacity Building," Humanitarianism, and the Future of U.S. Security Policy in Africa* (Carlisle, PA: Strategic Studies Institute, US Army War College, November 2007), 9.

66. James M. Jones, "A Commander's Perspective on Building the Capacity of Foreign Countries['] Military Forces," Testimony before the House Armed Services Committee, April 7, 2006, 5–6, http://www.dod.mil/dodgc/olc/docs/Test-Jones060407.pdf. On the GSPC's hostage taking (and the allegation of assistance from Algerian intelligence meant to draw the United States into the region), see Keenan, *The Dark Sahara.*

67. Donna Miles, "New Counterterrorism Initiative to Focus on Saharan Africa," American Press Forces Service, May 17, 2005, http://iipdigital.usembassy.gov/st/english/article/2005/05/20050517161156dmslahrellek0.6709864.html#axzz4EsxDqb2e.

68. US Department of State, *Country Reports on Terrorism 2005,* chap. 5, "Africa Overview," http://www.state.gov/documents/organization/65462.pdf.

69. Letitia Lawson, "U.S. Africa Policy since the Cold War," *Strategic Insights* 6, no. 1 (January 2007), http://calhoun.nps.edu/bitstream/handle/10945/11266/lawsonJan07.pdf?sequence=1; *Civilian-Military Operations Guide,* USAID Office of Military Affairs, Version 1.0, April 27, 2010, 15, http://star-tides.net/sites/default/files/documents/files/Civilian-Military%20Operations%20Guide.pdf; Miles, "New Counterterrorism Initiative to Focus on Saharan Africa."

70. QDR 06, 12. These activities are also referred to as "stabilization and reconstruction operations." See ibid., 36; SOCOM 2007, 10.

71. See "Pentagon Funds Diplomacy Effort," *Washington Post,* June 11, 2005.

72. Operation Enduring Freedom—Trans-Sahara, http://www.africom.mil/oef-ts.asp (no longer active; copy in author's possession).

73. Miles, "New Counterterrorism Initiative to Focus on Saharan Africa."

74. "About the Command," US Africa Command, http://www.africom.mil/about-the-command.

75. Ploch, "African Command," 4.

76. Transcript: "Mission, Not Location, Is AFRICOM's Goal, Deputy Tells Reporters in New York," press briefing with Ambassador Mary Carlin Yates Deputy to the commander for civil-military activities, 5 December 2007, http://www.africom.mil/NewsByCategory/transcript/6083/mission-not-location-is-africoms-goal-deputy-tells (22.08.16). Details of civil affairs activities undertaken by AFRICOM can be found at http://www.africom.mil/tags/civil-affairs-team, which provides a list of "Vignettes."

77. For the location of AFRICOM personnel, see "About the Command." For criticism of AFRICOM's establishment, see Stephen F. Burgess, "In the National Interest? Authoritarian Decision-Making and the Problematic Creation of U.S. Africa Command," *Contemporary Security Policy* 30, no. 1 (April 2009): 79–99.

78. Lutz Kleveman, *The New Great Game: Blood and Oil in Central Asia* (London: Atlantic, 2003), 34.

79. Department of Defense News Release, "Georgia 'Train and Equip' Program Begins," April 29, 2002, http://www.bits.de/NRANEU/Russia-Caucasus/georgia%20train%20and%20equip%20program.htm; "Republic of Georgia: Global Partner in Anti-Terror War," American Forces Press Services, May 15, 2002, reproduced at http://www.european-security.com/n_index.php?id=3148; Jaba Devdariani, "Georgian Officials Prepare to Tackle Pankisi Gorge Problem," Eurasianet.org, January 15, 2002, http://www.eurasianet.org/departments/insight/articles/eav011502.shtml; Ariel Cohen, "Moscow, Washington and Tbilisi Wrestle

with Instability in the Pankisi," Eurasianet.org, February 19, 2002, http://www.eurasianet.org/departments/insight/articles/eav021902.shtml; Paul Quinn-Judge, "Jihad Comes to Georgia," *Time,* February 15, 2002, http://www.time.com/time/printout/0,8816,203349,00.html; Irakly G. Areshidze, "Helping Georgia?" *Perspective* 12, no. 4 (March–April 2002), http://www.bu.edu/iscip/vol12/areshidze.html; Thomas Brady, "Georgia Invites United States to Chart Its Own Policy," Eurasianet.org, July 29, 2002, http://www.eurasianet.org/departments/insight/articles/eav072902a_pr.shtml.

80. Though it did not bear the formal "Operation Enduring Freedom" title, the program was described by EUCOM as "the Operation Enduring Freedom mission in the former Soviet Republic of Georgia" and "the OEF mission known as the Georgia Train and Equip Program," while, during his visit there, President Bush praised Georgia for the example it was setting in the War on Terror. See "Georgia Train and Equip Program Transitions to U.S. Marines," November 22, 2002, http://www.eucom.mil/media-library/article/21881/Georgia-Train-Equip-Program-Transitions-US-Marines; "Marines Assume Mission to Train Georgian Military," December 15, 2002, http://www.eucom.mil/media-library/article/21873/Marines-Assume-Mission-Train-Georgian-Military; and "Bush Praises Georgia for Setting Example, Supporting War on Terror," May 10, 2005, http://www.eucom.mil/media-library/article/21651/Bush-praises-Georgia-setting-example-supporting.

81. Department of Defense News Transcript, Assistant Secretary of Defense Clarke and General Peter Pace, February 27, 2002, http://fas.org/terrorism/at/docs/2002/Pace_Clarke02_27_02.htm.

82. Department of Defense News Transcript, Phone Interview with the Commander of the Georgia Train and Equip Program, May 30, 2002, http://fas.org/terrorism/at/docs/2002/Georgia_Waltemeyer.htm.

83. Department of Defense News Transcript, Secretary Rumsfeld Press Conference with Acting Georgian President Burdzhanadze, December 5, 2003, http://iipdigital.usembassy.gov/st/english/texttrans/2003/12/20031206134201attocnich0.2866632.html#axzz4EsxDqb2e; Department of Defense News Transcript, Background Briefing En Route to Georgia, December 5, 2003, http://archive.defense.gov/Transcripts/Transcript.aspx?TranscriptID=2773.

84. NEP Report, 8-12; Jerome Chen, "The List: The World's Largest Untapped Oil Fields," *Foreign Policy,* December 1, 2008, http://foreignpolicy.com/2008/12/01/the-list-the-worlds-largest-untapped-oil-fields; "Oil Fuels U.S. Army Role in Georgia," *Observer,* May 12, 2002.

85. "Roughly 2,000" is the number cited in Department of Defense News Transcript, Phone Interview with Commander of Georgia Train and Equip Program. Twenty thousand was the official total of the Georgian army in 2002. However, the lieutenant colonel responsible for coordinating the training with the US military, Nika Djandjgava, claimed that Georgia only had five thousand soldiers who were reliable. With barracks in a state of disrepair and salaries unpaid for months, deser-

tion was common, Djandjgava claimed. He described the GTEP as "a dream come true." See "U.S. Mans Outpost of Chaos in Georgia," *Economist Intelligence Unit,* Country Briefing, September 9, 2002, http://www.eiu.com.

86. Department of Defense News Transcript, Phone Interview with the Commander of the Georgia Train and Equip Program.

87. For example, the operation launched on August 25, 2002. See "Georgia Politics: Trying to Tame the Wild Pankisi Gorge," *Economist Intelligence Unit,* Country Briefing, August 26, 2002, http://www.eiu.com.

88. Examples include Teresa Ovalle, "Georgian Soldiers Take Care of Their Own," GTEP Public Affairs Office, August 22, 2003, http://www.eucom.mil/ media-library/article/21722/Georgian-Soldiers-Take-Care-Their-Own; Russ Harper, "Special Forces Soldiers Arrive in Georgia for Train and Equip Program," May 19, 2002, http://www.eucom.mil/media-library/article/21910/Special-Forces-soldiers-arrive-Georgia-Train-Equip; and Kathleen T. Rhem, "American Troops Training, Equipping Georgian Military," May 30, 2002, http://archive.defense.gov/ news/newsarticle.aspx?id=43997.

89. "Training for Iraq Boosts Security in Caucasus," American Forces Press Service, June 28, 2005, http://www.eucom.mil/media-library/article/21577/Training-Iraq-Boosts-Security-Caucasus. See also "U.S. Marines Train Georgian Military for Operations in Iraq," April 11, 2005, http://www.eucom.mil/media-library /article/21638/US-Marines-train-Georgian-military-operations-Iraq;and"EUCOM Issues Military Gear to Georgian Soldiers," May 23, 2005, http://www.eucom.mil/ media-library/article/21633/EUCOM-issues-military-gear-Georgian-soldiers.

90. "Georgian-American Ties Change Lives Forever," August 2, 2005, http:// www.eucom.mil/media-library/article/21522/Georgian-American-ties-change-lives; "Navy Doctors Reach Out to Georgian Community," September 13, 2005, http://www.eucom.mil/media-library/article/21473/Navy-doctors-reach-Georgian-community; "Task Force Explore Host Country," April 30, 2005, http://www.eucom .mil/media-library/article/21636/Task-force-explore-host-country; "U.S. Task Force Gives to Republic of Georgia School," November 17, 2005, http://www.eucom.mil/ media-library/article/21407/US-task-force-gives-Republic-Georgia-school.

91. Statement of Admiral Eric T. Olsen, US Special Operations Command, Before the Senate Armed Services Committee on the Posture of Special Operations Forces, March 4, 2008, 2, https://fas.org/irp/agency/dod/socom/posture2008.pdf.

92. "CIA to Expand Use of Drones in Pakistan," *New York Times,* December 3, 2009; "U.S. Now Trains More Drone Operators Than Pilots," *Observer,* August 23, 2009.

93. Ann Scott Tyson, "Sorry Charlie; This Is Michael Vickers's War," *Washington Post,* December 28, 2007.

94. For how things went wrong in Paraguay, see "Elite Troops Get Expanded Role on Intelligence," *New York Times,* March 8, 2006.

Acknowledgments

The idea for this collection came shortly after we hosted a conference at the University of Nottingham in September 2010, the success of which led us to believe that a selection of the papers would make for a great book on the different ways in which the United States has acted toward so-called peripheral areas in the years since 1945. It has taken far longer than originally envisaged for the collection to come together, but we think that the quality of the chapters demonstrates that this was a worthwhile wait.

Financial support for the conference came from a number of places, and we are hugely grateful to the Graduate School at the University of Nottingham, the dean of the Faculty of Arts at Nottingham, and the Paul Mellon Professorial Fund and Professor Tony Badger at Cambridge University.

At Kentucky, we have been very lucky to work with Andrew Johns, Stephen Wrinn, and Allison Webster—all of whom have been very enthusiastic about the project from the moment we contacted them and who have made the process of publication and of coordinating a wide range of academics as painless as it can possibly be. We also thank our copyeditor, Joseph Brown, for his careful work smoothing out the text and clarifying the references. The anonymous readers for the Press, meanwhile, made a series of smart suggestions that helped clarify certain themes in the book.

Beyond the people who contributed chapters to the volume, there were also a large number of people who gave papers, attended the conference, and chaired sessions over the course of the three days. Consequently, we would like to thank Campbell Craig, Pablo del Hierro, Michael Donoghue, Andrew Johnstone, Matthew Jones, Spencer Mawby, Paul McGarr, David Milne, Shannon Nix, Christopher Phelps, Tom Tunstall-Allcock, Mathilde von Bulow, and Arne Westad. Finally, it would not have been possible to put the conference on without the fantastic assistance of our three (then) doctoral students Hannah Durkin, Ben Offiler, and Sue Peng.

Contributors

Hal Brands teaches at the Sanford School of Public Policy, Duke University. He is the author of three books, most recently, *What Good Is Grand Strategy? Power and Purpose in American Statecraft from Harry S. Truman to George W. Bush* (Cornell, 2014). He has written widely on US foreign policy, grand strategy, Cold War history, and international security issues.

Simon Dalby, formerly at Carleton University, is now CIGI chair in the political economy of climate change at the Balsillie School of International Affairs and professor of geography and environmental studies at Wilfrid Laurier University, Waterloo, Ontario. He is the author of *Creating the Second Cold War* (Pinter, 1990), *Environmental Security* (University of Minnesota Press, 2002), and *Security and Environmental Change* (Polity, 2009).

Christopher R. W. Dietrich is assistant professor of history at Fordham University. He specializes in diplomatic history, intellectual history, and the history of international capitalism.

Philip Dow received his Ph.D. in 2012 from Cambridge University (Clare College) in the history of American foreign relations, under the guidance of Andrew Preston. His previous publications include "Romance in a Marriage of Convenience: The Missionary Factor in Early Cold War US-Ethiopian Relations, 1941–1960," *Diplomatic History* 35, no. 5 (November 2011): 859–95.

David Ekbladh is associate professor of history and core faculty in international relations at Tufts University. He is currently at work on a book tentatively titled "Look at the World: The Birth of an American Globalism in the 1930s." His first book, *The Great American Mission: Modernization* *and the Construction of an American World Order* (Princeton University Press, 2010), won the Stuart L. Bernath Prize of the Society of American Historians as well as the Phi Alpha Theta Best First Book Award.

Tanya Harmer is an associate professor of international history at the London School of Economics and the author of *Allende's Chile and the Inter-American Cold War* (2011), which won the Latin American Studies Association's Luciano Tomassini Prize in 2013.

Mary Ann Heiss is an associate professor of history at Kent State University. Her publications include *Empire and Nationhood: The United States, Great Britain, and Iranian Oil, 1950–1954* (Columbia University Press, 1997); coedited volumes on the recent history/future of NATO, intrabloc conflicts in NATO and the Warsaw Pact, and US relations with the Third World; and numerous essays in edited collections and professional journals, including the *International History Review* and *Diplomatic History.* Her current research explores the internationalization of decolonization against the backdrop of both Anglo-American relations and the United Nations in the period 1945–1963.

Ryan Irwin teaches US foreign relations history at the State University of New York, Albany. He is the author of *Gordian Knot: Apartheid and the Unmaking of the Liberal World Order* (Oxford, 2012) and is currently writing a book about liberal internationalism in the twentieth century. His writing explores the intersection of strategy and legitimacy, and his essays have been published in a variety of journals and periodicals, including *Diplomatic History,* the *International History Review, Foreign Affairs, History Compass, Passport,* and *Kronos.*

Robert J. McMahon is the Ralph Mershon Professor of History at Ohio State University. He is the author of several books, including *Dean Acheson and the Creation of an American World Order* (2009), *Limits of Empire: The United States and Southeast Asia since World War II* (1999), and *Cold War on the Periphery: The United States, India, and Pakistan* (1994). In 2001, he served as the president of the Society for Historians of American Foreign Relations.

Alan McPherson is professor of international and area studies, Cono-coPhillips Chair in Latin American Studies, and director of the Center for the Americas at the University of Oklahoma. He is the author of, among other books, *Yankee No! Anti-Americanism in U.S.-Latin American Relations* (Harvard, 2003) and *The Invaded: How Latin Americans and Their Allies Fought and Ended U.S. Occupations* (Oxford, 2014).

Andrew J. Rotter is the Charles A. Dana Professor of History and director of the Peace and Conflict Studies Program at Colgate University. He specializes in the history of US relations with Asia in the twentieth century. He is the author most recently of *Hiroshima: The World's Bomb* (Oxford University Press, 2009) and is currently at work on a study of two empires and the five senses.

David Ryan is professor and chair of modern history at University College, Cork. He has served as vice head of the College of Arts, Celtic Studies and Social Sciences and earlier as associate dean of the Graduate School. He is the author or editor of *US-Sandinista Diplomatic Relations* (1995), *US Foreign Policy in World History* (2000), *Frustrated Empire* (2007), and, with David Fitzgerald, *Obama, US Foreign Policy and the Dilemmas of Intervention* (2014). He is the coeditor of *The United States and Decolonization* (2000), *Vietnam in Iraq* (2007), *America and Iraq* (2009), and *U.S. Foreign Policy and the Other* (2015). He is completing a book on US collective memory and intervention since 1969.

Maria Ryan is an assistant professor of American history in the Department of American and Canadian Studies at the University of Nottingham. Her research interests are broadly in the field of post–Cold War US foreign policy, in particular, the development of neoconservatism; intellectuals and US foreign policy; humanitarian interventionism; the Bush administration and the global War on Terror; and the history of the CIA. She has written articles and book chapters on many of these topics. Her first book, *Neoconservatism and the New American Century,* was published by Palgrave Macmillan (New York) in 2010. She is working on a second monograph tentatively titled "'Full Spectrum Dominance': Irregular Warfare, and the War on Terror on the Periphery."

Bevan Sewell is assistant professor of American history at the University of Nottingham and coeditor of the *Journal of American Studies*. He is currently working on an intellectual biography of John Foster Dulles. His first book, *The US and Latin America: Eisenhower, Kennedy and Economic Diplomacy*, was published by I. B. Tauris in 2016, and he has published articles in the *English Historical Review*, *Diplomatic History*, the *International History Review*, and *Intelligence and National Security*.

Dustin Walcher is associate professor and chair of history and political science at Southern Oregon University. He is a specialist in international history, the history of US foreign relations, and inter-American affairs whose scholarship analyzes international economic policy, global capitalism, and social disruption. He is currently revising a manuscript that examines the link between the failure of US-led economic initiatives and the rise of social revolution in Argentina during the 1950s and 1960s.

Index